The National Park Service:
Responding to the September 11 Terrorist Attacks

Library of Congress Cataloging-in-Publication Data

McDonnell, Janet A., 1952-
The National Park Service : responding to the September 11 terrorist attacks /
by Janet A. McDonnell.
p. cm.
Includes bibliographical references and index.
1. United States. National Park Service. 2. September 11 Terrorist Attacks, 2001.
I. Title.

Cover: U. S. Park Police patrol New York Harbor after the attacks.

Inside cover, Maj. Tom Wilkins, U.S. Park Police, holds the American flag
during rescue operations at Ground Zero.

The National Park Service:

Responding to
the September 11 Terrorist Attacks

Janet A. McDonnell
National Park Service
Department of the Interior

Table of Contents

Preface

The terrorist attacks of September 11, 2001, and their aftermath left few Americans unaffected. As the federal agency with primary responsibility for protecting and preserving many of the nation's most significant cultural and historic sites, the National Park Service had a unique perspective and role in responding to this tragedy. The most profound personal impact within the Service was no doubt on those employees who either witnessed the attacks firsthand or were directly involved in the immediate response, but every national park was affected to one degree or another.

Park Service historians and ethnographers quickly recognized the need to record and preserve the experiences and perspectives of those who had witnessed or responded to the attacks. They conducted more than a hundred oral history interviews with Service employees throughout the country, in parks, regional offices, and the Washington headquarters. These unique interviews reveal the memories and interpretation of the event and aftermath in the words of those directly affected. In addition to conducting interviews, there was also a need to document and evaluate the official response of the National Park Service. With that in mind, I began to research the following questions: How did Service managers and staff respond at the national level and in the regional and park offices? What actions did they take and why? How did the attacks and their aftermath affect the way the Service and the parks operated? How did they affect park resources and the allocation of those resources? What impact did the attacks have on the way park staffs viewed their jobs and the way Americans viewed their parks? And finally, what lessons could the Service learn from this experience? What did the Service's response say about its values and responsibilities?

Simply put, my goal was to foster a deeper appreciation and understanding for the way the Service and its employees responded to the attacks and to create a detailed historical record of this unique and significant period in the Service's history. This history is also designed to provide

View of the Statue of Liberty overlooking New York Harbor.

Service managers and policymakers with information they might find useful in responding to future emergencies.

Writing this history presented some unique challenges. Many of the major decisions about the response operations were made in phone conversations or in meetings with little or no written record. A scarcity of written records meant a greater reliance on the oral history interviews that National Park Service historians and ethnographers conducted. This approach involved a certain amount of risk: memories can be faulty especially after experiencing such a traumatic event; oral accounts can sometimes be confusing or lack specific details.

The September 11 event was truly unique in nature and scope. For the first time in our history, American commercial airplanes were used as terrorist weapons. Never before had a terrorist attack within the United States resulted in so many casualties. The resulting story is complex, involving a broad range of perspectives, activities, and locations. When dealing with such a traumatic and chaotic event, even determining an accurate sequence of events can be difficult. Memories are powerful. Witnesses were often more likely to recall vividly their sense of shock and fear, the acrid smell of burning debris, or their images of wounded victims than to recall factual details. Yet both types of information are important for the historical record. "The lived experience is more complex than subsequent interpretations reveal," explains Mary Marshall Clark, the director of the Oral History Research Office at Columbia University.[1] The personal stories conveyed in the interviews reflect the horror of what witnesses experienced before these stories were turned into a more acceptable narrative.

This history reveals how the event strained Park Service resources, highlighted vulnerabilities in security, and brought into sharp relief the emotional and symbolic power of National Park Service sites, such as Independence Hall, the Statue of Liberty, and Manzanar. It also addresses deeply embedded cultural values. Weaving these threads together proved challenging: there were no historical prototypes or prior research upon which to draw.

Finally, without the perspective of time, it is difficult to interpret the full meaning and impact of the event. Yet it is important to capture personal stories and operational decisions while memories are fresh. This report provides a snapshot of a moment in time, a preliminary assessment, and it highlights the challenges of balancing security with the Service's statutory obligation to protect resources and provide for public enjoyment of those resources. It reveals the difficulty of making critical decisions in an uncertain and rapidly changing environment and the difficulty of responding to an emergency with a decentralized organizational structure. The goal was not to produce a definitive history of the response but to provide managers with a useful tool and future historians with a foundation upon which they can build.

This history would not have been possible without the tremendous support and cooperation from managers and staff throughout the Service. Early on, the Park Service's Northeast Region recognized the need to record the experiences and perspectives of employees affected by the attacks and launched a systematic effort to do this. Ethnographers Chuck Smythe and Mark Schoepfle conducted dozens of oral history interviews, which became valuable sources for this history. Doris Fanelli, Louis Hutchins, and George Tselos also conducted interviews.

Above all, I am indebted to the dozens of Park Service members who graciously shared their time, experiences, perspectives, and in a few instances, their frustrations and anguish, in oral history interviews with me and other Service historians and ethnographers. Many of their names are listed at the end. Rick Gale, Einar Olsen, Dennis McGinnis, Dennis Burnett, and others not only participated in interviews but also reviewed the draft manuscript and provided comments. Historians Ed Linenthal and Dwight Pitcaithley also reviewed the manuscript and provided thoughtful comments. I am grateful to Lise Sajewski who, using her love of language and considerable editorial skills, did much to improve the manuscript. My sincere thanks to Marcia Axtmann Smith for designing and producing this book with so much skill, creativity, professionalism, and patience. Working and consulting with the individuals mentioned above proved to be a truly rewarding experience.

Introduction

On the morning of September 11, 2001, a group of foreign terrorists launched an unprecedented, well-coordinated attack on the United States using as their weapons four California-bound commercial airliners, each loaded with the maximum amount of jet fuel for its long trip across the country. The first two hijacked planes slammed into the two tallest towers of the World Trade Center in New York City. These stunning 110-story glass-and-steel towers, which soared above the skyline in Lower Manhattan, had served as a major American business and commercial center. The third plane struck the Pentagon, and a fourth crashed in a field eighty miles southeast of Pittsburgh.

At 8:45 a.m. (EST) American Airlines Flight 11 carrying ninety-two people from Boston to Los Angeles crashed into the North Tower of the World Trade Center. Twenty minutes later, United Airlines Flight 175 with sixty-five passengers and crew also heading toward California ripped through the South Tower. At 9:40 a.m. (EST) American Airlines Flight 77, a Boeing 757 commercial airliner carrying sixty-four people and 30,000 pounds of fuel for its long flight from Dulles to Los Angeles, smashed into the west façade of the Pentagon with such force that it penetrated four of the building's five interior rings. The Federal Aviation Administration promptly banned takeoffs nationwide and ordered all flights that were in the air to land at the nearest airport. Then came the alarming news that United Airlines Flight 93 with forty passengers and crew en route to San Francisco had crashed in Shanksville, Pennsylvania. Not long after, reports circulated that this plane had been headed toward Washington, D.C., and heroic passengers had intervened to thwart this plan. Back in New York, shortly before 10:00 a.m. (EST) the South Tower of the World Trade Center crumbled to the ground killing most of those trapped inside and blanketing Lower Manhattan with a thick coat of debris and dust. Approximately a half hour later, the North Tower tumbled down as well. None of the passengers and crews on the planes survived. Thousands of people were injured or killed at the World Trade Center and Pentagon.

In its long history the National Park Service has rarely had to worry about war threatening the safety of its visitors or the integrity of the natural and cultural resources that are under its protection. The terrorist attacks and their aftermath had a profound impact on the national parks—and on the National Park Service and its employees. The attacks reaffirmed the importance of parks as venerated symbols American values and culture. The events, traditions, and values represented at the parks, particularly at the historic sites, took on new resonance for the American public and for employees struggling to come to grips with the nature and scope of the tragedy. The Statue of Liberty, St. Louis Gateway Arch, Liberty Bell, Washington Monument, and the other landmarks that the Service is charged with protecting help define Americans as a people. Yet, at the same time, the attacks exposed these venerated sites as potential targets.

The attacks and the response highlighted the critical role that the Park Service plays in the life of the nation and challenged the agency to reassess and reaffirm its missions, priorities, and resources. A careful study of the way leaders, managers, and staff responded reveals much about Service's culture, values, and responsibilities.

Though it is far too soon to identify and evaluate the long-term impact of the attacks, in some ways September 11 has been a transforming event for the National Park Service. The event prompted changes in the way the Service operates and is organized, and for many, gave the parks new meaning and significance.

I. National Park Service's Initial Response

Main Interior Building, Tuesday, September 11, 2001

Rick Gale, chief of the National Park Service's fire aviation emergency response and head of its incident management program, was sitting in Associate Director Richard (Dick) Ring's third floor office in the Department of the Interior's Washington, D.C. headquarters, when a call came in advising Ring to turn on the television. It would prove fortuitous that Gale who normally worked at the National Interagency Fire Center in Boise, Idaho, happened to be in Washington that day. Ring turned on the television just in time to see the second plane strike the World Trade Center in New York City. Gale headed back to his temporary office in the ranger activities division. Not long after, Ring received word that the Pentagon had been struck. He stepped outside onto his small balcony and glancing south saw an ominous cloud of smoke rising in the distance.[1]

Meanwhile, a few floors above, the acting chief of the Park Service ranger activities division, Dennis Burnett, was working at his computer when an employee ran down the hallway announcing that a plane had hit one of the World Trade Center towers. Burnett walked down to the vacant office of chief of ranger activities at end of the corridor, where he knew there was a television. After checking the news, he returned to his office. Moments later, he learned of the second plane attack. At that point, Burnett gathered his small staff, which included national law enforcement specialist Maj. Gary Van Horn, U.S. Park Police, and Search and Rescue Emergency Medical Services Coordinator Randall

American flag framed by the rubble at the World Trade Center after the attacks. Above, Pentagon damage.

Around 10:00 a.m. federal authorities ordered
government offices closed and approximately 260,000
federal workers in Washington began pouring out into the streets.

Coffman. They headed to the department's law enforcement security office, where they continued to monitor the television news coverage.[2]

Major Van Horn, an experienced career law enforcement officer, quickly recognized the need to immediately locate the Service's decision-makers and get them to a secure location in case there were incidents in the Washington area. He hurried back to his office and got on his police radio. After learning of the Pentagon attack, Van Horn became concerned about potential threats to the monuments and memorials on the National Mall. He climbed into his police cruiser and quickly drove to each of these monuments and memorials to conduct quick inspections and to make sure that Park Police officers were in position in the event of another attack. He spotted a suspicious package on the Memorial Bridge, a major route in and out of downtown Washington, and waited there until more officers arrived. After assuring himself that the bridge was secured, he returned to the Main Interior Building.[3]

Meanwhile, Burnett and other employees in Main Interior discovered that they could no longer make outgoing phone calls on either landlines or their cellular phones. Wireless networks had collapsed under the barrage of calls. When Burnett's daughter called to check on him a half hour after the Pentagon attack, he used this opportunity to establish what would become an important phone link. He asked his daughter to have the Eastern Interagency Coordination Center (EICC), a dispatch center located in Shenandoah National Park, call him. When the center contacted him, he asked the staff to continue calling every twenty minutes so that they could maintain a landline connection. Although phone service was severely restricted, Burnett was able to send an e-mail message to the regional chief rangers and to the dispatch center, informing them that the Washington headquarters had no communications capability.[4]

In his message, Burnett asked the dispatch center to become the agency's "eyes and ears." He directed parks and regions to channel all their messages for the Washington office through the center. Finally, he reported that the department had activated its continuity of operations plan and was relocating people in accordance with that plan. In another message he encouraged regional chief rangers to step up security at Park Service facilities and sites.[5]

The EICC had been established at Shenandoah National Park in Virginia in

1980 and had grown from a small center that coordinated responses to fires and local emergencies into a national coordination center. Combined with the coordination center was a communications center that provided emergency notifications of crisis situations and mobilizations for the Park Service, other federal agencies such as the Federal Emergency Management Agency (FEMA), and for senior department officials. While the communications center did the notifications, the coordination center directed the actual mobilization and demobilization of resources within the Service.

Upon learning of the attacks, the center's manager, Brenda Ritchie, an experienced emergency operations manager, immediately called in additional dispatchers to staff the communications center. Her first task was to contact senior department officials to find out where they were and verify that they were safe and to determine the status of all the parks and employees in the Park Service's Northeast Region. As already noted, initially officials in the Main Interior Building were unable to make outgoing calls, so the center called them every fifteen to twenty minutes. Faced with major communications problems, Ritchie quickly arranged to bring in a mobile satellite truck, a so-called cellular on wheels. The satellite truck and 150 cellular phones arrived within the first eight hours, and the center distributed the phones to key managers and operational staff. Bringing in the satellite dish on such short notice was no small feat and required unprecedented cooperation between two major telecommunications companies—Verizon and Sprint. As a result, phone service was

restored to most sections of the Main Interior Building.[6]

The center performed the communications role for both the Service and the Department of the Interior. It provided direct support to the parks and also to FEMA in New York and New Jersey. When the staff for the intelligence, coordination, and communications functions grew to more than twenty people, it became clear that the modest 1950s-era building that had housed the communications center in the past could not hold them all. Ritchie got approval to bring in a trailer to house the coordination center.[7]

Meanwhile, back in Washington, director of the National Park Service Fran Mainella; Pacific West Regional Director John Reynolds (who was acting as deputy director at the time); Associate Director for Administration Sue Masica; Associate Director for Cultural Resources and Partnerships Kate Stevenson; Dick Ring; Dennis Burnett; and others gathered in the deputy director's third floor office to plan a course of action. They quickly recognized the need to get to a safe environment where they would have effective communications.[8]

When Rick Gale joined the group, Reynolds introduced him to the director and recommended him to Mainella as someone with extensive experience in emergency response. Dick Ring suggested that Gale stay close to the director to enhance communication and coordination with the department. He also wanted Gale to coordinate the director's activities, communications, and directions regarding the emergency operations within the Service. The director quickly tapped Gale to go with her to meet with department leaders on the sixth floor. Gale would remain close to the director throughout the day and in the days that followed. He offered her advice on how best to organize the Service's response and laid out possible missions. In effect, Gale became a self-described sounding board for the director.[9]

Much like the rest of the country, in those first hours Service leaders were stunned by the attacks and struggled to understand the full scope and implications of what had happened. They were just beginning to receive some reports from the Park Police about its security-related activities and about the worsening traffic situation around the city. The leaders were not aware of any specific immediate threats to or attacks on any National Park Service areas, so they were not yet focused on planning a Service-wide response. They knew that Federal Hall and Castle Clinton National Monuments were located near the World Trade Center, but they did not yet know the status of those parks. Little information came out of New York in those first hours. Service leaders had concerns, but with landlines down and cellular phone system overloaded, they had little solid information and chose to proceed cautiously. Years earlier, as superintendent of Everglades National Park when Hurricane Andrew struck, Ring had learned that the best approach was to proceed slowly and to gather solid information before taking action. Since there were no reports of a park being struck, he believed the immediate task was simply to gather more information.[10]

The director issued "Emergency Operations Instructions," authorizing all regional directors, at their discretion, to reduce their staffs to essential personnel only. She specified that, if possible, parks should continue minimum operations with basic visitor contact services, provide updates on the incidents, and monitor television and radio reports. She directed that campgrounds remain open as appropriate. Finally, the director encouraged superintendents to advise their employees to become more security conscious.[11]

As the morning progressed, Service leaders learned that the federal government in Washington was shutting down its operations. Around 10:00 a.m. federal authorities ordered government offices closed and approximately 260,000 federal workers in Washington began pouring out into the streets.[12] Secretary of the Interior Gale Norton ordered the evacuation of the Main Interior Building and released a memo dismissing all nonessential employees for the remainder of the day. Her memo indicated that the dismissal would remain in effect the next day September 12, unless employees were informed otherwise.[13]

Continuity of Operations

When officials gathered in the deputy director's office, one of the first topics under discussion was the need to implement the Service's continuity of operations plan. The National Park Service headquarters, each regional and support office, and some individual parks had what is called a continuity of operations plan, which outlines specific measures to ensure that operations continue as smoothly as possible during an emergency. Park Service continuity of operations plans were designed to correspond to the department's continuity of operations

The National Park Service headquarters, each regional
and support office, and some individual parks had
what is called a continuity of operations plan,
which outlines specific measures to ensure that operations
continue as smoothly as possible during an emergency.

plan. The department's plan spelled out the succession of authority and provided for the removal of the secretary, deputy secretary, and each bureau head to a remote location well outside the Washington area. The plan specified that the National Park Service director would go to the same location as the secretary or to another location specified by the secretary.[14]

Initially the secretary wanted department and bureau leaders to go to what the plan designated as Site B—an office about ten miles away in Northern Virginia. Leaders considered Site B to be a safe location where they could organize the department's operations. The director and Rick Gale got in a car to drive to the site, but with the horrendous traffic congestion in downtown Washington it took them twenty minutes just to get out of the Main Interior Building's underground parking garage. As the minutes passed, Gale observed that with cellular phone systems overloaded, the director would be without any communications link for hours while she sat in traffic. The director agreed with his assessment. They got out of the car and went back up to the sixth floor. Soon after, the department set up operations in the department's National Business Center conference room in the basement, presumably the safest part

of the building. The large conference room became the department's coordination center. The director joined Deputy Secretary of Interior J. Steven Griles and other key department leaders there.[15]

Later in the day, the secretary decided to relocate to what the department's continuity of operations plan designated as Site C, an hour's drive outside Washington. As noted, the plan provided that the director and other bureau heads would join department leaders at this alternate site. The Service's own continuity of operations plan provided that its deputy director and other senior leaders would go to the Service's designated site in West Virginia. This facility had a conference room outfitted with extra phone lines and all the other equipment these leaders would need to continue their management functions. Staffs at both alternate sites quickly and efficiently organized to receive the senior managers.[16] At the request of department officials, a U.S. Park Police SWAT team came to the Main Interior Building and escorted senior department officials to Site C.[17]

Major Van Horn offered to escort the director to the alternate site, and being fairly new to the Service and unfamiliar with the site, she gratefully accepted. He led the way in his police cruiser, while the

Reflecting the White House's desire for the federal government to resume normal operations as quickly as possible, Secretary Norton made it clear that she expected as many parks as possible to be open on September 12.

director followed close behind in her own vehicle. They stopped at her home first so she could pack some extra clothing. While she did this, Major Van Horn went to his home where he quickly grabbed extra clothes and a couple sandwiches that his wife had prepared for him and the director. He went back to pick up the director and the two headed for Site C.[18] Meanwhile, Gale returned to his hotel room and, at the director's request, began contacting all the Service's senior managers to arrange for them to go to the designated West Virginia site the next morning.[19]

Once at the alternate site, department officials and bureau heads discussed the immediate challenges and made decisions about how to proceed. Their task was made more difficult because they had no clear sense of what sites were potential terrorist targets. They knew that economic centers, such as the World Trade Center, and military facilities, such as the Pentagon, were targets but did not know if any of what they considered to be the department's national "icons" were at risk. Since they did not know which sites, which national icons, were potential terrorist targets, initially they decided to increase security at all areas and to close some parks and facilities.[20] Service leaders immediately initiated twenty-four-hour security coverage at Boston Navy Yard where the USS *Constitution* was berthed, Independence Hall in Philadelphia, the Gateway Arch at the Jefferson National Expansion Memorial in St. Louis, Mount Rushmore, and at the major monuments and memorials in Washington, D.C.

The senior leaders at Site C also dealt with the question of whether employees should come to work the next day and, once the decision was made, how to get the word out to them. They tried to gather accurate intelligence information about potential threats in order to make informed decisions. They were prepared to stay at the alternate site as long as necessary. Later that evening when the initial frenzy had subsided, Van Horn quietly offered to escort the director back to the Washington area. Both agreed that returning to work in the Main Interior Building the next morning would send a strong message about the resilience of the federal government. After some discussion with department officials, the director decided to return. Meanwhile, in a televised address that evening, President Bush had announced that federal offices in Washington would be open for business the next day, September 12, so many other officials returned to Washington late that night as well.[21] In line with the president's address, the Office of Personnel Management announced that all federal agencies in the Washington area would reopen on September 12, though employees would be allowed to take unscheduled leave.[22]

Before leaving the alternate site, Major Van Horn asked the dispatch center to send a message from the director to all regional directors directing that the parks "as much as reasonable" assume normal operations on September 12. However, through delegation from the regional directors, park superintendents would have the discretion to limit or augment personnel and operations at sites where they deemed such measures appropriate. They were to grant nonessential personnel unscheduled leave. The memo went out to the field offices by e-mail.[23]

As soon as Gale received word that the director was returning to Washington, he began calling the associate directors back to advise them to cancel their plans to go to West Virginia. Around 10:00 p.m. Burnett sent word through the dispatch center in Shenandoah National Park that the secretary had canceled all activities at Site C. He advised Gale, Ring, and other Service managers to report for work in the headquarters building the next morning.[24]

Reflecting the White House's desire for the federal government to resume normal operations as quickly as possible, Secretary Norton made it clear that she expected as many parks as possible to be open on September 12. In a memo to department employees the morning of the 12th, she reiterated, "by providing uninterrupted service, we reaffirm that we will

not be intimated by acts of terrorism."[25] She announced that the monuments and memorials in Washington (except for the Washington Monument) had reopened at 11:30 a.m. and that the National Park Service sites were open, except for those in the New York City area. In a press release, she said, "Our focus remains on the safety of our visitors and our employees. We must remain vigilant as we provide the American people access to our nation's monuments, memorials, and parks for the solace and inspiration they provide." The secretary added that operations at the New York sites were more limited and Manhattan Sites remained closed. In closing, she wrote, "We encourage everyone to draw inspiration from our greatest national treasures and let them serve as reminders that this nation will endure and prosper."[26]

Bureau and department leaders, including Director Mainella, were back in their offices on the morning of the 12th. In an effort to reassure employees, Deputy Secretary Griles personally greeted them as they returned to work. All too soon, however, it became clear that this workday would be far from routine. Griles was in a meeting with the secretary when she received a call advising her that an unidentified and unaccounted for commercial airliner was heading from Canada toward Washington. Griles immediately directed that all employees move to the basement. Unfortunately, the department had no good mechanism for communicating with employees throughout the building. There was no public address system. No individual or office had specific responsibility for informing employees that they needed to evacuate to the basement cafeteria. Confused and anxious employees did not

understand why they were suddenly being sent there. When they arrived in the cafeteria, the scene was chaotic and reliable information was scarce. Officials tried to organize employees by bureau, but were unsuccessful.[27]

In the midst of the confusion, Griles and Mainella did what they could to calm employees and keep them informed. Griles explained the situation and offered employees the option of leaving. Meanwhile, Major Van Horn contacted the Park Police and determined that the information about an unidentified plane heading toward Washington was inaccurate. He also learned that the U.S. Air Force had sent up fighter pilots as an added precaution. Van Horn climbed up on a chair in the midst of the crowded cafeteria and used a hurriedly borrowed megaphone to convey this information.[28]

Notification of employees throughout the building was haphazard. There was an existing plan for evacuating the Main Interior Building in the event of a fire or bomb threat, but the plan did not provide for an alternate site for employees. There was no operations center identified for bureau heads that could provide employees

with information and instructions. No group or function had been identified as having primary responsibility for this task. The Service's head of risk management and employee safety, Richard (Dick) Powell, later emphasized that employees need to know where to go in an emergency. In the months after the attack, the department would develop a more detailed evacuation plan for Main Interior.[29]

Park Closures

Repercussions from the attacks were felt well beyond the Main Interior Building that first day. As news of the tragedy spread, virtually every unit of the National Park System grappled with the impact to one degree or another. At Independence National Historical Park, for example, park staff had the emotionally difficult task of explaining to visitors why the park was closing and giving them their first information about the terrorist attacks. Across the country, at Yosemite National Park, the superintendent decided to keep the park open. He immediately increased the ranger presence and the staff at the visitor center and the public information office. He also quickly dispatched rangers out to

Park rangers at Independence National Historical Park increase security after the attacks.

Hetch-Hetchy Dam, a major water supply source for the city of San Francisco. As at Independence, Yosemite staff had to perform the delicate task of informing visitors about the attacks.[30] Comforting distraught visitors in the midst of a national tragedy was a new and unfamiliar role for many park employees.

Superintendents had to carefully weigh a number of factors in deciding how to respond to the attacks. At Delaware Gap National Recreation Area, Deputy Superintendent Doyle Nelson closed the park and began implementing the park's continuity of operations plan even before receiving official word that government facilities would be closing. Nelson was not overly concerned that Delaware Gap might be a terrorist target, but he and his staff began shutting down operations in order to free up rangers for duty in other areas that had been more directly affected. That morning Nelson received calls from the Sandy Hook unit of Gateway National Recreation Area in New York requesting ranger assistance.[31]

Initially department leaders considered closing all 385 units in the National Park System. However, Rick Gale pointed out to the director that closing parks could sometimes require more resources than leaving them open. Full closure often required sweeping the backcountry areas and in some instances could be difficult to enforce. The director thus recommended to the secretary that they reduce services in the parks rather than implement a total closure. The secretary and director decided to keep the parks open, though there were exceptions. For example, all the units in the New York City area and all the national monuments and memorials in Washington were immediately closed.[32]

Other parks were closed temporarily as well, either because they were considered to be potential terrorist targets or because of their proximity to military or other sensitive installations.

At Golden Gate National Recreation Area in San Francisco, the Park Police instituted additional security measures within an hour of the attacks. The Park Police San Francisco field office, which operated on a twenty-four-hour basis, was in the midst of a shift change when the attacks occurred. Officers on the first shift were sent home but warned that they might be called back in to duty. There was immediate concern that the Golden Gate Bridge might be another terrorist target. California State operated the bridge, but since the footings stood on Park Service property, the Service was responsible for protecting the bridge's foundations. Park Police officials decided to secure the north and south Bay coastlines where the Golden Gate Bridge was anchored. Officers maintained seven fixed posts. Members of the criminal investigations section manned several of the posts along with horse mounted patrol officers. Implementing the closure took approximately one hour. Officers and supervisors cleared away the construction crews working on one side of the bridge and cut off all pedestrian access.[33]

The field office coordinated closely with the California Highway Patrol, Golden Gate Bridge District Police, San Francisco Police Department, Marin County Sheriff's Office, CALTRANS, and the San Francisco and Presidio Fire Departments. The field office doubled its patrols by using off-duty officers and extended tours of duty. The next day, the field office reported that things were "safe and running smoothly." They had closed Alcatraz, all visitor centers, and Fort Point under the Golden Gate Bridge and had halted pedestrian and bike traffic on the bridge.[34]

The day after the attacks, parks in New York City remained closed. Minute Man National Historical Park, which shared a boundary with Hanscom Air Force Base, and Boston Navy Yard in Boston National Historical Park remained closed. The U.S. Navy had immediately assumed the highest security level at the naval yard, and in response the park stepped up its security staffing and patrols.[35] Independence National Historical Park, Independence Hall, and the Liberty Bell were open, but all other visitor areas remained closed to the public. In the National Capital Region, officials suspended public tours at the White House indefinitely and closed the Ellipse area. Catoctin Mountain Park, site of the presidential retreat, Camp David, remained closed. Elsewhere, visitor centers at the Oklahoma City Memorial and at Organ Pipe Cactus National Park remained closed. At the request of the National Aeronautics and Space Administration, Canaveral National Seashore, a beach near the Kennedy Space Center, remained closed. At Dayton Aviation Heritage National Historical Park, a field located on Patterson Air Force Base was closed. Officials closed a short spur road to the observatory complex at Haleakala National Park in Hawaii at the request of the U.S. Air Force. Cabrillo National Monument in San Diego was closed because of naval base closures. At Golden Gate, both Fort Point and San Francisco Maritime National Historical Park remained closed.[36]

At the Navy's insistence, USS *Arizona* National Memorial remained closed to the public for six days following the attack, and the Navy set the security conditions for reopening. New security checkpoints were established and staffed by the Park Service and the Navy. The Navy required that the Service provide law enforcement officers to enforce security measures. This task was first accomplished by using law enforcement rangers detailed from other parks for twenty-one-day tours. Because of the high cost of using detailed rangers, the park hired three seasonal law enforcement rangers to meet the Navy's requirements.[37]

Parks in the Alaska Region, though open, faced special problems. Immediately after the attacks, the Federal Aviation Administration had grounded all commercial flights. Officials became increasingly concerned that the employees and visitors (particularly hunters) awaiting pick up by plane would run out of food or that their game would spoil. Also, since access to many of the parks in Alaska was by air only, some employees were stranded away from their permanent duty stations. Rangers stuck in the backcountry were running out of food.[38]

Two weeks after the attack, in New York City, Federal Hall National Monument, Castle Clinton National Monument, the Statue of Liberty, and Ellis Island remained closed, but Theodore Roosevelt Birthplace, St. Paul's Church, Hamilton Grange, and General Grant were open. Also still closed, in other parts of the country, were parts of the George Washington Memorial Parkway near the Pentagon, the Boston Navy Yard, a beach at Canaveral National Seashore, Fort Point, and the spur road at Haleakala.[39]

Support to the Department of the Interior

On the morning of September 11, department officials quickly identified high priority sites that they believed were potential terrorist targets to include some major Bureau of Reclamation projects in the West. They called upon the Park Service and other bureaus to provide security at the Main Interior Building and asked the Service to help protect some of the department's other high priority sites. The department's list of national icons included several Bureau of Reclamation dams. The bureau had no law enforcement or security personnel of its own except at Hoover Dam, so department officials asked the Park Service to provide law enforcement personnel to protect these dams. Meeting the Bureau of Reclamation's long-term security needs was a challenge. Service leaders found themselves in the difficult position of having to pull law enforcement rangers from their own key sites to provide the security the department requested.

Protecting Bureau of Reclamation sites presented two major problems for the Park Service: the first related to legal authority, and the second related to resources. The Service had no statutory authority on land outside park boundaries. It had no jurisdiction on many of the Bureau of Reclamation dam sites. Hoover and Davis Dams were located within the boundaries of Lake Mead National Recreation Area, but the legislation establishing the recreation area specifically excised the dams and related facilities. As a result, park rangers could

only provide law enforcement support under authority as deputy U.S. marshals. Each ranger had to be deputized as a special deputy U.S. marshal, a process requiring considerable time and effort. The Service had difficulty responding because only a small number of its rangers had been deputized.

Traditionally, the U.S. Marshals Service deputized the rangers for a single designated site for a specific period of time. Officials quickly discovered this practice was too restrictive because they needed the ability to transfer rangers from site to site. They began deputizing rangers for multiple sites for thirty days. Later, rangers were deputized for all department facilities, including the Main Interior Building, through December 31, 2003. Yet, even with the new, streamlined process, months later there remained a backlog of 500 to 800 applications for rangers waiting to be deputized.[40]

The Service sent several of its "special event teams" to secure the departmental icons, each with ten to twelve trained law enforcement rangers. Because of disruptions to commercial air travel, the Service tried to assign teams to nearby installations. These teams were fully equipped and ready to deploy on short notice. However, there was growing concern that the Service could not continue to rely on the relatively small number of rangers on special event teams who had been deputized. Four months after the attacks, park rangers remained on duty protecting these sites, and these special event teams, Burnett observed, had been "used to exhaustion."[41] By that time, some teams had been on three or four rotations at various dam sites in the West, and the Service had begun deploying individual rangers instead of teams. If there were not enough individual replacements, the teams had to extend their duty.[42]

Filling requests for law enforcement rangers at the Lake Roosevelt, Whiskeytown, and Lake Mead National Recreation Areas became increasingly difficult. On September 20, Pacific West Region Chief Ranger Jay Wells reported that he had no indication that additional rangers would be arriving soon and his rangers were "pretty well tapped out" with the coverage at the three recreation areas and their traditional firefighting assignments. Wells asked for assistance from other regions and warned that it was "getting to be a safety issue," particularly at Lake Mead National Recreation Area. If no relief came the following day, he added, the region planned to send a special event team to Lake Mead National Recreation Area that it had been holding in reserve in case it was needed in Washington, D.C., or New York City. Six rangers were providing twenty-four-hour security at Lake Mead, and the park was clamoring for more rangers. Ten rangers were stationed at the Bureau of Reclamation's Grand Coulee Dam at Lake Roosevelt National Recreation Area and four were assigned to the bureau's Shasta Dam project.[43]

Months later, the Lake Mead National Recreation Area superintendent reported that the post–September 11 security requirements had "heavily tasked" the park's protection division. At one point, the special event teams and park staff were providing maritime security above and below Hoover Dam and also staffing highway checkpoints east and west of the dam. In addition to securing the dams, the rangers still had

their ongoing mission of protecting visitors. Providing around-the-clock coverage at Hoover and Davis Dams had taken "a tremendous amount of manpower, time, and resources," he noted.[44]

Whiskeytown National Recreation Area faced similar challenges. On September 11, park rangers joined with local and state law enforcement agencies and the Bureau of Reclamation to enhance security at the bureau's critical Central Valley Project facilities located in or near Whiskeytown. This massive project supplied water for irrigation and provided flood control for the Sacramento River basin. It also generated and supplied a significant portion of the electrical power on the West Coast. The secretary had identified the Bureau of Reclamation's Shasta Dam as "a critical national asset." Whiskeytown staff provided continuous support to the Shasta Dam security personnel and helped them close off the dam and the surrounding area to public access. On several occasions the park's entire law enforcement staff participated in this operation. Park rangers managed security at the dam and supervised the twelve-member special event teams that rotated through every twenty-one days. As a result, the superintendent reported, "there has been a major reduction in proactive ranger patrol and resource protection/ education as a result of Whiskeytown's commitment to dam security."[45]

By mid-October, the visitor center at Lake Mead National Recreation Area had reopened, but tours of Hoover and Davis Dams remained suspended. The same was true at Shasta Dam at Whiskeytown National Recreation Area and Grand Coulee Dam at Lake Roosevelt National

Recreation Area.[46] The Service's support at Bureau of Reclamation projects and other department sites continued to have a great impact on its law enforcement resources and capabilities.

Conclusion

Much like every other federal agency, the National Park Service found itself ill prepared to respond to an emergency of the type and magnitude of September 11. The Service implemented its continuity of operations plan quickly, and for the most part, effectively that first day, but the implementation was not as smooth as officials would have preferred. Some officials evacuated reasonably quickly to designated alternate sites, but traffic congestion hampered the evacuation of others. With phone service disrupted throughout the city, contacting some officials was difficult.

The response also revealed some flaws in the Service's continuity of operations plan. The plan was somewhat dated and designed more for responding to a fire or bomb threat than a terrorist attack. Officials discovered that in some instances, particularly with the confusion and traffic gridlock they encountered, it might be more effective to shelter employees on-site than to evacuate them. Some leaders concluded that the Service needed a more flexible plan. At the same time, the response demonstrated that Department of the Interior and Park Service leaders understood their roles under the plan and were willing to pitch in and do whatever was required. "It was," Major Gary Van Horn said, "a combined effort of a lot of well-meaning, well-intentioned individuals." Decisions were made in a timely fashion and information flowed smoothly between department officials and Service representatives.[47]

As a result of the September 11 experience, Service leaders later brought in a group to revise and update the continuity of operations plan. Over a ten-day period, the consultants revised the plan to address the new security concerns and risk management concerns and added an even more remote alternate work site so that leadership could continue operations should another event occur in the Washington, D.C., area.[48]

While Service officials in the Washington headquarters grappled with the immediate issues of maintaining basic operations, enhancing security, and supporting the department, park superintendents throughout the country also faced the challenge of maintaining operations and keeping park employees, visitors, and resources safe. This challenge was particularly great in the Washington area and in New York City.

U. S. Park Police and park rangers in the Washington area responded immediately at the Pentagon and at treasured historic and cultural sites.

II. National Capital Region

While officials in the Main Interior Building struggled with the initial response, a few miles away at the U.S. Park Police and National Capital Region headquarters buildings in Washington's East Potomac Park, managers were already mobilizing. Together the region's Park Police and park rangers assisted in protecting the nation's leaders, Washington residents, and visitors; helped evacuate the city; cared for young children from the Pentagon day-care center; and secured some of the nation's most treasured historic and cultural sites.

U.S. Park Police Headquarters

On the morning of September 11, Deputy Chief John (Jack) Schamp was at his desk in Park Police headquarters pouring over reports related to an upcoming World Bank/International Monetary Fund meeting in Washington. An officer interrupted to inform him that a plane had struck the World Trade Center. Not long after, deputy chiefs Schamp, Benjamin J. Holmes, and Edward Winkel activated the chief's command post, a modest-size meeting room in the headquarters building outfitted with telecommunications equipment. Winkel was acting chief at the time. The Park Police chief's position had been vacant for some months and each of the three deputy chiefs alternated as acting chief for a three-month period. Park Police officials began discussing the immediate measures that should be taken to secure the monuments and memorials. About fifteen minutes later, the Park Police counterterrorism unit arrived at the center and would play a key role in disseminating

Securing the capital's memorials—including the Jefferson Memorial and Washington Monument— was an immediate priority for the Park Police of the National Capital Region. A Park Police helicopter, above, circles above the stricken Pentagon.

information and coordinating the Park Police response.

Acting Chief Winkel asked the acting operations division commander, Maj. Thomas Pellinger, and the acting commander for the special forces branch, Capt. Sal Lauro, to join the other officials in the command center. As Captain Lauro quickly drove from his office in the Navy Yard in southeast Washington toward Park Police headquarters and came over the Southeast Expressway, he saw an explosion in the vicinity of the Pentagon. When he pulled off the ramp to East Potomac Park, he saw smoke and flames rising from the direction of the Pentagon and heard a report that a plane had struck that building.[1] The acting chief and two deputy chiefs; Major Pellinger; captains Henry Berberich, Dan Walters, and Sal Lauro; and others who gathered in the command post discussed what needed to be done. Their most immediate concern was the security of the White House, as well as the need to evacuate and secure the national monuments and memorials. They alerted all units of the attack and contacted the Park Police New York field office where officers were already responding to the attacks at the World Trade Center.[2]

At the time of the attacks, organizationally, the U.S. Park Police came under the National Capital Region and its regional director, Terry Carlstrom. The two headquarters buildings were just a few yards apart. At one point early on, Regional Director Carlstrom strode over to the chief's command post where the Park Police officials were assembled. When he saw the command post operating smoothly, he indicated that he was satisfied with

their operations and would not interfere. He told the officers simply, "You've got it." One Park Police official later observed that he appreciated such a strong expression of confidence and support.[3]

The chief's command post had direct communication links to the FBI, White House Emergency Operations Center, District of Columbia Emergency Operations Center, and the Federal Emergency Management Agency's (FEMA) Operations Center. It also provided "real-time" information to its officers on the front lines and to the Interior department's law enforcement notification center, the dispatch center in Shenandoah National Park, U.S. Secret Service, Department of Defense, and metropolitan police department. Park Police officials had representatives on duty around the clock in the Secret Service, metropolitan police department, and the Arlington County/Pentagon command posts, who provided ready access to the information coming through those centers. Park Police detectives worked with the FBI, particularly on cases involving suspicious packages and people, contaminated mail, and bomb threats. The command post coordinated safe evacuation of cabinet members, park visitors, and commuters.[4]

Public information officers stationed in the command post responded to a steady stream of media inquiries and kept the public informed of increased security measures, road closures, and other issues. In the days following the attacks, the command post prepared a daily time line of events that was included in the daily briefing for Director Mainella. The post would remain in operation until Monday, September 17.[5]

The Park Police force mobilized fully. Managers initiated an emergency action plan calling in off-duty personnel, instituting twelve-hour shifts, bringing in extra personnel from outlying districts, and purchasing food and water. Many off-duty officers had already come in to work voluntarily. Some officers called in to see if they were needed or find out where to report, but the Nextel cellular communications system that Park Police managers used was overloaded. Some officers simply drove to locations where they thought they would be needed rather than wait for assignments. As a result, it took some time to determine where each officer was and which locations were covered.

The massive traffic congestion made it difficult for some officers to drive into work, particularly when they were in their private vehicles. The Park Police home-to-work vehicle program, which allowed officers to drive their service vehicle home at the end of their shift, proved to be extremely valuable both in Washington, D.C., and New York City. Officers who had their police vehicles at home were able to report in relatively quickly. Rather than respond to their normal duty station, these officers could be dispatched directly to critical areas. Driving police cars allowed officers to navigate through the traffic gridlock with greater ease. Their service vehicles had lights and sirens, and radios that allowed them to communicate. The home-to-work vehicle program greatly enhanced the park police's ability to deploy personnel rapidly. The percentage of officers participating in the program was relatively small at the time, but after September 11 officials expanded the program as more vehicles became available.[6]

Securing the White House, Monuments, and Memorials

Understandably, protection of the president was the highest and most immediate priority for the Park Police. They immediately deployed various units around the White House and the national monuments and memorials and began evacuation procedures. Minutes after the Pentagon was hit, Major Pellinger deployed the Park Police's mobile command post at Twelfth Street and Jefferson Drive on the National Mall. This mobile headquarters, a thirty-foot long recreational vehicle that contained a television, communications equipment, and meeting space, served as a key operations center. Pellinger began directing operations from the chief's command post, while Captain Lauro oversaw operations on the street.[7]

Park Police officers worked with the Secret Service and the metropolitan police to secure an area of several blocks around the White House. They implemented a full-scale closure of the roads around the White House. This task, which required a lot of manpower, had rarely, if ever, been done before. Captain Lauro had first received the new procedures for closures around the White House at the beginning of the Persian Gulf War in 1991 when he was a lieutenant working as shift commander. He had stuck the document into a binder and placed the binder in his briefcase, where it remained for ten years. When word came on September 11 that they were finally implementing the plan, he was able to quickly pull the plan out of his briefcase and begin executing the procedures.[8]

While one group secured the area around the White House, commander of the central district Capt. Henry Berberich and his officers secured the area around the Washington Monument. Lt. Pete Markland and several officers secured the Ellipse, and Capt. Dan Walters coordinated the closure of the Lincoln Memorial. Officers immediately closed not only the Jefferson and Lincoln Memorials and Washington Monument but also the Ellipse, White House sidewalks, and Lafayette Park. Fortunately, in addition to their own force, Park Police commanders were able to deploy forty officers who had been in the midst of riot training at a Park Police facility in southeast Washington when the attacks occurred. Officers initiated temporary road and pedestrian closures and increased patrols throughout the day in response to potential threats.[9]

Motorcycle Unit

The Park Police motorcycle unit typically had responsibility for providing security for the president, escorting dignitaries, and enforcing traffic regulations. Two members of the motorcycle unit, Lt. George Wallace and Sgt. Daniel Beck, were among the first uniformed law enforcement officers to arrive at the scene of the airline crash at the Pentagon. These two officers assisted with search and rescue of survivors, helped coordinate with Pentagon security, and performed other missions.[10]

Lieutenant Wallace was on the National Mall writing tickets when Sergeant Beck called his cell phone to tell him that a plane had hit one of the World Trade Center towers. Sergeant Beck called back a few minutes later to tell him that the second tower had been struck. At that point, Wallace climbed on his motorcycle and hurried back to Park Police headquarters. He knew some additional security measures would be put in place and that his unit might be called upon to assist with evacuations, road closures, and other missions.

Wallace was on the phone with another officer, when the officer informed him that there had been an explosion at the Pentagon. Beck and Wallace hurried outside, saw the thick smoke, and got on their motorcycles and rushed to the Pentagon. They arrived at the scene within minutes. Wallace later observed that President Bush had been scheduled to land at the Pentagon helipad later that morning, near the site where the plane slammed into the building. Wallace and other officers had been

Aerial photo of the Pentagon taken after the attack revealing some of the damage.

Some of the crew
grabbed their emergency
medical equipment and
ran toward the
Pentagon building.

assigned to escort the president from the helipad to the White House.

Lieutenant Wallace found what he described as "unimaginable" destruction at the Pentagon. He had witnessed catastrophic events before, but nothing had prepared him for the gruesome scene he encountered. At first, he saw no readily apparent signs of the plane except its outline in the side of the building. No airline parts stuck out of the building, and the surrounding debris field was small. Some of the injured were lying in the field near the helipad and people were running toward them to assist. Wallace tried to help the injured, but there seemed to be enough military personnel performing that task. So he ran up closer to the building where the fire department was starting to operate their hoses. Wallace and Beck, both volunteer firemen at one time and no strangers to firefighting operations, began pulling fire hoses. They moved near the entrance of the burning building and were preparing to enter to help rescue victims when one of the fire chiefs came out and announced that no one could go in because the structure was unsafe. A couple minutes later, as they were pulling back the hoses, the façade

of the building started to crumble and collapse. Wallace and Beck then helped evacuate people from the site because of concerns about another inbound plane. After about forty-five minutes of assisting at the Pentagon, Wallace and Beck got back on their motorcycles and began directing traffic away from the site.[11]

Aviation Unit

Lieutenant Wallace and Sergeant Beck were not the only Park Police officers to respond at the Pentagon in those first devastating minutes. Officers in the aviation section also played an important role at the scene. At the aviation hangar in southeast Washington along the Anacostia River, some of the crew were taking advantage of the warm weather and bright sunshine by washing the floor out in the aviation hangar with the door open. Meanwhile, in an open field next to the hangar, one of the helicopter pilots, Sgt. Kenneth Burchell, was conducting riot training for the Defense department's uniformed health services unit in preparation for the upcoming World Bank/International Monetary Fund protest demonstrations.

Two casualties are loaded on Eagle II.

One crew member saw the news account of the first plane hitting the World Trade Center and called in the others. Sergeant Burchell, his fellow pilot Sgt. Ron Galey, and a few others went inside to watch the television coverage. After seeing the second plane strike and noting the clear blue sky, they quickly concluded that the crash was not an accident. Burchell and Galey headed back out to the hangar. They heard a loud thud and looked up to see a column of smoke rising from the vicinity of the Pentagon. Burchell immediately ran back inside, yelling for his crew. Minutes later, the "aircraft crash phone" rang, setting off a distinctive horn alarm. The crash phone was a direct communications line from the control tower at Ronald Reagan Washington National Airport to the hangar so that the aviation unit can respond quickly to incidents at the airport. Sergeant Galey took the call. On the other end of the line, the air traffic controller indicated that a 757 commercial airplane had crashed in the vicinity of the Pentagon. Meanwhile, a call had also come in on the police radio indicating that the Pentagon had been attacked.

The helicopter crews scrambled to gather their equipment, get to the helicopters, and launch. The duty crew that day, which included Sergeant Galey, rescue technician Sgt. John Marsh, and Officer John Dillon, ran out to *Eagle I*, a Bell 412 helicopter, and took off within two or three minutes. Sergeant Burchell grabbed Sgt. Keith Bohn and two Defense department medics with Uniformed Services University and Health Sciences who were there for the training. They began installing a mass casualty kit on *Eagle II*, another Bell 412 helicopter, which

allowed them to carry four patients instead of two. The installation took a few minutes. Then *Eagle II* took off with pilots Burchell and Bohn, the two medics, aviation unit commander Lt. Philip Cholak, and assistant commander Sgt. Bernie Stasulli.[12]

Shortly after launching, *Eagle II* received its first report that there was an unauthorized aircraft inbound. *Eagle I* directed *Eagle II* to land at the Pentagon to conduct medical evacuations. *Eagle II* quickly landed on a paved roadway 150 to 200 yards from the area of impact. Some of the crew grabbed their emergency medical equipment and ran toward the Pentagon building. At this point, with the reports of an unauthorized inbound plane, Sergeant Burchell realized they needed not only to evacuate the casualties but also to be ready to get as many people as possible away from the site before there was another attack. Sergeant Bohn kept the helicopter engine running and Sergeant Stasulli stood outside to secure the landing zone. Stasulli was particularly concerned that people moving away from the building, particularly those who seemed somewhat dazed, would inadvertently step too close to the aircraft's tail rotor blades and be seriously injured. Meanwhile, Lieutenant Cholak, Sergeant Burchell, and the two medics moved closer to assess the situation. They initially anticipated ferrying hundreds of patients to hospitals all day long so they wanted to set up an orderly process for this first. They checked in with the triage officer who indicated that there were only eleven casualties in need of medical evacuation. Cholak and one of the medics went to the triage area to assist. Burchell headed back to get Sergeant Bohn to move the aircraft closer, which he did.

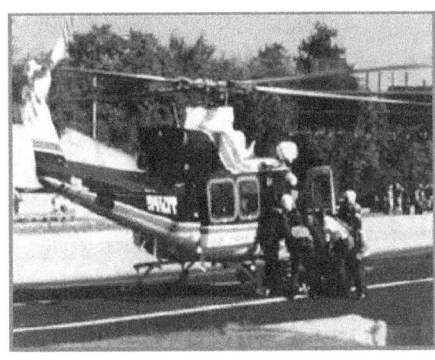

Although both crews saw many frightened and injured Pentagon employees fleeing the building, they saw others actually moving toward the burning building to help with the rescue operations. In contrast to other response operations in which they had participated, the crews were struck by the calm, orderly nature of the scene. They attributed this in part to the military training and discipline of many Pentagon employees. Sergeant Burchell found the response to be better organized than most. To illustrate this, he later recounted an incident soon after they landed where military personnel quietly spread out around the helicopter. When Lieutenant Cholak saw a number of military officers quietly encircle the aircraft, he became concerned that they might be injured by the tail rotor blade and directed them to move back. The officers immediately stepped back but calmly explained that they were simply securing the landing zone for him.

While the *Eagle II* crew stood by to transport the injured victims, *Eagle I* circled overhead. From the air initially the damage did not look extensive. The crew saw the fire and a great deal of smoke pouring from the building, but like Lieutenant Wallace,

they had difficulty identifying what was left of the hijacked airplane. The hole where the plane pierced the building appeared relatively small and there seemed to be little debris. The plane seemed at first to have simply disappeared into the building. On *Eagle I's* third pass over the building, however, Officer Dillon saw that the plane had penetrated from one ringed corridor of the building to the next, nearly reaching the center courtyard. Soon after, he and the others watched as the side of the building crumbled and collapsed.[13]

Eagle I was still circling overhead when the control tower at the airport warned of another unauthorized aircraft about twenty minutes out. Then just as *Eagle I* prepared to land, the air traffic controller radioed the crew that the smoke from the Pentagon had overtaken them and they were abandoning the airport control tower. In an unprecedented move, at the controller's request, *Eagle I* assumed control of the airspace for the entire Washington area. The task was simplified somewhat by the fact that the airspace had been closed down. The controller gave Sergeant Galey the radio frequency for the North American Aerospace Defense Command (NORAD), which had

Park Police and others prepare to transport injured victims at the Pentagon.

taken over control of the national airspace. Since NORAD typically only performs this function during wartime, the crews interpreted this shift as a strong indicator of the severe nature of the threat. No civilian plane would be allowed to fly in or out of the airspace without authorization from NORAD.[14]

Meanwhile, Burchell had asked Bohn to move the aircraft in closer, and they boarded two patients who were suffering from severe burns. As noted, *Eagle II* was prepared to carry four patients, but the triage officer did not have any other patients for transport at the time. The crew carried the patients to the MedStar unit of Washington Hospital Center, the region's only advanced burn center.

While *Eagle II* was at the hospital, *Eagle I* landed in the same area that *Eagle II* had vacated. Sergeant Galey was preparing to land when two F-16 fighter jets screamed past without warning. As soon as Galey landed, the two paramedics left the aircraft. The crew waited another ten minutes or so for additional patients. Sergeant Marsh came back and reported that there were no patients ready for transport but the helicopter should stand by. Then *Eagle I* received an update that the unauthorized inbound plane was now only a few miles out. They decided to move to a safer area a quarter mile from the Pentagon. The crew realized it could not conduct medical evacuations and provide command and control of the airspace at the same time, so they requested assistance from other departments that had helicopters which were equipped to transport injured patients, such as the Maryland State Police and Fairfax County Police Department.

They also asked that a metropolitan police helicopter be put in the air to provide command and control, and stood by for medical evacuations. The metropolitan police helicopter arrived and relieved *Eagle I* of its command and control function.

Sergeant Burchell had received the same reports of an inbound plane and knew there was an effort to disburse the aircraft at the scene. When it returned from the hospital, *Eagle II* set down at the western end of Memorial Bridge where it was somewhat sheltered by some trees and waited. The reported inbound plane never materialized. Not long after, both helicopters learned that there were no more patients to evacuate. Presumably some of the eleven had been taken away by ambulance.

After learning that there were no more patients to transport, *Eagle II* returned to the aviation hangar to pick up a Secret Service agent to patrol the airspace around the White House. As the helicopter climbed out of the Pentagon grounds, Sergeant Burchell spotted an F-16 fighter jet coming in from the opposite direction. He later recalled a particularly tense moment when the fighter jet flew by so low and close that he could see the brand name on the fighter pilot's sunglasses.[15]

The helicopters had microwave "downlink" capability that proved to be extremely valuable. With this technology, the crews could fly over a crime scene, demonstration, or other event and transmit instantaneous video images back to the chief's command post and other locations. Soon after *Eagle I* arrived on-site, the FBI asked the crew to turn on its microwave downlink. Dillon, who operated the downlink, found that in his first few passes over the Pentagon, the terrible images on the monitor looked so surreal that he occasionally had to take his eyes off the monitor and look down to confirm what he was seeing. The crew was able to transmit real-time images and information to people who needed them to make decisions.[16]

In addition to the downlink capability, the cameras on the helicopters could be switched to a forward-looking, infrared heat detection device known as FLIR. This technology proved to be extremely valuable. The fire department was having some difficulty getting its equipment to the proper locations to fight the fire. The crew took up the chief of the Arlington County Fire Department several times and flew low over the Pentagon so that he could locate the hot spots. The infrared imagery helped him locate the fire under the roof and enabled him to better position his firefighting crews and equipment. Flying in this environment was challenging because of the thick smoke, poor visibility, and the risk of inhaling hazardous materials, but *Eagle I* spent the next four or five hours flying overhead and transmitting video images to the FBI.

As the only aircraft on-site initially, the Park Police helicopters performed missions in support of the military. *Eagle I* also took up the commander of the 82nd Airborne Division so that he could get an aerial view that would assist him in deploying his troops around the building. By late afternoon, a number of military aircraft had arrived and the crews decided to complete their missions, leave the area, and go back to the hangar to refuel and prepare for whatever missions were ahead.[17]

During the recovery of victims from the Pentagon and collection of evidence, the unit supported the FBI with photo missions, crime scene search, and the use of the FLIR system in recovery of potential survivors. On September 11 and in the days following, the unit performed a number of missions in support of and in coordination with the FBI and Secret Service. The crews later described a new spirit of cooperation. *Eagle II* supported the Secret Service in protection of the president and White House and conducted additional flights in support of FBI. By the time *Eagle I* returned to the hangar, the *Eagle II* crew was already arranging to perform patrols for the Secret Service and to fly FBI agents out to Dulles International Airport, where the hijacked plane that flew into the Pentagon had originated. They were also developing their own plan for patrolling the metropolitan area.[18]

The crews spent the next few days patrolling along the Potomac River and checking bridges and overpasses in the city for potential threats. Major Pellinger deployed the aircraft around the White House. The areas around the White House and the U.S. Capitol were restricted airspace, and for several days the Park Police, in conjunction with the Secret Service, flew hourly around-the-clock security patrols around the White House and other restricted zones in the Washington area. Pellinger arranged for twenty-four-hour coverage for the monuments and memorials. Four months later, these patrols had ended, but crews continued to work twelve-hour shifts. As a result of the September 11 attacks, the unit's priorities changed. Security became "paramount," Ron Galey explained. As noted, the crews began to routinely conduct aerial checks of the monuments and memorials, something they had not done in the past in part because of concern that the noise would disturb tourists.[19]

The aviation unit's response activities involved a great deal of coordination with other departments and agencies. Fortunately, the crews had all the radio frequencies they needed to communicate effectively with the Arlington County Fire and Police Departments and the other agencies. They were also in frequent contact with Alexandria City and some of the other fire departments on the scene. They relayed information between fire departments on the ground that could not communicate directly with each other. The fact that the unit had experience dealing with the Arlington agencies, as well as Fairfax and Montgomery Counties, and had a good working relationship with those agencies made coordination easier.[20]

After September 11, the Park Police continued to use three-person crews for most missions. Although this approach added to their costs, they had found the three-person crews to be "invaluable." Crews could operate more efficiently and effectively with a third person. The helicopters were packed with sophisticated equipment such as the microwave downlink, FLIRs, video cameras, moving display maps, and radio communication equipment. The pilot had to devote all his attention to flying, and the second person had difficulty operating all this sophisticated equipment effectively. Three-person crews were ideal: one person flies the helicopter, the second operates the radios, and the third handles all the other equipment. The management sought to maintain the expanded crews for as long as possible. The Park Police also learned that

it was better to use 120- rather than 30-minute videotape because the tape compartment is mounted on the outside of the aircraft and changing tapes during an ongoing operation could be difficult.[21]

The contributions of the aviation unit were great both in the immediate aftermath and in the weeks that followed. As Sergeant Burchell observed, although the military had tremendous assets, "when you have an emergency in downtown Washington, D.C., ...you don't get Air Force Special Operations. You get two park policemen in a blue-and-white helicopter." The unit responded at the Pentagon within minutes of the attack and provided considerable support to the victims; to the military; and to various federal, state, and local agencies. "We did our part the best that we could," Burchell concluded.[22]

Evacuation of Cabinet Officials

Along with the response at the Pentagon, one of the earliest Park Police missions was to help evacuate and provide escorts for cabinet officials and other senior leaders. The Secret Service and the military had responsibility for evacuating cabinet members, but a decades-old plan stipulated that the Park Police would support the evacuation of these officials and secure the aircraft landing zones used in the evacuation. Officers had routinely practiced securing the staging area where cabinet officials were scheduled to gather so that they could be evacuated.

Shortly after 11:00 a.m. on September 11, Park Police officials learned that the White House had activated the evacuation plan. This was the first time in his twenty-four years as a Park Police officer that

Captain Lauro could recall the plan being activated. Park Police officers performed their assigned role and effectively cleared the designated staging area. Soon after the activation was canceled, but Park Police officers did escort a few officials and their staffs in a motorcade to a secure location. Later, Park Police officials conceded that providing escorts created some strain at a time when their officers were busy with other missions. As noted earlier, a Park Police special weapons and tactics (SWAT) team escorted the secretary of the interior and her senior staff to a secure location. They provided motorcycle officers and an escort vehicle to get them out of the city.[23]

Police cars and emergency vehicles were able move through the thick traffic much faster than private vehicles, and as a result, throughout the day, the Park Police received numerous requests for escorts. Officers also escorted President Bush, Vice President Richard Cheney, and Secretary of State Colin Powell. Traditionally, only the president and visiting dignitaries receive Park Police motorcycle escorts, not the vice president. However, after the attacks, officers began escorting the vice president to and from his office on a regular basis, which involved a significant commitment of resources. Motorcycle officers escorted the chairman of the Joint Chiefs of Staff, Gen. Henry H. Shelton, from Andrews Air Force Base to the Pentagon. One of the officers recalled the stunned expression on the general's face as they came up over a rise in the highway and he got his first view of the damage. The motorcycle unit also escorted the Montgomery County hazardous material unit down to the Pentagon.[24]

Traffic Management

In addition to their other missions, the Park Police are responsible for managing traffic on a number of bridges and roadways in Washington that are part of the National Park System, such as Memorial Bridge, George Washington Memorial Parkway, Rock Creek Parkway, and the Baltimore-Washington Parkway. All serve as major routes in and out of the city. Park Police officers took a number of measures to improve the flow of traffic and move people away from the downtown area more quickly. When the federal government released its employees that morning, many other downtown businesses and agencies did the same. With rumors about major disruption in the subway operations, the streets were jammed with several hundred thousand confused and alarmed commuters who were all trying to get out of the city as quickly as possible, creating what Deputy Chief Jack Schamp called "a monster traffic problem."[25] As traffic backed up around the city, workers trying to make their way home became increasingly anxious.

To help move traffic out of the downtown area faster and more efficiently, around 11:00 a.m. the Park Police decided to initiate the afternoon/evening commuting traffic patterns on all the major routes for which it had responsibility. This would direct traffic out of the city. Officers quickly reversed traffic lanes on Rock Creek Parkway making it one way outbound. They placed barricades across the entrances to the parkway but remained concerned that an inattentive or reckless driver might go around a barricade and enter traffic going the wrong direction. Lt. George Wallace could not recall any other instance where Park

Police had changed the traffic direction on Rock Creek Parkway outside of rush hour. Memorial Bridge and Clara Barton Parkway were restricted to outbound traffic only, and the southbound lanes of the George Washington Memorial Parkway were closed at Interstate 495. In some instances these historic parkways fed traffic onto city streets or state highways, where it jammed up. Park Police officials discovered that in the future they needed to coordinate more closely with the metropolitan police to improve the flow of traffic. Park Police representatives later worked with the metropolitan police and FEMA in developing detailed plans for the evacuation of the city.[26]

Additional Park Police Missions

In the days and weeks after the attacks, officers responded to reports of suspicious packages and vehicles, assisted the FBI with crime scene support, and cleared the core monument area of pedestrians and vehicles. They closed roads and increased patrols in response to potential threats. Whenever possible they responded to requests for uniformed patrols from agencies such as the Department of State, National Imagery and Mapping Agency, U.S. Army Corps of Engineers, CIA, and National Security

Agency. When a piece of the airplane that had struck the Pentagon was discovered some distance away at Arlington Cemetery, Park Police officers quickly secured the site until the FBI arrived.[27]

Park Police canine units helped sweep for bombs at the Little Falls Pumping Station and the Washington Aqueduct in northwest Washington. These critical facilities provided drinking water to the city. Two SWAT teams and canine units deployed at Camp David provided security for the president. Between September 11 and September 23, officers responded to roughly seventy reports of suspicious vehicles, packages, and persons. Through all of this, officers continued their day-to-day operations, which included investigating crimes, enforcing traffic and environmental restrictions, and assisting citizens.[28]

Park Rangers Respond

Working closely with the Park Police in Washington was a significant contingent of law enforcement rangers from the National Capital Region. Shortly after 9:30 a.m. on September 11, the region's chief ranger, Einar Olsen, was sitting in a meeting at the Anacostia Naval Station in southeast Washington with representatives from the Environmental Protection Agency,

Department of Defense, and FBI. The meeting had just begun when suddenly a number of pagers began going off around the room. One Defense representative, who had left the room to take a phone call, bolted back in to announce that the Pentagon had been hit. The other participants rushed to the window and saw smoke in the distance.

Olsen drove quickly back to his office, arriving at the regional headquarters ten minutes later. Soon after, he and others who were meeting in the regional director's office heard a loud explosion. At the time they feared there might have been another attack, but the noise was actually the sonic boom from a U.S. Air Force fighter jet that had scrambled from Langley Air Force Base in southeast Virginia. Faced with uncertain threats, Regional Director Terry Carlstrom decided to close the regional office and send employees home. The headquarters was located a short distance from the Pentagon and some of the national monuments and he was anxious to get employees away from the area in case there was another attack. As with the other federal workers released early from the office, headquarters employees were unsure how to get home with the disruptions in mass transportation and traffic gridlock. Some ended up taking off on foot.

As noted earlier, the Park Police were already mobilizing because they had primary responsibility for the security of the national monuments and memorials. Olsen recommended that the region put all its law enforcement rangers on alert to assist.[29] Under the Service's decentralized organizational structure, park superintendents have ultimate authority over their personnel. Olsen recognized that in an emergency this

system could impede the ability to mobilize and transfer resources. He recommended that Carlstrom "regionalize" the park law enforcement rangers so that Olsen would not have to secure approvals from individual superintendents before deploying those rangers. This would give Olsen the flexibility and authority that he needed to shift resources within the region. The regional director gave him an emergency delegation of authority to put rangers under regional control, so that he could move them around in response to the immediate requirements. Carlstrom thus placed the region's law enforcement rangers under Olsen's direct command. Unfortunately, Olsen found that he had no way to communicate with many of these rangers. This dilemma, he said, became a "major issue."[30]

With the authority issue resolved at least temporarily, Olsen walked next door to the Park Police headquarters and offered the assistance of the region's law enforcement rangers. Regional officials were concerned about possible future attacks on the monuments, the White House, or other facilities for which they were responsible. They also realized that Park Police resources were stretched thin. They agreed that Olsen would try to get some fifteen rangers and that the Park Police would relay assignments for them.

With the phone systems overwhelmed, Olsen was forced to rely on a radio system based out of a vehicle to communicate. He used one of the emergency vehicles in the parking lot outside the headquarters to contact the regional communications center in western Maryland. The center, which coordinated ranger activities throughout the National Capital Region, had only become a twenty-four-hour operation six months earlier. In response to Olsen's call, the center put out a message informing parks that there was a regional emergency and all rangers were under the region's authority. The center then called all the outlying parks where rangers worked.

Olsen decided to establish a staging area at the headquarters of the George Washington Memorial Parkway. This was a convenient location, outside the congested downtown area but near major roads, so there was easy access. He advised the communications center to call the George Washington Memorial Parkway headquarters and direct them to prepare to be the staging area. Olsen then got in his vehicle and began working his way through what he described as "horrendous" traffic in Washington. By that time, federal offices had closed contributing to the traffic congestion, and even emergency vehicles were having difficulty navigating through the city. All of the major bridges providing direct access to the parkway were clogged, so Olsen spent the next hour slowly weaving his way north and west through downtown Washington and into Maryland up to the American Legion Bridge. He crossed the bridge into Virginia and drove south on the George Washington Memorial Parkway until he reached the park headquarters.

Meanwhile, the park's superintendent, Audrey Calhoun, had set up the staging area. Rangers were already arriving from other parks as far away as Antietam National Battlefield, Monocacy National Battlefield, Harpers Ferry National Historical Park, C&O Canal National Historical Park, and Catoctin Mountain Park. As soon as the first seven rangers

arrived, Olsen asked the communications center in Maryland to contact Park Police headquarters to get the first assignment for the rangers, and the Park Police relayed the assignment back through the center.[31]

The first assignment was to send rangers to the Columbia Island portion of the George Washington Memorial Parkway to assist the children who had been evacuated from the day-care center at the Pentagon when the attack occurred. Roughly fifty adults and children from the day-care center had crossed the footbridge by Columbia Island Marina, which is under Park Service jurisdiction, and were sitting in a grass field known as the Lyndon Baines Johnson Memorial Grove. Olsen led the seven rangers down the parkway in a convoy because they were unfamiliar with the area. He described the trip down the parkway as "very eerie" and quiet. The rangers passed checkpoints but saw almost no traffic.[32]

The convoy reached its destination around noon. Olsen left Dwight Dixon, a district ranger from C&O Canal National Historical Park, in charge of the squad and returned up the parkway to the staging area. At Lyndon Baines Johnson Memorial Grove, Dixon found dozens of small children, including infants and toddlers. His team quickly set up a protective perimeter around the children and blocked one lane of westbound traffic on the George Washington Memorial Parkway to increase safety. The rangers were not equipped to transport such a large number of children. Eventually, they stopped an empty tour bus and asked the driver to help transport the children to a Virginia Department of Transportation facility near the Navy Annex just south of the Pentagon. Rangers carefully loaded up the children, blankets, and other items and escorted the bus to the facility. Once there, they helped move children, staff, and portable cribs into the building. Someone brought in baby formula to feed the infants and lunch for everyone else. The rangers set up a security zone around the building and waited for the parents to claim their children. By 5:30 that evening all of the children had been picked up, and after determining that there were no additional assignments, Dixon and the other rangers drove home.[33]

National Mall

While Dixon's team was busy caring for the young children from the Pentagon daycare center, enough rangers had arrived at George Washington Memorial Parkway headquarters to form a second squad. The Park Police gave the rangers another assignment—to report to the mobile command post located on the National Mall at Twelfth Street and Jefferson Drive in northwest Washington. About 2:00 p.m. Olsen led a second convoy down the parkway, across the Theodore Roosevelt Bridge, and into Washington. After receiving a briefing at the command post, the rangers led by Manassas National Battlefield Park Ranger Gil Goodrich were assigned to provide security and enforce closures along the National Mall and at the Jefferson Memorial. The squad was released later that evening after enough Park Police officers had arrived to replace them.

As rangers from outlying parks assisted the Park Police on the National Mall, employees from National Capital Parks–Central were also hard at work in the same area. National Capital Parks–Central rangers immediately evacuated and closed all park sites. The site manager for the National Mall, Lance Hatten, was in the midst of giving a presentation at the Old Post Office Tower on Pennsylvania Avenue, when a Park Police officer informed him of the attacks in New York City. By the time he returned to his office at the ranger station, the National Mall area was already being evacuated and traffic was in near gridlock. Faced with a great deal of uncertainty and horrible traffic congestion, tourists looked to the rangers on the Mall for advice about what to do, where to go, and what road to take. Unfortunately, in this confusing situation the rangers had little information to provide. Hatten released his employees around noon. Later that afternoon, Hatten and the superintendent of National Capital Parks–Central visited the various sites to make sure that they were secured.[34]

Meanwhile, while others fled the scene at the White House the morning of the attacks, Presidents' Park grounds crews remained on duty. In anticipation of the president's return to the White House by helicopter, they removed picnic tables that had been set up on the south lawn for a planned afternoon event to create a landing space. President's Park rangers and volunteers helped clear the area around the White House and comforted anxious visitors. Maintenance employees set up additional security barricades.

That evening, National Capital Parks–Central maintenance staff installed snow fence to close off the periphery of the Jefferson and Lincoln Memorials and the area around the base of the Washington Monument. They installed snow fencing and about ten miles of temporary chain-link fence in the National Mall area. Days later, when the decision was made to close the entire Ellipse, the maintenance crew worked from 5:00 p.m. on Sunday until 8:00 a.m. the next morning off-loading and placing Jersey barriers at the entrances.[35]

Catoctin Mountain Park

While some of the region's rangers and Park Police officers supported operations in the Washington area, others took assignments at Catoctin Mountain Park, site of the presidential retreat, Camp David. In the first hours after the attacks, park staff tried to contact the regional headquarters but failed to reach anyone in the chain of command. They began to route their communications through the region's communications center in western Maryland. Initially Catoctin managers decided not to release the staff because they thought they might be needed for security-related missions. The park, in fact, never received a call from the regional office directing it to close. Not until the next morning did employees learn that neighboring parks had released their employees.

The day of the attacks the Secret Service requested assistance from the park's rangers and from the Park Police to provide twenty-four-hour security at Camp David. When the president evacuated from Washington, D.C., to Camp David, the region sent additional park rangers to enforce various security perimeter zones around that area. This Park Police and ranger support included additional patrols, manning four checkpoints, and closing the central portion of the park. The security situation intensified a day or two later

when the president, vice president, cabinet members, and other senior officials began a series of high-level meetings at Camp David. Security became a long-term assignment. During the months that followed, the Park Service would institute more than fifty-six days of twenty-four-hour closures at various areas of the park.

During the closures, typically four rangers were needed each day to man posts and patrol. At the same time the staff was taxed with additional foot and vehicle patrols outside its normal duty hours, whether there was a visit in progress or not. Two shifts a day were needed to cover these patrols. The additional patrols were not covered by any reimbursable agreements with the Secret Service. The park did not usually operate twenty-four hours a day, seven days a week, and had not budgeted or staffed for such operations. Managers had to draw on emergency law and order funds. Catoctin Mountain Park Superintendent Mel Poole observed that people did not immediately associate Camp David with Catoctin, so it was difficult to convince them that the park was as important as the Statue of Liberty or Independence Hall because the president and vice president were frequently in residence. A year earlier, the park had been cut from ten law enforcement positions to eight.[36]

When park managers needed additional rangers from other parks, they submitted their request to the regional communications center. Though this twenty-four-hour dispatch center had been operating for only a year, according to Poole, it had proved itself to be "one of the best things that this region has done in many, many years." If the center could not fill the request, the request went to the Eastern Interagency Coordination Center (EICC) in Shenandoah National Park. There was also a less formal process for sharing and coordinating resources within the region. For example, on September 12, Poole informed the regional director that Catoctin would quickly exhaust the existing ranger resources, and the regional director mentioned another park that might have some available resources. So Poole informed the regional communications center that this park might have some rangers available who could meet his need. Having this unofficial communications system in addition to the official one, Poole noted, "makes us more efficient."[37]

The security mission prompted Catoctin Mountain Park to draw on rangers from throughout the National Capital and Northeast Regions to fill shifts. Rangers came from as far away as the Gettysburg, Fredericksburg, and Spotsylvania battlefields, Delaware Water Gap, and Valley Forge. As a result some of the outlying parks in the National Capital Region were stripped of most of their protection rangers and forced to close gates and buildings temporarily.[38]

After September 11 attacks, the National Capital Region embarked on a comprehensive effort to enhance its emergency response capability, focusing increased attention on safety, training, employee and public information, planning, mobilizing resources, and logistical support. It also took steps to improve communications among the parks, specifically establishing radio links and expanding the use of satellite phones.

Conclusion

The success of the region's response to the September 11 attacks can be attributed to a number of factors: the superb cooperation between the region's law enforcement rangers and the Park Police; the willingness of parks to share their ranger resources; and the dedication of individual law enforcement rangers and Park Police officers who worked extended duty hours, sometimes for weeks and even months. The region's law enforcement rangers and the Park Police had worked together in the past during demonstrations or other special events. With this event, however, said Capt. Sal Lauro, the number of rangers who supported the Park Police and the speed of their response was unprecedented.[39]

Another key to the successful response in Washington was the close cooperation between the Park Police and the police and fire departments in Arlington County, Alexandria, and Fairfax County in Virginia, as well as with various federal entities. Over the years, the Park Police, particularly its special forces branch, had often worked closely with the Secret Service, U.S. Capitol Police, FBI, and various local jurisdictions—metropolitan police, metro transit police, Arlington and Fairfax Counties. The strong relationships that Park Police had forged with those entities enabled them to work effectively as a team on September 11.

The role that park rangers and Park Police played in evacuating government leaders, protecting the public, and securing some of the nation's most revered monuments and memorials was unprecedented. The same remarkable level of dedication and cooperation would characterize the response of Park Police and park rangers in the New York City area.

III. New York City

While Park Service employees in the Washington area struggled
to respond to the terrorist attacks, many of their fellow employees in
New York City were also grappling with the immediate impact. Some
employees in New York personally witnessed the attacks on the World
Trade Center; some were directly involved in caring for victims; and
still others participated in search and recovery operations at the site of
the collapsed towers, known as Ground Zero. Many of the roughly 450
National Park Service employees at the twenty-one Park Service sites in
New York Harbor were profoundly affected by the events of September
11.[1] The units most affected were no doubt two units of Manhattan Sites,
the Statue of Liberty, Ellis Island, and Gateway National Recreation
Area. Park staffs and the Park Police New York field office played a
significant role in the response.

U.S. Park Police New York Field Office

The Park Police field office in New York City traditionally provided law
enforcement services at all the units in Gateway National Recreation
Area as well as at Statue of Liberty National Monument and Ellis Island.
Field office commander Maj. Thomas Wilkins was at his residence at
Fort Wadsworth, across the harbor from Manhattan, when he saw television coverage of the first plane slamming into the tower. Grabbing his
binoculars, he hurried up to the overlook near the Verrazano Bridge
where he would have a clear view of Lower Manhattan. Capt. Neal
Lauro (brother of Capt. Sal Lauro), who was district commander for the

*Opposite page, the World Trade Center towers soared as a backdrop to
Liberty Island before the September 11 attacks.
Above, the United Airlines plane circles before tearing through the second tower.*

Park Police responded quickly at the various park units in New York City and spent much of their free time participating in the rescue operations at Ground Zero.

Staten Island Station, the Statue of Liberty, and Ellis Island, learned of the attack from his son who was on a bus heading into Manhattan. Capt. Neal Lauro and two of his officers, Lt. Dave Buckley and Sgt. Frank Abbatantuono, who were in his office at the time, drove to the overlook where they joined Wilkins and a few others. Against the brilliant blue sky, they could see smoke and fire pouring out of one of the trade towers. Together they watched as a second plane swept in low across the harbor and slammed into the second tower.

Watching this second attack, they quickly concluded that this event was no accident. A minute after the building was hit, the jarring sound of the explosion reached them. The officers said little. They all came to the same conclusion that the Statue of Liberty was a potential target for another attack, and they would be in a better position to respond if they were at Ellis Island. Captain Lauro immediately contacted the commander at the Statue of Liberty and directed him to evacuate the island. Lauro, Buckley, and Abbatantuono quickly got back in the car and drove to Ellis Island. Eight or nine officers were on duty at the Statue of Liberty and at Ellis Island at the time. Lauro's most immediate concern was to do everything possible to prevent

another attack. He got on the phone and the radio giving instructions and arranging to bring off-duty officers back into work. Buckley who commanded the field office's SWAT team made a call to ask the Park Police dispatcher to direct his team to go to Ellis Island.[2]

Before leaving for Ellis Island, Captain Lauro ordered the closure of Fort Wadsworth. Major Wilkins began coordinating with U.S. Coast Guard officials to institute security measures at the post. Fort Wadsworth housed the command center for the Coast Guard's New York Harbor operations, an Army Reserve center, a Defense Logistics Agency facility, and the foot of the Verrazano Narrows Bridge. As a result, security concerns for the area were particularly great. Officers immediately closed the back gate and placed guards at the main entrance to control access. A police lieutenant was assigned to serve as liaison and help the park and the Coast Guard put in place appropriate security measures.[3]

Major Wilkins had just dropped in on a Coast Guard briefing when the first tower collapsed. He returned to the overlook in time to see the second tower collapse. At that point, he decided to drive into Manhattan to the New York Police

Department (NYPD) command post at One Police Plaza. Thick gray ash coated his windshield as he came across the Brooklyn Bridge. He pulled up at One Police Plaza and with the electrical power out climbed eight floors to the command post, where representatives from various state and local agencies were gathering. The major thought his presence in the command post would enhance communications and coordination with other agencies. He believed it was important to have a Park Police representative in the command center with enough authority to make quick decisions if necessary, and he was confident that his two district commanders, Capts. Neal Lauro and Marty Zweig, could handle the operations in their areas. Wilkins's primary role at the NYPD command post was to inform the other representatives of the resources that the Park Service had available. Later, he also relayed information about injured firefighters who had been taken to Ellis Island.

While Major Wilkins performed his tasks at One Police Plaza, the Park Police field office continued operating under its normal structure. At 9:15 a.m. the field office had notified all off-duty personnel to report for duty immediately. Some officers had difficulty coming in to work because of traffic congestion and road closures. As in Washington, D.C., officers enrolled in the home-to-work program had an easier time driving in. Captain Lauro continued to oversee missions at Staten Island, the Statue of Liberty and Ellis Island, and Captain Zweig, district commander for the Brooklyn and Queens unit, remained at Floyd Bennett Field dispatching Park Police throughout the area. Zweig quickly called in additional officers, closed off Floyd Bennett Field, and dispatched several boats to Manhattan. The Park Police field office was able to deploy its officers and boats to different areas based on information that Wilkins relayed from One Police Plaza.[4]

The Park Police marine unit included a forty-one-foot patrol boat *(Marine 4)*; twenty-six-foot Whaler patrol boat *(Marine 3)*; twenty-five-foot Sea Ark patrol boat *(Marine 5)*; thirty-foot Intrepid patrol boat *(Marine 2)*; and twenty-seven-foot Glacier Bay patrol boat *(Marine 1)*. Fire Island National Seashore dispatched two boats with rangers to assist the Park Police with marine operations. The Park Police vessels quickly formed a security perimeter around Ellis Island and Liberty Island and

Above, Park Police assist with debris removal at Ground Zero.

helped evacuate employees and residents on Liberty Island. The marine vessels transported wounded police and firefighters, and frightened civilians from the Battery Park area to Ellis Island. The marine unit evacuated the Secret Service's entire New York field office from 7 World Trade Center and also carried doctors, nurses, and supplies that had been prepositioned on Ellis Island into Manhattan.

A couple days after the attack, as Officer David Moen and two other officers patrolled on *Marine 5*, they noticed one of the buildings near the South Cove marina starting to collapse. Thousands of frightened rescue workers from Ground Zero suddenly began running. *Marine 5's* crew saw some deputy U.S. marshals running toward the water to escape. The crew motioned them toward the boat and held a line around the dock so the eight deputies and a construction worker could jump onto the boat. During this process, one deputy fell into the water and quickly went under. The crew pulled him out and took the deputies safely out into the harbor and to Ellis Island.[5] The marine unit played a key role in the response. "Without

the boats," Officer Moen explained, "we would have felt like we were helpless." Without the boats, he said, traveling in and out of Manhattan would have been "next to impossible." The boats allowed the Park Police to travel back and forth from Manhattan to Jersey and from Staten Island. Having a direct link by water allowed them to get where they were needed much faster. The marine unit coordinately closely with the Coast Guard and provided support to the Coast Guard and other agencies. The boats provided escorts, enforced safety zones, and transported personnel between Ellis Island and Manhattan.[6] Throughout the response, Park Police officers continued to work closely with the staffs at Manhattan Sites, the Statue of Liberty, Ellis Island, and Gateway National Recreation Area.

Manhattan Sites

Manhattan Sites, an urban park in the New York City area made up of six separate sites (Castle Clinton National Monument, Federal Hall National Memorial, General Grant National Memorial, Hamilton Grange National Memorial, Saint Paul's Church

Above left, view of burning trade towers from New York Harbor.
Above right, Park Police vessel patrols the harbor.

National Historic Site, and Theodore Roosevelt Birthplace National Historic Site), was one of the most immediately and dramatically affected units in the National Park System. All six sites were briefly closed to the public immediately after the attacks and two of these remained closed for weeks after. The impact on Federal Hall National Memorial and Castle Clinton National Monument was particularly great. Federal Hall, located on Wall Street in the center of the financial district just a few blocks east of the World Trade Center, became a disaster shelter moments after the trade towers collapsed. The small staff provided shelter and aid to an estimated 250 people fleeing the smoke, dust, and debris that rained down on the streets of Lower Manhattan.[7]

Interpretive Ranger Laura Brennan had arrived at Federal Hall before 8:00 a.m. to prepare for the regular 9:00 a.m. opening. Promptly at 9:00 a.m. she and maintenance laborer Daniel (Danny) Merced opened the doors to visitors. When they walked outside, they were startled to find the front steps completely covered with papers and burning debris. A large column of smoke loomed overhead. They headed back into the building so Merced could make sure the burning debris did not start a fire on the roof. As they walked toward the stairs

they heard the loud boom of the plane hitting the second tower. They hurried back to the front door where they saw what they described as hundreds of people running down the narrow Wall Street. One passerby screamed that the World Trade Center had been struck. Although no one on the staff could yet fully comprehend what was going on, they decided to secure the building as a precaution.

While Brennan called down to nearby Castle Clinton National Monument to find out what was going on, Merced and maintenance mechanic Archie Johnson walked up the street to get a glimpse of the damaged trade center. After witnessing the gruesome scene and assessing the situation, they returned to Federal Hall and asked for permission to go home. By that time the radio was reporting major disruptions in traffic and public transportation around the city so they decided to stay put. Meanwhile, Christopher Keenan, supervisory park ranger at General Grant National Memorial and the only commissioned law enforcement officer for the Manhattan Sites, was in a government van driving into Lower Manhattan hurrying to the regularly scheduled monthly staff meeting at Federal Hall. As he headed south he saw a huge cloud of smoke coming from the World Trade Center. He pulled over to let fire engines pass. He later vividly recalled seeing the faces of those firefighters and cheering them on. Tragically, many of the first firefighters to rush to the scene would later be trapped when the trade towers collapsed. As Keenan continued on at a much slower pace, frantic strangers ran directly into his van. He heard a thunderous explosion and screaming and wondered what was going on. When he could progress no

The small staff at Federal Hall provided shelter and aid to an estimated 250 people fleeing the smoke, dust, and debris that rained down on the streets of Lower Manhattan.

farther because of road closures and traffic, he parked the van in Battery Park, grabbed his riot helmet, and set off on foot for Federal Hall.

The superintendent had not yet arrived at Federal Hall, so the chief of interpretation for Manhattan Sites, Steven Laise, took charge temporarily. After hearing news of the second attack on the radio, he directed the staff to close down the building. Laise and Keenan carefully searched the building inside and out for explosives and suspicious packages. They were outside when the first tower collapsed. Shortly after the collapse, people came running down Nassau Street and Wall Street, frantically trying to outrun an enormous cloud of dust and debris, a scene that Brennan later compared to something out of a *Godzilla* movie. The dark cloud moved faster than the people could run. As the darkness overtook them, they found it increasingly difficult to breathe and desperately sought shelter. Keenan, Merced, and Laise, who were at the Nassau Street entrance, began grabbing people and shoving them into Federal Hall. They slammed the door behind them.

The small basement quickly filled with strangers covered with gray dust and soot. Suddenly Brennan and the others felt the building "rumble." They had no way of knowing at the time that the frightening "rumble" they experienced was caused by the collapse of the first tower. Concerned about the safety of her coworkers upstairs, Brennan ran from the basement to the third floor staff offices. The third floor was the least secure area in the building because of all the windows. As Brennan hurriedly moved the staff off the third floor, she noticed a dark cloud had engulfed the building.

Johnson and Merced had decided to head home, but they did not make it very far. When Johnson opened the back door to leave, more people rushed into the building seeking shelter. He spotted a large cloud of debris and quickly closed the door. When he reopened the door, it was pitch black outside. He heard women yelling from across the street, ran over to assist, and brought them inside.

Meanwhile, out on the street, eyes stinging Merced was overtaken by the dust cloud when the South Tower collapsed. The

View of Federal Hall National Memorial along Wall Street.

dust aggravated his chronic asthma, and he began to have difficulty breathing. As Merced tried to push down his own fears and struggled for breath, frightened strangers who had seen him speaking to a police officer minutes earlier and seen his uniform now approached him. A few frantic strangers grabbed onto him screaming for help. As Merced tried to calm them, he concluded that he had no choice but to bring them back to Federal Hall. Although he was only two blocks from Federal Hall, the smoke was so thick that he temporarily lost his bearings. He had to feel his way along a wall leading the others until he found the doorway. By the time he reentered the building, he was covered from head to toe with dust and dirt. After showering and changing into a clean uniform, he noticed that other strangers had already taken refuge in the basement. Merced grabbed some rags and pulled the bottled water machine from the maintenance shop area out into the basement so that people could clean off some of the dust and ash. The staff handed out cups of bottled water. They took turns standing by the door to let in the people who continued to seek shelter.[8]

The staff left the air-conditioning on, but this seemed to draw in even more dust. As more people entered the building, the basement filled with dust, making it increasing difficult for them to breathe. Fortunately, the park had recently received a large shipment of dust masks for its maintenance staff, which the staff now handed out. The air quality in the now crowded basement continued to deteriorate. The staff realized that they needed to get the visitors out of that area. They asked those who were coated with dust to brush themselves off and then move up to the first floor where the air was better. They moved those who needed medical attention to the second floor where the air was better still. Meanwhile, the staff had to deal with fear and uncertainty. They heard on the radio about the attack on the Pentagon and worried about additional attacks. With the New York Stock Exchange just across the street there was some concern that they were perilously close to a potential target.[9]

Manhattan Sites superintendent, Joseph Avery, on his way to the monthly staff meeting was delayed in traffic. He parked on a side street near Federal Hall and began running. The overpowering dust and smoke turned his blue coat gray and forced him to take temporary refuge in a nearby building. By the time he arrived and went through the side entrance, he found his staff already busy caring for the stranded guests. Roughly 150 visitors were in the cramped basement covered with dust, with another 100 sheltered on the first floor. Some were crying. Some were washing themselves off as best they could with water and paper towels. Many had cuts and other minor injuries, several had asthma, some were understandably very distraught, and two women indicated they were pregnant and in need of a place to rest. One asthmatic was having a particularly difficult time breathing. Fortunately, Keenan and Brennan both had emergency medical training. Brennan performed first aid up in the rotunda area, while Keenan tended to those who remained in the basement. Federal Hall had little in the way of first-aid supplies and Keenan regretted that in his haste to get there earlier that morning, he had left his emergency medical kit behind in his vehicle.

People huddled on the floor while staff members did everything they could to make them comfortable and calm them. Some visitors were panicky, while others stared blankly into space. Still others settled into the benches in the Peter Zenger Room, the only windowless room, and to provide a diversion Merced put in a film that park staff used for interpretation. He also took one of the pregnant women who was complaining of pain down to the maintenance area where she could put her feet up and be more comfortable. He even shared his own asthma medication with the young woman who was having much difficulty breathing. Another sympathetic staff member gave a pair of sneakers to a woman who had literally run out of her shoes in her frantic effort to escape the dust and debris. The sight of well-dressed women in business suits barefoot with their legs cut up left an incongruous and unforgettable image for staff members. The staff managed to get a working phone line and allowed their guests to call family members to let them know that they were okay. Few had any idea where they were. People had run blindly into the building and some were interested in learning about the site, so Johnson gave them a tour. The routine tasks of showing the interpretive film and leading a visitor tour must have seemed somewhat surreal under these circumstances.

The force of the tower collapse shook open some of the building's old windows allowing dust to stream in. More than an inch of dust piled up on the first floor. People were terrified. The staff let them go up to the second floor. When the second tower fell, people did not hear the loud rumble as with the first one because the dust and debris hanging in the air muffled the sound.

But they heard a gush of air pass and saw the sky become completely dark. More people rushed in from outside. Desperate strangers seeking refuge broke out a window facing Wall Street.[10]

With so many people to care for, the staff asked the Park Police for help. Capt. Marty Zweig sent two officers to Federal Hall. Sgt. Clyde Solomon had just dropped his children off at school when the dispatcher directed him to respond to Federal Hall. He and Officer Bekim Cobaj drove their police van through the smoke of Lower Manhattan to Federal Hall. The staff was relieved to see the two officers who arrived in their SWAT uniforms. The officers joined the staff in trying to calm and reassure the visitors. They helped identify those in greatest need of medical attention. While Sergeant Solomon helped the staff move the injured to the second floor, Officer Cobaj went in search of medical assistance. Officials had set up triage centers with medical personnel in certain parts of the city. One of these centers was a few blocks away at the Federal Reserve Bank. The two officers used their police van to transport the injured, sick, and pregnant to this triage center where the most critical patients were placed in ambulances and carried to the hospital.

After helping transport the injured to the Federal Reserve Bank, Keenan returned to Federal Hall where Merced brought his attention to a hot dog cart across the street that had been abandoned. After checking for suspicious packages, Keenan, Merced, and Solomon took bread, soda, and other packaged food from the cart to give to the hungry and thirsty people inside.

By early afternoon, some of the dust had settled and the visitors began to head home. Solomon distributed dust masks and advised them to walk across the Brooklyn Bridge, which seemed to be the safest route out of town for pedestrians. By around 1:30 p.m., after the last visitors had departed, Johnson, Merced, and Brennan began their long, somber walk home. Avery, Laise, and a couple others stayed behind to inspect the building for major structural damage. Laise and Avery finally left at 5:00 p.m. Solomon and Cobaj remained on-site until around 10:00 p.m. and then used their van to shuttle firefighters closer to Ground Zero. Keenan would remain on duty at Federal Hall through the night. During the night the cooling tower on the roof overflowed because dust had blocked the drains. The chief of maintenance at the Statue of Liberty, Peter O'Dougherty, came over around midnight to address the problem.[11]

The next morning transportation was still disrupted and parts of Manhattan remained closed off. Despite this situation, thinking that he might be needed a determined Danny Merced slowly made

his way in to work. He relieved Keenan around 9:00 a.m. Park Police officers were on-site, but Merced and Sheila Hamilton were the only staff members to come in that day. Hamilton handled the phones while Merced cleaned the building. He made sure that the basement area and bathroom were clean and available to policemen and firemen working in the area.

Federal Hall remained closed on September 13, but Keenan and Avery came in to assess the damage. They conducted a preliminary examination of the building's structure to determine whether a more extensive evaluation would be needed. More than an inch of dust and debris blanketed the roof. On September 11, the air-conditioner had pulled the dust into the air-conditioning ducts and filled the building with dust. The two men concluded that the building's interior would have to be professionally cleaned using hazardous material procedures and equipment before the staff could be allowed to return.[12]

The imposing building was a solid masonry structure of granite and marble that had stood since 1842. It was so sturdy that the lowest floor had been designated an air

Park Police canine unit on duty at Federal Hall after September 11.

Although Federal Hall was solid masonry, constructed of granite, the force of the crumbling trade towers and the resulting dust and debris caused significant damage.

raid shelter during the Cold War. However, the powerful seismic waves following the collapse of the towers caused serious structural damage. The force of the collapse caused a significant expansion of pre-existing horizontal interior cracks along the west wall running parallel on the basement and first floor. Vertical cracks extended above the interior doors and through the lintels.[13] Over the next few days, the staff slowly resumed operations. Within roughly a week, phone service, electrical power, and water supply were fully operational and the broken windows had been replaced. Contracts were negotiated for cleaning the interior and the heating/air-conditioning system. Cleaning was particular challenge because the asbestos that had been used in the construction of trade towers permeated the area.

Preliminary estimates indicated that the cost of stabilizing the cracks could reach $15 million. Other needed repairs included replacing the filters, gearbox, and chiller fan unit in the cooling tower on the roof; replacing glass in the skylight above the rotunda and in a Wall Street window; removing dust and debris from the roof and gutters; replacing soiled carpet in the

basement; and cleaning more than twenty dust-filled air handler units. Reopening the site also hinged on providing adequate security for the site, the public, and the staff. Park Police officers were stationed at the site twenty-four hours a day, and security guards operated a magnetometer and inspected packages.[14]

Just south of Federal Hall, Castle Clinton National Monument also struggled with the impact of the attacks. Castle Clinton is a circular structure that had been built in the nineteenth century to defend New York Harbor. It is located in Battery Park at the southern tip of Manhattan, less than a mile southwest of the World Trade Center. Site manager Charles Markis arrived at 8:15 a.m. on September 11 anticipating another routine day. He had no way of knowing that this day would quickly become anything but routine. With the mild temperatures and clear skies, a number of visitors had already gathered outside when Markis and other rangers opened the doors to the public promptly at 8:30. The site manager returned to his office, which looked out onto the central parade ground in Battery Park. At approximately 8:45 a.m. he noticed people pointing as they looked north

Workers remove dust and debris from the entrance to Federal Hall.

toward the World Trade Center and became curious. He stepped outside his door and looked up to see one of the trade towers in flames. Soon after the staff began to see papers from the offices and other debris floating in the air.

Back inside, Markis heard a radio announcement that there had been some kind of accident at the trade center and began to think about evacuating his staff. A call came in from the regional office directing the site to close. The first Circle Line boat that carried visitors to the Statue of Liberty and Ellis Island was scheduled to depart at 9:00 a.m. and passengers were already boarding. Markis walked over to the ticket office and directed the manager to get the passengers off the boat. He also instructed his staff to clear visitors from the site, from the bookstore, restrooms, and museum area. After clearing out the visitors, they secured the back door.

The site manager and a few others were outside the building preparing to secure the doors when they saw the second plane fly overhead and dive into the second tower. Then came the chilling realization that they were under attack. Markis went back inside

to close up his office and discovered that they had no telephone or electrical service. He and his staff decided to evacuate. As they prepared to leave, they heard a loud explosion. Not knowing at the time that a tower had collapsed, they feared that the noise might be a bomb or missile. Then they saw a huge debris cloud fast approaching and realized it was not safe to leave. The small group of employees and partners hurriedly took refuge in the site manager's office, donning dust masks that he pulled from a supply closet. With no telephone service, electrical power, or batteries for the radio, they were completely cut off, without communications. They heard another explosion as the second tower collapsed and heard the sirens and fighter jets overhead but could only surmise what was happening. Peering out through a small window they saw a frightening mix of ash, concrete, business cards, stationary, and other debris rain down. The sky turned black. Markis tried to calm his staff as they sat in the dark imagining the worst.

The police were not letting civilians go north of Battery Park so a number of people were huddled outside around the

Castle Clinton on the southern tip of Manhattan was less than a mile from the World Trade Center.

Staff at the Manhattan Sites set aside
their own fears and safety concerns
to provide food, water, shelter, and medical assistance
to the victims of the attacks.

monument where the dust and debris were thickest. The staff could hear their voices, but Markis concluded it would not be wise to invite them in. He worried that the burning debris he had seen would ignite the wood shingle and truss roof that covered the perimeter of Castle Clinton. If there was a fire, he knew his small staff could retreat to the cellar, but they would not be able to take care of more people. The staff remained secluded in Markis's office for about an hour and a half under the rain of dust and debris. When the sky began to clear, they went out to look around. One of the first things they did was look to reassure themselves that the Statue of Liberty still stood.[15]

The ticket office manager and one of the Circle Line owners had a cell phone with a radio function so they were able to contact the Circle Line boat captains and ask them to bring the boats in to help evacuate people. Two Circle Line boats from across the East River where they were tied up arrived, and the staff provided the crews with dust masks. As with Federal Hall, the incident highlighted the importance of having a supply of dust masks on hand for emergency situations. Authorities used the seawall behind Castle Clinton as a staging area and commandeered all boats in the harbor to

evacuate people from Lower Manhattan. Circle Line boats carried people to New Jersey.

The experience also highlighted unexpected problems. Castle Clinton's restrooms had been renovated with electronic flush mechanisms. These mechanisms could not function without a power supply, so the staff was unable to draw water into a sink or flush a toilet. None of the drinking fountains functioned because emergency responders had tapped into the water system and the water pressure was low. Also, without electricity to operate the pump, sewage backed up within twenty minutes, so the staff could not allow the public to use the restrooms. They later allowed some limited access to the restrooms and distributed some bottled water. When the situation calmed down, the staff began to leave. Markis, the last to leave, began to walk home around 1:00 p.m.

Communications remained disrupted for days after the attack. The site manager could only contact employees who lived in New Jersey and Connecticut by cell phone. The city closed off the part of Manhattan south of Fourteenth Street. The military established a staging area for the National Guard in Battery Park. Staff members were temporarily placed at other sites. Markis later took a position at Sagamore Hill National Historic Site and did not return to Castle Clinton as site manager.[16]

Unlike Federal Hall, which sustained significant damage, Castle Clinton came through attacks "in remarkably good condition."[17] It reopened a few weeks later without any special cleaning or additional security personnel, though the sale of Statue of Liberty ferry tickets at Castle Clinton was suspended temporarily.[18]

September 11 was a defining experience for employees at Manhattan Sites, particularly at Federal Hall and Castle Clinton. Superintendent Avery was justifiably proud of his staff, describing them as patient, kind, and comforting. Staff members put aside their own fears and safety concerns to provide food, water, shelter, and medical assistance and to calm panicky and occasionally hysterical victims. For example, despite his own serious asthma condition, Danny Merced worked continuously filling the water machine and helping the visitors. Fellow employee Archie Johnson found himself drawing on his Vietnam experience that day as he went around calming individuals and making sure that everyone was all right. "Help your fellow man was just— that was the day to do that, you know," he explained.[19] Steve Laise explained that in helping people that day, staff members drew on the Service's "strong tradition of service." "It's been that way ever since 1916, when the Park Service was created, that rangers are there to help people," he added. "If it's deep in the wilderness and somebody's lost, or if it's in Lower Manhattan and somebody's seeking shelter, that's our job. That is what a park ranger does." Christopher Keenan, too, felt the personal

satisfaction of knowing that he had done "exactly what I was supposed to do."[20]

For some, the experience changed the way they viewed their fellow workers. It forged a tighter bond among park staff. They felt renewed respect and appreciation for each other. "I could have been no prouder if they were my children or my best friend because they hung in there, man. They really hung in there," said Johnson. "I know that when push comes to shove and you need them," he added, "they'll be there for you." Managers expressed great pride in the way the staff pulled together and responded to the crisis, especially the maintenance employees and rangers. "We could have shut our doors and went home," Keenan said. "We didn't. We stayed on, and I'm very proud of us."[21]

In the weeks that followed, some of those who had taken refuge in Federal Hall that traumatic day either sent notes or came back to thank the staff personally. Another gentleman sent a poignant thank-you note on behalf of his daughter, a young attorney who had taken shelter at Federal Hall. It was not unusual for strangers to stop Merced and Johnson on the street to thank them for their efforts that day. One woman who had escaped the trade center returned to thank and embrace a Castle Clinton ranger who had led her safely to a boat that carried her to New Jersey.

Federal Hall reopened to the public on October 15, but with new security measures in place. Visitors now went through magnetometer screening. Before September 11, the Park Police provided support at Federal Hall only in response to special circumstances as needed. Now they had a continual presence there. Castle Clinton did

not reopen until nearly a week later, on October 22, because of the Army Reserves occupying Battery Park. Visitation did not immediately return to its pre–September 11 level. Federal Hall and Castle Clinton had always been considered secondary destinations for visitors to Manhattan. To further complicate matters, transportation in Lower Manhattan was disrupted for some time. With the major attractions in Lower Manhattan gone or closed and Ellis Island and the Statue of Liberty closed, fewer visitors came to Federal Hall in November 2001 than in November 2000.[22]

Manhattan Sites was left with significant concerns. The first was the high cost of stabilizing the structure of Federal Hall and implementing the additional security measures required at Federal Hall and Castle Clinton. The magnetometers, X-rays, and Park Police or protection rangers required at those sites added significantly to costs. Months later, Superintendent Avery reported, "Manhattan Sites continues to suffer from inadequate funding and FTE [staff positions]...."[23]

Senior staff of the House and Senate Appropriations and Authorizations Committees toured both Federal Hall and Castle Clinton, and Congress later appropriated $16.5 million to repair and rehabilitate Federal Hall. Counterterrorism funds made possible the installation of surveillance cameras at Castle Clinton and Federal Hall. As noted, security guards, magnetometers, and X-ray machines were employed. A radio system was purchased for park communications and the park acquired two emergency response vehicles. Castle Clinton received a surveillance camera and public address system.[24]

Statue of Liberty and Ellis Island National Monuments

Federal Hall and Castle Clinton were just two of the Park Service sites in the New York City area that were directly affected. Education specialist Park Ranger Vincent DiPietro was assembling children's coat racks for the education room in the main building at Ellis Island when he heard an explosion. He went outside and stood with a few others scanning the Manhattan skyline. Soon they saw flames pour out the windows of one of the trade towers and thick black smoke rising. It was eerily quiet,

View of the main building at Ellis Island. After the second plane struck the trade towers, park staff evacuated the building and gathered at the flagpole.

> As employees gathered near the flagpole, park officials worried that the Statue of Liberty might be attacked and decided to evacuate nearby Liberty Island.

he recalled, as they waited to see what would happen next. DiPietro waited to hear the sound of sirens responding as they had after an attack on the World Trade Center a few years earlier, or to see the smoke diminish as sprinkler systems kicked in and firefighters responded. Yet, nothing seemed to happen for the next fifteen or twenty minutes.

Meanwhile, dozens of employees gathered at the fuel dock, the best spot on the island for viewing Lower Manhattan. They watched a second plane fly in low directly overhead, so low they could see its United Airlines logo. The fact that it was a commercial airliner struck DiPietro as odd. The plane sailed in at an angle around the second tower and directly into the imposing structure as if to cut it in half. It appeared to explode inside the building as if, DiPietro vividly recalled, "the building just swallowed up that airline." Witnesses stood in stunned disbelief. More than a few described watching the plane hit as "surreal," much like watching a movie. "It was as if someone had just hit you over the head with a two-by-four," DiPietro explained, "and you're just shaking your head and thinking—What just happened? Did we all see the same thing?"

Suddenly, the staff knew that this scenario was no accident. Something was horribly wrong. Their minds simply could not absorb the horror of what they had just seen. Some started running back and forth, not knowing where to go or what to do. Others grabbed their cell phones and began calling loved ones. For some, there was the uneasy feeling that the event they had just witnessed could affect them directly. In the back of their minds, they knew that both the Statue of Liberty and Ellis Island could be targets.

After the initial shock, managers and staff began to mobilize. They started to receive reports of other attacks and began preparing an appropriate response. After watching the second plane strike, few, if any, employees, were comfortable remaining inside. Getting everyone out of the building and accounting for them was paramount. Protection rangers quickly evacuated the building and gathered employees on the lawn near the flagpole at the front of Ellis Island. Unfortunately, those standing near the flagpole were in direct sight line of the smoke and burning towers, which added to the emotional distress of some. Standing near the flagpole, horticulturist Alfred Farrugio was struck by the fact that the seagulls, which normally circled the patio area outside the cafeteria scavenging for food, were on the ground. The seagulls sat perfectly still with their heads tucked into their bodies, as if they knew that something was terribly wrong.

Meanwhile Assistant Superintendent Frank Mills quickly moved to stop traffic from coming across the bridge that connects the island to Liberty State Park in New Jersey. He positioned himself at the gate with the keeper of his weapon unsnapped, determined not to let anything cross the bridge. Park Police officers relieved him a few minutes later and he assumed the role of incident commander making sure that structures were in place for the emergency medical operations. Only later did he realize that if terrorists had driven a rental truck filled with explosives across, there was little he could have done to stop them.[25]

As employees gathered by the flagpole, park officials decided to evacuate nearby Liberty Island believing the Statue of Liberty might be at risk. Park Police officers evacuated the island and then surrounded it with a cordon of boats. Capt. Neal Lauro even pulled his own officers off the island because he knew that they could not prevent an attack from another plane. If the threat came by boat, however, they could take certain measures to defend the island. Fortunately, this early in the morning no visitors had yet arrived on Liberty Island and the number of residents was fairly small, so the evacuation went smoothly.

Back at Ellis Island, perhaps as many as 150 or 200 employees stood on the seawall behind what is known as the "wall of honor," waiting to evacuate. They spotted a speedboat charging toward them. Some

wondered if the boat was a kind of suicide bomber because it ignored warnings to turn away and raced through a sign that said no docking permitted. Thinking they were under attack, terrified employees, some hysterical, began running to the opposite side of the island. Knowing how close they were to the site of the attacks and feeling somewhat isolated on the island, they felt particularly vulnerable.

When the first plane hit the North Tower, boat captain Alfred Arberg was at the Marine Inspection Office next to the Staten Island Ferry in Battery Park changing the oil in the generator on *Liberty IV.* This sixty-four-foot vessel usually carried staff and VIPs to Ellis and Liberty Islands. Captain Arberg launched the boat and as he headed toward Ellis Island, he received a call directing him to the Statue of Liberty to evacuate the staff and residents. Normally the staff boat went to Ellis Island first and then Liberty Island. After loading passengers at Liberty Island, Arberg headed on to Ellis Island. Passengers who tried to get off at Ellis Island were instructed to remain on the boat and go home. Some Ellis Island employees also got on the boat. Unfortunately, the staff boat deposited its passengers in Battery Park just as the first tower collapsed, and they suddenly found themselves in the midst of the dust and ash and hysteria. Police directed them onto the Staten Island Ferry, which dropped them off in an unfamiliar area to make their way home from there as best they could. Once at Staten Island, some were taken in temporarily by staff who lived at Fort Wadsworth. In hindsight, Assistant Superintendent Cynthia Garrett later conceded that the decision to take that first group of employees to Manhattan had not been thought out carefully.[26]

While the first load of passengers made their way home, Captain Arberg had returned to Ellis Island, picked up a second group of employees, and headed back to Manhattan. By that time, however, the second tower had collapsed and people were jumping off the dock at Battery Park to escape the dust and debris. When Arberg saw the situation, he turned the boat around and brought his passengers back to Ellis Island.

After Arberg returned to Ellis Island, Chief of Maintenance Peter O'Dougherty directed him to put *Liberty IV* back in its berth and placed the sixty-five-foot *Liberty II* in service. *Liberty II* was a wider vessel with an open front normally used for hauling garbage, so it could better accommodate gurneys for the seriously injured. Arberg headed back across the harbor to Manhattan with O'Dougherty and two emergency medical technicians on board to help with the evacuation of Lower Manhattan. They stood by for half an hour, but there were so many boats that *Liberty II* was not needed and they returned to Ellis Island. The fire department commandeered another vessel, *Liberty III*, to carry firemen to and from the North Shore Marina. *Liberty IV*, which could carry up to eighty people, was later used to transport emergency personnel from Brooklyn Navy Yard to Lower Manhattan.[27]

As Arberg carried that first group of park employees and residents to Lower Manhattan, Statue of Liberty Superintendent Diane Dayson was making her way into work. The only car access to Ellis Island was through Liberty State Park and New Jersey officials had restricted access, causing her some delay. By the time she arrived, the second plane had struck and the towers were near collapse. Dayson's most immediate concern was the safety of her employees. Some employees who were anxious to get home and reconnect with loved ones as quickly as possible left the island, while others wanted to stay and help when they learned that evacuees from Lower Manhattan would be arriving. The superintendent and the other managers wanted to limit the number of employees on Ellis and Liberty Islands because of concerns about additional attacks. Managers asked those staff members who were involved in visitor protection services or had some first-aid skills or emergency medical training and could help with a planned triage center to stay. They advised the others to go home. However, some employees who lived in New Jersey were unable to get home because of bridge and road closures. Dayson and the boat captains discussed possible locations where the boats could safely drop off staff members and put them in a position to get transportation home. Some were deposited in Upper Manhattan and other boroughs in New York City.

Capt. Neal Lauro and two of his officers had arrived and established a command center at Ellis Island. Assistant Superintendent Garrett and no doubt many other employees were very glad to see the officers that day. Lauro, Dayson, and Garrett would work side by side throughout the day as they determined what needed to be done. The spirit of cooperation remained strong as they coordinated the response.[28]

In a hastily established triage center, Ellis Island employees cared for hundreds of wounded trade center victims, and injured rescue workers, firemen, and police who arrived by boat from Manhattan.

Early on, the Park Police received word that Ellis Island would be used as a triage center for victims from Lower Manhattan. The idea of using the island as a triage center was not new. The Secret Service had previously identified Ellis Island as a possible evacuation point for special major events scheduled in New York City. The island was considered a good evacuation site because of its proximity to Lower Manhattan and because of the land bridge connecting it to New Jersey.[29]

Park staff immediately began preparing for the arrival of the first victims. Maintenance workers carried chairs outside and set up the triage center at the front of the island with tables and portable toilets. Staff started amassing emergency medical gear on the front lawn. Not long after, boats from NYPD, U.S. Army Corps of Engineers, and other agencies began arriving with trade center victims, as well as injured rescuers, firemen, and policemen. Staff members described the people coming off the boats as "walking wounded." Although most arrivals did not have serious physical injuries, many were scared, disoriented, and coated with dust. They came off the boat, said one staff member, "grasping for air, coughing, looking like they had been through a snow storm, a sugar factory, dust and everything covering their bodies."

Some struggled with broken limbs and respiratory problems; others appeared to be in shock. A few were soaked with jet fuel. Months later, park employees recalled vivid images of seeing people in business attire walking around shoeless, in torn clothing, with stunned, vacant expressions on their faces. One staff member noted that even if he had not seen the smoke and fallen towers, he would have known that terrible destruction had occurred simply by watching the victims come off the boats.[30]

An emergency medical services team from a Jersey City hospital assisted with the triage center. Officials organized three teams, and a fairly organized process evolved. One group made up of the Jersey City emergency medical team, first responders, and a few staff members with emergency medical training provided medical treatment. A second group did what they could to calm people and make them comfortable; and the third group addressed basic needs such as food, water, diapers, and restroom facilities.

While the emergency responders and a few staff members tended to the medical needs, others did what they could to comfort the victims and make them comfortable until New Jersey officials could transport them to a hospital. Boats carrying victims from

Lower Manhattan radioed ahead to let staff know if they had any serious burn victims, so that the emergency medical team would have gurneys and stretchers ready. One boat arrived after another, each carrying fifty to seventy passengers. As each new arrival got off the boat, he or she was wetted down with a hose to remove the dust and soot. Joan Kelly, a secretary at the park, then recorded their names, address, telephone numbers, time of arrival, and the phone number of a contact. Kelly passed the information on to Paula Castro who entered it into a computer database. Another employee maintained a list of boats and their arrival times. The names of the refugees were organized by the name of the boat on which they arrived. The information was ultimately provided to the Park Police and NYPD to help families and friends locate the refugees. One employee, drawing on his previous emergency training, placed a piece of tape around each person's wrist with his or her name and social security number as an identifier. After recording the names, staff directed the arrivals to a shaded area with chairs were they could get out of the sun and provided them with water and sandwiches. The park's concessionaire and some employees prepared and brought out food for the visitors. Staff handed out T-shirts provided by the concessionaire to replace the dust coated or torn clothing worn by some victims. They also fashioned baby diapers out of T-shirts and distributed makeshift baby bottles. After a few hours, refugees who did not need medical attention were transported by bus to Liberty State Park and later to Brooklyn.

Some of those coming through the triage center shared heart-wrenching stories about what they had experienced that morning. Some were in tears. Kelly described the frustration many staff members no doubt felt that day. "You felt like you wanted to make it all better for them and you couldn't," she explained. A few visitors left particularly lasting impressions. Kelly recalled a frightened little girl with a heart condition to whom she gave special attention. Daniel Brown recalled a stunned female police lieutenant who was anxious to contact her sister to let her know that she was safe. Brown placed the call for her and took satisfaction in knowing that he had brought some comfort to the lieutenant and her family. After a grateful hug from the lieutenant he moved on to assist others.

By some accounts as many as 275 people had come through the triage center that day, some of them badly burned. Fifty of these were transported to local hospitals. Dozens of trained medical personnel were positioned on the island and a long row of ambulances lined up on the New Jersey side of the bridge stood ready to transport the injured. Tragically, the devastation at the trade center was so great that the large numbers of injured victims they expected never materialized. As hours passed and relatively few injured arrived, some employees began to feel increasingly helpless and disappointed.[31]

Dayson spent much of the day out in front of the main building supporting her staff. Periodically she came inside to try to contact the regional office. There was no phone service, and with power disrupted, no computers or television. Fortunately the Park Police had radio contact with NYPD and could find out what was going on in the city. The superintendent found that tending to the injured while ensuring the safety of her staff was no easy task.

Later in the day, employees who lived in New Jersey were finally able to go home. As the last of the injured were taken away and operations were winding down, the park received a call saying the island might be needed as a morgue. Dayson and a few others stayed to make the arrangements. O'Dougherty and his maintenance crew hurriedly set up a temporary morgue in one of the large storage buildings on the island. They cleared out the building and set up lighting. Various self-contained morgue-type units were brought over from New Jersey and staged on the island. The temporary morgue was never used and later when it became clear that few bodies would be recovered from Ground Zero, it was demobilized. By early evening there was little left to do and most of the staff had headed home. O'Dougherty, who felt particular responsibility as the facility manager, stayed on duty all night to make sure all the equipment and lights operated properly. The concessionaire remained all night as well, preparing food for the few who remained. Dayson later praised her staff for "putting our emotions aside and our fears and anguish to deal with the moment at hand... to serve the victims that were brought over from the World Trade."[32]

The park remained closed for the next few days and managers directed employees to stay home. Frank Mills, one of the few employees to report for work the next day, had positive experiences with the Service's peer counseling program in the past and was anxious to address the issue of employee assistance and counseling. By September 13, members of the

Service's critical incident stress debriefing team were on their way to provide support to employees in the New York City area. Six peer counselors arrived at the park on Friday afternoon and began work the next day, meeting with Ellis Island and Statue of Liberty employees. These employees had to deal with the trauma of witnessing the attacks and the collapse of the towers. Some mourned the loss of a familiar skyline. They had to come to grips with not only sight of the destruction, but the strong odor, a smoky, burnt smell, that permeated Lower Manhattan, what one employee called "the smell of tragedy." On the day most employees returned to work, they found their supervisors lined up to greet them, as if they were VIPs, a reception Castro later described as "heart-warming."

Each employee carried indelible memories of that day, memories easily triggered by a particular action, image, or even smell. Months after the attacks as Vincent DiPietro straightened up the front desk, he noticed the cancellation stamp normally used for the Park Service's passport program. Apparently no one had touched the stamp since that fateful day because the date on it still read "September 11." DiPietro decided to save the stamp as a tribute. "It's like one thing that froze that day in time," he explained.[33]

The issue of reopening Ellis Island and the Statue of Liberty was complex and troublesome. The question was not just when to reopen but how to do so in a safe and secure manner. In those first weeks, Diane Dayson participated in a number of conference calls with the regional director and Director Mainella. They discussed the impact of the tragedy on the staff and on operations as well as the measures needed to improve security. Later, Northeast Regional Director Marie Rust came to Fort Wadsworth and met with staff from Manhattan Sites, Gateway National Recreation Area, and the other parks in New York Harbor. Officials tried to determine how best to get the parks back in operation.[34] As islands, both sites were vulnerable to attack by boat and air. Their staffs had watched transfixed as the plane had swooped low overhead before slamming into the second tower and had seen the towers collapse. They were understandably concerned about air traffic and keenly aware that the Statue was a potential terrorist target.

Reopening the Statue of Liberty was a particularly thorny issue. Park officials reviewed the existing information about how long it would take to evacuate visitors from the various parts of the building safely. Having this information and knowing that the Statue was a potential target, managers questioned whether the Service could do enough to guarantee the safety of visitors. With only one way up and down, managers were left pondering how they would get people out safely in an emergency. Service leaders realized that they needed to take extreme care not to put visitors in the same position as those who had been trapped on the top floors of the trade towers.

Assistant Superintendent Garrett observed that the park was "forever changed" by the events of September 11. On some level employees had already lived with the realization that Ellis Island and the Statue of Liberty were potential targets, but the attacks brought this reality home more

forcefully. Employees understandably became more cautious or even suspicious in the way they viewed visitors. Reflecting the new dilemma faced by managers at a number of parks, Statue of Liberty officials struggled with the issue of enabling people to experience the park's rich resources while at the same time keeping them and the Statue safe. Like managers at other parks, Garrett had to learn more about security than she ever imagined. The Service's mission had always been to balance preservation with use, but now managers had to weigh security concerns as well. Finding the right balance, she conceded, was "unbelievably complex."[35]

Before reopening either Ellis or Liberty Islands, officials had to develop effective procedures for screening visitors. Managers had to make decisions about security inspections and where to place the metal detector and X-ray machine. They had to develop a screening plan that would satisfy the director, the regional director, and others. It would take months of planning and the recommendations of many experts before the park felt comfortable moving forward. Officials adopted off-site screening. In the past officials screened visitors with a magnetometer after they arrived at the Statue of Liberty. Now they decided to screen visitors with X-ray machines and a magnetometer at Battery Park and Liberty State Park, before they boarded the Circle Line boats to go to Ellis Island or Liberty Island.

Security changes brought an increased role for the Park Police. Off-site screening required the presence of Park Police, even though a private security firm operated the equipment. In addition, before September

11, the Park Police marine unit's role at the Statue of Liberty had been limited. Park Police officials had received authorization and funding to buy a boat for law enforcement purposes at the Statue of Liberty, but the boat had no dedicated crew. It was manned by what were called "incidental operators," specially trained individuals who could be pulled temporarily to do this. After September 11, the marine unit continued its patrols and played an integral role in maintaining a security zone around the Statue of Liberty.[36]

Superintendent Dayson and her staff spent many hours working with security experts from outside the Park Service who advocated a slow, methodical approach to reopening. She sometimes felt she did not have enough support for this approach from Service leaders who to her seemed more focused on visitation than security. Service leaders, she explained, were feeling pressure from concessionaires who complained about losing money because of the closure and from private foundations that complained the closing impeded their fund-raising efforts. Before the attacks, more than five million people visited the park each year, and concessionaires wanted to see that level of visitation again. They wanted full open access to the Statue

of Liberty. From their perspective, off-site screening slowed the flow of visitors. Dayson later observed that she felt pressure to reopen before she believed the park was as safe as it could be.

Dayson preferred instituting security systems slowly and methodically. She wanted the Secret Service and local police to conduct security assessments and make their reports. Then, based on their recommendations and on a series of meetings with Washington and regional officials, they would determine how best to phase in these security measures. She would then share the plan with the city, the concessionaires, and the other partners, ask them to help fund it, and discuss how they might recoup their losses. The property in Battery Park where the screening occurred belonged to the city, and the park needed authorization from city officials to install temporary structures to house its metal detectors and X-ray machines. The property at Liberty State Park where visitors entering from New Jersey would be screened belonged to the state of New Jersey. The park's screening operations significantly affected its partners and strained relationships that had been cultivated over the years. Instead of giving partners a complete plan to review to get their support, the

> Park managers soon discovered
> that there was a delicate balance between
> protecting park resources and visitors and
> contributing to the response effort.

Service implemented temporary measures. City officials complained that the huge tent in Battery Park obstructed the view of the harbor just as they are beginning to revitalize the park. Everything was, she said, "haphazardly done" in order to meet the immediate need of reopening.[37]

Officials continued to regard the Statue of Liberty as a potential target, and though visitors were allowed to walk around the island, the Statue itself remained close. The decision about reopening the Statue ultimately would be made at the highest levels of government, after the introduction of enhanced security measures. On the positive side, with the Statue closed, Garrett pointed out, visitors benefited from a "more intimate experience" of it. Rather than simply riding the elevator up inside the Statue, they walked around Liberty Island, read the wayside exhibit signs, and enjoyed a quieter, more contemplative experience. The park changed the way it interpreted the New York City skyline. It began giving interpretive talks off-site at Battery Park and Liberty State Park. While visitors waited to be screened, guides described what they would experience at Ellis Island and talked to them about the skyline.[38]

Although Ellis Island reopened to the public months after the attacks, the inside of the Statue of Liberty would not reopen for several years. The temporary closure at Ellis Island and prolonged closure at the Statue of Liberty gave staff the opportunity to catch up on routine maintenance projects. At Ellis Island, they painted bathrooms, refurbished the historic floors, and undertook other long overdue maintenance projects. The museum program was able to significantly reduce its backlog of cataloging. Over time officials developed a visitor use and protection plan for the Statue of Liberty that would provide visitors with increased access, and with the new security measures in place the Statue was scheduled to reopen in August 2004.[39]

Gateway National Recreation Area

Gateway National Recreation Area also felt the powerful impact of the attacks. The park encompasses more than 26,000 acres of sandy beaches, marsh, wildlife sanctuaries, recreational and athletic facilities, historic structures, and airfields in several Park Service units surrounding New York Harbor. When the attacks occurred, the superintendent of the Jamaica Bay unit of Gateway National Recreation Area, William (Billy) Garrett, quickly contacted

Capt. Marty Zweig. They began coordinating with the FBI and NYPD to accommodate their needs. At the request of the police department, Jamaica Bay officials closed all entrances to Floyd Bennett Field, which housed the police department's special operations division and served as the department's central staging area in that part of Brooklyn. The police department blocked the front gate with garbage trucks and Jersey barriers. The park had an existing agreement with the police for the city to use parts of the airfield for their helicopters and other special programs. The FBI asked to use some of the storage space at Floyd Bennett Field. FBI and park officials discussed the FBI storing parts there or using some of the aviation hangars as temporary morgues. Eventually the FBI used one small hangar. Park Police officers provided security for an FBI evidence-collection site at the airfield. While anxious to accommodate the FBI and the metropolitan police, Garrett and Zweig had to carefully weigh the potential impact on park resources and address the need to reopen the site to visitors and resume normal operations.[40]

With so many agencies eyeing Floyd Bennett Field as a potential staging area for their support functions, Garrett discovered that the idea that the field was part of the National Park System somehow got lost. He had to continually assert that it was a national park and should be treated appropriately. Like many other park managers, he discovered there was a delicate balance between protecting the park and contributing to the response effort. He wanted to support the response effort but also leave the park in a position where it could resume normal operations as quickly as possible. Ultimately the park and the metropolitan police forged a cooperative relationship and communication between the two improved.

The park also supported the American Red Cross. The American Red Cross operated a major food preparation operation out of a hangar on Floyd Bennett Field for nearly four months after the attacks. At one point, the relief agency was preparing ten thousand meals a day for relief workers at Ground Zero. The presence of the American Red Cross, however, proved to be a drain on park resources. Park staff had to quickly arrange housing for more than one hundred Red Cross workers as well as

View of building 7 at the World Trade Center after the attack.

maintain the restrooms and the electrical power for them.[41]

At Fort Wadsworth in the Staten Island unit of Gateway National Recreation Area, Superintendent Shirley McKinney quickly took steps to enhance security on September 11. Capt. Neal Lauro assigned an officer to help her address security issues at Staten Island. McKinney's responsibilities included Great Kills Park with its marina and Miller Field, located near one of the major thoroughfares on Staten Island. She directed the ranger in charge at each site to clear out visitors and close their sites, with help from the Park Police. "It was really a good team effort," she observed. After personally visiting each site and assuring herself that her employees were all right, she returned to Fort Wadsworth.[42]

The metropolitan police ultimately used a historic hangar at Miller Field as a command center and as an equipment-staging area for two months. The mayor of New York City and the governor of New York used it as a landing area for their helicopters.

By legislation, the Park Service was the lead agency for the Fort Wadsworth complex, so final decisions about security rested with McKinney. Decisions about security were complicated by the fact that the park's partners at Fort Wadsworth, specifically the Coast Guard, Army Reserve, and the Defense Contract Management Agency, had very different missions. No protocol existed for an event of this kind, but McKinney did what she could to accommodate the varied security needs. In addition the Coast Guard's mission was to protect the New York Harbor. To do this job, Coast Guard officials had to be able to communicate

quickly and effectively with the crews on their vessels. Because of their grave concern about the security of their communications equipment, they often operated under a higher threat level than the Park Service, U.S. Army Reserve, or Defense Contract Management Agency. The Coast Guard also set up a temporary camp to support the two hundred additional personnel brought in to protect the harbor. At the Coast Guard's request, park managers temporarily closed Fort Wadsworth and instituted a 100 percent identification check at the main entrance. The post would remain closed for two months.[43]

Much like her counterpart at the Jamaica Bay unit, Billy Garrett, McKinney found herself in the position of reminding other agencies (and a particular Coast Guard captain) that Fort Wadsworth was a national park and she needed to allow public access. The Coast Guard captain agreed to the reopening but installed barricades around the Coast Guard property within the post. McKinney stationed a person at the main gate to provide security and asked the captain to remove his personnel. She felt strongly that a visitor's first contact should be a Park Service representative in the green-and-gray uniform, not an officer in a blue uniform carrying a gun. The captain understood her concerns. When the war in Afghanistan began and the Coast Guard threat level went back up, however, she had to close the park again. The closure lasted until December 2001. Again, balancing the need for security with the park's fundamental missions proved difficult. When fishermen protested the closure, McKinney worked out a compromise that would allow them access but only after recording their fishing permit and license numbers.

> The response in the New York City area
> clearly demonstrated the close connection
> between these parks and their surrounding communities
> and the value of having protected areas and facilities
> that can be used to support other agencies during emergencies.

McKinney had high praise for her staff at Staten Island. "I think we are stronger as a result of it," she concluded.[44]

At the Sandy Hook unit of Gateway National Recreation Area, business manager David Luchsinger went to North Beach for a firsthand view of the trade towers when the attacks occurred. He immediately contacted the Coast Guard station at Sandy Hook. The Coast Guard indicated that they needed to borrow the park's forty-one-foot patrol boat, named the *George B. Hartzog, Jr.* after one of the Service's former directors. The boat and crew assisted the Coast Guard by transporting volunteer New Jersey firefighters and a Coast Guard admiral and his staff to New York City. Coast Guard officials also asked for help patrolling New York Harbor. That evening, Luchsinger, along with three other park employees and a Coast Guard representative, took the boat out into the harbor and positioned themselves at the foot of the Verrazano Narrows Bridge. Armed with automatic weapons, the crew chased and intercepted unauthorized vessels attempting to sneak into the harbor.

Park managers decided to close the Sandy Hook unit to provide additional security for the Coast Guard station at the tip of Sandy Hook. The park closed on September 11 and partially re-opened at the end of the week under heightened security to include Jersey barriers at park entrances. Portions of the park remained closed much longer because of their close proximity to the Coast Guard facilities.[45]

Conclusion

Weeks after the attacks, Fort Wadsworth, Miller Field, and parts of Floyd Bennett Field remained closed to the public. Superintendents from the parks in the New York City area met on Friday, September 14, to discuss transportation, peer counseling for employees, security and law enforcement, and other important issues and to assess the current situation at the various sites. A few days later, Statue of Liberty and Ellis Island employees gathered at Ellis Island for the first time since September 11 and shared their emotional stories. On September 19 the Director Mainella addressed roughly three hundred Park Service employees from the New York area who had convened on the main floor of the Ellis Island museum. The director, along with the Northeast Regional director and her deputy, visited Ground Zero. They also visited Federal Hall and the New York Stock Exchange, one of the Park Service's partners. The visit no doubt gave these leaders a fuller appreciation not only of the impact of the attacks on the parks and park employees but also of the pressing security concerns.[46]

Although park employees resumed their tasks and all the park sites in the New York City area except for the Statue of Liberty reopened to visitors, there was no sense that things had returned to normal. Managers and staff struggled with new feelings of vulnerability. As one superintendent observed, "the emotional scars will last a lifetime." Months after the event managers and staff still struggled to describe the shock they felt that day and the difficulty they had accepting what had happened. As Joseph Avery noted, "You just did not believe what you were being told hardly. Or you didn't believe it could happen. It was bewilderment. It was confusion." Laura Brennan echoed that they were all in "total disbelief, much like—this can't be happening."[47]

The fear and uncertainty remained long after for some employees. Vincent DiPietro observed, "Not many people go home knowing that the place [where] they work influences so many other people for good or bad" or that the place they work generates so much hatred that terrorists would be willing to kill employees and visitors. Statue of Liberty Assistant Superintendent Frank Mills, too, described a new element of uncertainty. "I think we've learned that the National Park Service plays a role in the community, in the local community as well as in the national community....But I think mostly we learned that we are vulnerable." The American people, said Mills, went to parks for comfort and were met by competent, caring Park Service staff. They found

they could rely on the parks when they needed them.[48]

The response in the New York City area clearly demonstrated the close connection between these parks and their surrounding communities and the value of having protected areas and facilities that can be used to support other agencies during emergencies. The response in New York, much like the one in Washington, D.C., was characterized by and strengthened by the close cooperation between the parks and the Park Police and the outstanding service of park managers and staff and Park Police officers. At the same time, the Park Service's experience dealing with the Coast Guard and NYPD highlights the complexities created when agencies with contrasting missions and functions are housed inside park boundaries.

IV. Incident Management

As park managers and staffs in Washington, D.C., and New York City struggled to respond in those first chaotic hours after the attacks, senior leaders in Washington took the extremely important step of activating the Service's incident management system, its organizational structure and procedures for responding to extraordinary events. This decision would ultimately have a huge impact on the nature, effectiveness, and success of the Service's response operations.

Convening Incident Management Teams

Associate Director Dick Ring was among those who encouraged officials to immediately activate the Service's national all-risk incident management team to coordinate the response. He recognized that the headquarters' function had been disrupted and no orderly plans were in place to address that situation. He had learned through his experience with other major incidents that during an emergency, existing plans were quickly tossed aside. Incidents and events rarely unfold as anticipated, Ring observed, and the existing plan usually addressed the previous event, not the immediate one. The established, routine organizational structure was not the appropriate structure for responding to an emergency: the regular staff did not necessarily have the necessary skills, and the normal operating processes were not designed for the speed and coordination required during an emergency. No organization set up to provide routine day-to-day services, Ring explained, was designed to operate effectively in an emergency environment. The incident

*View of Main Interior Building in downtown Washington, D.C.
The rolling hills of Shenandoah National Park stood in stark contrast
to the turmoil in Washington, D.C.*

> The incident management system was the most effective tool that the Service had to quickly deploy people who were pretrained to handle any kind of event.

management system was the most effective tool that the Service had to quickly deploy people who were pretrained to handle any kind of emergency situation or event. Particularly with the temporary relocation of the headquarters function to West Virginia, the Service needed people who could respond quickly to rapidly changing circumstances and coordinate effectively with department senior leaders.[1]

Rick Gale, who had served as the incident commander for both the Yellowstone fires in 1988 and Hurricane Andrew in 1992, also recognized the need to convene and preposition the national incident management team so that it could respond quickly if needed. Initially, Gale, Dennis Burnett, and others opposed staging the team in Washington because the situation was so uncertain. They discussed convening the team at Shenandoah National Park, safely away from the chaos, where it would have ready access to the dispatch center. Moreover, three of the team's key members (Greg Stiles, Dennis McGinnis, and Chester Mikus) were already based at the park. On the Director Mainella's behalf, Gale instructed the dispatch center activate the team.

Incident Commander Skip Brooks, chief of maintenance for Colonial National Historical Park in southeast Virginia, was meeting with York County officials when Greg Stiles called to alert him that the team might be activated. Team member Dennis McGinnis, chief of maintenance at Shenandoah National Park, was on vacation in the Outer Banks of North Carolina having his hair cut in a local barbershop when he saw the planes strike the World Trade Center on television. McGinnis, who served as the team's operations section chief, was one of the few members who had responded to every incident since the Pearl Harbor commemorative event in 1991. He immediately contacted the dispatch center and confirmed that the team was being activated. McGinnis then drove to Colonial National Historical Park to meet up with Brooks and they headed to Shenandoah National Park. When the two men arrived at the park later that night, they initially were instructed to go to the alternate site where department leaders had gathered. Not long after, they were told to remain at the park. By midnight four team members were at the park. They formally began operations early the next morning.[2]

Team members had always been confident that they could be on-site within 24 hours, but this assumption hinged on being able to use commercial air transportation. The events of September 11 taught them not to make this assumption again. As noted earlier, all commercial flights were temporarily grounded, and team members scattered around the country had great difficulty responding. Brooks found himself two to three days behind schedule because of delays bringing in his team members. Although each team member had a designated alternate, filling the positions proved difficult. For example, Stiles, the team's planning section chief, was pulled to work for the department, leaving Brooks temporarily with a key position vacant. Stiles' alternate from Zion National Park in Utah did not arrive for two and a half days. The finance section chief spent three days driving across country from Arizona to Chicago and then caught a flight after air traffic resumed. It took the team's information officer nearly a week to travel from the West Coast. Members of a regional incident team helped fill the gap until the national team, known as a Type 1 team, was fully established.

The alternate incident commander, J.D. Swed, drove from Indiana to join the team as Brooks's deputy. In addition to Brooks, Swed, and McGinnis, the team included Aniceto (Cheto) Olais as planning section chief, Bob Howard as logistics section chief, Kim Glass (later replaced by Ruth Kohler) as finance section chief, and Debee Schwarz as information officer. Gale served as the team's agency representative, the incident command system's advisor to the director.[3]

That first night in Shenandoah National Park, Brooks found it difficult to communicate effectively with officials in Washington, D.C. He decided that his team needed to be in Washington, with another team established in Shenandoah as a backup. Although officials initially had wanted the team safely outside the Washington area, by the afternoon of September 12 they had concluded that the immediate threat of another terrorist attack had subsided, and the team needed to be physically closer to support the leadership more effectively. The team began operations in the Main Interior Building early on September 13, working out of the ranger activities office. A few days later, they moved across the street to the top floor of the South Interior Building, into a well-equipped facility with phones and computers. It was the same facility the team had occupied earlier when they had worked on the Service's facilities management software. By the end of the week, forty team members were at work in Washington.[4]

The team's arrival in Washington took some pressure off headquarters officials and the small ranger activities staff. The team was able to establish itself quickly and provide the needed oversight and staff support. With the decentralized authority and limited law enforcement staff in the Park Service, Maj. Gary Van Horn observed, "We really couldn't get done all that needed to be done at [the Washington headquarters] without calling in a Type 1 incident team."[5] The headquarters was in the midst of a move to a nearby building on G Street, and all their operational plans were in boxes. Despite this, Brooks found that the ranger activities division knew exactly what to do and implemented the all-risk plans.

With the activation of the team, the Park Service moved to the forefront in the Department of the Interior's response because it was the only bureau in the

> Each incident management team operated
> under a "delegation of authority," which defined
> its mission and authorized its operations.

department with an all-risk incident system and the needed resources. The Service had more resources for responding to this kind of incident in the form of law enforcement personnel, heavy equipment, and heavy equipment operators than any other bureau.[6]

Incident Management System

The Service's incident management system had been in place approximately twenty years. Its structure was loosely based on a military model of an incident commander with staff reporting directly to an incident commander. The typical staff includes an information officer, safety officer, operations section, logistics section, and planning section. Although the Service initiated the system years earlier specifically to respond to wildland fires, in 1985 it adopted the system for responding to all types of emergency operations, so called all-risk incidents. Since that time, the system had been used to respond to a large number of events and incidents, both large and small, and it has been used occasionally on an interagency basis. For example, in 1988 officials used the system to deploy roughly 12,000 people to respond to the major fire in Yellowstone National Park. They also used an incident team to develop

the implementation plan when the Service underwent a major reorganization in the mid 1990s.

The system was rooted in the concept of bringing in a preestablished team specifically trained and experienced in incident management to oversee a particular incident or event so that the affected park, region, or national organization could focus on its normal day-to-day operations. Members trained, exercised, and deployed as part of a team so that they did not lose valuable time becoming familiar with each other and with the operating procedures. They were trained and equipped to handle a broad range of responsibilities to include planning, logistics, and public affairs. All had completed training at the Federal Law Enforcement Training Center.

Under the all-risk incident management system, teams were organized at the local, regional, and national levels. A so-called Type 1 team operated at the national level, while Type 2 teams functioned at the regional level. There was an Eastern Type 2 team, for example, that was three deep, meaning three individuals were designated for each position. Two of the three individuals assigned to each position were from the Park Service's Southeast Region, and

> The Service had more resources for responding
> to this kind of incident in the form of law enforcement personnel,
> heavy equipment, and heavy equipment operators
> than any other bureau.

the third was from the Northeast Region. Type 3 teams were formed at the park level, though not all parks had them. Teams at each level had the same five-person core that included section chiefs for operations, planning, and logistics, as well as information and safety officers. By the time individuals worked their way up through the system from Type 3 teams to Type 2 to Type 1, they were seasoned professionals with extensive operational experience.

Delegation of Authority

Each incident team operated under what was called a "delegation of authority" letter authorizing its operations. A team typically developed the delegation of authority in partnership with the official who called them in. Depending on the scope and nature of the incident or event, the delegation of authority was signed by a park superintendent, a regional director, deputy director, or the director. Because the September 11 response was a major, national event, Director Mainella signed the delegation of authority letter, which conveyed her expectations to the team. The director's letter delegated to the team "authority and responsibility to manage the continuity of operations for the National Park Service." This broadly written delegation of authority gave the team the authority to act on the director's behalf as well as the equally important authority to expend funds. It also specified the actions they could not take without the approval of the director or her designated representative.[7]

Typically, after the delegation of authority was signed, the incident team established its objectives and developed a plan for its operations. During the September 11 response, Brooks's team found itself continually revising the operational plans. The objectives, which could be fluid, described what the team wanted or planned to do in a specific period of time known as the "operational period." To establish the objectives, management worked with the advisor agency administrator (and for the September 11 event they worked with a representative from the secretary of the interior's office). Then the team developed strategies and tactics that would enable them to meet their objectives. The "tactics" were the specific task the operational staff performed to attain the objectives. During the response, the objectives and the tactics frequently changed, sometimes on a daily basis. The team put together an incident action plan (a notebook) that laid out the incident objectives, command and control structure, delegation of authority, phone numbers for contacts, and other important information. The objectives, strategies, and tactics were all rooted in that original delegation of authority.

The director's delegation letter for September 11 outlined nine "responsibilities," which ultimately became the team's objectives. The team's first responsibility was to "protect human life and operate safely." When appropriate, the team was to notify managers and supervisors of the potential need to provide employees with alternative work sites or other accommodations. Team members were to analyze information about the "overall situation" and determine the best measures for maintaining essential operations while keeping employees safe. In addition they were to help develop and coordinate information about ongoing response operations for employees in the Washington office. Particularly significant, the delegation of authority directed the team to coordinate its activities with the department as needed. The team was to keep members of the Service's National Leadership Council informed of significant events and gather all the information about the parks that the director or her representative requested. Also significant, the authorization specified that the team was to keep

its costs below $100,000 unless the director approved an increase. Finally, the letter designated Rick Gale as the director's representative for this incident.

The requirement to coordinate with the department was a unique and ultimately very significant provision. This situation was the first time that the national team had been asked to provide such extensive resources in supporting the department. Although the team had worked with the department in the past and had supported department officials during the transition to the new millennium (known as the Y2K event), the September 11 incident was very different. With Y2K, the team had focused on safeguarding a process rather than supporting an operation with rangers, equipment, and other resources. The director had given the team responsibility for looking at the Service resources and response activities from a national perspective and to prioritize resources. The delegation letter specified that the team would be financially accountable and operate safely.[8]

Role and Activities of the Type 1 Team

During the September 11 response, the Type 1 team's primary role was to develop plans and gather information. Its job was to identify available resources and provide the director with clear, accurate information that would allow her to make informed decisions about responding to the incident. Its goal was to give the director a reliable "snapshot" of all the resources she had available at a particular moment in time. She, in turn, conveyed this information to the department. Though the team "never shoveled any dirt or moved any material," Gale explained, its role in planning was "vital."[9]

The team quickly became the agency focal point for gathering, consolidating, and updating information about the status of individual parks. Within the first twenty-four hours, the center at Shenandoah had set up a process in which every park unit would, by phone or fax, provide a regular update of their closures and planned special events. The center used the information to generate a status report. They faxed the report to the Type 1 team and the team used it to brief the director. The report changed over time as headquarters officials requested certain types of information. Early on September 12, officials directed all park units to report to the Type 1 team the special events planned from September 12 to October 1 with a brief description of those events and any changes to park status as they occurred.

The center also received numerous requests for law enforcement rangers and tried to use the existing national fire system to fill these requests. But initially some park units were reluctant to release resources and the center had difficulty filling all the requests. There were conference calls to discuss the security priorities, but initially no real priority system was in place. Brenda Ritchie

and her staff had no national database they could use to easily identify and locate available resources, so they created their own. The regional law enforcement specialists directed their parks call the center each day with information about resource availability. Park Service areas reported in twice a day and later once a day. The team collected the information and prepared reports twice a day.[10]

Director Mainella was keenly interested in what was going on in the parks, how they were doing, what parks were opened, and which ones were closed. Skip Brooks briefed the director and senior staff twice each day, at 7:30 a.m. and around 5:00 p.m. After the morning briefing, the director then took the information to her 8:15 a.m. departmental meeting. On weekends, Brooks called her at home to keep her informed.

The director also held daily conference calls with the regional directors and associate directors at noon eastern standard time. In this forum, regional directors reported on the situation in their parks and the status of their resources. Participants discussed key issues and shared updated information that the director in turn provided to the secretary. Gale and Brooks participated in these calls. During these calls, the director or regional directors occasionally asked Brooks or Gale to follow up on specific issues or questions. Brooks found these conference calls particularly useful because they provided information that he did not get anywhere else. After the first or second week when the situation had stabilized somewhat, the director scaled back the conference calls to every other day.[11]

The team established an effective system for identifying law enforcement rangers, equipment, and other types of Service resources. Working with facility management experts, the team developed templates that could be used in concert with the existing Park Service facility management software to help identify and track emergency resources (e.g. people, equipment) in a national emergency. Team members contacted each of the 385 units in the National Park System at the time and asked the chief rangers or chiefs of maintenance to identify their available resources. They tried to gather the information in a logical sequence so it could be entered into the existing Facilities Management Systems Software (FMSS, also known as MAXIMO). This computer software allowed them to track a variety of resources throughout the Service. As the facility manager at Shenandoah National Park, Dennis McGinnis was already well acquainted with the MAXIMO system. Other members were also familiar with the system.[12]

In addition to identifying and obtaining needed resources, team members gathered critical information and disseminated it to high-level officials in the Interior department, Director Mainella's senior staff, and employees in regions and parks. They prepared reports on status of parks (based on information from dispatch center) for directorate and secretariat and coordinated the flow of information to the dispatch center.

The team also performed security-related missions. The team's operations section contacted all regional safety officers and risk managers to determine if evacuation plans were in place for their regional offices

and if safe havens had been established for employees. Another, much more narrowly focused, security-related task was to evaluate security at the Main Interior Building, as well as at Park Service offices at 1800 G Street, 800 North Capitol Street in northwest Washington, D.C., and later the Accounting Operations Center in Reston, Virginia. Brooks brought in a group to conduct the security analysis under McGinnis's direction. The team soon found that much of the security work for the Main Interior Building had already been done and was under review at the departmental level, so they concentrated on evaluating security at the G Street and North Capitol facilities. They also drafted an evacuation plan for the Accounting Operations Center in Reston. By the end of its first week, the team had completed a security evaluation for the department and continued its security and risk assessment of Park Service offices in Washington.[13]

Managers were particularly concerned about the inadequate security at the G Street location. Approximately 130 Service employees had moved into new offices on G Street the weekend before the attacks as part of a larger effort to free up space for a planned renovation of the Main Interior Building. Major Van Horn and Risk Management Manager Dick Powell led the effort to address these concerns. After the terrorist attacks, officials decided to move those employees back into Main Interior. Brooks's team hurriedly located a furniture supplier and negotiated a purchase agreement. The furniture was installed in the headquarters building by the time employees arrived on Monday, September 18. The team's logistics element knew how to perform these tasks quickly,

> Initially, the process of gathering information from hundreds of individual parks was not as smooth or as precise as officials would have liked.

and the contracting officer had $5 million authority. The department also ordered various resources, everything from tables to law enforcement rangers, through the team perhaps because, as one team member contended, the team could get these resources more efficiently. The team and senior officials focused primarily on the security of parks, buildings, and monuments. Although Powell tried to draw more attention to employee health and safety issues, he found that he had little success in this effort until the discovery weeks later of the first anthrax-laden letter.[14]

The information-gathering process was not as smooth or precise as officials would have liked. Occasionally, there were discrepancies between the information the team provided to the director in its report and information in the daily electronic Service-wide newsletter called *Morning Report* put out by the ranger activities division. Brooks became increasingly concerned about these discrepancies and asked the *Morning Report*'s editor, Bill Halainen, to join his team. Halainen's primary function was to ensure that timely, accurate information was conveyed to the field through the *Morning Report*. After he joined the team, there were fewer discrepancies between the information in the *Morning Report* and the

park status reports that Brooks provided to the director.[15]

In those first critical days, team members compiled a list of significant dams located within Park Service areas as well as a list of heavy equipment and operators available within a day's drive of New York City and the Pentagon. They collected and provided information about staffing levels and availability for the Park Police in Manhattan.

The team compiled status reports on parks and dams and compiled resource availability lists organized by region. For two weeks after the attack, team members continued to call every park to established a comprehensive list of qualified people (e.g. people with law enforcement commissions or EMS certification) and equipment (e.g. front loaders, backhoes) that could be used in emergencies. The focus was on resources similar to those needed in past incidents such as the Yosemite floods and Hurricane Andrew. By September 27 the team had contacted nearly every park unit.[16]

After the first week, officials brought in an incident team from the Southeast Region to assist with the extensive communications requirements. They also wanted the team to serve as a backup in case there was another attack in Washington. With the director's approval, Brooks mobilized the eastern incident management (Type 2) team, headed by Incident Commander Robert (Bob) Panko from Everglades National Park, and directed them to Shenandoah National Park. Panko's team was in place on September 20. The primary function of this seven-person team was to support the Service's expanded communications operations at the dispatch center and serve as a backup in the event that the Type 1 team had to be evacuated from the Washington area. Shenandoah National Park Superintendent Doug Morris gave Panko's team a limited delegation of authority, which authorized it to coordinate the flow of information, provide support to the expanded dispatch operations, and use park facilities and resources. However, even though the superintendent signed the delegation of authority, the Type 2 team reported directly to Brooks who retained the overall delegation of authority from the director.[17]

Brooks's team completed its standard fourteen-day tour, and on September 25 a new Type 1 team under Incident Commander Eddie Lopez assumed responsibility for managing the incident. During its tenure, this team either completed or assisted with the following tasks. It produced a Service-wide emergency resource inventory of law enforcement rangers, emergency medical service's personnel, boat operators, maintenance mechanics, electricians, plumbers, carpenters, equipment operators, and specific types of heavy equipment for all the parks. It compiled daily status reports for units affected by closures or restrictions related to the terrorist attacks. Team members reviewed and updated the Service's continuity of operations plan and assisted

in completing a risk assessment for the South Interior Building.

At this point, Lopez's team recommended that it transition to a smaller organization which could provide limited incident support indefinitely. It recommended that officials demobilize Panko's Type 2 team in the near future and demobilize most of Lopez's team by October 3. It also recommended that officials detail personnel to the Washington headquarters to provide continued incident support and deactivate most of the expanded dispatch function at Shenandoah National Park on October 3. Having completed its missions, Panko's team officially ended its operations on September 28. Lopez's Type 1 team did demobilize on October 3, and there was a transition from a national incident management team to another team for a few more weeks to provide logistical and financial support. After October 12, all requests for resources related to the ongoing security operations would be handled through the Service's normal procedures for ordering resources.[18]

Type 2 Incident Management Team—Northeast Region

While the Type 1 team mobilized at the national level, the Northeast Region called in a Type 2 team to support its response. Much like officials in Main Interior, after learning of the first attack, Regional Chief Ranger Robert (Bob) Martin and others gathered around a television in a conference room in the regional headquarters in Philadelphia. Martin, who had come to the chief ranger job fairly recently after a seven-year vacancy in that position, began discussing what needed to be done with the other staff. The small group that had gathered around the television quickly formed an ad hoc incident command team and set up a command post. This team included representatives from interpretation, operations, and law enforcement.

With commercial flights grounded, Regional Director Marie Rust found herself stranded in Florida, and the acting regional director, Associate Director for Park Operations Dale Ditmanson, was out of the office, so Martin temporarily assumed responsibility for directing the region's response. He would serve as incident commander until the Type 2 team arrived. After contacting Dennis Burnett in Washington, Martin and others began planning their immediate response. When Ditmanson arrived later that morning, officials began to discuss a more long-term strategy and made plans to activate the region's incident management team. Martin sent e-mail messages to all the park chief rangers encouraging them to become more vigilant about security and to consider possible evacuations and measures to secure their parks. The region asked all the parks to report their available resources. Ditmanson requested that the Type 2 team under Incident Commander Rick Brown immediately come to Philadelphia to coordinate the response for the regional director.[19]

Until Brown's team arrived, the original team with Ditmanson, Martin, Clark Guy, Jimmie Moore, Russ Smith, and Kathy Dilonardo would continue to oversee the response. Martin assigned one of the managers as a public information officer to respond to media queries. Team members worked well into the evening answering questions from the press, contacting parks

about their planned openings and closures on September 12, determining the availability of various skills within the region like heavy equipment operators and emergency medical technicians. Martin and Moore remained in the command post all night so that they could respond quickly if necessary. Shortly before dawn, Martin received word that the decision had been made to reopen the parks on September 12 and his team began notifying the parks.

The Type 2 team was able to mobilize more quickly than the Type 1 team in part because its members were closer geographically and less dependent on air transportation. Regional staff set up a command center for the team in one of the training rooms in the Philadelphia Support Office. They worked through the night to install phones and computers so that Brown's team would be able to begin work as soon as it arrived. The team formally took over operations in Philadelphia early the morning of September 12. It included Planning Section Chief Carl Merchant, Operations Section Chief Will Reynolds, Safety Officer Ben Morgan from Everglades National Park, Public Information Officer Paul Pfenninger, and Chester Mikus. Morgan, who was in Manhattan at the time of the attack, had contacted the team knowing that they would need a safety officer.

Pfenninger, an interpretive program manager at Shenandoah National Park, had learned of the terrorist attacks on the radio while in his car that morning. He immediately called into the communications center to offer assistance. At noon, he received a call back informing him that his Type 2 team had been activated. That evening Pfenninger and Mikus, also from

*The incident management structure
could be rapidly expanded, contracted, and tailored to
fit the size and nature of a particular event.*

Shenandoah National Park, set off for Philadelphia. They arrived at their hotel around midnight. When they showed up for work at the regional headquarters early the next morning they were quickly tasked to gather information about parks in the region that had been affected and available resources. Since the park units in Manhattan were without communications, the first challenge was to establish connections using cell phones and e-mail. A Philadelphia company donated cellular phones with a two-way radio feature that proved useful.[20]

As noted, the Type 2 team had responsibility for coordinating the region's response. More specifically, its task was to assist parks, develop contingency plans, and help get information out to the public. Martin worked closely with the team and together they began formulating a plan of action. Team members began contacting each park in the region to get a status report and identify those parks in need of additional security—in effect to do a risk assessment. They then provided this information to their counterparts on the Type 1 team in Washington, D.C., so that the information could be passed on to the director. The team's primary responsibility was to gather information about park closures

and upcoming events and transmit it to the communications center in Shenandoah National Park, which had a direct link to the Type 1 team. Information flowed primarily from the Type 2 team incident commander to the Type 1 incident commander, though the various section chiefs occasionally communicated with their counterparts directly. The two teams were in constant communication. The members were familiar with each other and had a good rapport.

Regional leaders decided to keep the team at the Philadelphia headquarters where it had access to computers, telephones, and all the resources and support it needed from regional managers and staff rather than send it to New York City. Some team members visited the parks in Manhattan to assess the situation firsthand, but for the most part they relied on televised news broadcasts and information gathered by phone. They were in daily contact with Park Service employees in Manhattan. Operations Section Chief Reynolds, a law enforcement ranger, worked with security issues and coordinated with the Park Police and the FBI. The FBI fed information to Park Police representatives who in turn provided information to the team. The team presented briefings to Ditmanson each morning and afternoon and occasionally participated in conference calls with Marie Rust. The team conducted briefings, handled questions, and occasionally made operational decisions. It had the authority to transfer resources within the region.[21]

Conclusion

The Type 1 and Type 2 teams played a vital role in shaping and implementing the Service's response to the events of September 11. Although the all-risk incident management system had never before been used in response to a terrorist attack, Dennis Burnett, Rick Gale, and other managers expressed great satisfaction with its overall effectiveness. One of the major strengths of this system was its tremendous flexibility. The general framework and guidelines for the system had enough flexibility that decision-makers and operators could respond effectively to a broad range of incidents and events. The incident management structure could be rapidly expanded, contracted, and tailored to fit the size and nature of a particular event. This allowed managers to bring in additional staff from around the country in response to expanding mission requirements or to reduce staff as an incident drew to a close. The teams were made up of seasoned professionals who were trained to deal with fires, earthquakes, and even hurricanes and had worked with each other for years.[22] They were well prepared to respond quickly to a variety of emergencies.

In addition to its flexibility, incident management system freed up personnel at every level to focus on their normal day-to-day operations. "Once the team hits the ground and gets going and has some clear assignments," Paul Pfenninger explained,

"the positive things are that they can take the stress away from the employees that are working at the park." Also the system brought greater organization and continuity to the situation and made ordering resources easier. On the other hand, the teams sometimes created stress for the existing staffs by coming in and taking over.[23]

Although the system worked well, some speculate that it might have functioned more effectively at the regional level than at the national level in Washington. The September 11 response posed unique challenges for the Type 1 team. The normal means of communication and transportation were not available. As noted earlier, with planes grounded and rail service disrupted, bringing in team members from around the country proved difficult. Team members needed to be on-site quickly to accomplish the objectives, but for the first few days Skip Brooks had no finance person or planning section chief. Although Brooks had high praise for the system, its success, he said, depended on team members having the necessary tools. Typically his team completed its action plan within the first twenty-four hours, but in this instance his team could not develop a plan until all its members arrived several days later. The shortage of staff and resources for those first two to three days was a matter of serious concern for Brooks and others. Because developing the action plan took three or four days, he explained, the team was already behind. Dennis McGinnis recommended that leaders take the necessary steps to ensure that proper mechanisms were in place to bring in team members more quickly in the future. Although plans later developed to deal with the transportation problem, there remained a need for greater redundancy in positions on the team. Having continuity in these positions was particularly important. Personal relationships were critical to the success of the incident management system. Members needed to be able to trust the information they provided and received was accurate.

The team also faced the challenge of tapping all the resources required. Under the incident management system, the team issued what was called a resource order (a request for a person or equipment, etc.) and the dispatch center called parks to identify and order that resource. During this response, the team had difficulty filling these resource orders. Some park officials were understandably reluctant to release resources because of concern about potential threats to their own sites. Some parks, such as Independence National Historical Park, tried to respond to requests for resources but were already struggling to meet their own security needs. As might be expected, parks farther away from high threat areas tended to be more willing to share their personnel. Also, superintendents might not have understood initially that the resources were not only to help other parks, but also to support the Bureau of Reclamation. Whatever the reason, the reluctance to share resources made it difficult to get these resources into the system so they could be transferred to other areas with higher priority. Occasionally, some coaxing from the director was required.[24]

In addition to communications and resource challenges, team members found themselves struggling to meet all of the expectations of department and Service officials, especially when these expectations were, as McGinnis noted, "growing geometrically day by day." The greater the team's success, the more people called on it. With officials pulling the team in different directions, Brooks conceded, "It was difficult at times to meet everybody's needs."[25]

Defining the relationship of the incident command system to the normal organizational structure also posed a challenge. The relationship was generally fairly clear when the incident command system performed separate functions that did not interfere with the normal operations of the agency or when normal operations ceased. When both organizations were functioning but some of the agency's normal mission and functions had been disrupted or scaled back, defining the relationship between the two became more difficult, confusing, and time consuming. Inserting the team in the middle of existing bureaucracies sometimes created resistance. One team member recommended that the Service do more to educate managers about the team's purpose, function, and responsibilities. The delegation of authority letter clearly stated that the team would perform only the specific tasks that the director assigned. The team was designed to free managers and staff to focus on their day-to-day operations. However, at times managers were reluctant to hand off some of their responsibilities to team members, and this reluctance created tensions. In some instances, the team simply had to work around certain individuals.[26]

Finally, some of the Service's most experienced incident managers are nearing retirement, and the agency stands to lose a great deal of experience and institutional knowledge in the coming decade. The Type I team already has several vacant positions. Brooks recommended that the Park Service develop and execute a recruiting strategy to fill the void and designate someone in the Washington headquarters to manage the teams, oversee funding and recruiting, and ensure ongoing training and exercises. The Service, he explained, needed a structure in place to support the rangers who are called up, house them, provide action plans and direction, and handle finances and the media. For fire response, a specially designated center in Boise, Idaho, directed the response, but the Service had nothing comparable for all-risk response.[27]

Eddie Lopez's team recommended that Service leaders enhance the response capabilities of the Type I and Type 2 teams and the nine regionally based "special event teams." Specifically, the team recommended that managers fill all the existing vacancies on the Type I and Type 2 teams, schedule training, develop standard operating procedures, and consider establishing an additional Type I team. At the time, the Service had six regionally based Type 2 teams capable of rapidly mobilizing in their geographic regions. Finally, Lopez's team recommended that Service leaders review administrative policies that might impede response, such as the policies concerning pay caps and back-filling positions.[28] Despite the challenges, the incident management system proved to be an invaluable tool for Service leaders and had a huge impact on the effectiveness of the Service's response.

V. Challenges

While the incident management teams grappled with the challenges of setting up their operations and carrying out their missions, problems with communications, coordination, and funding continued to hamper the Service's response.

Communications

One of the most difficult and sometimes least successful aspects of the Service's response to the attacks was in the area of communications. In the first hours after the attacks, there were difficulties with almost every aspect of communication, from notifying employees about evacuations and closures to gathering intelligence and sharing information. Communications lines within the Washington headquarters broke down or were nonexistent. As noted earlier, the department had no public address system and no formal systems in place to inform employees that Main Interior was being evacuated or to direct them to the basement. Other than phone and e-mail, the Service had no communications link between offices or buildings in Washington, D.C. When employees were directed to the basement of Main Interior on the morning of September 12, Park Service employees at the nearby G Street office and at 800 North Capitol Street were not immediately notified.

Communication outside the Washington headquarters was not much better. Although some regional and park offices did an excellent job of communicating with their employees and reviewing their emergency procedures in the first hours after the attacks, in others there was confusion. Some parks had difficulty contacting their regional offices and

Park Police officers in New York City relied heavily on their radio communications.

some regional offices had difficulty contacting personnel in the headquarters. The *Morning Report* proved useful for Service-wide internal communications, but even when distribution of the report increased briefly to twice a day, it could not fill the need for real-time information and instant communications. The *Morning Report* had never been designed for that role. Not all employees read this report on a daily basis or even had access to it on computers.

As noted earlier, on September 11, many landlines in the Washington, D.C., and New York City areas were either down or overloaded and cellular phone systems functioned sporadically or not at all. Service leaders quickly learned that in an emergency they could not rely on the regular telephone system to meet their communications needs. Officials throughout Main Interior had great difficulty calling out of the building. Senior leaders found themselves relying to some extent on information that Maj. Gary Van Horn was able to get from the Park Police using his police radio. With landlines unavailable, Type i team members also had difficulty getting all the information they needed during the first forty-eight hours. The situation did not improve significantly until the dispatch center in Shenandoah National Park set up a satellite dish and distributed cellular phones linked to that satellite. Although the situation improved in the Washington area, the Northeast Regional office continued to have difficulty communicating with its field offices.[1]

Officials found that initially the Government Emergency Telecommunications System (GETS), a restricted emergency phone system, provided the only reliable means of communication. Unfortunately relatively few managers had access to this system, and in those first chaotic hours not all of them immediately thought about using their GETS access cards. Operations became easier later in the day when managers began using priority phones lines in the directorate offices. GETS access was particularly useful to the senior leaders who evacuated to West Virginia that first day and to Type i team members. The Park Police also found the system useful. At one point, using GETS was the only way they could consistently make long-distance calls on landlines. Park Police officials recommended that in the future all key personnel have GETS access.[2]

Communications problems were particularly severe in New York City in part because the main telephone switch for Lower Manhattan had been located in the basement of one of the collapsed trade towers. Its destruction left some areas such as Fort Wadsworth without phone service for several weeks. Although Park Police used cellular phones and other means to compensate, the problems occasionally hampered operations. Initially, the police relied mostly on radio communications. Cellular phones became a "lifeline," said Capt. Marty Zweig.[3]

Nextel cellular phones, which had a "direct connect" feature that functioned much like a two-way radio or walkie-talkie, proved to be invaluable for employees throughout the National Park Service, particularly for the Park Police. A number of the officers, detectives, and supervisors had Nextel phones. Deputy Chief Jack Schamp described these phones as a "very effective tool," which allowed commanders to

In the first hours after the attacks,
there were difficulties with almost every aspect of communication,
from notifying employees about evacuations and closures
to gathering intelligence and sharing information.

communicate effectively with each other and supervisors to communicate with their officers. However, even the Nextel phone system occasionally became overloaded. Also, although the Park Police used Nextel for operational matters, it was not a secure system. Park Police officials later recommended that a satellite phone be available at major sites in the New York field office.[4]

With the disruptions in both traditional and cellular phone service, the Park Police and park rangers relied more heavily on radio communications. Yet, this system had its own weaknesses. As with cellular communications, radio communications can be scanned by outsiders and are not secure. In addition, Park Police officers and park rangers in the Washington, D.C., area could not communicate with each other by radio because they operated on different frequencies. Most rangers did not have the Park Police frequency on their portable radios. Signals from the portable radios that rangers carried could not reach the National Capital Region's communications center in western Maryland because there were no radio repeaters in the Washington area. The signals from the radios in their service vehicles could reach the communications center, but just barely. With phone lines

jammed, rangers could only contact the Park Police by going through the regional communications center, a time-consuming process. Regional Chief Ranger Einar Olsen observed that the regional communications center was "critical" in organizing and communicating with personnel on September 11.[5]

Radio communications in the New York area were complicated by the fact that personnel at the Statue of Liberty operated on a different radio system than neighboring Park Service sites. Gateway National Recreation Area operated on a VHF band, while the Statue of Liberty system used a UHF band. Although the Park Police could operate on a UHF frequency from Brooklyn, generally communication was difficult. They could talk to the dispatchers who, in turn, could talk to people at the Statue of Liberty and Ellis Island. However, Maj. Thomas Wilkins's radio would not operate from inside the building at One Police Plaza, so he had to rely on Nextel and landlines when they were operational. He found that he could only communicate with his station commanders 50 percent of the time. "There were a lot of different channels of communication going on and there wasn't always good overlap," Wilkins conceded.[6] Not until months later were Park Police officers all on the same frequency.

Coordination

Even when phone lines and radios operated smoothly, sharing information effectively within the Service and with the department remained a major challenge. Senior managers had considerable difficulty acquiring the timely, accurate intelligence information that they needed, particularly information concerning potential threats to parks. With no established mechanism in place to systematically gather such intelligence, the information they received was often spotty.

The Park Police served as a major source of intelligence information for both department and Service leaders. As noted earlier, Park Police representatives in various operations centers around the Washington area shared information with the military, FBI, Secret Service, metropolitan police, and other agencies. Every morning, Major Van Horn contacted each representative by phone to gather the latest information. These agencies shared information well, but the Service did not get the highly classified information that would come from the National Security Administration or the CIA.

The Park Police also assigned a detective to an FBI counterterrorism task force who relayed intelligence information to individuals with the proper clearance, and some of this information was passed on to the department. This FBI task force, however, was not strictly an intelligence-gathering mechanism and was not designed to provide agencies with the most current intelligence on a regular basis. Personal contacts that the Park Police had established over the years proved to be a valuable asset because intelligence information is often relayed through personal contacts to specific individuals. Most sources are reluctant to share information with someone they do not know personally and trust.[7]

The chief's command post transmitted information to Major Van Horn and to the department's operations center as appropriate. Van Horn, in turn, provided department and Service leaders and the Type I team with as much information from the Park Police as he could, particularly information concerning potential threats to parks, and he coordinated closely with the department's office of security and law enforcement. The Type I team had its own representative in the chief's command post who conveyed information. Park Police officials later reported that, "The ability of the Force to access this type of information during this critical time played a significant role in the coordination of emergency services and the safe evacuation of department personnel as well as visitors to our monuments and memorials." Occasionally tensions surfaced when department or Service officials who asked the Park Police for classified information found their request denied because they lacked the proper security clearance or the requisite "need to know."[8]

Transmitting intelligence information in a timely, efficient manner from the Washington headquarters to the individuals in the field offices responsible for protecting the parks also proved difficult. The Park Service had to develop its own process to convey information to its field offices. As an added complication, few employees in park and regional offices had the level of security clearance they needed to receive this type of information. Nor did most field offices have the secured phones and fax machines they needed in order to receive such information. Even if Service leaders had been able to gather more security-related information, they would have difficulty conveying it to the parks because there was no secured communications system. To acquire intelligence information, individual parks for the most part had to rely on relationships they had established previously with the local FBI office, Secret Service, other federal agencies, or state and local agencies.

Managers in regional and park offices concluded that they needed to coordinate better with the intelligence community. Regional officials in Philadelphia found that they could not get from Washington the intelligence information, particularly information about potential threats to parks, that they needed in order to make carefully considered decisions about staffing and resources. They decided to bring in some of the region's special agents and place them in the counterterrorism task force that had been set up Philadelphia and Boston to help coordinate the flow of information into those places. As a result, regional officials were able to quickly access any information affecting a park's security. These special agents were able to communicate with their counterparts at other agencies. As trained investigators, they understood the language.[9]

Conveying security-related information was but one aspect of more general problems with the flow of information. Park Service officials continued to struggle with the timeliness and accuracy of the information that came into the Main Interior Building, something that experienced incident managers insist should not have happened after the first few days. Under the existing structure, information flowed from parks and regions to the communications and coordination center in Shenandoah National Park, from the center to the Type I team, from the Type I team to Park Service headquarters, and from that headquarters to the department. Such a complex communications chain increased the risk of transmission errors.

As Director Mainella's representative to the Type I team, Rick Gale was responsible for providing her with the information she needed to make effective decisions or to provide to the department leaders. He conceded that there were occasional "glitches." There were alternative communications sources and mechanisms and sometimes the director and other officials received inconsistent or inaccurate information. At that point, she would appropriately question which information was correct. She did not always receive the accurate, precise information that she needed to take to department leaders.[10]

Department leaders who remained at the alternate site also had to be kept informed. The director insisted that Skip Brooks send information to these officials by fax twice a day, but sometimes he would later discover that no one had picked up the information. Communications glitches like this were not uncommon. People occasionally complained that they had not received the information that the team had sent.

The director required a great level of detail, no doubt in part because she needed to pass that information on to department leaders. For the Type I team, getting that detailed information from park rangers and maintenance employees through their superintendents and regional offices was not easy. The team had to make sure that everyone involved understood the director's requirement for detailed information and do its best to ensure that the information was accurate. Although the team constantly strove to provide her with the most detailed, current, and accurate information possible, the information varied depending on reporting methods and the time of day it was reported. The difference in time zones sometimes contributed to the confusion, and not all parks followed the prescribed format for reporting the information. As a result, the team found errors in the information that first week. Initially there were also occasional problems with the way the dispatch center interpreted the information it received, but these problems were addressed within the first weeks.

Brooks later indicated that with information changing so rapidly planning became more difficult. Sometimes the flow of information to the team was too slow and occasionally Brooks became concerned when things did not come together the way they should. Brooks observed that during Hurricane Andrew the team lost all its phone systems and had to get a satellite. It took three days, but once the phone links and satellite were in place, the team had a better handle on the movement of resources than it did with the September 11 event.[11]

The Service's primary conduit for information was the communications and coordination center at Shenandoah National Park, but at times the demands for information

and resources were so great that they threatened to overwhelm the center. It was not always able to respond to the requests for information or resources quickly enough. The dispatch center transmitted two reports each day, one listing current park closures and the other with status reports on all parks. The reports sometimes contained inconsistent and contradictory information.[12]

The dispatch center was in an increasingly difficult position. Its staff had a critical role in providing information, but as Dick Ring observed, "often they were not allowed to play it." Rather than go through the center as procedures dictated, some officials in the directorate or secretariat began calling parks, regions, or the dispatch center directly to get information or request resources. This further complicated the flow of information and occasionally created confusion.[13]

Requests for information poured into the dispatch center. The Type I team and various department officials all clamored for information. Yet, accurate up-to-date information was not easy to come by. Some parks neglected to phone in their reports at the designated time. Information changed depending on the time of day it was reported. Officials in Washington might get more current information directly from someone they knew in a park that conflicted with what the dispatch center provided.

In the center's defense, it was very difficult for the center to perform its coordination and communications functions effectively for the Service and department when the staff was busy setting up its communications structure. Lacking an established plan to follow, the center had to improvise to a great extent. Brenda Ritchie later recommended establishing a permanent facility rather than ramping up the center every time there was an event. Other managers recommended devoting more resources to telecommunications and other modern technology.[14]

Just as there were communications difficulties, there were occasional problems coordinating the response within the Service and between the Service and the department. Some officials in this relatively new administration had never dealt with an event of this nature and were unfamiliar with the capabilities that existed within the Park Service for responding, particularly its incident management system. Even those familiar with the Service's response capabilities were sometimes reluctant to turn responsibility over to an outside management team. Feeling personally responsible, they tended to turn to the normal day-to-day organization, which as noted earlier was not designed to respond to emergencies. As a result, officials spent more time than necessary figuring out what needed to be done and how to organize the response.

Some department and Service leaders were never totally comfortable with turning aspects of the operation over to an incident management team. Department officials never adopted an incident management system and structure, and though Park Service leaders adopted the system and convened a team, they never delegated enough authority for it to "do fully what it was designed to do." In the early stages of an event, Ring explained, leaders needed to know enough about emergencies to set clear objectives and then back out. The department and

Park Service responses, he asserted, would have been much more effective if leaders had fully employed the incident management system.[15]

At a meeting with department officials, Service representatives suggested creating a unified command system that would operate under the department's direction. The Service had successfully used a unified command system before, when it coordinated with the FBI during the Bridal Trail murder investigation in Shenandoah National Park. Department leaders rejected this proposal. As noted, they might simply have been reluctant to adopt a system that was unfamiliar. They understandably might also have been concerned that the incident team could not acquire critical resources quickly enough, and indeed this was sometimes the case.[16]

In addition to encouraging the department to adopt an incident management system, Service managers offered to share their own Type 1 team. Again the department declined. Some Service leaders later maintained that the department's decision hampered coordination, resulted in duplication of effort, and ultimately made the Service's response more difficult. They recommended in the future the department adopt an incident command system and utilize it fully. The department would be much better positioned for its homeland security mission, they argued, if it did not have to deal with the day-to-day operations. Yet, some managers were simply unwilling to relinquish control or had other reservations. They tried to order resources and enhance security but had no efficient mechanism in place to do this. As a result, interactions between Service and

There was no seamless mechanism for funding
as there was with fire incidents. Beyond the issue of
funding authority, there was the very real concern about
whether the Park Service and the other bureaus would be
reimbursed for the costs associated with the response.

department managers sometimes became strained. In an effort to promote better coordination, the Type 1 team placed a representative in the department's command center and worked hard to ensure that the representative had access to the most current information.[17]

Although efforts to improve coordination with the department had some success, supporting department requirements was neither simple nor easy. This support involved compromises, particularly when it came to allocating the Service's law enforcement ranger resources. Service managers constantly had to balance the department's need for law enforcement rangers to provide security at its sites with their responsibility to protect the parks. Rick Gale, acting on the director's behalf, often made the final determinations about resources. Ultimately, the Park Service met the department's needs, but the department's lack of familiarity with the incident command system created confusion. The response highlighted the need to better educate senior management about the potential role and contributions of the incident management system. For senior managers to feel comfortable and confident about bringing in an incident team with which they had never worked, Brooks

noted, they must first fully understand how the system worked.

The response also revealed the need for the Service to better integrate its activities with those of the department. The lack of adequate cooperation between the Service and the department expressed itself in various ways. On at least one occasion three different department officials submitted four requests to the Park Service for the same information. In other instances, department officials informed Service leaders they did not want the Service's resources and declined their offer of assistance from its incident management team, but then they ordered those resources directly from individual parks. The Service, for its part, might not have always done all that it could to coordinate well with the department.[18]

Director Mainella, too, reiterated the need for an organized structure that could be automatically activated for this type of response. She recommended that the department's office of managing risk and public safety help bureaus solve their emergency operations policy problems, coordinate interagency issues, provide technical assistance, and represent the department to the Federal Emergency Management Agency. The office of managing risk and public safety chose not to use the incident command system. For several days, it struggled to organize emergency management.

The response highlighted many lessons learned in the areas of communication and coordination. Department law enforcement lacked a centralized organizational structure. At the time of the attack, the department's small six-person law enforcement security team was located in the office of managing risk and public safety. The secretary and senior managers had no meaningful single point of contact during an emergency. The historic lack of a prominent departmental law enforcement office resulted in, what the department's inspector general described as, "a void in leadership, coordination, and accountability in the law enforcement program." The department's bureaus operated their own law enforcement programs with little oversight and direction from the department, creating a "state of disorder" in the structure and operation of law enforcement throughout the department. The post–September 11 environment magnified the organizational and management problems of the department's law enforcement component. To address the problem, in late October, the secretary appointed a deputy assistant secretary for security and established a new office of law enforcement security.[19]

Funding

In addition to the problems of communications and coordination, Service managers had to grapple with the fundamental question of how to pay for the response. At the time of the attacks, the department had no national contingency authority for emergency funding. Nor did the Service have any emergency funding authority, except for wildland fire response. With wildland fires, the Service had the authority to establish an account and begin expending funds immediately so managers could begin recording expenses, but there was no comparable authority for other types of emergencies. There was no seamless mechanism for funding as there was with fire incidents. Beyond the issue of funding authority, there was the very real concern about whether the Park Service and the other bureaus would be reimbursed for the costs associated with the response. If Congress did not later authorize a supplemental appropriation to cover the emergency expenditures, the agency would be forced to take the money from land acquisition or some other source or perhaps delay certain construction projects.

The funding issue caused confusion throughout the Service. Some parks and regions used the emergency law and order funding provided by the Washington headquarters. Managers in the National Capital Region initially struggled with how for fund the additional ranger assignments. Ultimately, they determined that the unit receiving the support would bear the cost. Months after the event, Congress still had not appropriated additional funds to cover past and future expenses related to the response, and Service managers reprogrammed funds to cover some of the costs.[20]

The dispatch center faced its own funding challenges. It had no established account and regular budget to fund its operations but rather received funding only for specific emergencies. When a fire occurred and the National Interagency Fire Center in Boise, Idaho, asked the center to order personnel for a fire event, the center had a series of account numbers that it could assign to send people out. But this arrangement was not the case for other types of emergencies. The center lost valuable time grappling with the funding issue. Brenda Ritchie observed that it was expensive to use emergency accounts and set up the center each time there was an emergency. It would be more cost effective, she argued, to have a permanent facility and an established account. Moreover, without an established account, the center could not sign contracts for services or lease equipment, both critical actions in responding to an emergency.[21]

Funding has often been an issue when responding to incidents and emergencies. Bringing in and maintaining the Type 1 team involved considerable expense. The director's original delegation of authority included a $100,000 funding cap, and the team made every effort to keep costs within that cap. After the first few days, however, Brooks realized that the team's operating costs would quickly exceed $100,000. He explained the situation to the director and asked her to lift the cap. The director agreed to consider removing the cap but only after Brooks provided her with adequate documentation indicating why this action was necessary and what the additional expenditures covered.

In his presentation to the director, Brooks explained that the team had already exceeded the initial operating cost ceiling of $100,000. He pointed out that since the original authorization, the team's missions and responsibilities had expanded, to include help developing an evacuation plan for the secretary and her key staff. On September 20, the director agreed to lift the $100,000 cap in the delegation of authority and replace it with a provision to "keep costs commensurate with the needs of the incident."[22]

Unfortunately the original cap had sometimes forced the team to focus more attention on funding issues than on the immediate requirements of the situation. The dilemma was whether operators should base their decisions and actions on costs or ignore the cost because some item or some personnel action was needed for safety and security. For example, although Brooks needed to bring his team members in as soon as possible so they could begin to plan and execute the response, he decided not to bring them in by charter airplane because of the cost. If not for the cap, he could have brought his resources in more quickly and accelerated the response.[23]

To complicate the funding issues, initially the department assured its bureaus that their expenses would be covered and directed them to take the appropriate action regarding employee safety and protection of facilities and resources. Days later the department informed its bureaus that each would have to cover its own costs, and in the case of the Park Service, each park unit would have to absorb much of the expense. Since bureaus and parks were in the last two weeks of the fiscal year, budgets were tight.[24] The department's reversal had what was described as a somewhat "chilling" effect on the service's response. The decision sometimes caused managers to hesitate and to second-guess expenditures because of concern about money.

The Service had existing statutory authority to spend money on missions related to a national disaster or national emergency, but as with wildland fire response, the issue was who would ultimately pay the bill. Without a supplemental appropriation from Congress, as mentioned before, there was the risk that the agency later might have to trade off some major construction projects. However, Ring explained, "If you try and hedge how you operate in an emergency based on having those questions answered at that point in time, you will almost certainly impair the effectiveness of your emergency operation." In the emergency phase, typically the first few days, he insisted, managers must simply agree to do whatever was necessary to meet their emergency objectives and worry about funding later. During the September 11 response, the funding constraints during the emergency phase hampered the team's ability to accomplish its tasks. Concern about costs and expenditures contributed to hesitation in making decisions, micromanagement, and second-guessing. Concern about funding delayed actions to communicate more effectively and deploy resources longer than necessary. During the short-term emergency phase, Ring argued, operators should spend whatever was necessary to respond effectively to the immediate emergency and sort out funding issues later.[25]

The Park Police faced similar funding problems. Again, there was no emergency fund and existing operational funds were scarce because it was late in the fiscal year. There was an established procedure to request what was called emergency law and order funding, which included a cap on the amount of the request. If the Washington office approved the request, the funds were transferred from other projects and places. Park Police costs were wrapped into the department's request to Congress for

supplemental funding, and later the Park Police received some additional funding. In their after-action report, Park Police leaders emphasized how important it was that managers know funding is available for these type of emergencies. They recommended that an emergency operations fund be established which could be immediately accessed with the approval of the assistant secretary for policy, management, and budget.[26]

In the weeks after the attacks, managers worked to prepare a supplemental appropriation request for Congress. They instructed parks to establish holding accounts and start charging costs against it, believing that the money would eventually be reimbursed. Congress ultimately provided some additional funding for the Service's internal expenses and for its support to the Bureau of Reclamation. The department received $92 million in supplemental funding from Congress. More than $63 million of this money was allocated to the Park Service to provide relief for the costs associated with increased security and emergency construction related to security at "icon" parks.[27] However, the broader issue of funding emergency response operations remained unresolved.

A year after the attacks, Congress established Flight 93 National Memorial to honor the passengers and crew.

VI. Aftermath

The September 11 attacks and their aftermath had profound and lasting affects on the national parks, park employees, visitors, and on the National Park Service. Although park units in New York City and Washington, D.C., might have felt the most intense and extensive impact initially, virtually every unit was affected to one degree or another. The attacks and the response also affected the organizational structure and processes of the Service. As one writer explained, "The attacks not only changed us as a nation, but also deeply affected the National Park Service and the sites under its care." In the wake of the tragedy, park employees acknowledged this change. They spoke of adjusting to "a new normal."[1]

The terrorist attacks prompted the creation of a new unit in the National Park System. A year after the attacks, Congress established Flight 93 National Memorial to commemorate the heroic passengers and crew of Flight 93 who gave their lives on September 11, 2001, to thwart what many believe was a planned attack on the nation's capital. At the direction of Congress, the open field near Shanksville, Pennsylvania, where the commercial airliner went down became a unit of the National Park System. Service representatives worked with the local community, assisted with public meetings regarding the future of the site and provided advice and technical assistance.

Opposite page, these words from the Franklin Delano Roosevelt Memorial assumed new meaning for park employees and visitors. Above, visitors left tokens of remembrance at the Flight 93 crash site in Pennsylvania.

Service leaders as well as park managers and staff around the country instituted new or enhanced security measures and became more security conscious.

Impact on Parks and Visitors

The terrorist attacks reaffirmed the status of parks as symbols of fundamental American values but also exposed them as potential targets. Though security concerns were not new to the Park Service, it now had to address vastly increased terrorist threats that could jeopardize the safety of its visitors and employees and the integrity of the natural and cultural resources for which it was responsible.

By all accounts, the attacks prompted greater security awareness among Service leaders, park managers, and park staff. A number of parks, particularly those considered to be at greatest risk, instituted new security measures to include an increased law enforcement presence, surveillance cameras, and metal detectors. Gateway National Recreation Area reported, "Security would become an issue, not only for us, but for our tenants and for other agencies that would call on us for help...we still witness the evolution of concerns generated on that terrible day." There were major, easily visible, security enhancements at the monuments and memorials on the National Mall, such as the installation of barriers and increased screening of visitors. Immediately after the attack,

park employees encircled the Washington Monument with concrete Jersey barriers and installed barriers on the east side of the Lincoln Memorial. The Service installed magnetometers at the White House Visitor Center and at the Washington Monument. Independence National Historical Park installed metal detectors and introduced new security procedures with restricted access. Parks near or bordering military installations, such as Sandy Hook unit of Gateway National Recreation Area and Minute Man National Historical Park in Massachusetts, stepped up their security.[2]

As managers instituted new or enhanced security measures, park employees around the country became much more security conscious, particularly in the way they viewed visitors. Employees became more observant and vigilant. Valley Forge National Historical Park staff, for example, began to look for "red flags," things that did not "look right," such as a visitor carrying a briefcase. "I think we all look at things a little bit differently," said one employee. The staff at Yosemite National Park, too, became more attuned to potential threats. "I think we're all thinking about things in a little bit different way," the superintendent explained. Security-conscious employees at Shenandoah National Park and Delaware

Water Gap National Recreation Area found themselves observing visitors more closely.[3]

Along with the increased emphasis on security, the events of September 11 prompted an immediate and significant overall decline in park visitation. Fear of commercial air travel, reduced flight schedules, disruptions in the economy, and high gasoline prices contributed to the drop in visitation. In 2001, roughly 280 million people visited park units, five million less than in 2000. Almost all of this loss occurred in the last quarter of 2001, after the September attacks. The sudden drop in international visitors had a particular impact on the large scenic parks in the West. *USA Today* reported that Grand Canyon had 60,000 fewer bus passengers in October 2001. Visits to Independence National Historical Park dropped from 4.8 million in fiscal year 2001 to 4.35 million in fiscal year 2002. Curtailment of school-sponsored trips, decreased foreign travel, and the general decline in domestic tourism contributed to this drop.

While overall visitation dropped off, particularly among travelers from overseas, more Americans were visiting parks closer to home. Statistics showed that visits to large, popular sites such as the Grand Canyon and Yosemite declined by more than 20 percent, but parks in or near major urban areas experienced dramatic increases. For example, visits to Shenandoah National Park, a few hours drive from the Washington area, increased 22 percent. Visits to sites that inspired patriotism, such as the historic battlefields and Mount Rushmore, also increased. Valley Forge National Historical Park reported a decrease in visitors from outside the local community, such as those brought by tour companies, while the number of visits from locals increased. Visitation to Valley Forge eventually began to climb.[4]

For Americans who visited parks after the tragedy, the sites often took on new meaning and assumed greater significance. The parks became increasingly important to the American public as places of healing and reflection. The events of September 11, noted Director Mainella, "underscores the value of parks as places of healing and introspection and of the high value of large federal open spaces." As the Park Service's chief of communications, David Barna, explained, "This is where the public goes to renew their spirit." A refuge manager at Jamaica Bay Wildlife Refuge found that many visitors just wanted a quiet place for reflection. They expressed a new level of appreciation for the park. Yosemite staff

found that visitors came seeking solace, a sense of security, and a place of reflection.[5]

Visitors from the Washington area who arrived at the entrance stations at Shenandoah National Park on the afternoon of September 11 explained to rangers that they needed to get away from the city and from nonstop news accounts of the tragedy. Visitation to the park spiked shortly after the attacks. Shenandoah National Park visitors came not only seeking a break from television news but also seeking comfort. The interpretive staff sensed that the visitors had an emotional need to connect with the park and changed their behavior in response. Instead of taking their usual fifteen-minute breaks, the interpreters used the time to move around and connect with visitors. Instead of giving a thirty-minute talk, they looked for more personal, creative ways to help visitors establish personal connections to the park. The chief of interpretation observed that visitors seemed more interested in finding meaning in the park.[6]

The events, traditions, and values represented at many sites had new resonance for both visitors and park employees who were struggling to come to grips with the attacks. For example, as site manager Lance Hatten walked through the outdoor Franklin Delano Roosevelt Memorial the morning after the attacks doing a routine check, he happened to glance up at a quote carved into one of the granite walls: "FDR—freedom from fear." Suddenly this simple, eloquent quote took on a powerful, new meaning for him. In the week after the attack, people gathered on the National Mall for candlelight vigils in expressions of patriotism and unity. They used chalk to write statements about freedom and democracy on the pavement. Hatten saw opportunity amidst the tragedy. In the past, he said, Americans had sometimes taken for granted the meaning of these sites, but September 11 gave them the opportunity to reconnect with these places. Visitors to Fort McHenry in Baltimore told the staff that they came out of a sense of patriotism. The superintendent reported, "Visitors come to look at the flag and experience solace and quiet at Fort McHenry."[7]

Manzanar National Historic Site in California, where Japanese Americans had been detained after Pearl Harbor, was another site that assumed new meaning.

This monument at Manzanar is inscribed, "This is the place of consolation for the spirit of all mankind."

Visitors began to leave September 11 "offerings" at the site. A huge American flag was hung on the existing Manzanar Relocation Center signs. Smaller flags suddenly appeared around the cemetery, left there, Superintendent Frank Hays explained, "as a kind of recognition of the site as an important part of the civil rights story." The park, said Hays, had a unique role advancing a public dialog about racism, civil rights, and other controversial subjects. Hays quickly recognized the connection between September 11 and Manzanar and the "obvious parallels" between Pearl Harbor and the terrorist attacks. The morning of the attack, he anticipated getting media requests to address the connection between what had happened to Japanese Americans at Manzanar and the current climate of suspicion surrounding Arab Americans. He and other park staff wanted to ensure that in their future interpretation, they allowed visitors to make the connection. September 11 prompted discussion about the Constitution that for Hays reaffirmed the relevance of Manazanar and provided park interpreters with a common context they could use to explain that relevance. The park received a number of media inquiries. The CBS *Sunday Morning* television program filmed a segment with reporter Charles Osgood highlighting the connection between September 11 and the Japanese-American experience after Pearl Harbor.[8]

The terrorist attacks prompted changes in interpretation at some parks. Staff at Valley Forge National Historical Park used the tragedy as an opportunity to address new interpretive themes. Interpreters traditionally talked about the experiences of an army in the field, the local Quaker popula-

tion, and the pacifist Germans. The attacks prompted them to rethink this approach. The way the park interpreted issues of national defense changed and the dialog with visitors became more provocative. The staff encouraged visitors to reflect on not only what the soldiers did at Valley Forge but also on how the principles of the American Revolution had shaped us as a people. Independence National Historical Park Supervisory District Ranger Frances Delmar found that more visitors came to Independence Hall seeking answers than at any time she could recall. They wanted to learn about constitutional issues, such as balancing individual freedoms with national security. Park staff was able to provide historical context for the questions visitors raised.[9]

In addition to giving new meaning to parks and prompting changes in interpretation, the September 11 event and its aftermath illustrated the way parks, particularly those in dense urban areas, were and continued to be an integral part of their surrounding communities. This was especially true in the New York City area. Sites such as Federal Hall and Ellis Island sheltered and cared for their neighbors on September 11. A number of New York sites allowed other agencies to use their facilities and open spaces.

Managers at Gateway National Recreation Area were keenly aware of the park's role and responsibilities as part of the surrounding community. On September 23, 2001, the park co-sponsored a prayer vigil at Fort Tilden with community groups and churches in Rockaway, New Jersey. It provided space for the Rockaway Chamber of Commerce and other organizations that

were collecting donated clothing and other items for World Trade Center victims. Later, when Flight 587 crashed in Rockaway, the New York Police and Fire Departments and the Transportation Safety Board temporarily used park facilities. "We're part of the community, while at the same time we're part of a federal system, a national system of parks," Superintendent Billy Garrett explained. He believed it was important to have programs that lent support to the parks neighbors. After learning of plans for a memorial service for victims of the crash, Garrett approached the local chamber of commerce and offered support. Park staff helped organize the event (sponsored by the city of New York and attended by 5,000 people), helped with traffic, and helped with the clean up afterward. Garrett gave the introductory remarks using the opportunity to remind people of the value of parks as places for people to come together. As an expression of the increased level of cooperation, the park signed a cooperative agreement with the police department allowing it to use the airfield in future disasters.[10]

Yosemite National Park, too, was keenly aware of its role in the broader community.

When President Bush called for a national day of remembrance and a moment of silence, Superintendent David Mihalic began to think about how his park could participate. He arranged for a public display of a fire engine, a rescue vehicle, a patrol bicycle, a ranger patrol car, one of the concessionaire's security vehicles, an ambulance from a local hospital clinic, and a couple horse patrol rangers. The staff put out flags and white banners that said "In Remembrance" and invited visitors to sign them. By noon, hundreds had gathered around the display. At the designated moment of silence, all of the park's shuttle buses pulled over to the side of the road and stopped. A uniformed ranger quietly brought her horse out into the middle of the crowd and all the emergency vehicles turned on their red lights. Staff and visitors stood in silence for a moment. Then the red lights were turned off and bus service resumed. Visitors of all ages and backgrounds left their signatures on a banner of 140 feet of plain brown and white craft paper. As Mihalic explained, "People were tying the National Park idea to the whole moment." Yosemite later sent one of the signed banners to Manhattan

A candlelight vigil, sponsored in part by Gateway National Recreation Area, was held at Fort Tilden on September 23, 2001.

> The dramatic increase in homeland security requirements created a strain on the National Park Service's law enforcement capability.

Sites as a symbol of support for their colleagues. "It's not just the World Trade Center story," Mihalic observed. "It's not just the Pentagon story. It's not just the hole in the ground in some rural county in Pennsylvania. It's something like blowing up the *Maine* or like the *Arizona* or like the bridge at Concord. It's something that... transcends us as a nation." It is a national story, he added, and the Park Service's role was to preserve and tell the national story.[11]

Shortage of Law Enforcement Personnel

In the aftermath of the attacks, the National Park Service grappled with severe shortages in its law enforcement capability. At the time, the Service had approximately 1,500 commissioned law enforcement rangers (not including seasonal rangers) and roughly 600 Park Police officers. More than 200 of the law enforcement rangers became involved in special assignments resulting from the attacks. Half of these people were assigned outside of their home parks, including sixty-one at Bureau of Reclamation dam projects, fourteen at the Interior department's Washington headquarters, and twenty-five at Independence National Historical Park, Boston National Historical Park, USS *Arizona* National

Monument, and other parks. Their assignments generally were twenty-four hours a day, seven days a week, for two to three weeks at a time. A report by Interior department Inspector General Earl E. Devaney noted that for months after the attacks, most of the protection rangers and Park Police officers assigned to "icon" parks worked twelve-hour shifts, seven days a week. "We have a concern about the long-term effectiveness of the protection staff and the officers who operate under these intense conditions," the report noted. According to the inspector general, with the exception of Boston Navy Yard, no icon park had received a significant increase in permanent rangers since September 11 and many parks were operating with smaller protection forces than before the attacks.[12]

Some parks already had existing cooperative relationships with neighboring parks that enabled them to share resources. For example, Boston National Historical Park had relationships with Minute Man National Historical Park, Cape Cod National Seashore, and Springfield Armory National Historic Site. Independence National Historical Park had ties with Valley Forge National Historical Park, Gettysburg National Military Park, and Assateague Island National Seashore.

Initially their chief rangers shared resources with each other somewhat informally. As the response continued, however, "special event teams" were going out for their third or fourth rotation and there was growing concern for their health and well-being. As a result, some superintendents began holding back their resources. Managers realized they needed a larger pool of people. Parks that were already understaffed became increasingly reluctant to release rangers for duty elsewhere. As time went on, some parks started to feel that they were contributing more than others. "We really don't have a real understanding of what the National Park Service wants from us," said Regional Chief Ranger Bob Martin, "in this period of terrorism." They were not sure what help the Service expected from them during the national emergency.[13]

The Southeast Region initially used its special event teams but they were being called out repeatedly. Regional leaders decided they could no longer rely solely on these teams, they needed to tap other available resources. They asked each park prepare a minimum staffing plan to reveal the shortfalls that would occur if its law enforcement rangers were dispatched elsewhere. Then the superintendents were to identify the specific resources they would need to provide the minimum level of protection and release the rest to support the national response. After the superintendents completed this plan and the regional director approved it, the parks released all other available law enforcement rangers to meet Service-wide requirements.[14]

Having by far the largest law enforcement contingent within the department at the time, the National Park Service was called upon to do "some extraordinary things" after the attacks, Maj. Gary Van Horn observed. The Service was asked to perform functions that it had not performed in the past, or at least not to the same degree, such as providing extended security for Bureau of Reclamation sites in the West. These new homeland security requirements prompted managers to think more about how to respond rapidly to several locations with enough personnel to provide protection at the request of the president, department, or Service leaders. The Service was such a decentralized organization that aside from deploying its special event teams in response to specific requests, it relied on individual rangers who were available in other parks. Managers expressed frustration with the inability to identify individuals who could respond rapidly and provide security until others could be brought in. The September 11 experience convinced leaders that they could not rely solely on special event teams; they needed to be able to draw on other resources as well.

Not until September 11 did managers fully realize how desperately short the Service was in law enforcement personnel. Some now worried that the Service would burn out hardworking, dedicated law enforcement personnel and put additional strain on their families. Van Horn emphasized that regional chief rangers needed the authority and ability to call up law enforcement rangers on short notice, without having to go through the various levels of management for approval. In a crisis, managers needed to have pre-identified individuals in different parks and direct line authority to call them on duty immediately. In an emergency, there is no

New homeland security requirements
prompted managers to think more about
how to respond rapidly to several locations with enough
personnel to provide protection at the request of the
president, department, or Service leaders.

time to get permission from a number of people. Van Horn recommended having a direct line of authority within law enforcement during emergencies.[15]

Well before the attacks, a series of studies and reports had documented a significant shortfall in law enforcement personnel. Over the previous four years, reports from Congress, the department's inspector general, the International Association of Chiefs of Police, and the National Academy of Public Administration had addressed the issue of the increasing resource and visitor protection demands and their impact on law enforcement, fire protection, emergency services, and other protection duties. These studies revealed inadequacies both in the Park Police and the law enforcement ranger programs. They emphasized the need for increased staff, new training, and additional resources.

A congressional report on law enforcement within the Service called the Thomas Report had concluded that the Service needed 1,295 additional rangers. The National Academy of Public Administration had made an assessment of the law enforcement programs. A study by the International Association of Chiefs of Police identified need for 615 additional law enforcement rangers (roughly the equiv-

alent of seasonal staff). The Park Police had indicated a need for an additional 200 officers. The studies had received little attention and had not sparked any major reforms or initiatives at the bureau or department level. No new law enforcement positions had materialized. Meanwhile, according to *Federal Times*, the number of reported incidents had grown by 39 percent from 1999 to 2000 for the Park Service and other bureaus. The situation only grew worse when rangers were pulled for homeland security missions. Acting Chief Ranger Dennis Burnett explained, "Basically, we're overworking an already overstressed workforce." Rangers, he said, were trying to meet the new security needs, "as well as the day-to-day protection of the resources in the national parks that we're charge with protecting according to Congress."[16]

Responding to requests for rangers for long-term security assignments was a major challenge. While the number of requests for assistance grew significantly, the number of rangers had not kept pace. To illustrate the seriousness of the problem, Einar Olsen explained that in a recent six-month period, the National Capital Region had lost 20 percent of its rangers. The ranger force was often asked to perform special assignments, he added, "but we're in dire

Months after the attacks, officers in Washington
continued to work extended shifts to cover
routine assignments and the additional security
at the monuments and memorials.

straits." Because of the security assignments, parks were being asked to reduce their normal staffing levels. As a result, said Olsen, "We're providing just the very basic public safety needs in the parks and things such as resource protection are really taking the backseat now."[17]

Catoctin Mountain Park was just one example of the problem the region faced. The park had lost two of its ten rangers in the previous year, and Superintendent Mel Poole worried about burnout. One major lesson he saw coming out of September 11 was that the Service needed a significant increase in ranger law enforcement personnel. "If September 11 was not a wake-up call," Poole warned, "I don't know what would be." Ranger Dwight Dixon observed that even under normal circumstances staffing the park and providing the necessary protection was difficult. The response time grew longer. "If you're highly visible you can probably deter a lot of crime, just from being seen," Dixon explained, "and if there's only one or two rangers spread out over a 165-mile district, it's not inconceivable that some visitors may come here fairly regular and never see a ranger." A visible ranger force, he explained, helped deter and ultimately reduce car break-ins, vandalism, and other crimes in the park. With

the reduced force after September 11, the number of incidents increased.[18]

Parks in the Northeast Region grappled with similar shortages. For example, Shenandoah National Park sent rangers to assist temporarily at Shasta and Hoover Dams and to provide security at Independence National Historical Park, Boston National Historical Park and the Main Interior Building. These assignments left the park short staffed and falling further behind in its work plan. Even with some funding available to pay for overtime and to hire assistance, Ranger Rick Childs said, "There are some traditional functions that just cannot be done as a result of this." The park had to cut back the hours and the area of coverage. During certain times of the day, rangers could not patrol as large an area. Nor could they always provide some of the services that they had in the past, such as assisting a visitor with a disabled vehicle. With lighter coverage, managers had to draw the rangers close in, leaving fewer rangers to patrol the periphery. No major tasks were ignored, but the rangers focused their response in the more developed, heavily visited areas such as Skyland and Big Meadows. Patrols in the extreme outlying areas in the north and south were less frequent. Homeland security assignments typically involved twelve-hour days, for either fourteen or twenty-one days, plus a travel day on each end. This meant rangers were away from their home parks for twenty-three or twenty-four days at a time and were tired when they returned. By late fall the rangers working overtime were showing signs of fatigue.[19]

At Valley Forge National Historical Park as many as three protection rangers (representing 25 percent of its ranger force) worked outside park at one time. Two rangers left for the sky marshal program and a third relocated when her husband took a position with that program. In fiscal year 2002, Upper Delaware Scenic and Recreational River sent eleven people to support homeland security–related missions and assist other areas, which reduced its available staff during peak visitation season. The drain on the protection staff prompted joint river patrols with other divisions and agencies in order to promote visitor safety.[20]

Much like the ranger force, the Park Police, too, was stretched thin as officers took on additional security missions. Months after the attacks, officers in Washington continued to work extended shifts to cover routine assignments and the additional security at the monuments and memorials. Weeks of twelve-hour shifts proved draining, and eventually the officers became tired. Though very proud of the professionalism of the officers, Deputy Chief Jack Schamp conceded that maintaining the desired level of alertness among officers who were working extended shifts for a prolonged period was a challenge. The Park Police after-action report highlighted "extreme staffing shortages." The Park Police, it noted, could

not maintain closures without significant overtime. These extended hours led to exhaustion and "reduced long-term effectiveness."[21]

Officers in the New York field office worked many hours of overtime to protect the Statue of Liberty and Federal Hall. Eight months after the attack, they were still working ten- to twelve-hour shifts, sometimes six days a week. The first signs of burnout started to appear. "We've been able to accomplish our mission, but it has been close," Capt. Neal Lauro said.[22]

To make the situation worse, both the ranger force and the Park Police lost trained personnel to the new sky marshal program. This was a federal program, established as a result of the September 11 attacks, to place trained armed law enforcement personnel on commercial flights. The Service could not compete with the higher salaries that the newly created Transportation and Security Administration offered its sky marshals. Capt. Sal Lauro estimated that ten to fifteen officers left in a one-month period. In the first two months that the Transportation and Security Administration was hiring, the New York field office lost fourteen officers, roughly 10 percent of the force. Since these officers had already been through training at the Federal Law Enforcement Training Center, they could easily transition into sky marshal jobs, with only a single week of additional training.[23]

The expanded security missions and functions and the loss of officers ultimately slowed the force's response time. Deputy Chief Schamp conceded that the overall quality of Park Police services had been affected. Fewer officers were available to patrol the streets, parkways, and parks. In Washington, the specialized patrols felt the greatest impact. There were fewer mounted patrols on the horse trails in Rock Creek Park. Some of the undercover officers who had watched for car break-ins and assaults had been put in uniform and assigned to fixed posts. Some training and other programs in Washington were postponed or canceled. Outlying patrols were modified because of the shortage of personnel. With more officers focused on the monument area downtown, patrols in the outlying areas such as Dupont Circle in northwest Washington became less frequent.[24]

The New York field office faced similar challenges. Not since *Operation Desert Storm*, a decade earlier, had Park Police officers been at Federal Hall on an extended basis. In the past, officers had provided support to Manhattan Sites only for limited periods during special events or investigations. After September 11, they assumed a continual presence. The expanded Park Police role in New York after September 11 strained the force and left it with position vacancies.

Even before the attack, the New York field office had difficulty meeting all the requirements placed upon its officers. The staff in the field office was operations oriented. The office had only a small three-person administrative staff to support more than one hundred officers. As a result, officers had had to take on nonoperational, collaborative duties. For example, one lieutenant, a shift supervisor responsible for supervising operations on the street, also handled radio communication and fleet management. His duties included ordering emergency equipment and overseeing

training. The officer had three full-time "jobs" in addition to his duties as shift supervisor. There were other similar cases. Maj. Thomas Wilkins observed, "They have a tremendous amount of responsibility and really not very much support in order to accomplish what they need to accomplish." He praised his staff for doing an "excellent job" in a difficult situation. The increased security requirements forced the New York field office to push back training and semiannual firearms qualifications. Wilkins worried that despite his staff's hard work it would not be able to provide the same level of service it had in the past.[25]

The New York field office's SWAT team had played an important role helping with triage on Ellis Island and patrolling the perimeters of Ellis and Liberty Islands. The team, said Lt. Dave Buckley, was an "integral part" of the overall protection plan. In the months after the attacks, however, six people left the field office's Emergency Services Unit (as the team was now called), four of these to become sky marshals. With so few members left, the unit was disestablished.[26]

At the same time, the field office was assuming a more visible role in the Northeast Region. When dealing with security issues at the Statue of Liberty, Wilkins worked directly with the regional director and associate regional director and even with the director and the secretary. These individuals all took a personal interest in the Statue's security plan. With a relatively new Park Service director and no permanent Park Police chief at the time, Wilkins found that he had difficulty focusing attention on the severity of the staffing problem

and the planning for security at the Statue of Liberty.

Wilkins received additional funding for enhanced security but did not receive a commitment of increased personnel until months later. He had difficulty conveying the significance of the fact that he had lost fifteen people at a time when the workload had increased significantly. Wilkins did not believe Park Police officials in Washington understood the severity of the situation until April 2002 when he informed them that the field office could not support any of the upcoming scheduled events in the city, such as the five-borough bike tour. Nor could he support reopening the Statue of Liberty.

On the bright side, the centralized structure of the Park Police made allocating resources both in New York and in Washington, D.C., easier. Wilkins was able to pool resources, for example, pulling officers from Gateway National Recreation Area and directing them to the Statue of Liberty. He concluded, "Your people are your strength. They are what make the organization."[27]

Multi-region Coordination Group

Although the National Park Service responded to the attacks quickly and effectively and had enough resources to handle the immediate threat, leaders became increasingly concerned that they might not have enough law enforcement resources to respond appropriately to the increased security requirements over the long term. Months after the attacks, the requirement to protect park sites, Bureau of Reclamation dams, and the Main Interior Building was beginning to take a toll. In addition, the Service had committed itself to providing more than one hundred rangers to support the upcoming 2002 Winter Olympics in Utah. The Service was competing with other federal agencies for the same law enforcement/protection candidates, and despite its best efforts, it continued to have difficulty filling vacant positions. Leaders recognized that they could no longer simply react to individual requests for ranger resources, they needed to have a more effective Service-wide system in place to determine priorities and allocate resources.

Recognizing the growing strain on resources, on October 5, 2001, Deputy Director Deny Galvin convened a management assessment team to develop a plan for how the Service could best respond with its law enforcement personnel in the post–September 11 environment. This small group headed by Rick Gale and made up of ranger activities division staff and regional chief rangers met in Main Interior over the Columbus Day weekend in October 2001 to develop what was termed a strategic assessment. In their assessment the team would address the issue of how the Service could best respond with its law enforcement personnel in the face of national security threats while still fulfilling its responsibilities of protecting its sites, employees, and visitors. It would also lay out alternative approaches to addressing the shortage of law enforcement rangers in the long term.

The team spent the holiday weekend developing an assessment of the current situation and a plan to allocate resources effectively on a large scale. They acknowledged that the existing system for allocating resources had not been efficient. At any given time, approximately two hundred law enforcement rangers were working outside their own parks and another hundred were working extended shifts in their own parks. Team members concluded that they needed a process similar to the national fire response system to identify, deploy, and manage resources.[28]

With the national wildland fire response, managers had a system in place based on clearly defined threat levels. As the level of fire threat increased and additional resources were required to respond to the treat, park operations were reduced or drawn down. The levels went from level one where a fire or fires affected a single region to the highest level, level five, when parks were closed so that the Service could respond to the particular fire emergency. There had never been a similar system of stages or levels of response in place for national security. Committing resources at level one was relatively easy, Dick Ring explained, but that task becomes increasingly difficult at levels two, three, four, and five. Describing in advance the trade-offs and impacts at each level, he added, was "critically important." But, as noted, no such system was in place on September 11. The guidance from leadership was to send all the personnel and other resources that were requested but also to maintain their normal level of operations and keep the parks open. This task became inherently impossible. To make matters worse, no one authorized the parks to hire additional personnel to backfill vacant ranger positions. As a result, some parks found themselves struggling with conflicting demands they could not possibly meet. Park managers wanted and needed information and guidance concerning the trade-offs that were authorized and the level of emergency that existed.[29]

In its assessment report, the team reiterated the Service's statutory responsibility to protect park property and the public. This task was even greater, the report emphasized, because the Service was responsible for protecting many high-visibility national icons and parks that housed elements of public utility infrastructure. Invoking the familiar drawdown concept used in national fire response, the team laid out predefined levels of personnel commitment based on the level of threat severity. The team's proposal would require park chief rangers and superintendents to identify acceptable drawdown levels and identify

> Some regional chief rangers found that allocating park resources became easier with the creation of the multi-region coordination group.

protection staff who could be freed up for deployment elsewhere.

In addition to the drawdown concept, the team's proposal incorporated other aspects of the existing fire response system. The fire response system included individual coordination centers around the country that fed resources into the firefighting system. There was a multi-agency coordination group made up of representatives of various federal agencies that established priorities and allocated resources for fire response. This group had the ability to draw on resources of the Bureau of Land Management, Forest Service, Bureau of Indian Affairs, and other federal agencies. Experienced senior rangers recognized that a similar system could be used to feed rangers into homeland security missions. They argued that with the increased security missions the Service could no longer continue to react in a piecemeal fashion to individual requests for law enforcement rangers. Rather, the Service needed an integrated structure or system to set priorities and allocate resources, similar to the multi-agency coordination group that existed for fire response. The team presented its final assessment to Deputy Director Galvin on October 9, 2001, and later Galvin formally presented the team's assessment to the Service's National Leadership Council.[30]

On November 4, 2001, Service leaders adopted the team's recommendation and established a multi-region coordination group to coordinate the mobilization of resources for the ongoing security operations within the Service. Initially the group worked out of a coordination center in Portland, Oregon. Later it moved to the Columbia Cascades Support Office in Seattle. Mark Forbes from the support office served as coordinator.

Over a period of a few weeks, the ranger activities division along with the multi-region coordination group developed the criteria for a drawdown and an exercise for parks to go through to identify the resources they could temporarily make available to other parks. The regional chief rangers developed a national emergency response plan to organize and coordinate all the law enforcement resources to handle the current emergency and future emergencies. The plan described five distinct levels of preparedness and response, ranging from normal operations to national emergency, the level to be determined by the director. All parks were required to prepare drawdown plans to keep the minimum staff required and release the other rangers for security assignments elsewhere.

The emergency response plan would be used in the future to manage any national crisis or large-scale emergency to "ensure a unified and coordinated response."[31]

Director Mainella approved the Service's national emergency response plan on November 16, 2001. In transmitting the plan to the regional directors, she explained that the additional task of providing protection assistance at some department facilities had "taxed the normal operation of our national parks." To date, she added, the Service had successfully met the department's immediate short-term emergency needs for law enforcement personnel through voluntary reassignments from the parks, but long-term commitments required a mandatory program. These measures, she continued, would enable leaders to manage and allocate resources effectively during any national emergency or significant incident. In accordance with the plan, she asked regional directors to have parks develop drawdown plans within two weeks. These plans would help parks determine how many rangers or Park Police officers needed to remain in the park and how many could be made available to support the national protection priorities.[32]

Under the Park Service's emergency response plan, the director would declare a specific level of response based on the requirements the department placed on the Service. The director determined that the Service would respond up to a certain level of impact on the parks. Then the multi-region coordination group would serve as a broker to ensure that the demands were evenly distributed among parks and that no parks were disproportionately affected. An individual park superintendent was under guidance from his or her regional director to release resources up to that specific level of impact. When superintendents reached that level of impact, they would inform their regional director or regional chief ranger, so that a negotiation or brokering process could begin.[33]

Some regional chief rangers found that allocating park resources became easier with the creation of the multi-region coordination group. With the drawdown plan, all personnel who were not needed to provide support at the very basic levels were considered available for emergency operations to move around as needed. Every park submitted a list of a reasonable amount of resources considering what they had available. Einar Olsen, however, found that the National Capital Region simply did not have many rangers available for assignments outside of their own parks even at the highest response levels. He did not believe Service leaders fully recognized the strain on the ranger force. "In terms of shifting resources and priorities in the agency," Olsen added, "I've seen no difference at all."[34]

Developing the multi-region coordination group and the national response plan were major accomplishments. In the Northeast Region, Chief Ranger Bob Martin expressed pride in the regional chief rangers. They had only been together as a group since May 2001 when the last two vacant chief ranger positions were filled. Yet, they had taken on new, challenging issues and formed a cohesive group.[35]

In addition to the emergency response plan, in the aftermath of the attacks there were several major initiatives at the department and Service level that affected the law enforcement program. At the director's request, Deputy Director Don Murphy organized a task force to review the previous law enforcement studies and resolve a number of law enforcement issues. The task force made up of Steve Calvery, Dick Ring, Dennis Burnett, a few regional directors, and some Park Police officials, held its first meeting in February 2002. Members spent the first meeting developing a long-term agenda and discussing the future of the Service's law enforcement program.

Secretary Gale Norton established the Law Enforcement Review Panel to evaluate the law enforcement reforms the inspector general had recommended in a January 2002 report, "Disquieting State of Disorder: An Assessment of Department of the Interior Law Enforcement." On July 19, 2002, she formally approved more than twenty measures proposed by the review panel to improve law enforcement throughout the department, including the appointment of a deputy assistant secretary for law enforcement and security. The measures were largely consistent with those recommended in the inspector general's report.

The secretary made it clear that she expected immediate action on the directives that affected the National Park Service. Not long after, Director Mainella outlined a series of reforms. "We must now demonstrate our commitment to move beyond planning and begin to take action," she explained. The director also created the new associate director for resource and visitor protection position to coordinate the diverse protection ranger functions. This associate director would be considered the functional "chief ranger" of the National Park Service and would provide leadership and policy direction for various park ranger functions.[36]

The aftermath of September 11 ultimately brought significant changes to the Service, its parks, and its people. Many of these changes were positive, though not all. Park visitation declined but the sites and the values they represented assumed new meaning and significance. In some instances, existing bonds between individual parks and their local communities were reinforced and strengthened. The attacks contributed to a shortage of law enforcement personnel and revealed weaknesses in the Service's procedures for allocating resources, but they also prompted promising reform and organizational change.

As a result of the terrorist attacks and the increased emphasis on homeland security, many park rangers who had been commissioned as law enforcement officers were drawn to a greater degree into security and law enforcement functions as part of their day-to-day responsibilities.

Conclusion

Much has been learned as a result of the events of September 11—and even more remains to be understood and analyzed. The attacks and their aftermath clearly demonstrated the importance of the large federal areas and facilities with controlled access in supporting emergency response. Floyd Bennett Field with its open areas and storage facilities, for example, became an important staging area; Federal Hall became a place of critical refuge for people fleeing the collapse of the trade towers; and Ellis Island served as a triage center.

The use of park property to support the response effort was readily apparent and relatively easy to document. Less apparent and more difficult to measure was the immediate and long-term impact of the response on park resources. Park rangers have always played a critical role in preventing crime and catching criminals in the act. Chief rangers in the parks warned that if they met the current requirements for drawing down their protection rangers they would not have enough rangers to catch poachers or adequately protect archeological sites. Some senior managers expressed concern that the monitoring and protection of natural and cultural resources in the parks had declined because rangers had been drawn away for homeland security missions elsewhere.[1]

More than a year after the attack, managers were still trying to determine the extent to which the shortage of protection rangers had jeopardized natural and cultural resources. No one had yet conducted a comprehensive study of the impact on cultural and natural resources in the parks. The protection rangers were traditionally the "eyes and

Interacting with visitors remains an important function for park rangers and Park Police.

ears" of the parks, and resource managers often relied on them to detect and report changes, such as trees that had been cut or bloodstains from a deer. These rangers had not been out in the parks, particularly in the more remote areas, to the same degree as before September 11 and thus were not able to report the necessary information about resources. "We know there are impacts. We know they are out there, but...you have to be out there to see it and observe it or else you have to wait until somebody tells you about it," said the Southeast Region's Chief Ranger Judy Forte. Though the full impact of the September 11 response on park resources had not yet been revealed, some senior rangers speculated that crime had probably increased and some resources had been lost in the absence of protection rangers.[2]

Also difficult to quantify was the impact of the attacks on the role of the park ranger. Traditionally the park ranger functioned as something of a generalist who fulfilled many diverse roles and responsibilities. As a result of the terrorist attacks and the increased emphasis on homeland security, many park rangers who had been commissioned as law enforcement officers were drawn to a greater degree into security and law enforcement functions as part of their day-to-day responsibilities. The Service had already begun to focus more on law enforcement as a separate function, but after September 11 the pressure to narrow the park ranger's function from a generalist to more of a law enforcement function increased. The inspector general reported that with the additional security responsibilities the role of the protection ranger had "made a significant exemplary shift." Some managers and employees questioned the

appropriateness of using these park rangers as guards. The inspector general concluded that requiring police officers and protection rangers to perform sentry duties for extended periods of time was not in the best interest of the officers or the department itself.

Forte, like many other rangers, had come into the Park Service with the generalist view that her job primarily was to protect and interpret park natural and cultural resources. Her duties included search and rescue, interpretation, trail work, firefighting, and other tasks. Law enforcement was just one aspect of the generalist ranger function. After the September 11 response, she said, the career of the park ranger became more protection oriented. For years, the Service had assumed the benefits of the generalist ranger to the agency, but now it was weighing the benefits of generalist rangers against the need for homeland security. As regional chief ranger, Forte found herself spending more time on law enforcement, emergency services, and security than in the past and coordinating more with other law enforcement bureaus. "Homeland security is what is hot on people's minds right now," she stated simply, "and that's where we are."[3]

One side benefit from the increased emphasis on security in the nation and in the National Park Service was that it prompted a greater appreciation for police, firefighters, and other law enforcement representatives. The public held Park Police in higher esteem after September 11, much as they did other police and firefighters. New York City officials became more aware of the Park Police's contributions, inviting Maj. Thomas Wilkins to participate in a citywide counterterrorism subcommittee. Within the Service as well there was greater appreciation for Park Police. Parks that in the past discouraged a visible police presence, now found that visibility reassuring.[4] One New York Park Police officer observed that September 11 "really showed the American people that no matter where the danger is we're going to be there." Deputy Chief Jack Schamp noted that the public image of the Park Police had improved. The Interior department, he believed, had a better understanding of the role and missions of the Park Police, such as ensuring the safety of the secretary of the interior. Capt. Neal Lauro expressed what was probably the sentiment of many officers. "I was never as proud to wear the uniform as that day," he said. His brother, Capt. Sal Lauro, also expressed great pride in the way the officers had performed. Secretary Norton presented the Park Police with a unit citation for their response to the events of September 11.[5]

Much like the Park Police, protection rangers were also viewed a little differently after the attacks. The public became increasingly aware that security was part of the park rangers' mission. Rangers in the Northeast Region were instructed to maintain a high level of visibility in part because their presence reassured visitors.[6] The green-and-gray ranger uniform became an even more powerful symbol of security and protection. Thousands of Americans who visited parks were reassured when they saw uniformed rangers. The power of the uniform as a symbol of safety and protection was perhaps most dramatically and poignantly illustrated immediately after the attacks in New York when people on the streets desperately fleeing the smoke and debris grabbed on to Danny Merced after spotting his uniform.

The Service has always faced the challenge of balancing its responsibility for protecting visitors with its fundamental mission of preserving resources and providing for the public enjoyment of those resources. This task became much more complex and difficult as a result of the September 11 attacks. In the aftermath, the Service struggled to adjust the effects of heightened security. The Park Service had always been involved in security, Dick Ring observed, but the level of resources and attention devoted to that activity increased significantly. Managers struggled to find ways to ensure that the security efforts did not disrupt visitor services, normal park activities, or the normal enjoyment of the parks. The Park Service worked with and provided support to the Bureau of Reclamation, the Navy, and other agencies, so its workload had increased.[7]

The long-term impact of the attacks on the National Park Service mission, resources, functions, and culture remains unclear. Some veteran responders viewed September 11 as a transforming event for the Service. "I think we've got to balance being able to protect our resources, our visitors, our employees, and then also letting our visitors enjoy the parks," Skip Brooks explained. Rick Gale noted that the attacks could be a transforming event for the Service if it incorporated the lessons it had learned. He encouraged Service leaders to continue to look at innovative ways to allocate resources and address staffing shortages, to focus less on obstacles and more on opportunities. The greatest challenge, he conceded, was to think strategically, to look ahead, and develop a proactive approach in dealing with incidents and potential threats.[8]

The National Park Service had reason to feel proud of its response. The actions of many individual Service employees represented the very highest standards of service and dedication. The efforts of the staff at Federal Hall, Ellis Island, and elsewhere on September 11 certainly reflect their outstanding performance. The service and dedication to duty was also reflected in the dozens of law enforcement rangers who spent weeks away from their homes and families working long hours to support the response. It was reflected in the Park Police officers who worked extended hours for weeks and sometimes months. It was reflected in the actions of employees who spent their extra hours searching for victims at Ground Zero, like Gateway National Recreation Area Ranger Theresa Marie Cervera. On September 11 Cervera, who had arrived early for a 9:00 a.m. first-aid/CPR class, was birdwatching at the Great Kills section of Staten Island. After witnessing the attack through her binoculars, she rushed to Ground Zero to assist. Once there, someone placed a stethoscope in her hand and she immediately went to work treating injured firefighters and police. Cervera worked through the night treating injured rescue workers and shouldered the grim task of digging for victims. In the following weeks, she drove to Ground Zero each evening after her regular duty hours and worked until midnight.[9]

Certainly one the most dominant themes of the National Park Service's response was that of parks and park employees around the country pulling together and supporting each other. In New York City and Washington, D.C., rangers and Park Police provided support to each other. Parks as far south as Assateague Island in Maryland sent up boats to patrol around the Statue of Liberty. As Officer David Moen observed, people put their personal differences aside and worked together as a team. New York and Boston area parks received assistance from rangers from Assateague Island National Seashore, Cape Cod National Seashore, Colonial National Historical Park, Fire Island National Seashore, Richmond National Battlefield, Petersburg National Battlefield, Upper Delaware Scenic and Recreational River, Delaware Water Gap National Recreation Area, Gettysburg National Battlefield, Shenandoah National Park, and Blue Ridge Parkway. "We didn't have the numbers that we needed and we couldn't provide as much assistance as maybe we would like to or maybe the department would have liked us to provide," Dennis Burnett conceded, "but I think that we were in place and ready to respond with a phone call." He aptly summed up the Service's response by saying, "We did what had to be done and I think we got it accomplished."[10]

The Service clearly demonstrated that despite staffing shortages and communications problems, it could respond effectively to the attacks. Yet, in ways recounted earlier, the attacks might have left the National Park Service forever changed. In the span of a single morning, its mission and functions became more complex and the challenge of protecting its parks, its people, and its visitors became much more difficult.

Notes

Unless otherwise noted, copies of all interview transcripts and all files cited below are located in the administrative history files, National Register, History, and Education, National Park Service (NPS), Washington, D.C.

Preface

[1]Mary Marshall Clark, "The September 11 Oral History Narrative and Memory Project: A First Report," *The Journal of American History*, 89, no. 2 (September 2002): 569-79.

I. National Park Service's Initial Response

[1]Richard Ring, interview by Janet A. McDonnell, May 29, 2002, p. 2; Richard T. Gale, interview by Janet A. McDonnell, December 12, 2001, p.1.

[2]Dennis Burnett, interview by Janet A. McDonnell, January 29, 2002, pp. 1-2.

[3]Maj. Gary Van Horn, interview by Janet A. McDonnell, February 26, 2002, p. 2.

[4]Burnett, interview, pp. 4, 6.

[5]Dennis Burnett, e-mail to Bill Halainen, September 11, 2001, 8:38 a.m., file: 9/11 documents. [Time indicated on e-mail does not appear to be accurate.]

[6]Brenda Ritchie, interview by Janet A. McDonnell, January 23, 2002, pp. 1-3, 6, 37; Mel Poole, interview by Mark Schoepfle, December 17, 2001, p. 36.

[7]Ritchie, interview, pp. 10-11, 3-4, 13.

[8]Burnett, interview, pp. 2, 7.

[9]Ring, interview, p. 13; Gale, interview, pp. 1-2, 6, 10.

[10]Ring, interview, pp. 3-4, 7-8.

[11]Director Fran Mainella, memo, "Emergency Operations Instructions, September 11, 2001," NPS *Morning Report*, September 11, 2001, supplemental special edition, file: *Morning Report* [hereafter cited as *Morning Report*].

[12]Michael Grunwald, "Terrorists Hijack 4 Airliners, Destroy World Trade Center, Hit Pentagon, Hundreds Dead," *Washington Post*, September 12, 2001, www.washingtonpost.com [accessed March 12, 2003].

[13]Burnett, interview, pp. 2-3; Secretary Gale Norton, memo, September 11, 2001, referenced in *Morning Report*, September 11, 2001, supplemental special edition.

[14]Burnett, interview, pp. 7, 9.

[15]Gale, interview, pp. 2, 3, 5; Van Horn, interview, p. 3.

[16]Ring, interview, p. 4; Gale, interview, pp. 4-5; Van Horn, interview, p. 6; Eastern Interagency Coordination Center (EICC) Log, September, 11, 2001, 1415 hours, file: incident management; Director Fran Mainella, memo (draft) to assistant secretary for policy, management, and budget," n.d., file: 9/11 documents.

[17]Commander, Planning and Development Unit, memo to Acting Chief, U.S. Park Police, "After-Action Report on Terrorist Attacks on World Trade Center/Pentagon," September 12, 2001, file: USPP [hereafter cited as USPP, "After-Action Report"].

[18]Van Horn, interview, p. 7.

[19]Gale, interview, p. 4.

[20]Van Horn, interview, 9.

[21]Ibid., pp. 11-12; Burnett, interview, p. 14.

[22]EICC Log, September 12, 2001, no time, file: incident management; "Workers Offered Leave As Government Reopens," *Washington Post*, September 12, 2001, www.washingtonpost.com [accessed March 12, 2003].

[23]Ring, interview, p. 25; EICC Log, September 11, 2001, 2227 hours, file: incident management; SHEN Communications Center, memo to all regional directors, "Normal Operations," September 11, 2001, file: *Morning Report*.

[24]Gale, interview, p. 4; EICC Log, September 11, 2001, 2145 hours, file: incident management.

[25]*Morning Report*, September 13, 2001, morning edition.

[26]Department of the Interior (DOI), press release, "Washington Area Monuments Reopen," September 12, 2001; *Morning Report*, September 13, 2001, morning edition.

[27]Director Fran Mainella, memo (draft) to assistant secretary for policy, management, and budget, n.d; Gale interview, pp. 6, 16; Van Horn, interview, p. 12; Richard Powell, interview by Janet A. McDonnell, April 30, 2002, pp. 6, 8; Ring, interview, p. 5.

[28]DOI, "September 11," *People, Land and Water*, 8, no. 6 (September/October 2001): p. 19; Van Horn, interview, p. 13; Ring, interview, p. 6.

[29]Director Fran Mainella, memo (draft) to assistant secretary for policy, management, and budget, n.d.; Powell, interview, pp. 7-8.

[30]Frances Delmar, interview by Doris D. Fanelli, March 15, 2002, p. 8; David A. Mihalic, interview by Louis Hutchins, February 4, 2002, pp. 11-16.

[31]Doyle Nelson, interview by Chuck Smythe, May 13, 2002, pp. 4-6, 8.

[32]Gale, interview, pp. 10-11.

[33]U. S. Park Police (USPP), "Lessons Learned," n.d., p. 1, file: USPP; Deputy Chief John D. Schamp, interview by Janet A. McDonnell, April 17, 2002, pp. 22-24.

[34]USPP, "The Force's Response," September 13, 2001, file: USPP; Gretchen Merkle, e-mail to John D. Schamp, February 12, 2001, file: USPP.

[35]Superintendent's Annual Narrative Report (SANR), Boston NHP, FY2001.

[36]"Park Status Report," September 12, 2001, file: incident management; Ibid., September 14, 2001; *Morning Report*, September 14, 2001, afternoon edition.

[37]SANR, USS *Arizona* NM, FY2001.

[38]EICC Log, September 12, 2001, 1200 hours, file: incident management; Ibid., 1700 hours.

[39]"Park Status Report," September 27, 2001, file: incident management; *Morning Report*, September 26, 2001; Ibid., September 28, 2001.

[40]Burnett, interview, pp.17-23; Einar S. Olsen, interview by Janet A. McDonnell and Gary Scott, December 13, 2001, p. 24; Gale, interview, pp. 24-25; Judy Forte, interview by Janet A. McDonnell, January 29, 2002, p. 7.

[41]Burnett, interview, pp. 21-22.

[42]Forte, interview, p. 8.

[43]Chief Ranger Pacific West Region (PWR), memo to PWR Directorate, September 20, 2001, file: incident management; Jay Wells, fax to Skip Brooks, September 20, 2001, file: incident management.

[44]SANR, Lake Mead NRA, FY2001.

[45]SANR, Whiskeytown NRA, FY2001.

[46]"Parks and Monuments: Some Open, Some Not," *New York Times*, October 14, 2001.

[47]Van Horn, interview, pp. 6, 16-18; Ring, interview, p. 5; Gale, interview, pp. 4-5.

[48]Burnett, interview, p. 10; Gale, interview, p. 29; Dennis McGinnis, interview by Janet A. McDonnell, December 5, 2001, p. 34.

II. National Capital Region

[1]Capt. Sal Lauro, interview by Janet A. McDonnell, March 28, 2002, p. 3.

[2]Sal Lauro, interview, p. 3; Schamp, interview, April 17, 2002, p. 4.

[3]USPP, "After-Action Report"; Schamp, interview, pp. 1-3, 6, 33.

[4]Maj. Thomas Pellinger, interview by Mark Schoepfle, March 29, 2002, pp. 3, 5-6,10-11, 22-23; Sal Lauro, interview, pp. 22-24; Schamp, interview, pp. 10-11.

[5]USPP, "Lessons Learned," p.2; *Morning Report*, September 16, 2002; "U.S. Park Police Lead Interior Security Efforts in New York, Nation's Capital," *People, Land and Water*, 8, no. 6 (September/October 2001): p. 23; Chief's Command Post, memo, "Daily Summary Report", September 17, 2001, file: USPP.

[6]USPP, "After-Action Report"; USPP "Lessons Learned," p. 3; Schamp, interview, pp. 25-26; Capt. Neal Lauro, interview by Janet A. McDonnell, May 7, 2002, p. 22; Sal Lauro, interview, pp. 6, 48.

[7]Chief's Command Post, memo, "Daily Summary Report", September 11, 2001, file: USPP; Pellinger, interview, pp. 2, 3, 5; Sal Lauro, interview, pp. 5, 39-40.

[8]Sal Lauro, interview, pp. 27, 34-35.

[9]Ibid., pp. 5-6; USPP, "Lessons Learned," p. 2; USPP, "The Force's Response"

[10]"U.S. Park Police Lead Interior Security Efforts in New York, Nation's Capital," p. 22; USPP, "The Force's Response."

[11]Lt. George F. Wallace, interview by Mark Schoepfle, January 16, 2002, pp. 2-7, 12-13.

[12]Sgt. Ron Galey, interview by Janet A. McDonnell, December 17, 2001, pp. 1-3; Sgt. Kenneth Burchell, interview by Janet A. McDonnell, December 17, 2001, pp. 2-5; Sgt. Bernard T. Stasulli, interview by Janet A. McDonnell, December 10, 2001, pp. 3, 5; Bill Lane, "NCR Contributes to September 11th Help Efforts,"n.d., file: USPP.

[13]Burchell, interview, pp. 7-12, 20-21; Galey, interview by McDonnell, p. 3; Stasulli, interview by McDonnell, p. 9; Officer John Dillon, interview by Janet A. McDonnell, December 10, 2001, p. 3.

[14]Galey, interview by McDonnell, pp. 4-5; Stasulli, interview by McDonnell, p. 7; Dillon, interview, p. 10; Sgt. Bernard T. Stasulli, interview by Mark Schoepfle, January 16, 2002, p. 6.

[15]Burchell, interview, pp. 12-15, 18; Stasulli, interview by McDonnell, pp. 7-8; Lane,

"NCR Contributes to September 11th Help Efforts"; Stasulli, interview by Schoepfle, p. 7; Galey, interview by McDonnell, pp. 5-8.

[16] Galey, interview by McDonnell, p. 8; Dillon, interview, p. 2.

[17] Dillon, interview, pp. 4, 6; Burchell, interview, p. 27; Galey, interview by McDonnell, pp. 10-12.

[18] USPP, "The Force's Response"; Galey, interview by McDonnell, p. 16; USPP, "Lessons Learned"; Dillon, interview, p. 4; Burchell, interview, p. 19.

[19] Dillon, interview, pp. 6-7; Galey, interview by McDonnell, pp. 13-14; "U.S. Park Police Lead Interior Security Efforts in New York, Nation's Capital," pp. 22-23; Pellinger, interview, p. 9.

[20] Galey, interview by McDonnell, p. 9; Dillon, interview, pp. 11-12.

[21] Galey, interview by McDonnell, p. 19; Stasulli, interview by McDonnell, pp.15-17.

[22] Burchell, interview, pp. 25-26.

[23] Sal Lauro, interview, pp. 12-13; Schamp, interview, p. 8; USPP, "Lessons Learned," p. 2; USPP, "After-Action Report"; Sgt. Robert MacLean, e-mail to *Morning Report*, September 12, 2001, 6:45 a.m.; Chief's Command Post, "Daily Summary Report" (time line), September 11, 2001, 1020 hours, file: USPP; Ibid., 1125 hours; Ibid., 1356 hours; USPP, "The Force's Response."

[24] Pellinger, interview, pp. 4, 7; USPP, "The Force's Response"; Wallace, interview, pp. 7-8, 17, 19.

[25] Schamp, interview, p. 6.

[26] Wallace, interview, p. 15; USPP, "Lessons Learned," p. 2; Chief's Command Post, "Daily Summary Report" (time line), September 11, 2001, 1120 hours, file: USPP; Ibid., 1158 hours; Pellinger, interview, pp. 3, 22-23; Sal Lauro, interview, pp. 8-9; Schamp, interview, p. 32.

[27] Pellinger, interview, pp. 9-10; "U.S. Park Police Lead Interior Security Efforts in New York, Nation's Capital," p. 22; USPP, "The Force's Response"; Sal Lauro, interview, p. 12.

[28] USPP, "The Force's Response"; "U.S. Park Police Lead Interior Security Efforts in New York, Nation's Capital," p. 23; Sal Lauro, interview, pp. 9, 16; USPP, "Lessons Learned."

[29] Olsen, interview, pp. 1-5.

[30] Ibid., pp. 6, 32-33.

[31] Ibid., pp. 6-11.

[32] Ibid., pp. 10-11.

[33] Dwight Dixon, interview by Mark Schoepfle, pp. 2-3, 5-7; Olsen, interview, pp. 11, 14.

[34] Olsen, interview, pp. 15-16; Lance Hatten, interview by Mark Schoepfle, February 27, 2002, pp. 4, 9, 14.

[35] "Highlights of September 11th for National Capital Region," n.d., file: 9/11 documents; Sean Kennealy, interview by Mark Schoepfle, December 18, 2001, pp. 8-9.

[36] Mel Poole, interview by Mark Schoepfle, December 17, 2001, pp. 5-8, 15, 17, 20-21, 23-26; SANR, Catoctin Mountain Park, FY2001; Olsen, interview, pp. 16-17.

[37] Poole, interview, pp. 34, 40, 42.

[38] Olsen, interview, pp. 17-18.

[39] Sal Lauro, interview, pp. 21-22.

III. New York City

[1] *Morning Report*, September 15, 2001, afternoon edition.

[2] Maj. Thomas Wilkins, interview by Janet A. McDonnell, May 8, 2002, pp. 1-2; Neal Lauro, interview, pp. 1-2; Lt. Dave Buckley, interview by Janet A. McDonnell, May 7, 2002, pp. 2-5.

[3] Wilkins, interview, pp. 4-5; Neal Lauro, interview, p. 9; "U.S. Park Police Lead Interior Security Efforts in New York, Nation's Capital," p. 22.

[4] Wilkins, interview, pp. 6, 12; "U.S. Park Police Lead Interior Security Efforts in New York, Nation's Capital," p. 22; USPP, "Lessons Learned," p. 3; Capt. Martin L. Zweig, interview by Chuck Smythe, December 11, 2001, pp. 1, 6-8.

[5] Zwieg, interview, pp. 7-8, 10; USPP, "The Force's Response"; *Morning Report*, September 13, 2001, morning edition ; Wilkins, interview, p. 13; *Morning Report*, September 15, 2001, afternoon edition. [By some accounts, there were seven U.S. marshals and two construction workers.] Officer David Moen, interview by Janet A. McDonnell, May 7, 2002, pp. 5-8; Neal Lauro, interview, p. 9; "U.S. Park Police Lead Interior Security Efforts in New York, Nation's Capital," p. 22.

[6] Moen, interview, pp. 10-12.

[7] Daniel Merced, interview by Chuck Smythe, December 19, 2001, p. 28; *Morning Report*, September 12, 2001, morning edition; SANR, Manhattan Sites, FY2001.

[8] Laura Brennan, interview by Chuck Smythe, December 20, 2001, pp. 6-8, 10-12; Merced, interview, pp. 5-13, 23; Archie Johnson, interview by Chuck Smythe, January 23, 2002, pp. 5-7; Christopher Keenan, interview by Chuck Smythe, December 20, 2001, pp. 6-7, 11, 14, 16-17; Steven Laise, interview by Chuck Smythe, December 19, 2001, pp. 5-6.

[9] Johnson, interview, pp. 8, 17, 28; Sgt. Clyde Solomon, interview by Janet A. McDonnell, May 8, 2002, p. 2; Laise, interview, pp. 6, 8.

[10] Joseph Avery, interview by Chuck Smythe, January 23, 2002, pp. 5, 14; Keenan, interview, pp. 17-18, 22, 26; Brennan, interview, pp. 13-16; Laise, interview, pp. 6-8, 14; Merced, interview, pp. 14, 17, 20-22; Johnson, interview, pp. 9-11; Zweig, interview, p. 13.

[11] Cynthia Garrett, interview by George Tselos, June 6, 2002, p.18; Zweig, interview, p. 13; Solomon, interview, pp. 1-5, 7, 9; Keenan, interview, pp. 27, 29-31, 36; Laise, interview, pp. 8-9, 20-21; "U.S. Park Police Lead Security Efforts in New York, Nation's Capital," p. 22; Merced, interview, p. 18; "Nomination for the USPP Certificate for Sergeant Clyde E. Solomon and Officer Bekim Cobaj," n.d., file: USPP; Johnson, interview, pp. 26, 34; Avery, interview, p. 6; Peter O'Dougherty, interview by Mark Schoepfle, February 1, 2002, pp. 9, 26; Steven Laise, e-mail to Janet A. McDonnell, February 11, 2004.

[12] Keenan, interview, pp. 37, 40, 42; Merced, interview, pp. 34, 36; Laise, interview, pp. 11-13.

[13] *Morning Report*, September 13, 2001, afternoon edition; Ibid., September 14, 2001, afternoon edition; Avery, interview,

p. 14; Laise, interview, pp. 15-16; SANR, Manhattan Sites, FY2001; Steven Laise, e-mail to Janet A. McDonnell, February 11, 2004.

[14]Northeast Region Type 2 Team, "Daily Status Report," September 18, 2001, Operation Secure Parks, Box 1 of 2, file: Status Reports; SANR, Manhattan Sites, FY2001.

[15]Charles Markis, interview by Louis Hutchins, February 26, 2002, pp. 4-14, 17, 21.

[16]Markis, interview, pp. 16-23, 35, 38, 40.

[17]Northeast Region Type 2 Team, "Daily Status Report," September 18, 2001, file: incident management.

[18]SANR, Manhattan Sites, FY2001.

[19]Avery, interview, p. 13; Keenan, interview, p. 32; Johnson, interview, pp. 11-12, 15.

[20]Laise, interview, p. 18; Keenan, interview, p. 38.

[21]Johnson, interview, pp. 43-44; Laise, interview, pp. 18-19; Keenan, interview, pp. 51, 54-55.

[22]Johnson, interview, p. 19; Avery, interview, pp. 20, 29; Merced, interview, pp. 55-57; Laise interview, pp. 27, 29, 30; SANR Manhattan Sites, FY2001.

[23]SANR, Manhattan Sites, FY2001.

[24]Ibid., FY2002.

[25]Vincent DiPietro, interview by Mark Schoepfle, February 1, 2002, pp. 2-8, 22; Paula Castro, interview by Mark Schoepfle, pp. 3-4; Alfred Farrugio, interview by Mark Schoepfle, January 30, 2002, pp. 4-5; Frank N. Mills, interview by Mark Schoepfle, January 31, 2002, pp. 3, 5, 16, 25-26; O'Dougherty, interview, p. 3.

[26]Castro, interview, pp. 4-5; Joan Kelly, interview by Mark Schoepfle, p. 3; O'Dougherty, interview, pp. 5-6; Neal Lauro, interview, p. 3; Diane Dayson, interview by Mark Schoepfle, January 28, 2002, pp. 3-4, 8-10; Cynthia Garrett, interview, pp. 5-6; Alfred Arberg, interview by Mark Schoepfle, February 1, 2002, p. 3.

[27]Arberg, interview, pp. 4-6, 14-19; O'Dougherty, interview, p. 10; SANR, Statue of Liberty/Ellis Island Immigration Museum, FY2001; Mills, interview, p. 30.

[28]Cynthia Garrett, interview, pp. 12, 14; Dayson, interview, pp. 3- 4, 7-8, 11-12; Mills, interview, p. 28; Castro interview, p. 11; Neal Lauro, interview, pp. 8, 15.

[29]Dayson, interview, pp. 4-5; Neal Lauro, interview, pp. 3-4.

[30]O'Dougherty, interview, pp. 7-8; DiPietro, interview, pp. 14-15, 20; Dayson, interview, p. 5; Cynthia Garrett, interview, p. 12; Daniel T. Brown, interview by Mark Schoepfle, January 29, 2002, pp. 5-6.

[31]Kelly, interview, pp. 4-9; Castro, interview, p.12; Brown, interview by Mark Schoepfle, January 29, 2002, pp. 18-20; Dayson, interview, pp. 7, 9, 12-15, 17; Mills, interview, p. 33; Cynthia Garrett, interview, p. 10; Neal Lauro, interview, pp. 12-13; USPP, "The Force's Response"; "U.S. Park Police Lead Security Efforts in New York, Nation's Capital," p. 22; Morning Report, September 13, 2001, morning edition; Ibid., September 15, 2001, afternoon edition; Ibid., September 12, 2001, morning edition; DiPietro, interview, pp. 22-23.

[32]Dayson, interview, pp.14-16, 18-21; O'Dougherty, interview, pp. 19, 23; Mills, interview, p. 29; "U.S. Park Police Lead Security Efforts in New York, Nation's Capital," p. 22.

[33]Mills, interview, pp.15, 27; *Morning Report*, September 13, 2001, afternoon edition; Northeast Region Type 2 Team, "Daily Status Report," September 18, 2001, file: incident management; Castro, interview, p. 17; DiPietro, interview, p. 50.

[34]Dayson, interview, pp. 21, 23-26.

[35]Cynthia Garrett, interview, pp. 20-24; DiPietro, interview, p. 28.

[36]Dayson, interview, pp. 26-27; Schamp, interview, p. 28; Wilkins, interview, p. 14.

[37]Dayson, interview, pp. 29-52.

[38]Cynthia Garrett, interview, p. 26; Dayson, interview, pp. 64-65.

[39]Dayson, interview, pp. 21-23; O'Dougherty, interview, p. 32; "Secretary Norton Announces New Visitor Plan for Statue of Liberty," *Arrowhead*, 11, no. 2 (Spring 2004): 1; "Statue of Liberty Reopening Date Announced," June 30, 2004, www.inside. nps.gov/printheadline.cfm?type [accessed July 6, 2004].

[40]Zweig, interview, pp. 13-14; William Garrett, interview by Chuck Smythe, February 24, 2002, pp. 15-17; www.nps/ gov/remembrance [accessed May 5, 2003]; Northeast Region Type 2 Team, "Daily Status Report," September 18, 2001; "U.S. Park Police Lead Interior Security Efforts in New York, Nation's Capital," p. 22.

[41]William Garrett, interview, pp. 18-21; www.nps/gov/remembrance [accessed May 5, 2003].

[42]Shirley McKinney, interview by Chuck Smythe, January 25, 2002, pp. 1-2.

[43]McKinney, interview, pp. 4, 7-8, 23; Northeast Region Type 2 Team, "Daily Status Report," September 18, 2001; *Morning Report*, September 15, 2001, afternoon edition; www.nps/gov/remembrance [accessed May 5, 2003].

[44]McKinney, interview, pp. 11-16, 24-25.

[45]David Luchsinger, interview by Chuck Smythe, January 23, 2002, pp. 5-8, 12,15; *Morning Report*, September 14, 2001, afternoon edition.

[46] www.nps/gov/remembrance [accessed May 5, 2003]; Northeast Region Type 2 Team, "Daily Status Report," September 18, 2001; Mills, interview, pp. 13-14; Dayson, interview, pp. 21, 23-26.

[47]Avery, interview, p. 11; Brennan, interview, p. 8; SANR, Gateway NRA, FY2001; *Morning Report*, September 28, 2001.

[48]DiPietro, interview, p. 49; Mills, interview, pp. 61, 67, 77-78.

IV. Incident Management

[1]Ring, interview, pp. 9-11, 19.

[2]Gale, interview, pp. 6, 8; Skip Brooks, interview by Janet A. McDonnell, June 12, 2002, p. 1; Ritchie, interview, p. 8; Dennis Burnett, e-mail to Bill Halainen, September 11, 2001, file: 9/11 documents; McGinnis, interview by Janet A. McDonnell, pp. 2, 7-9, 16; EICC Log, September 11, 2001, 1501 hours, file: incident management; *Morning Report*, September 12, 2001, morning edition.

[3]Brooks, interview, pp. 2-4, 9; McGinnis, interview, p. 16; Paul Pfenninger, interview by Janet A. McDonnell, January 23, 2002, pp. 14-15; Operation Secure Parks, "Organization Assignment List."

[4]McGinnis, interview, pp. 12, 16; Gale, interview, p. 11; Brooks, interview, p. 13; *Morning Report*, September 13, 2001, morning edition.

[5]Van Horn, interview, p. 19.

[6]Brooks, interview, p. 7; McGinnis, interview, pp. 4-5, 11.

[7]Director Fran Mainella, memo to Skip Brooks, "Delegation of Authority, NPS Continuity of Operations," September 13, 2001, file: incident management; Brooks, interview, p. 8; McGinnis, interview, p. 4.

[8]Brooks, interview, pp. 3, 8-9; McGinnis, interview, pp. 2-4, 14-15; Director Fran Mainella, memo to Skip Brooks, "Delegation of Authority, NPS Continuity of Operations"; Operation Secure Parks, "Narrative Update and Discussion of Incident Management Operations."

[9]Gale, interview, pp. 12-13, 29; McGinnis, interview, pp. 5-6, 12.

[10]Ritchie, interview, pp. 11-12, 15-16; Bill Halainen, e-mail to SHEN EICC, September 12, 2001, file: incident management; *Morning Report*, September 12, 2001, supplemental special edition; *Morning Report*, September 18, 2001.

[11]Brooks, interview, pp. 6, 14-15, 26, 31-32; Gale, interview, pp. 13, 17; McGinnis, interview, p. 29.

[12]McGinnis, interview, p. 4; Brooks, interview, p. 29; Gale, interview, pp. 13-14.

[13]Operation Secure Parks, "Narrative Update and Discussion of Incident Management Operations"; Brooks, interview, p. 35; McGinnis, interview, p. 34; *Morning Report*, September 19, 2001.

[14]McGinnis, interview, pp. 23-24; Gale, interview, p. 15; Powell, interview, pp. 10, 22, 28; *Morning Report*, September 19, 2001.

[15]Brooks, interview, pp. 30-31; McGinnis, interview, p. 31.

[16]"Incident Objectives," September 14, 2001, file: incident management; *Morning Report*, September 19, 2001; Ibid., September 25, 2001; Ibid., September 26, 2001; Ibid., September 27, 2001.

[17]Brooks, interview, pp. 5, 23-24; Operation Secure Parks, "Narrative Update and Discussion of Incident Management Operations"; Shenandoah National Park (SHEN)Superintendent, memo to all employees, "Eastern Incident Management Team Activities," September 20, 2001, file: incident management; SHEN superintendent, memo to Robert Panko, "Limited Delegation of Authority, Operation Secure Parks Incident," September 20, 2001, file: incident management.

[18]*Morning Report*, September 23, 2001; Operation Secure Parks, "Transition Plan and Recommendations," October 1, 2001 (Approved October 2, 2001, by Acting Director Denis Galvin), file: incident management; Robert Panko, memo to SHEN Superintendent, "Closeout of Limited Delegation of Authority, Operation Secure Parks," September 28, 2001, file: incident management.

[19]Robert Martin, interview by Janet A. McDonnell, February 5, 2002, pp. 1, 3, 5, 11; EICC Log, September 11, 2001, 1600 hours, file: incident management; Ibid., 1320 hours; McGinnis, interview, p. 10.

[20]Kay Dilonardo, e-mail to Chuck Smythe, April 4, 2002, file: 9/11 documents; Martin, interview, pp. 5-6, 10; Pfenninger, interview, pp. 4-5, 7, 14, 22.

[21]*Morning Report*, September 12, 2001, morning edition; Kay Dilonardo, e-mail to Chuck Smythe, April 4, 2002; Russ Smith, e-mail to Northeast Region, September 12, 2001, 11:18 a.m; Martin, interview, pp. 13, 37; Pfenninger, interview, pp. 7-9, 11, 15-16, 18, 23; McGinnis, interview, pp. 10, 29; Brooks, interview, p. 15.

[22]Burnett, interview, pp. 12-13; Gale, interview, pp. 7, 14, 29-30; McGinnis, interview, pp. 9, 15, 29; Brooks, interview, pp. 39-40.

[23]Pfenninger, interview, p.17, 19.

[24]Martin, interview, p. 37; McGinnis, interview, pp. 16, 19, 37-39; Brooks, interview, pp. 3, 17, 21, 37-48; Pfenninger, interview, p. 10.

[25]McGinnis, interview, p. 22, 36; Brooks, interview, p. 20.

[26]Ring, interview, pp. 15-16; Martin, interview, p. 16; McGinnis, interview, p. 20.

[27]Brooks, interview, pp. 43-45, 48.

[28]Operation Secure Parks, "Transition Plan and Recommendations."

V. Challenges

[1]McGinnis, interview, 17-18; Martin, interview, p. 9.

[2]Director Fran Mainella, memo (draft), to assistant secretary for policy, management, and budget, n.d.; Burnett, interview, p. 5; Van Horn, interview, p. 16; McGinnis, interview, pp. 17-18; USPP, "Lessons Learned," p. 2.

[3]Zweig, interview, p. 31.

[4]Schamp, interview, pp. 15-16; USPP, "Lessons Learned," p. 2; Sal Lauro, interview, p. 51; Wilkins, interview, p. 9; Zweig, interview, pp. 31-33; Neal Lauro, interview, pp. 6-7.

[5]NPS, "Lessons Learned," (draft), November 13, 2001, pp. 13-14; Sal Lauro, interview, p. 50; Olsen, interview, p. 37.

[6]Wilkins, interview, pp. 11-13.

[7]Sgt. Robert MacLean, e-mail to *Morning Report*, September 12, 2001, 6:45 a.m.; USPP, "The Force's Response"; Van Horn, interview, pp. 20-22; Schamp, interview, pp. 20-21.

[8]McGinnis, interview, 33; USPP, "After-Action Report"; Schamp, interview, p. 18; Sal Lauro, interview, p. 52.

[9]Van Horn, interview, pp. 22-23; Brooks, interview, p. 33; Powell, interview, pp. 24-25; Martin, interview, pp. 16-18, 39.

[10]Gale, interview, pp. 18, 22; NPS, "Lessons Learned," (draft), p. 17.

[11]Brooks, interview, pp. 16, 22-23, 28-29, 31, 39-40; McGinnis, interview, pp. 26-27.

[12]Brooks, interview, pp. 28-29; NPS, "Lessons Learned," (draft), p. 17.

[13]Ring, interview, p. 16; NPS, "Lessons Learned," (draft), p. 17.

[14]Ritchie, interview, pp. 32-35, 39; Gale, interview, p. 22; Martin, interview, p. 41.

[15]Ring, interview pp. 12-15; Director Fran Mainella, memo (draft) to assistant secretary for policy, management, and budget, n.d.

[16]Brooks, interview, pp. 11-12, 20, 28-29.

[17]Gale, interview, pp. 14-15; Martin, interview, p. 36; McGinnis, interview, p. 25; Brooks, interview, p. 16.

[18]Brooks, interview, pp. 9-10, 50; Gale, interview, pp. 22, 33-34, 37.

[19]Director Fran Mainella, memo (draft) to assistant secretary for policy, management, and budget, n.d.; DOI, Office of the Inspector General (OIG), *Disquieting State of Disorder: An Assessment of Department of the Interior Law Enforcement,* January 2002, Report no. 2002-I-0014, file: IG reports.

[20]Gale, interview, p. 21; Olsen, interview, p. 20.

[21]Ritchie, interview, pp. 25-28, 39-40.

[22]McGinnis, interview, pp. 39-40; Brooks, interview, p. 18; Director Fran Mainella, memo to Skip Brooks, September 20, 2001, "Delegation of Authority, NPS Continuity of Operations." [This documentation took the form of a report called Operation Secure Parks, "Narrative Update and Discussion of Incident Management Operations," September 21, 2001, file: incident management.]

[23]Brooks, interview, pp. 47-48.

[24]Director Fran Mainella, memo (draft) to assistant secretary for policy, management, and budget, n.d.

[25]Ring, interview, pp. 13, 17-18.

[26]Sal Lauro, interview, pp. 36-37; USPP, "Lessons Learned," pp. 3, 5.

[27]Martin, interview, pp. 33-34; DOI, OIG, *Assessment of Security at the National Park Service's Icon Parks,* August 28, 2003, Report no. 2003-I-0063, p. 5, file: IG reports.

VI. Aftermath

[1]Todd Wilkinson, "On the Homefront," *National Parks Conservation Association Magazine,* April/May 2002; Delmar, interview, p. 26.

[2]*An Act to Authorize a National Memorial to Commemorate the Passengers and Crew of Flight 93,* September 24, 2002, 107th Congress, Public Law 107-226; SANR, Gateway NRA, FY2002; Pellinger, interview, p. 16; Delmar, interview, pp. 21, 26; Martin, interview, p. 13.

[3]Ronald Boice, interview by Doris D. Fanelli, April 5, 2002, pp. 21, 23; William Troppman interview by Doris D. Fanelli, April 5, 2002, pp. 11, 18, 29; Mihalic, interview, pp. 38, 43; Nelson, interview, pp. 13, 20-22; Rick Childs, interview by Mark Schoepfle, May 6, 2002, p. 19.

[4]"National Park System Visitation Report," *New York Times,* May 7, 2002; "For U.S. Tourists, Vacation's a Walk in the Park," *USA Today,* April 18, 2002, www.usatoday.com [accessed April 22, 2002]; SANR, Independence NHP, FY2002;

"A Year Later the Travel World is Still Spinning," *Washington Post*, September 8, 2002; Troppman, interview, pp. 14, 23.

[5]Wilkinson, "On the Homefront"; NPS, press release, "Media Report on Security at NPS Sites," March 10, 2003, www.inside.nps.gov [accessed March 10, 2003]; Don Reipe, interview by Chuck Smythe, December 19, 2001, p. 10; Mihalic, interview, p. 24.

[6] Tracy Thetford, interview by Mark Schoepfle, April 4, 2002, p. 10; Pfenninger, interview, pp. 24-25, 28.

[7]Hatten, interview, pp. 18, 32, 39; "American History Lessons," *Washington Times*, August 7, 2002.

[8]Frank Hays, interview by Chuck Smythe, May 21, 2002, pp. 4, 12-19, 25, 30.

[9]Troppman, interview, pp. 12, 20, 26; Delmar, interview, pp. 27-28.

[10]William Garrett, interview, pp. 22-26, 36; www.nps/gov/remembrance [accessed May 5, 2003].

[11]Mihalic, interview, pp. 26-35, 44.

[12]*Morning Report*, November 28, 2001; DOI, OIG, *Assessment of Security at the National Park Service's Icon Parks*, Report no. 2003-I-0063, pp. 8-9.

[13]Burnett, interview, pp. 23-24; Martin, interview, pp. 19-20, 28-29.

[14]Forte, interview, pp. 5-6.

[15]Van Horn, interview, pp. 24-28.

[16]*National Leadership Council Journal*, November 15, 2002, file: 9/11 documents; Schamp, interview, pp. 43-46; Martin, interview, p. 28; Burnett, interview, p. 30; DOI, OIG, *Disquieting State of Disorder: An Assessment of Department of the Interior Law Enforcement*, Report no. 2002-I-0014, p. 20; International Chiefs of Police, *Policing the National Parks: 21st Century Requirements*, 2000, chap. 5.

[17]Olsen, interview, pp. 22-23.

[18]Poole, interview, pp. 23-24, 47-48, 50; Dixon, interview, pp. 19-22.

[19]Childs, interview, pp. 6-10, 12-14.

[20]SANR, Valley Forge NHP, FY2002; SANR, Upper Delaware SRR, FY2002.

[21]Schamp, interview, pp. 27-28, 33-35; Pellinger, interview, p. 14; Sal Lauro, interview, pp. 34, 38; USPP, "Lessons Learned," p. 5.

[22]SANR, Gateway NRA, FY2002; Wilkins, interview, p.16; Neal Lauro, interview, pp. 19-21.

[23]Sal Lauro, interview, p. 38; Wilkins, interview, pp. 16-17.

[24]Schamp, interview, p. 30; Pellinger, interview, p. 12.

[25]Neal Lauro, interview, p. 5; Wilkins, interview, pp. 15-19.

[26]Buckley, interview, pp. 1-2, 7-8, 11.

[27]Wilkins, interview, pp. 19, 21-24.

[28] Management Assessment Team, "Assessment of Strategic Alternatives for National Park Service Protection Response," October 9, 2001; Gale, interview, p. 22; Martin, interview, p. 21; Burnett, interview, p. 25; NER, Bob Martin, "Thank you to NPS for Post–9/11 Support," www.inside.nps.gov [accessed October 7, 2002], file: 9/11 documents.

[29]Ring, interview, pp. 23-25.

[30]"Assessment of Strategic Alternatives for National Park Service Protection Response"; Martin, interview, p. 22; Burnett, interview, p. 24; Gale, interview, pp. 22-23.

[31]*Morning Report*, November 28, 2001; Burnett, interview, p. 29; Olsen, interview, p. 18; NPS, "Emergency Response Plan," November 7, 2001, p. 2.

[32]Director Fran Mainella, memo to all regional directors, "National Emergency Response Plan," November 16, 2001; *Morning Report*, November 28, 2001.

[33]Ring, interview, pp. 25-26.

[34]Forte, interview, p. 4; Olsen, interview, pp. 32-34.

[35]Martin, interview, p. 42.

[36]"Daily Headlines: Law Enforcement Task Force—First Meeting Report," file: 9/11 documents; "Secretary Approves Measures to Improve DOI Law Enforcement," www.inside.nps.gov/printheadlines [accessed July 25, 2002], file: 9/11 documents; Director Fran Mainella, memo to National Leadership Council, "Law Enforcement Reform Actions," December 9, 2002, file: 9/11 documents.

Conclusion

[1]Ring, interview, p. 22; Martin, interview, pp. 30-32.

[2]Forte, interview, pp. 9-10; Martin, interview, pp. 31-32.

[3]DOI, OIG, *Assessment of Security at the National Park Service's Icon Parks*, Report no. 2003-I-0063; Forte, interview, pp. 12, 14-15, 19-24.

[4]Wilkins, interview, pp. 24-26; Neal Lauro, interview, pp. 23-24; Sal Lauro, interview, pp. 59-60; Buckley, interview, pp. 17-18.

[5]Moen, interview, p. 10; Schamp, interview, p. 38; Neal Lauro, interview, p. 29; Sal Lauro, interview, p. 47; Secretary of the Interior, memo "Unit Citation USPP National Park Service," n.d., file: USPP.

[6]Martin, interview, pp. 25-26.

[7]Ring, interview, p. 20.

[8]Brooks, interview, p. 41; Gale, interview, pp. 30-32, 35.

[9]Theresa Cervera, interview by Chuck Smythe, January 24, 2002, pp. 3-7.

[10]Burnett, interview, pp. 26, 32-33; Moen, interview, p. 12; *Morning Report*, September 15, 2001, afternoon edition.

Oral History Interviews

Copies of all interview transcripts listed below can be found in the administrative history files, National Register, History and Education, National Park Service, Washington, D.C.

Amato, Tito. Interview by Chuck Smythe. New York, NY. January 23, 2002.

Arberg, Alfred. Interview by Mark Schoepfle. New York, NY. February 1, 2002.

Avery, Joseph. Interview by Chuck Smythe. New York, NY. January 23, 2002.

Bohn, Sgt. Keith. Interview by Janet A. McDonnell. Washington, D.C. December 17, 2001.

Boice, Ronald. Interview by Doris D. Fanelli. Valley Forge National Historical Park, Pennsylvania. April 5, 2002.

Brennan, Laura. Interview by Chuck Smythe. New York, NY. December 20, 2001.

Brooks, Gregory P. Interview by Janet A. McDonnell. Colonial National Historical Park, VA. June 12, 2002.

Brown, Daniel T. Interview by Mark Schoepfle. New York, NY. January 29, 2002.

Buckley, David L. Interview by Janet A. McDonnell. New York, NY. May 7, 2002.

Burchell, Sgt. Kenneth S. Interview by Janet A. McDonnell. Washington, D.C. December 17, 2001.

Burnett, Dennis. Interview by Janet A. McDonnell. Washington, D.C. January 29, 2002.

Castro, Paula. Interview by Mark Schoepfle. New York, NY. January 30, 2002.

Cervera, Theresa Marie. Interview by Chuck Smythe. New York, NY. January 24, 2002.

Childs, Rick. Interview by Mark Schoepfle. Shenandoah National Park, VA. May 6, 2002.

Dayson, Diane. Interview by Mark Schoepfle. New York, NY. January 28, 2002.

Delmar, Frances. Interview by Doris D. Fanelli. Philadelphia, PA. March 15, 2002.

Dillon, Officer John. Interview by Janet A. McDonnell. Washington, D.C. December 10, 2001.

DiPietro, Vincent. Interview by Mark Schoepfle. New York, NY. February 1, 2002.

Dixon, Dwight. Interview by Mark Schopfle. Catoctin National Park, MD. January 14, 2002.

Farrugio, Alfred. Interview by Mark Schoepfle. New York, NY. January 30, 2002.

Gale, Richard. Interview by Janet A. McDonnell. Washington, D.C. December 12, 2001.

Galey, Sgt. Ronald A. Interview by Janet A. McDonnell. Washington, D.C. December 17, 2001.

Garrett, Billy. Interview by Chuck Smythe. New York, NY. January 24, 2002.

Garrett, Cynthia. Interview by George Tselos. New York, NY. June 6, 2002.

Hanley, Joanne. Interview by Chuck Smythe. Telephone Interview. May 6, 2002.

Hatten, Lance. Interview by Mark Schoepfle. Washington, D.C. February 27, 2002.

Hays, Frank. Interview by Chuck Smythe. Telephone Interview. May 21, 2001.

Johnson, Archie. Interview by Chuck Smythe. New York, NY. January 23, 2002.

Kelly, Joan A. Interview by Mark Schoepfle. New York, NY. February 1, 2002.

Keenan, Christopher. Interview by Chuck Smythe. New York, NY. December 20, 2001.

Keneally, Sean. Interview by Mark Schoepfle. Washington, D.C. December 18, 2001.

Laise, Steven C. Interview by Chuck Smythe. New York, NY. December 19, 2001.

Lauro, Capt. Sal. Interview by Janet A. McDonnell. Washington, D.C. March 28, 2002.

Lauro, Capt. Neal. Interview by Janet A. McDonnell. New York, NY. May 7, 2002.

Luchsinger, David. Interview by Chuck Smythe. New York, NY. January 23, 2002.

Markis, Charles A. Interview by Louis Hutchins. New York, NY. February 26, 2002.

Martin, Robert R. Interview by Janet A. McDonnell. Washington, D.C. February 5, 2002.

McGinnis, Dennis. Interview by Janet A. McDonnell. Washington, D.C. December 5, 2001.

McKinney, Shirley. Interview by Chuck Smythe. New York, NY. January 25, 2002.

Merced, Daniel. Interview by Chuck Smythe. New York, NY. December 19, 2001.

Mihalic, David A. Interview by Louis Hutchins. Yosemite National Park, CA. February 4, 2002.

Mills, Frank W. Interview by Mark Schoepfle. New York, NY. January 31, 2002.

Moen, Dave. Interview by Janet A. McDonnell. New York, NY. May 7, 2002.

Murphy, Christopher. Interview by Janet A. McDonnell. New York, NY. May 8, 2002.

Nelson, Doyle. Interview by Chuck Smythe. Delaware Water Gap National Recreation Area. May 13, 2002.

O'Dougherty, Peter. Interview by Mark Schoepfle. New York, NY. February 1, 2002.

Olsen, Einar S. Interview by Janet A. McDonnell and Gary Scott. Washington, D.C. December 13, 2001.

Pellinger, Maj. Thomas. Interview by Mark Schoepfle. Washington, D.C. March 29, 2002.

Pfenninger, Paul M. Interview by Janet A. McDonnell. Shenandoah National Park, VA. January 23, 2002.

Poole, Melville. Interview by Mark Schoepfle. Catoctin National Park, MD. December 17, 2001.

Powell, Richard C. Interview by Janet A. McDonnell. Washington, D.C. April 30, 2002.

Reipe, Don. Interview by Chuck Smythe. New York, NY. December 19, 2001.

Ring, Richard G. Interview by Janet A. McDonnell. Washington, D.C. May 29, 2002.

Ritchie, Brenda. Interview by Janet A. McDonnell. Shenandoah National Park, VA. January 23, 2002.

Schamp, John D. Interview by Janet A. McDonnell. Washington, D.C. April 17, 2002.

Solomon, Sgt. Clyde E. Interview by Janet A. McDonnell. New York, NY. May 8, 2002.

Stasulli, Bernard. Interview by Janet A. McDonnell. Washington, D.C. December 10, 2001.

Stasulli, Bernard. Interview by Mark Schoepfle. Washington, D.C. January 16, 2002.

Thetford, Tracy. Interview by Mark Schoepfle. Shenandoah National Park, VA. April 4, 2002.

Troppman, William. Interview by Doris D. Fanelli. Valley Forge National Historical Park, PA. April 5, 2002.

Van Dorn, Maj. Gary. Interview by Janet A. McDonnell. Washington, D.C. February 26, 2002.

Waite, Lt. Bryan. Interview by Janet A. McDonnell. New York, NY. May 7, 2002.

Wallace, Lt. George. Interview by Mark Schoepfle. Washington, D.C. January 16, 2002.

Wilkins, Maj. Thomas. Interview by Janet A. McDonnell. New York, NY. May 8, 2002.

Zweig, Capt. Martin L. Interview by Chuck Smythe. New York, NY. December 11, 2001.

Photo Credits

Unless noted below, all photographs are credited to the National Park Service.

p. 1 – DOD

p. 14 – Photodisc

p. 15 – U.S. Government

p. 18 – DOD by Tech Sgt. Cedric H. Rudisill

p. 19 – U.S. Army

p. 21 – U.S. Government

p. 32 – Photodisc

p. 33 – NPS by Eugene Kuziw

p. 46 – Photodisc

p. 60 – Photodisc

p. 88 – Marcia Axtmann Smith

p. 94 – NPS by Don Reipe

Index

the graveyard, regidor of public works, etc.). From the town of Tlacotepec, municipal authorities carry out tasks which, according to national laws, should apply to the entire municipality, although in the Mixteca as well as other regions of Oaxaca, each town in the municipality has traditionally been self-governed (Hernandez-Diaz and Martinez 2007).

The independence of each settlement is accentuated by the fact that every town is entitled to agricultural land. In the case of Tlacotepec, this entitlement has made the Communal Property Commission, which regulates access to communal agricultural land and is independent of the ayuntamiento, an important local institution. Land is formally held communally, but each *comunero,* or entitled beneficiary citizen, has a title of possession that is issued by the commission. The main functions of the commission have changed as agricultural production in Tlacotepec has decreased. Migration in particular has left few people to work the fields at the same that the costs of agricultural investments such as fertilizers, seeds, and labor have become too expensive for those who remain. Of those Tlacotepenses who continue to farm, most employ traditional techniques to grow corns and beans, often for subsistence. Although most agriculture is for subsistence, farmers with a surplus and those needing money urgently will often sell their crop in the market of the nearby city of Santiago Juxtlahuaca.

The communication services of the municipality are concentrated in the town of San Miguel Tlacotepec, where there is a public phone, a privately owned telephone booth, and a little over 100 private landlines in homes. Cellular phones have become increasingly common and are the only form of telecommunication available to the inhabitants of the towns outside of the municipal capital. Internet access is available only in the capital, in two specific privately owned locales. Computers given by a U.S.-based donor were no longer in use in 2011. Television and radio are widely available (INEGI 2010). The telegraph and mail services, in disuse in other places, are still alive in the town of San Miguel Tlacotepec. Inhabitants of surrounding communities within the municipality go to Tlacotepec to receive packages and letters sent by family members living in other parts of Mexico and the United States. The fact that an important part of remittances is received through this mechanism keeps the telegraph office alive at the seat of municipal government. At the cabecera there is a telegraph office which receives the remittances sent by migrants to their families in Tlacotepec. Table 1.1 shows the level of monthly remittances received at the office.

Table 1.1 Monthly number and total of remittances sent in 2008

Month	Total remittances (in Mexican pesos)	Number of remittances sent
January	249,842	80
February	309,217	73
March	470,576	106
April	371,326	105
May	465,793	134
June	448,137	114
July	522,792	116
August	315,864	91
September	579,587	156
October	249,842	80
November	249,842	80
December	249,842	80
TOTAL	*4,482,660*	*1225*

Source: Telecom telegraphs, San Miguel Tlacotepec.

Of special interest in Table 1.1 are the high quantities received in July and September, the months in which the patron saint festivals are held. Our research finds that migrants sent more money to their families during these in order to participate in the festivals.

While the intensity of migration from San Miguel Tlacotepec has grown in recent decades, elders recall that the first Tlacotepense migrants left to work in the fields of the neighboring state of Veracruz in the 1950s. Around the same time, the wealthiest families of Tlacotepec began to migrate to Mexico City. Shortly after, other families with fewer resources left Oaxaca for other parts of Mexico, settling mostly in Mexico City and agricultural areas in the states of Sinaloa and Baja California. From these northern Mexican states, Tlacotepenses began to cross the border to the United States, settling in northern San Diego County, especially the cities of Vista, Oceanside, San Marcos and Escondido, beginning in the 1970s. At first, the international migration of Tlacotepenses followed a circular pattern, with male migrants shuttling back and forth between work in the United States and their families in Mexico. This circular migration was the most common pattern until the late 1980s. As one migrant from Tlacotepec put it: "… I would temporarily leave and come back, from 1983 to 1989 that was the routine, leave, come back, leave, come back. In 1989 I left permanently, I took my family and have not gone back to this day."

There are several reasons for the shift from circular migration to the more permanent settlement that has become the norm for Tlacotepenses in the

United States today. The 1986 Immigration Reform and Control Act (IRCA) gave legal status to many undocumented immigrants in the United States, including Tlacotepenses who began to lay down permanent roots. Another factor was the movement of Tlacotepenses out of the agricultural sector. For the first wave of Tlacotepense migrants, agriculture was the main, if not only, labor option. Recent arrivals, however, have opted for other job opportunities. As a migrant from Tlacotepec recounts: "The first time [I worked in the United States] it was in the fields. I was there about two days, but I didn't like it and I decided to leave, and I found work in a factory, where I was better off." The availability of these stable, fulltime jobs has facilitated the settlement process for many Tlacotepenses and at the same time has limited the opportunities for circular migrations, which were much more common for those employed in seasonal farming (Appleby, Moreno, and Smith 2009). A third factor leading to a decline in circular migration has been the increase in border enforcement measures (see Chapter 2). As the border crossing experience has become more difficult and expensive, Tlacotepense are increasingly staying for longer periods of time to avoid the physical dangers and financial costs of multiple crossings.

Today, Tlacotepense social networks within the United States ease the settlement of migrants, providing a support structure that makes longer stays less difficult. This process is exemplified by Arturo, a Tlacotepense migrant who lived over 20 years in the United States: "I had a brother in the city of Vista, California. When I arrived there I realized it was a sanctuary of many Tlacotepenses. There were already many people [from Tlacotepec] living [in Vista] … I liked it so from the day I arrived there I didn't leave."

Growing settlement in the United States drives the abandonment of houses. Figure 1.3 shows abandoned houses on virtually every block.

Figure 1.3 Abandoned Houses in San Miguel Tlacotepec

■ = abandoned house

With the U.S. economic crisis of recent years, there has been a growing concern, in Mexico in general and in Oaxaca in particular, about the fates of migrant families in the United States. This concern led to speculation about a possible massive return of Mexicans from the United States to their places of origin. At the end of 2008 the Mexican Secretary of Labor declared that the government expected the return of around 200,000 migrants within a 12-month period due to the U.S. economic crisis. The main concern was that this return would add to the 1.9 million unemployed in Mexico in the same period. A month after the Labor Secretary issued his statement, members of Congress and the Interior Secretary agreed on the need to design a preventive program in the case of a substantial return of Mexican migrants caused by the U.S. economic crisis. The predicted massive return of Mexican migrants never materialized. Given that the recession was affecting both the United States and Mexico, the general perception remained among migrants that the United States offered more economic certainty than Mexico (Aguilar et al. 2010). Even with a decrease in the employment available, most migrants chose to remain in the United States.

While most migrants have chosen to remain in the United States, their quality of life has suffered, and not only for economic reasons. The condition of vulnerability, especially for undocumented Mexican migrants, has intensified as a result of interior immigration enforcement measures by federal, state and local governments. Migrants have faced growing difficulties in finding employment and have lived under a constant fear of deportation (see Chapter 3).

However, these challenges have not stopped all Tlacotepense migrants from creating a vibrant sense of community on both sides of the border. Soccer games, birthday parties, *quinceañeras*, fundraisers, and the patron saint festival continue to bring together Tlacotepenses. Some still return home for visits, particularly for the patron saint festival and the holiday season, a phenomenon we were able to observe during our fieldwork. Although the lives of Tlacotepenses in the United States and those who depend on their remittances in Tlacotepec have become more and more challenging in recent years, many continue to thrive, leading lives increasingly shaped by the realities of migration today.

KEY FINDINGS

The chapters that follow can be read independently as studies of specific topics related to the migrant-sending town of San Miguel Tlacotepec and its satellite receiving town of Vista in California. Together, the chapters form a comprehensive, multidisciplinary case study with findings that engage key topics in the study of international migration.

Chapter 2, *U.S. Border Enforcement in an Era of Economic Uncertainty: the Limits of Deterrence and Legal Alternatives*, examines the impact of literal walls – border walls and other methods of deterrence – on the flow of migrants from Mexico to the United States. The authors find that these walls, which they label immediate deterrence, largely fail to keep out Tlacotepense migrants who attempt to cross without papers, a finding consistent with previous MMFRP studies (FitzGerald, Alarcon, and Muse-Orlinoff 2010; Cornelius, D. S. Fitzgerald, and Borger 2009; Cornelius and Lewis 2007; Cornelius, FitzGerald, and Fischer 2007; Cornelius et al. 2010; Cornelius, D. S. Fitzgerald, Hernandez-Diaz, et al. 2009). But the literal walls that make up immediate deterrence are only part of the story, as remote deterrence leads many potential Tlacotepense migrants to decide against leaving home in the first place. Fear of the dangers of crossing the border often form a mental wall, leading fewer Tlacotepenses to head north.

Chapter 3, *"They Want Us to Go Back to Mexico": Tlacotepenses Living Under the Radar in North San Diego County*, contributes to understanding the ways undocumented migrants adapt to hostile local policies that deal with immigrants. The chapter reveals the strategies employed by migrants to remain undetected and to deal with the everyday fear of interaction with authorities, which could lead to deportation. The authors suggest that the restrictive interior enforcement measures adopted by the local, state and federal governments may impede their social incorporation and cohesion and ultimately send a double message of both rejection and a pressure to assimilate. In the end, the policies create a wall, isolating Tlacotepenses from the broader U.S. communities in which they live. Tlacotepenses come to rely ever more on each other to navigate a society which excludes them in important ways.

Chapter 4, *The "parties" between us: Migrant participation in the local politics of San Miguel Tlacotepec*, analyzes the specific form of local indigenous government in place in San Miguel Tlacotepec, focusing particular attention on a binational migrant organization – the FIOB –that is a significant political actor across Oaxaca and California. This chapter argues that the form of local indigenous government in Tlacotepec has become so flexible that it has recently become nearly identical to what it traditionally tried to distance itself from: the party system rooted in the political institutions of the non-indigenous Mexican population.

In chapter 5, *Discount transnationalism: Recession and the transformation of cross-border ties*, the authors argue that the U.S. economic crisis has modified how migrants form and maintain their relations across the U.S.-Mexican border. Tlacotepenses have adjusted the way they participate in transnational activities, often choosing less expensive ways to participate than they may have during better economic times, a phenomenon the authors call "discount transnationalism." The chapter argues that although the recession has generated certain restrictions when it comes to financing and participating in such activities, it has not led Tlacotepenses to cut ties transnational ties completely, but instead has forced them to find ways to adapt to the new financial realities that they face.

In chapter 6, *A House Divided: Family Separation and Education*, the authors study the impact of family separation on the educational success of Tlacotepenses. To evaluate this educational success, the authors analyze the results of our survey on student's aspirations, attainment, and grades. The chapter relates various forms of family separation (whether neither, one or both parents are absent from the household) to outcomes of educational success. Surprisingly, the form of separation that is most associated with student's success – one parent in the United States (usually the father) and the other at home with the children – is one that has become increasingly common as increased border enforcement measures have made cyclical returns nearly impossible for Tlacotepense migrants (Cornelius, D. S. Fitzgerald,

Hernandez-Diaz, et al. 2009). Certain kinds of separation in this case actually drive Tlacotepense students' education success.

Chapter 7, *Migration and Mental Health in a Binational Mixteco Community*, also finds that crossing the wall that separates the United States and Mexico is associated with positive outcomes. Examining the mental health of migrants, returned migrants and non-migrants, the authors find that the first group –migrants currently living in the United States – has lower rates of depressive symptomology. The authors argue that while the border wall separates migrants from their hometown, the social networks of fellow Tlacotepenses in the United States provide a buffer against mental health problems. These buffering effects of social networks, combined with the so-called "healthy migrant" effect (by which the healthier are more likely to migrate in the first place) and the "salmon bias" effect (by which those who are sick return home) explain the fact that current migrants show better mental health outcomes than do returned migrants and those who have never left Tlacotepec.

Chapter 8, *A Town Without Water is Dead: Migration and Responses to Ecological Change*, focuses on the problems resulting from the lack of potable and irrigation water in San Miguel Tlacotepec. The long-standing water problems have not been solved because of the often opposing agendas of actors who might take them on. Much like in chapter 4, the divisions that separate Tlacotepenses into factions have led to a situation in which there are many proposed solutions, but not enough combined resources or political will to make changes. These divisions are often between migrants and non-migrants – walls between people exacerbated by walls between countries.

CONCLUSION

San Miguel Tlacotepec, with its long history of migration to the United States, is a community that becomes more divided with each passing year. Tlacotepenses without documents continue to remain in the United States longer before returning home. The realities of daily life for Tlacotepenses who have lived 10, 20, 30 or more years in the United States – not to mention their U.S.-born children – find themselves more attached to Tlacotepense-origin neighbors and more removed from those who remain in Tlacotepec itself. Relationships between Tlacotepenses are often strained by the distance that separates them. As both chapter 4 and chapter 8 show, there is often tension between migrants and non-migrants. Whether over local politics or the availability of water, there are stark contrasts in the views of Tlacotepenses living in Mexico and those outside of the hometown.

But it would be inaccurate to say that Tlacotepenses in the United States and those in Mexico remain completely divided. Indeed, this study in many ways shows a picture of creativity to get around walls put in the way of Tlacotepenses. Among those in the United States, restrictive policies threaten to create walls that keep Tlacotepenses separate from the U.S. communities in which they live. While Chapter 3 shows the creative strategies Tlacotepenses use to navigate around these policies, it also makes clear that the ultimate effect of such policies is to impede these migrants' incorporation into the host society. Tlacotepenses come to rely more than ever on fellow migrants, afraid to go beyond the walls that such policies put in place. Yet Tlacotepenses refuse to remain trapped. In spite of restrictive local policies, in spite of the border wall, and in spite of the years that many have been gone from their hometowns, vibrant connections remain between Tlacotepenses on both sides of the border. As chapter 5 shows, many have to settle for discount transnational activities, but they continue to find ways to remain connected to those in their hometown.

The conflicts between various Tlacotepense factions are a barrier to town projects, but without migration, the town would be worse off in many ways. One example is education. As the authors argue in chapter 6, Tlacotepense students with one migrant parent often do better than those with no migrant parents and those with both parents absent. While the walls that separate parents from their children present emotional and psychological challenges for all involved, the resources that migrants can send to their families can provide the boost that sees Tlacotepense students succeed in school.

Throughout this book, a clear picture emerges of an ever-increasing number of walls being put up around Tlacotepenses. Border enforcement measures, restrictive local policies, and the economic recession all put up potential walls that threaten the vibrant Tlacotepense community. Yet with creative adaptations, the community on both sides of the border remains strong, with Tlacotepenses connected to those who live close by as well as those who live thousands of miles away.

Acknowledgments

We are grateful for the generous support for this project provided by the Ford Foundation's Mexico City office, University of California Office of the President, the Office of Research Affairs and Eleanor Roosevelt College at the University of California, San Diego, and the *Instituto* de *Investigaciones Sociológicas* at the Universidad Autónoma Benito Juárez de Oaxaca. We are most thankful to the people of San Miguel Tlacotepec whose hospitality and kindness made this book possible.

WORKS CITED

Aguilar, Arturo, Georgia Hartmann, David Keyes, Lisa Markman, and Max Matus. 2010. "Coping with La Crisis." in *Mexican Migration and the U.S. Economic Crisis: A Transnational Perspective*, edited by Wayne A. Cornelius, David Fitzgerald, Pedro Lewin Fischer, and Leah Muse-Orlinoff. Boulder, CO: Lynne Rienner Publishers.

Alvarado Juárez, Ana Margarita. 2008. "Migración y pobreza en Oaxaca." *El cotidiano* 148(23):85–94. Retrieved September 19, 2012.

Appleby, Clare, Nancy Moreno, and Arielle Smith. 2009. "Setting Down Roots: Tlacotepense Settlement in the United States." Pp. 63–85 in *Migration from the Mexican Mixteca: A Transnational Community in Oaxaca and California*, edited by Wayne A. Cornelius, David S. Fitzgerald, Jorge Hernandez-Diaz, and Scott Borger. Boulder, CO: Lynne.

Besserer, Federico. 1999. *Moisés Cruz. Historia de un transmigrante*. Mexico City: Universidad Autónoma de Sinaloa/Universidad Autónoma Metropolitana.

Besserer, Federico. 1996. *Un viaje por las aproximaciones teóricas a las comunidades transnacionales y cuatro tarjetas postales de la Comunidad de San Juan Mixtepec*. Zamora, Michoacán.

CONAPO. 2005. *Índices de marginación*. Mexico City: Consejo Nacional de Población Retrieved (http://www.conapo.gob.mx/work/models/CONAPO/indices_margina/margina2005/IM2005_principal.pdf).

CONEVAL. 2011. *Pobreza en México y las Entidades Federativas*. Mexico City: Consejo Nacional de Evaluación de la Política de Desarrollo Social Retrieved (http://web.coneval.gob.mx/Informes/Interactivo/Medicion_pobreza_2010.pdf).

Cornelius, Wayne A., David Fitzgerald, Pedro Lewin Fischer, and Leah Muse-Orlinoff, eds. 2010. *Mexican Migration and the U.S. Economic Crisis: A Transnational Perspective*. Boulder, CO: Lynne Rienner Publishers.

Cornelius, Wayne A., David FitzGerald, and Pedro Lewin Fischer, eds. 2007. *Mayan Journeys: The New Migration from Yucatan to the United States*. Boulder, CO: Lynne Rienner Publishers.

Cornelius, Wayne A., David S. Fitzgerald, and Scott Borger, eds. 2009. *Four Generations of Norteños: New Research from the Cradle of Mexican Migration*. Boulder, CO: Lynne Rienner Publishers.

Cornelius, Wayne A., David S. Fitzgerald, Jorge Hernandez-Diaz, and Scott Borger, eds. 2009. *Migration from the Mexican Mixteca: A Transnational Community in Oaxaca and California*. Boulder, CO: Lynne.

Cornelius, Wayne A., and Jessa M. Lewis, eds. 2007. *Impacts of Border Enforcement on Mexican Migration: The View from Sending Communities.* Boulder, CO: Lynne Rienner Publishers.

FitzGerald, David, Rafael Alarcon, and Leah Muse-Orlinoff, eds. 2010. *Recession Without Borders: Mexican Migrants Confront the Economic Downturn.* Boulder, CO: Lynne Rienner Publishers.

Fox, Jonathan, and Gaspar Rivera-Salgado. 2004. "Indigenous Mexican migrants in the United States." San Diego: Center for U.S.-Mexican Studies, UCSD/Center for Comparative Immigration Studies, UCSD.

Hernandez-Diaz, Jorge, and Juan Martinez. 2007. *Dilemas de la institución municipal: Una incursión en la experiencia oaxaqueña.* Oaxaca: Universidad Autónoma Benito Juarez de Oaxaca.

Hirabayashi, Lane Ryo. 1986. "The Migrant Village Association in Latin America: A Comparative Analysis." *Latin American Research Review* 21(3):7–29. Retrieved February 19, 2011.

INEGI. 2010. *II Conteo de Población y Vivienda.* Mexico City: Instituto Nacional de Estadística, Geografía e Informática.

Kearney, Michael. 1994. "Desde el indigenismo a los derechos humanos: Etnicidad y política más allá de la mixteca." *Nueva Antropología* (46):49–67.

Méndez Morales, Sara. 2000. "Características de la migración femenina temporal en la mixteca oaxaqueña." Pp. 251–280 in *Migración y relaciones de género en México*, edited by Dalia Barrera Bassols and Cristina Oehmichen Bazán. Mexico City: GIMTRAP and UNAM.

Méndez y Mercado, Leticia Irene. 1985. *Migración, decisión involuntaria.* Mexico City: Instituto Nacional Indigenista.

Rivera-Salgado, Gaspar. 1999. "Mixtec Activism in Oaxacalifornia Transborder Grassroots Political Strategies." *American Behavioral Scientist* 42(9):1439–1458. Retrieved September 20, 2012.

Romero Frizzi, Ma. de los Angeles. 1996. *El sol y la cruz : los pueblos indios de Oaxaca colonial.* Tlalpan, D.F. [Mexico]; Col. Alpes, D.F. [Mexico]: CIESAS ; INI.

Ruiz Quiroz, René, and Lucía Cruz Vásquez. 2009. *Estadísticas de la Población Migrante Oaxaqueña.* Oaxaca: Instituto Oaxaqueño de Atención al Migrante.

Schiller, Nina Glick. 1997. "The Situation of Transnational Studies." *Identities* 4(2):155–166. Retrieved September 20, 2012.

Spores, Ronald. 1984. *The Mixtecs in ancient and colonial times.* Norman: University of Oklahoma Press.

Velasco Ortiz, Laura. 2002. *El regreso de la comunidad: migración indígena y agentes étnicos*. Mexico City: El Colegio de México y el Colegio de la Frontera Norte.

Velasco Ortiz, Laura. 2000. "Migración, género y etnicidad: mujeres indígenas en la frontera de Baja California y California." *Revista Mexicana de Sociología* 62(1):145–171. Retrieved September 19, 2012.

2 U.S. Border Enforcement in an Era of Economic Uncertainty: The Limits of Deterrence and Legal Alternatives

JASON FISCHBEIN, KRISTOPHER MALABAD, SANDRA ACOSTA,
CHRISTOPHER DUEÑAS, INDIRA VELASCO VILORIA

> *I don't think it will stop. It might deter people like me, who are very cautious. But a lot of people that have made up their mind, they are tired of not having money, of not finding a job; they say 'Let's go. If they kill us, then they kill us.' And that wall, we might not be able to jump it, but there will be coyotes that will dig a kilometer-long hole. And they will do it. They will do it because they know there is money to be made.*
> — Javier, a middle-aged undocumented migrant

Beginning in the 1990s, the U.S. government sharply intensified its immigration enforcement policies along the Southwestern border. Operation Hold the Line in El Paso, Texas (1993), Operation Gatekeeper in San Diego, California (1994), and Operation Safeguard in Tucson, Arizona (1994) inaugurated a period of concentrating Border Patrol resources along the border line in an attempt to deter undocumented entry (Cornelius, 2006). The number of Border Patrol agents grew from 5,900 in 1996 to 20,500 in 2010. The proposed 2012 DHS budget for Customs and Border Protection (CBP) soared to $11.8 billion from $5.9 billion in 2003, and to $5.8 billion from $3.3 billion for Immigration and Customs Enforcement (ICE) (DHS, 2012). New fencing and sophisticated surveillance systems were also added amid enthusiasm for increased enforcement from both Republicans and Democrats in Congress.

How successful have U.S. policies been at deterring unauthorized migration? Two ways of assessing the extent to which border control policies deter unauthorized migration include *immediate deterrence* (turning back illegal crossers at the border line through Border Patrol apprehensions) and *remote deterrence* (measures that deter potential migrants from deciding to leave their homes in the first place). Based on the survey evidence from Tlacotepec, we argue that border enforcement policy has been ineffective at immediate

19

deterrence. Ninety-six percent of Tlacotepenses who had ever attempted to enter clandestinely were eventually able to do so, a success rate that has changed little since 1965. However, there is some evidence that many members of the community are deterred from ever trying to migrate without papers in the first place because of the high costs of paying for a coyote, fears of the physical dangers of crossing the border region without papers, and the lack of available jobs in the United States. The legal immigration system in practice is closed to those who do not have close family members in the United States.

IMMEDIATE DETERRENCE

Estimates of unauthorized immigration are notoriously plagued with methodological challenges. Census data and the American Community Survey can be used to approximate the total *stock* of unauthorized migrants in the United States using the "residual method" accounting for legal immigration flows, the numbers of citizens, and births and deaths (Bean et al., 2001). It is inherently difficult to measure the deterrent effect of government policy on unauthorized migration *flows* using Border Patrol statistics, however. The agency only reports apprehension events, not the total number of individuals detained, which is an important distinction because many migrants are detained on multiple attempts to enter. The number of successful entries and the number of individuals who successfully enter is unknown. Changes in the number of apprehensions by the Border Patrol since the 1990s have coincided with considerable economic volatility, making it difficult to assess the independent effect of border enforcement on the number of apprehensions.

In 1993, at the beginning of the recent period of concentrated border enforcement, annual apprehensions totaled about 820,000. Increased enforcement measures pushed apprehension up to 1.6 million in 2000, but the economic downturn beginning in 2007 played a role in the decline of apprehensions to 541,000 in 2009 and 463,000 in 2010 (DHS, 2011).[1] The Pew Hispanic Center estimates that only 150,000 unauthorized immigrants from Mexico arrived annually during the period from March 2007 to March 2009, down from an annual average of 500,000 in the early 2000s (Passel and Cohn 2010). At the same time, the increase in physical barriers around metropolitan areas such as San Diego and El Paso has led undocumented migrants to shift their clandestine entry attempts to more desolate and dangerous locations. One perverse consequence of these policies has been the death of more than 5,000 migrants along the border since 1994, an average of one migrant a day (Jimenez, 2009).

Although the increase in resources devoted to border enforcement has been dramatic, many undocumented migrants continue to cross. A previous benchmark known as "operational control," defined as the ability to prevent

---

1 Although these numbers include apprehensions on all U.S. borders, nearly all took place along the Southwest border.

all unlawful entry into the United States, was scrapped by the Obama administration in 2011. The Government Accountability Office claims that less than half of the southern border is under operational control, and Homeland Security Secretary Janet Napolitano announced that using the term operational control is "obsolete" because the expectations inherent in operational control are predicated on an impossibly high standard (*Washington Times*, 2011).

Survey data from Tlacotepec and its satellite communities in the United States in 2007 and 2011 capture retrospective data on successful and unsuccessful entries since 1965, providing the basis for a detailed case study of how immigration enforcement measures have affected migration patterns.

Table 2.1 Percentage of Tlacotepense Clandestine Migrations by Mode of Entry, 1965 to 2010

Mode of Entry	1965-1986	1986-1993	1994-2001	2002-2010
Walking	90.5	86.5	54.4	74
Swimming	0	0	1.5	1.4
Hidden in Vehicle	0	5.8	13.2	9.6
Using Fake/ Borrowed Documents	0	0	8.8	6.9
Other	9.5	7.7	22.1	8.2
N	21	52	68	73

Table 2.1 shows that 16.5 percent of respondents who entered between 2002 and 2010 reported entering the United States clandestinely through a legal port of entry, either by hiding in a vehicle or using fake or borrowed legal documents. Despite an increase in crossings through legal ports of entry following the 1986 Immigration Reform and Control Act, and with greater intensity after 1994, the vast majority of Tlacotepenses continue to enter the United States by walking through the desert and mountains. While walking across the border through deserts and mountains poses the greatest physical risks to migrants, it is the cheapest alternative, and thus remains the most viable option for many undocumented migrants. Clandestine migration through legal ports of entry has a variety of advantages over the alternatives. Not only is it the quickest and least physically-demanding mode of entry, but it is also generally considered to be a safer investment than other entry

methods (Spener 2009, 124). In Tlacotepec, 38.3 percent of the population was apprehended at least once on their most recent undocumented migration when crossing through the desert or mountains, while only 22 percent of Tlacotepenses were apprehended at least once on their most recent clandestine journey when crossing unauthorized through legal ports. Nevertheless, entry through a legal port of entry has its drawbacks. A migrant apprehended when crossing through a legal port of entry is more likely to incur incarceration and formal deportation, and migrants caught feigning U.S. citizenship are permanently barred from naturalizing (U.S. Sentencing Commission, 2009).

The average price paid by a migrant crossing through a legal port of entry was $2,850, while the average price paid by a clandestine migrant walking through the desert or mountains was $1,587. Although crossing through a legal port of entry can be much more expensive than crossing through the desert, doing so can give the migrant a substantially higher chance of crossing the border without being apprehended. Opting to take this more effective mode of entry can often save the migrant money that would be wasted in failed attempts. Migrants who make unsuccessful clandestine attempts are often returned to Mexican border cities such as Tijuana and Ciudad Juárez, where migrants must pay for food, living accommodations, and transportation—expenses that can be avoided if initial clandestine attempts are successful (Hicken, Fischbein, Lisle 2011).

Table 2.2 Propensity of Tlacotepense Unauthorized Migrants to Cross at a Port of Entry, 1985-2010

(Intercept)	1.160
	(0.800)
Number of Family Members in the U.S.	0.124
	(0.090)
Age	-0.072*
	(0.025)
Male	-1.292*
	(0.025)
Year Crossed	
1985 –1994	0.560
1994 - 2001	(0.512)
	-0.029
2002 - 2010	(0.588)
	0.711
Married	(0.603)
	0.053
Has Children	(0.690)
McFadden's R-squared	0.150
N	138

Who chooses to cross illegally through ports of entry along the border? Table 2.2 shows that migrants crossing in the first wave of concentrated border enforcement between 1994 and 2001, and those crossing in the second wave between 2002 and 2010, were no more likely than earlier migrants to cross at a legal port of entry. Women and young people were significantly more likely to cross clandestinely through a legal port of entry during the entire period.

Table 2.3 Likelihood of Tlacotepenses Being Apprehended at Least Once During a Clandestine Attempt to Enter the United States, 1965-2010

(Intercept)	-0.936
	(0.493)
Trip Number	0.017
	(0.048)
Age	-0.005
	(0.013)
Male	0.694*
	(0.333)
Year Crossed	
Pre-1986	
1986-1993	-0.213
	(0.305)
1994-2001	0.052
	(0.272)
2002-2010	-0.600
	(0.320)
Used a coyote	-0.063
	(0.237)
Month Crossed	
January - March	
April – June	0.265
	(0.262)
July – September	-0.260
	(0.292)
October – December	0.259
	0.319
McFadden's R-squared	0.029
N	423

Table 2.3 shows that men are more likely than women to be apprehended, largely due to the fact that Tlacotepense women migrate illegally through legal ports of entry (hidden in vehicles or using fraudulent documents) more frequently than men. There has been no statistically significant change in the likelihood that unauthorized migrants will be apprehended in the 2002-2010

cohort, despite the border buildup. One likely explanation for this is that coyote usage in Tlacotepec has increased along with increased border enforcement. Fifty-three percent of Tlacotepenses used a coyote in the period from 1986 to 1993, 72 percent from 1994 to 2001, and 87 percent from 2002 to 2010.

A 2010 study (Hicken, Fischbein, Lisle 2011) of a migrant-sending community in Tlacuitapa, Jalisco, found that apprehensions of clandestine migrants from that community were significantly correlated with the month in which they attempted to cross the border. Migrants from Tlacuitapa were apprehended far more infrequently when crossing clandestinely in the winter months, likely due to the Border Patrol's policy of decreasing line-watch hours from the months of October to December when migrants have historically returned to Mexico for vacation. Apprehension rates in Tlacotepec, however, do not demonstrate this trend. One possible explanation why Tlacuitapenses were apprehended less frequently than their Tlacotepense counterparts during the winter months is that while Tlacotepenses enter clandestinely through California more often than in any other region, Tlacuitapenses enter most frequently through the state of Texas, where border enforcement intensity may vary seasonally.

Figure 2.1 Apprehension Rates and Rates of Eventual Crossing Success of Tlacotepenses, 1965-2010

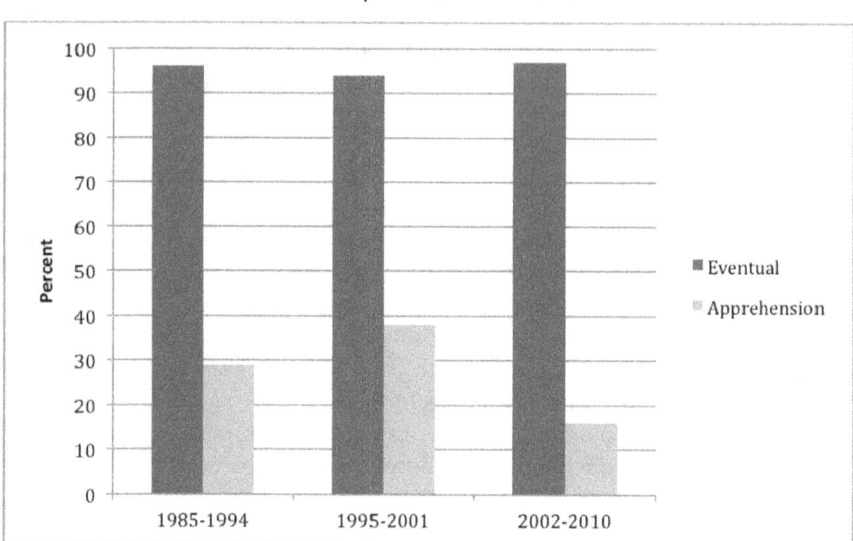

N=182

The lack of operational control by U.S. authorities along the border is evident in the high rate of success reported by clandestine migrants from Tlacotepec. The survey evidence from Tlacotepec suggests border enforcement has not been very successful at keeping undocumented migrants from crossing the border. Ninety-six percent of all Tlacotepenses who have ever attempted to cross the border illegally were able to do so successfully, and since 1965, there has been little variation in eventual rates of successful crossing. Although nearly all Tlacotepenses who attempt to cross clandestinely are ultimately successful, many are apprehended along the way. As Figure 2.1 indicates, from 1986 to 1994, about 27 percent of Tlacotepenses were apprehended at least once when crossing the border illegally. As border enforcement intensified in the 1990s, the apprehension rate in Tlacotepec rose to over 37 percent. By 2002, however, the rate of apprehension in Tlacotepec decreased to pre 1990s levels, stabilizing at 25 percent, presumably because undocumented migrants and their smugglers have adapted successfully to the new strategies of the U.S. Border Patrol.

In sum, there is little evidence that border enforcement policies are creating immediate deterrence in Tlacotepec. Migrants are using coyotes and increasingly entering clandestinely through legal ports of entry to circumvent the obstacles put in their way by the

REMOTE DETERRENCE

Remote deterrence entails efforts intended to dissuade potential migrants from ever deciding to leave their homes in the first place (FitzGerald and Alarcón, forthcoming). U.S. border enforcement, along with the recession and border banditry, appear to have created a deterrent effect on the migration plans of some prospective migrants such that they never leave their hometowns in the interior to try crossing the border. Asked whether they planned to migrate to the United States in the coming year, about 13 percent of Tlacotepenses without legal authorization to do so indicated they had plans in 2011, down from 18 percent who indicated such plans in the 2007 Oaxaca survey.[2] This decrease is evidence of a remote deterrent effect interacting with the economic downturn that has dried up jobs for migrants in the United States.

KNOWLEDGE OF BORDER ENFORCEMENT

What do migrants know about the border enforcement measures put in place in recent years? Their level of knowledge of increased border enforcement was assessed by asking them to name up to three actions the U.S. government has taken since 2007 to keep undocumented migrants from entering the United States. More than 61 percent of respondents indicated knowledge of at least one enforcement measure.[3] As shown in Figure 2.2, respondents indicated the most familiarity with newly-constructed fencing along the border, and with a recent increase of Border Patrol agents patrolling the border. Sixty-two percent of respondents indicated knowledge of either more miles of fencing or more Border Patrol agents, while about 38 percent of respondents said they had no knowledge of recent policy initiatives

---

2 The intent to migrate within Mexico was more common than the intent to migrate to the United States in our 2011 survey. Nineteen percent of Tlacotepec residents aged 15-45 who do not have U.S. immigration papers said they intended to migrate within Mexico, compared to 10 percent who said they intended to migrate to the United States.

3 Coded responses included more miles of border fencing, cameras and infrared detectors, more Border Patrol agents, incarceration upon capture, UAV (unmanned aerial vehicle) patrol drones, and "other."

Figure 2.2 Respondent Knowledge of Increased Border Enforcement, 2011

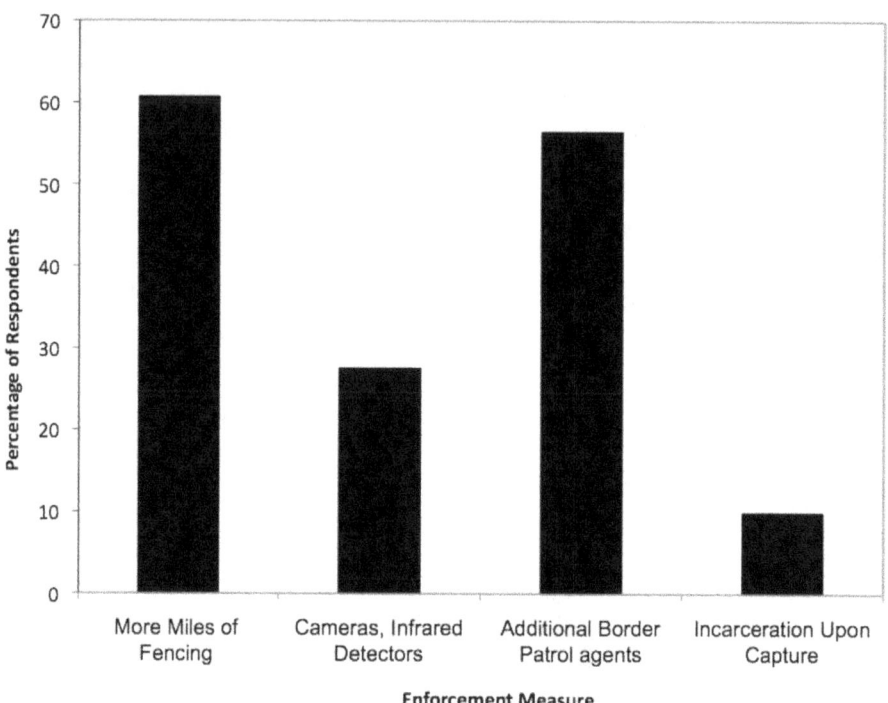

N= 557

SOURCES OF CONCERN FOR UNAUTHORIZED MIGRATION

Respondents were asked to rank from a list up to three factors that would most worry an unauthorized migrant attempting to cross the border.[4] Border crime topped the list of concerns regarding unauthorized migration to the United States,[5] followed closely by the Border Patrol and extreme climate. As indicated in Figure 2.3, 25 percent of respondents indicated border crime as their primary concern, an increase from 18 percent reported in the 2007 Oaxaca study. This increase reflects concern over the stemming from Mexican

---

4 Respondents were asked to rank order up to three factors that would most worry a migrant attempting an unauthorized entry into the United States, in the order which would most worry the prospective migrant. The options were: border crime, extreme climate or other natural hazards, the Border Patrol, being incarcerated in the United States if caught, Mexican police, not finding work in the United States, and the border wall itself.

5 Border crime first emerged as the primary concern for unauthorized migration in the MMFRP's 2010 survey in Tlacuitapa, Jalisco (Hicken, Fischbein, Lisle 2011, p.19).

president Felipe Calderon's attempts to take on the country's drug traffickers, which has led to 35,000 deaths, primarily in northern Mexico, between December 2006 and December 2010 (FitzGerald and Alarcón, forthcoming). Border crime is a pressing concern for potential migrants as drug syndicates vie for control of illicit drug markets and access to trafficking routes between Mexico and the United States, which include pathways for migrants seeking clandestine entry.

Figure 2.3 Sources of Concern About Clandestine Entry: First Response

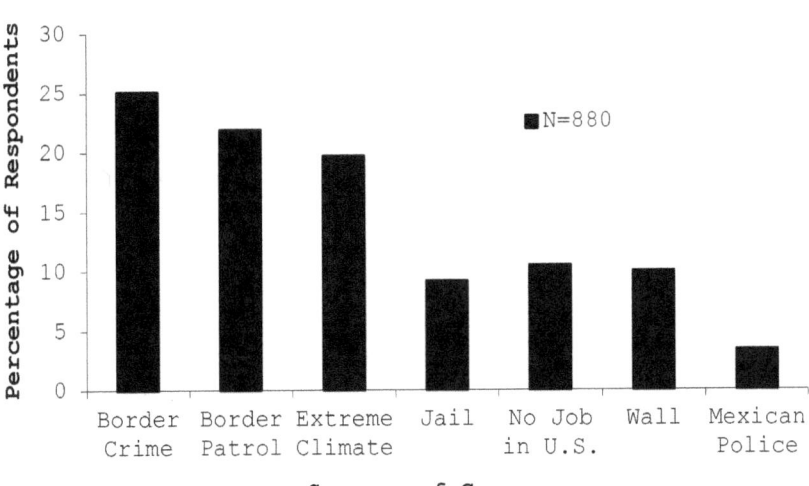

As border crime has emerged as Tlacotepenses' primary concern associated with clandestine migration, anxieties pertaining to the extreme desert climates of the U.S.-Mexico border have moved down in relative importance in comparison to previous MMFRP studies. As indicated in Table 2.4, about 20 percent of respondents indicated extreme climate as their primary concern associated with undocumented migration, in significant contrast to the 42.9 percent of respondents who indicated extreme climate as their top concern in the 2007 Oaxaca survey. In spite of this finding, border crime, Border Patrol, and extreme climate were again reported as the top three concerns associated with clandestine migration (as indicated in Table 2.4), while incarceration, fears of not finding work in the United States, and the border wall itself did not rank highly among concerns (see Figure 2.3). All of these concerns lead over 90 percent of respondents to report that clandestine migration is "very dangerous." With fears of border crime emerging as the top concern for unauthorized entry to the United States, migrants are increasingly concerned with the potential risks of clandestine entry.

Table 2.4 Tlacotepenses' Primary Concern Regarding a Clandestine Entry, 2007-2011

Ranking	2007	2011
1st	Extreme Climate (42.9%)	Border Crime (25.1%)
2nd	Border Patrol (23.6%)	Border Patrol (21.9%)
3rd	Border Crime -18%	Extreme Climate (19.7%)
N	652	588

PERCEPTIONS OF THE U.S. ECONOMY

Many Tlacotepenses are aware of the poor state of the U.S. economy and have delayed plans to migrate until the situation improves. Asked to describe the economic situation in the United States, nearly 54 percent indicated that it was "somewhat bad" or "very bad." Over one-fifth of respondents indicated that someone in their household had returned to Tlacotepec from the United States since 2007 due to lack of work.

When asked about the ease or difficulty of finding work in the United States, over 94 percent of respondents indicated that it was "very difficult" or "somewhat difficult" to do so. Among respondents who said it is "very difficult" to find work, over 90 percent indicated no plans to migrate to the United States in 2011. Among those who said it is "somewhat easy" to find work in the United States, 78 percent indicated no plans to migrate. When the same question was restricted to the answers of respondents without U.S. documentation papers, almost 89 percent indicated no plans for migration when answering it is "very difficult" to find a job within the United States. There is a palpable concern about the economic conditions of the United States within the Tlacotepense community. When asked to offer advice to potential migrant youth, Javier Sanchez, a Tlacotepec resident who has lived in the United States for 5 years, advised: "They shouldn't go … because right now the economy is poor. When there was a strong economy, yes, they needed workers. But not now."

DECIDING TO MIGRATE CLANDESTINELY

The economy, however, does not tell the entire story of why emigration rates have declined. Border enforcement policies influence whether, how, and where Tlacotepense migrants enter the United States clandestinely. Though immediate deterrence at the U.S.-Mexico border is largely ineffective, there are indicators that remote deterrence is affecting the modes and locations of entry utilized by clandestine migrants. For example, of those Tlacotepenses who migrated clandestinely since 2002, 87 percent of them reported using a coyote on their most recent undocumented journey. That so many now feel the need to use the services of a coyote is its own specific form of remote deterrence. Because employing a coyote is a very expensive investment, an average of $1680 for crossers between 2005 and 2010, those migrants who can afford a coyote will hire one, while without access to the necessary funds will be deterred from undertaking a clandestine journey in the first place.

What other evidence is there that U.S. border enforcement deters Tlacotepenses from planning to migrate? As reported in Table 2.5, a series of logistic regression models measured the effects of knowledge and perceptions of border enforcement on the intent to migrate to the United States among individuals aged 15 to 45, the prime migration age cohort, in San Miguel Tlacotepec.[6] Among the respondents, those who were undocumented, male, had previous migration experience, and had personal knowledge of someone who had died crossing the border were more likely to report that they in-tended to migrate to the United States in the coming year. While the last find-ing sounds counterintuitive, intending migrants likely have denser networks of U.S.-based friends, as well as family and friends who are *former* migrants. Even after controlling for the density of potential migrants' current family ties to the United States, intending migrants were more likely to know someone who has died in a crossing attempt.

Importantly, respondents who reported that crossing the border clandes-tinely is very dangerous were significantly less likely to report an intention to cross in 2011. Danger at the border can be partly attributed to border crime associated with Mexican drug violence, but the border is also dangerous as a direct consequence of U.S. enforcement strategy, which has aimed to concen-trate resources in urban areas and hope that the extreme heat of the deserts, cold of the mountains, and swift waters of the Rio Grande and All-American Canal will deter migrants from crossing in nonurban areas (Hicken, Fischbein, Lisle 2011, 22). In this sense, border enforcement is having a remote deterrent effect, as more migrants choose not to run the risk of crossing through a desert border with enhanced enforcement and criminal elements standing in the way of successful and safe entry to the United States.

---

6 Respondents were asked if they personally knew anyone who had died crossing the border, how they would rate the difficulty of evading the Border Patrol on a four-point scale, and how they would rate the level of danger of crossing the border without papers on a four-point scale.

In addition to perceptions of border danger, those who reported that the U.S. economy was "somewhat bad" or "very bad" were significantly less likely to report an intention to migrate, as the poor job market of the United States draws fewer migrants to pursue work. The complex interplay of U.S. enforcement measures (which indirectly contribute to dangerous conditions along the border) with the force of an economic recession and an ongoing drug war in Mexico have contributed toward stemming the flow of unauthorized migration.

Table 2.5 Predictors of Plans to Migrate in the Next Year among Tlacotepenses Aged 15 – 45 Who Have Never Received Legal Permission to Enter the United States

	m1	m2	m3	m4	m5	m6	m7
(Intercept)	-0.265	-0.096	-0.176	-0.163	-0.287	-0.229	-1.046
	(2.466)	(2.463)	(2.506)	(2.656)	(2.466)	(2.665)	(2.922)
Age	-0.260	-0.268	-0.199	-0.312	-0.257	-0.248	-0.198
	(0.176)	(0.175)	(0.179)	(0.180)	(0.176)	(0.183)	(0.198)
Age-squared	0.004	0.004	0.003	0.005	0.004	0.004	0.003
	(0.003)	(0.003)	0.003	0.003	0.003	0.003	0.003
Male	0.971*	0.927*	0.826*	0.989*	0.989*	0.790	0.852
	0.403	0.405	0.416	0.402	0.407	0.422	0.453
Never married	-0.152	-0.234	-0.150	-0.690	-0.121	-0.895	-0.962
	0.721	0.721	0.714	0.800	0.724	0.806	0.856
Has children	-0.160	-0.424	-0.155	-0.700	-0.128	-1.126	-1.171
	0.734	0.748	0.732	0.781	0.739	0.805	0.855
Number of family in the U.S.	-0.158	-0.142	-0.181	-0.172	-0.160	-0.184	-0.166
	0.132	0.132	0.134	0.134	0.132	0.138	0.141
Has never	1.167*	1.210*	1.202*	1.348*	1.184*	1.518*	1.637*

migrated to U.S.	(0.462)	(0.463)	(0.463)	(0.475)	(0.466)	(0.484)	(0.513)
Wealth in Mexico[7]	0.135	0.150	0.140	0.150	0.140	0.210	0.191
	(0.254)	(0.253)	(0.261)	(0.254)	(0.254)	(0.263)	(0.281)
Knows someone who died trying to cross	1.076*		1.183		1.520*		
	(0.509)		(0.514)		(0.558)		
Very dangerous to cross	-1.184*		-1.437*		-1.492*		
	(0.457)		(0.497)		(0.545)		
Difficult to cross[8]	0.991		1.336		1.665		
	(0.806)		(0.854)		(0.930)		
Knowledge of border enforcement	-0.126		0.017		-0.095		
	(0.399)		(0.433)		(0.465)		
U.S. economy is bad[9]					-1.183		
					(0.463)		

---

7 The wealth variable is constructed from the battery of questions which asked about what assets people have in their house. The wealth score is computed by extracting the first component of a principle component analysis of the remaining questions. It is the linear combination of responses that accounts for the maximum amount of variance in the data. This is a standard method for computing wealth indices.

8 The "difficult" variable is constructed from anyone who responded that it was either somewhat or very difficult to cross the border.

9 The "U.S. economy" variable is constructed from anyone who responded that the state of the U.S. economy was either somewhat or very bad.

Easy to find job in U.S.					0.567 (0.774)		
Lack of a return migration due to job loss within household					0.019 (0.479)		
N	395	393	393	384	395	381	352
McFadden's R-squared	0.088	0.105	0.113	0.102	0.088	0.153	0.200

LEGAL MIGRATION

Critics have often argued that the estimated 6.7 million unauthorized Mexicans should "get in line" to come with legal papers, but they fail to assess the many obstacles that stand in the way of efforts to enter legally—obstacles that are more pronounced in poverty-stricken towns like Tlacotepec (FitzGerald and Alarcón, forthcoming). Tlacotepenses often lack financial resources, skills, and knowledge of the U.S. legal immigration system, and even many of those who could potentially enter legally under a family sponsorship are unwilling to wait ten or more years for a legal permanent residency (LPR) visa. The U.S. legal immigration system does not put numerical caps on the immigration of U.S. citizens' parents, spouses, and unmarried children under the age of 21. Other family categories, including the immigration of family members of LPRs, are subject to annual numeric caps. Typically, if a Mexican national is related to a potential U.S. sponsor, he or she usually will have to wait for a longer time than nationals of most countries to gain legal permanent residency (FitzGerald and Alarcón, forthcoming). For example, the unmarried sons and daughters of U.S. citizens over the age of 21—the first preference cap—have to wait 19 years to receive a visa. This is about 14 years above the average wait time of this preference category for nationals of most other countries. Migrants from Mexico are subjected to a long backlog for LPR visas, and the annual quota of 25,620 LPR visas (excluding immediate relatives as U.S. citizen sponsors) is minimal in alleviating the high demand for them. The end result is that Mexican migrants end up waiting longer for legal documents than do other nationals, leading few who wish to reunify with family in the United States and obtain a job immediately to pursue this route.

Close family ties to a U.S. citizen or legal permanent resident is the main avenue through which a Tlacotepense could likely qualify to obtain an immigrant visa. Since only about 20 percent of the respondents in our study are U.S. citizens, many Tlacotepenses' prospects of securing legal documents through family reunification are severely limited. Out of the 70 authorized Tlacotepense migrants in our study, only 37.1 percent said they received their LPR status through their parents.

Another path to legal migration is employer sponsorship. However, being sponsored by an employer is even more difficult for low-skilled workers, who make up the majority of the Tlacotepense population. Few farmers take advantage of the H-2A temporary agricultural worker visa, of which 150,000 were given in 2009, because the existing unauthorized population in the United States is willing to work cheaply. Furthermore, the H-2A visa is only for temporary stays and is not an avenue for legal permanent residency. Another visa open to low-skill workers is the H-2B non-agricultural visa. In 2009, 66 percent of these visas were awarded to Mexican nationals. However, the H-2B visa, like its counterpart, is seasonal and must be continually renewed (Fitzgerald and Alarcón, forthcoming). Only 8 individuals in our study claimed to have had either an H2A or H2B visa. Employer sponsorship is rarely an avenue for legal migration for the Tlacotepense community.

Out of the Mexican-born population in our sample who entered the United States clandestinely on their last migration, 32.4 percent eventually obtained legal permanent residency and 21.1 percent had become U.S. citizens. Currently, the main route for legalization for Tlacotepenses is through family reunification, which has numerous hurdles for migrants who are not immediately related to a U.S. citizen. With few prospects for another large-scale legalization program such as the Immigration Reform and Control Act (IRCA) of 1986, migrants who travel to the United States clandestinely are unlikely to secure papers at a later date.

These impediments to legalization explain why very few Tlacotepenses even submit applications for LPR status. Only 18.9 percent of all those surveyed replied that they applied at one point in time for any type of visa to enter the United States. Of those who went to the United States, only 28.7 percent who were unauthorized on their last trip ever made attempts to secure any type of visa. Vincent, an undocumented migrant who has lived in Vista, California for 14 years, said that after a consultation with an immigration lawyer, he concluded that his pursuit of LPR status would be futile. The attorney told him, "We can fill out your paperwork, but we are not sure if they are going to accept you. Are you going to pay me $600 monthly for three years? Four years?" Vincent said, "It was too much money for nothing ... for no guarantee.'" Expensive lawyer fees coupled with no guarantee of acquiring LPR status makes following this route unattractive for many migrants.

Tlacotepense migrants also describe growing anti-immigrant sentiment in the United States and perceive it to be a disadvantageous time to enter the

United States and wait for a new legalization program. Luis, a migrant who obtained his LPR visa through IRCA, explains how the political climate has changed since 1986 by declaring: "They are not going to pass another amnesty nor are they going to pass what they call the DREAM Act[10] because that implies that they will bring more people ... and right now, what they want is to get rid of those without documents." These anxieties, along with the bureaucratic difficulties of securing legal documents, combine to create an environment in which legal migration is not open for most potential migrants.

CONCLUSION

The border enforcement efforts of the U.S. government are not effectively stemming the undocumented migrations of Tlacotepense migrants. Ninety-six percent of all Tlacotepenses who have ever attempted to cross the border clandestinely were able to do so successfully—including 95 percent of those who tried to cross without papers since 2002—and only 35 percent of Tlacotepenses were apprehended one or more times on their most recent undocumented journey. Although clandestine migrations through legal ports of entry have higher success rates, the prohibitive cost of this method of crossing leads the majority of Tlacotepenses to continue to enter illegally by walking through the extreme climates of the Southwestern deserts and mountains.

There is greater evidence of remote deterrence. Migrants with previous migration experience and those migrants who are more enmeshed in existing migrant networks are more likely to attempt a clandestine migration, while those migrants who feel that it is very dangerous to cross the border (90 percent of the Tlacotepense community) are significantly less likely to pursue clandestine entry. Importantly, Tlacotepenses with negative views of the current state of the U.S. economy are also less likely to migrate illegally.

Border crime registered as the foremost fear when Tlacotepenses were asked to report their top concerns associated with clandestine migration. Anxieties pertaining to extreme temperatures and the Border Patrol were also prominently reported by Tlacotepenses, further bolstering the view that remote deterrents are indeed swaying Tlacotepenses' migration behavior. The influence of the economic recession and border enforcement have an interactive effect. The cost of hiring a coyote continues to be very high, and the economic crisis means that fewer Tlacotepenses living in the United States are able to finance the trips of their friends and family who hope to join them there.

---

10 The DREAM (Development, Relief, and Education for Alien Minors) act would allow undocumented children a path to obtaining a LPR visa if they graduate from a U.S. high school and attend an institution of higher education for two years, along with other qualifications.

Finally, most Tlacotepenses do not view legal migration as a viable option. Lacking financial resources, advanced skills, and exact knowledge of the process of securing legal papers, few Tlacotepenses are likely to meet the criteria necessary to secure legal status. Even in cases where family reunification is feasible, Tlacotepenses have little incentive to wait more than a decade for the legal migration process to run its course. In the absence of a more streamlined path to legality, undocumented migration will continue and is likely to increase when economic conditions improve.

WORKS CITED

Bean, F. D., R. Corona, R. Tuiran, K. A. Woodrow-Lafield, and J. Van Hook. 2001. "Circular, invisible, and ambiguous migrants: Components of difference in estimates of the number of unauthorized Mexican migrants in the United States," *Demography* 38:411-22.

Borger, Scott. 2009. "Estimates of the Cyclical Inflow of Undocumented Mexicans to the United States." CCIS Working Paper No. 181. La Jolla, CA: Center for Comparative Immigration Studies, University of California, San Diego.

Cornelius, Wayne A., David S. Fitzgerald, and Jorge Hernandez-Diaz. 2009. *Migration from the Mexican Mixteca: A Transnational Community in Oaxaca and California.* La Jolla, CA: Center for Comparative Immigration Studies, University of California, San Diego.

Cornelius, Wayne A. 2001. "Death at the Border: Efficacy and Unintended Consequences of Immigration Control Policy," *Population and Development Review* 27: 661-85.

Department of Homeland Security (DHS). 2011. "FY 2012 Budget in Brief." Washington, DC: Office of Homeland Security, January 27, 2011. http://www.dhs.gov/xlibrary/assets/budget-bib-fy2012.pdf

Department of Homeland Security(DHS). 2011. "Securing America's Borders: CBP Fiscal Year 2010 in Review Fact Sheet." 2011. Washington, DC: U.S. Customs and Border Protection, March 15, 2011. http://www.cbp.gov/xp/cgov/newsroom/fact_sheets/cbp_overview/fy2010_factsheet.xml

FitzGerald, David, and Rafael Alarcón. Forthcoming. "Migration: Policies and Politics." In *Mexico and the United States: Possibilities of Partnership,* ed. Peter H. Smith and Andrew Selee, manuscript, Center for U.S.-Mexican Studies, University of California, San Diego, under consideration at Lynne Rienner Publishers.

FitzGerald, David S., Rafael Alarcón Acosta, and Leah Muse-Orlinoff, eds. 2011. *Recession Without Borders: Mexican Migrants Confront the Economic Downturn.* La Jolla, CA: Center for UC San Diego Center for Comparative Immigration Studies.

Jimenez, Maria. 2009. *Humanitarian Crisis: Migrants Deaths at the U.S.-Mexico Border.* American Civil Liberties Union of San Diego and Imperial Counties/Mexico's National Commission of Human Rights. www.aclu.org/files/pdfs/immigrants/humanitariancrisisreport.pdf

Orrenius, P. M., and M. Zavodny. 2005. "Self-Selection among Undocumented Immigrants from Mexico," *Journal of Development Economics* 78, no. 1: 215-40.

Passel, Jeffrey S., and D'Vera Cohn. 2009. "Mexican Immigrants: How Many Come? How Many Leave?" Washington, DC: Pew Hispanic Center.

Spener, David. 2009. *Clandestine Crossings: Migrants and Coyotes on the Texas-Mexico Border*. Ithaca, NY: Cornell University Press.

US Sentencing Commission. 2009. "Immigration Primer." http://www.ussc.gov/training/Immigration_Primer2009_April.pdf

3 "They Want Us to Go Back to Mexico": Tlacotepenses Living Under the Radar in North San Diego County

ANGELA S. GARCÍA, GLORIA MOLINA-ESTOLANO, MOHAMMAD OMAR QURESHI, FERNANDO RIEDEL, RAFAEL SOLIS, ESTEFANÍA CASTILLO BALDERAS

> *In the last year, I have noticed that there are a lot of checkpoints. Earlier this year, a lot of Mexicans gathered with signs and were warning people that came off the freeway that there was a checkpoint ahead. People are terrified.* — Paula, 35-year-old resident of Escondido

Tlacotepenses traditionally migrate to San Diego's North County, a region with an array of local immigration measures. From proposed rental housing bans and day laborer ordinances to local-federal enforcement partnerships and mandated E-Verify usage, cities across North County have busily entered the realm of immigration policy activism.[1] Combined with federal interior enforcement efforts, these local immigration policies create a restrictive environment for unauthorized immigrants. This chapter presents one of the first empirically-based studies of immigrants' responses to local restrictions and interior enforcement in their destinations. Combining survey data with extensive qualitative interviews, our analysis indicates that exclusionary policy contexts mediate immigrant incorporation. Reacting to legal threats and hostile reception, immigrants go underground: they hold negative perceptions of local law enforcement, associate routine activities like driving and walking with anxiety and deportation, and develop strategies of avoidance and fitting in to mitigate the discovery of unauthorized status.

In order to provide context to this study, the chapter begins by outlining the development of subnational policies of immigration across the United

---

1 E-verify is a system run by the Department of Homeland Security that electronically compares information from employment forms with government records to determine U.S. work eligibility.

States. An overview of the restrictive measures in North County follows. Next, we discuss the relatively poor relationship between Tlacotepenses and the local law enforcement of their destination locales. The chapter concludes with an analysis of the ways that fear of deportation permeates into daily life. Immigrants strive to avoid contact with authorities entirely, and do this by developing strategies to live under the radar. However, the practices Tlacotepenses engage in to avoid detection also negate their broader incorporation into receiving society.

IMMIGRATION POLICY AND INTERIOR ENFORCEMENT: FROM D.C. TO SAN DIEGO

States and localities frequently formed their own immigration policies in early American history. This practice ceased in the late nineteenth century, when a series of Supreme Court rulings articulated the doctrine of plenary power and declared the regulation of immigration a federal competency (Martin and Schuck 2005; Motamura 1990). From this period forward, the federal government has controlled the policy decisions around who may enter the United States and under what conditions, as well as the enforcement of those policies.[2] Despite this federal authority over immigration policy, since the late twentieth century an increasing number of states and localities have developed immigration and enforcement measures of their own, producing legislation that ranges from accommodating to restrictive (NCSL 2011).[3]

In exploring the contemporary motivations for subnational jurisdictions to enter the immigration policy and enforcement arena, some scholars point to a combination of rising levels of unauthorized immigration and ineffective or absent federal immigration legislation (Cornelius 2010: vii; Ramakrishnan and Wong 2008). Others focus on the demographic growth of the Latino and foreign-born share of the population, especially in untraditional U.S. destinations (Furuseth and Smith 2010; Espenshade et al. 2007). The partisan composition of receiving communities also appears to play a role in whether states and localities take a restrictive legislative stance towards immigration and enforcement (Ramakrishnan and Wong 2010), as do the motivations of elected officials, some of whom act as policy entrepreneurs that build their political

---

2 As the Supreme Court considered the Chinese Exclusion Act of 1882 and the Geary Act of 1892 in Chae Chan Ping v. United States (1889) and Fong Yue Ting v. United States (1893), it first articulated the plenary power doctrine. Later rulings, such as Hines v. Davidowitz (1941) and LULAC v. Wilson (1995) uphold this federal plenary power by limiting subnational governments' abilities to create immigration policy.

3 In the literature on subnational immigration activism, initiatives classified as accommodating seek to expand immigrants' local rights, benefits, and integration into the receiving community. Those categorized as restrictive attempt to constrain immigrants' local rights, benefits, and integration, often by conditioning access on immigration status or even national origins.

careers on restricting immigration (Doty 2003; Singer, Wilson, and DeRenzis 2009).

The formulation of subnational immigration measures has contributed to tensions between different levels of government as well as legal disputes over whether states and localities should be formally involved in immigration and enforcement policy-making, given the federal government's authority over this arena (Varsanyi 2010). Restrictive legislation is particularly polemical, with litigation often reaching federal appeals courts. At the state level, for example, California's Proposition 187 of 1994 curtailed public benefits, health care, and education for the unauthorized (State of California 1994). The measure passed with the support of Californian voters, though immediately afterward legal challenges citing violation of federal plenary power successfully blocked most of the proposition (Wroe 2008: 101-104; Martinez HoSang 2010: 196-197). Under the Obama administration, the Department of Justice (DOJ) has filed suit against highly punitive state-level immigration policies. Following Arizona's Senate Bill 1070 of 2010 and Alabama's House Bill 56 of 2011, for example, it challenged the states' measures, arguing that they conflict with federal immigration law and undermine the plenary power of the federal government (DOJ 2011).

At the local level, restrictive measures are also subject to legal dispute. For example, the city of Hazleton, Pennsylvania passed an ordinance in 2006 to make the municipality "one of the most difficult places in the United States for illegal immigrants," according to Mayor Louis Bartletta (quoted in Preston 2006). Hazleton's ordinance established English as its official language and outlined procedures to revoke the licenses of businesses employing unauthorized immigrants and to fine the landlords who rent to them (City of Hazleton 2006). In doing so, the city pushed the federal courts to weigh in on the role of local municipalities in determining immigration policy. Much like California's Prop 187, Hazleton's policy was struck down due to its infringement on the federal government's plenary power. Nevertheless, the city's activism inspired over sixty local governments to pass punitive measures of their own (Englund 20007: 884), including North County's Escondido, Oceanside, and Vista. These locales are home to 63 percent of the study sample (or 202 immigrants), 68 percent of who are unauthorized, and thus more vulnerable to restrictive policy and federal interior enforcement in their destinations.

In October 2006, the Escondido City Council passed an ordinance that prohibited landlords from renting housing to unauthorized immigrants. Facing a lawsuit and a temporary injunction by a federal judge, the city rescinded the ordinance in December 2006 (Isackson 2006a, 2006b). [4] Escondido then turned to driver's license checkpoints—first established in 2004—as an alternative tool to restrict unauthorized immigration (Breier 2010; Guidi 2011). Positioned on

---

4 In 2007, the state of California passed Assembly Bill 976, which prohibited local governments from requiring landlords to check renters' immigration status.

a main thoroughfare to screen for valid driver's licenses and small infractions, the checkpoints are part of an enforcement scheme that is strongly criticized by civil rights groups who argue that they subject unlicensed immigrants to automobile impoundment as well as potential deportation (Marosi 2011).[5]

Another restrictive effort in Escondido is a pilot program that stations Immigration and Customs Enforcement (ICE) officers—those charged with apprehending and deporting unauthorized immigrants—in the Escondido Police Department. Initiated in May 2010, this program allows ICE agents to respond to events in Escondido as varied as traffic stops and gang sweeps (Marosi 2011).[6] Pablo, an unauthorized Tlacotepense migrant who lived in Escondido for several years, believes he was a victim of this police-ICE collaboration. Arrested for riding his bike on the sidewalk, Pablo was later questioned by ICE and deported. The latest move towards restriction in Escondido came in March 2011, when the city council approved a resolution requiring the city to use E-Verify, a system run by the Department of Homeland Security that electronically compares information from employment forms with government records to determine U.S. work eligibility, and encouraged businesses to also utilize the tool (City of Escondido 2011).[7]

Escondido's neighbors in North County have also embraced restrictions. In April 2011, the Oceanside City Council supported the drafting of a resolution requiring all contractors with the city to use E-Verify (City of Oceanside 2011).[8] Vista's City Council approved an ordinance targeting day laborers, many of whom are Mexican immigrants, in June 2006. With this measure city leaders, seeking to reduce or eliminate the congregation of day laborers in the jurisdiction, required employers to register with the city before hiring short-term workers (City of Vista 2006; Rodriguez and Gaona 2006). In the months prior to the passage of the ordinance, a local chapter of the Minutemen frequently protested at a day labor hiring site in Vista, pressuring the City Council to act (Varsanyi 2008: 36). Although Vista's day laborer measure faced criticism, with civil rights groups charging that it intimidated unauthorized immigrants and served as a pretense for detaining them, the city settled legal

---

5 As of writing, California's state Legislature was debating two Assembly bills, 1389 and 353, which would prevent law enforcement agencies from seizing an unlicensed driver's vehicle if a licensed driver is available to retrieve it.

6 Because the program developed behind closed doors and without a formal memorandum of understanding, the precise extent to which federal immigration enforcement agents are involved in local Escondido police operations is unclear. See "Immigration agents accompany police on some calls," in the June 27, 2010 San Diego Union Tribune, http://www.signon-sandiego.com/news/2010/jun/27/immigration-agents-accompany-local-police-some-cal/

7 A bill to prohibit local governments from making E-Verify mandatory for employers within their borders, AB 1236, was working its way through the California assembly at the time of writing. At the federal level, E-Verify is mandatory for business contracting with the federal government, though HR 2164, introduced in the House of Representatives in June 2011, would mandate the use of E-Verify for all employers in the Nation.

8 As of writing, Oceanside had yet to pass its E-Verify resolution.

challenges to the ordinance that claimed it was unconstitutional and had discriminatory intent (Isackson 2007). The day laborer measure therefore remains in force.

In North County San Diego, Tlacotepense immigrants are subject not only to the restrictive measures proposed and enacted in municipalities like Escondido, Oceanside and Vista but also the federal government's interior enforcement. Under the Obama administration, ICE set a record for overall removal of unauthorized immigrants in the 2010 fiscal year, with almost 400,000 deportations nationwide. Of those deported, 73 percent were Mexican nationals. This unprecedented rate reflects an increase of over 23,000 removals compared to the 2008 fiscal year, the last equivalent period entirely under the Bush administration (DHS 2010a; DHS 2010b).

San Diego County's participation in Secure Communities, a federal ICE initiative that checks the fingerprints of jail detainees against immigration databases, played a part in this deportation spike. In May 2009, the San Diego jurisdiction became the first in California to join the program and facilitate the identification of unauthorized immigrants detained in area jails (ICE 2011).[9] In addition, the Border Patrol maintains a significant presence in North County. Because of its proximity to the U.S.-Mexico border, Border Patrol agents do not need a warrant or probable cause to conduct a routine search for unauthorized migrants in the area.[10] These federal interior enforcement actions combine with restrictive local-level policies to shape a hostile receiving environment for Tlacotepenses in North County.

While subnational immigration policies are steadily expanding across the United States, little is known about how these initiatives directly affect unauthorized migrants living restrictive destinations. Scholars have yet to produce systemic evidence of how migrants react to local policy that attempts to restrict unauthorized immigrant communities (García et al. 2010). How do immigrants negotiate the policy constraints of their receiving communities, and what are the mechanisms through which local contexts shape immigrants' lives? The numerous restrictive measures in North County San Diego affect Tlacotepenses in broad and significant ways, as we describe in the following sections.

---

9 In August 2011, the Department of Homeland Security (DHS) announced the termination of Secure Communities Memorandums of Agreement with state and local governments. DHS initially entered into these agreements as a way to encourage voluntary participation in the initiative. The announcement followed attempts by the governors of Massachusetts, New York, and Illinois to terminate their agreements because of concern that the program fails to target serious unauthorized immigrant criminals (Semple and Preston 2011). DHS now argues that the agreements are not necessary to operate Secure Communities in subnational jurisdictions. The agency plans to have the program active in every state by 2013 (DHS 2011).

10 Federal regulations designate Border Patrol agents as immigration officers and define these agents' jurisdictions as within the "reasonable distance" of 100 miles from the border (8 CFR 287.1; Haddal 2010: 30). Because San Diego's North County falls well within this range, Border Patrol agents may operate freely there.

THE IMMIGRANT-POLICE RELATIONSHIP

The multiple immigration ordinances of North County are continually evolving. Challenges to these measures' legality are interwoven with the multiscalar dynamics of the policies in which different levels of government—federal, state, county, and local—play a role. Although these factors complicate a detailed understanding of the political climate towards unauthorized immigrants in the area, Tlacotepenses are often well informed about the local policies in their destinations as well as federal enforcement tactics. Pedro, an unauthorized Tlacotepense living in Escondido, described the various local policies proposed in North County in depth. He concluded that "the authorities are squeezing us more than before. They want to clear us out. They want us to go back to Mexico." While all Tlacotepenses are not as informed as Pedro, at the very least they demonstrate a firm understanding that many localities in North County do not take an accommodating approach to immigration.

Migrants' social networks play a vital role in channeling information about restrictions in their destinations. Jorge, a 20 year-old Tlacotepense who recently lived in Vista, recalled that he became aware of the city's day laborer ordinance through his cousin: "He told me that it wasn't safe to look for work that way anymore. He heard there were Minutemen and police at the spot where we used to wait for jobs." Spanish language media and the Mexican consulate in San Diego also help migrants gain knowledge about restrictive environments of their destinations. The local newspapers *Hispanos Unidos* and *La Prensa San Diego*, for example, carry frequent coverage of immigration measures and interior enforcement activity in the region. In February 2011, the Mexican consulate organized a town hall-style meeting in Escondido with the police chief, who addressed the city's vehicle checkpoints and the importance of reporting crime (Secretaría de Relaciones Exteriores 2011). The information Tlacotepenses gain through these varied sources allows them to make knowledgeable decisions about when and how to interact with local law enforcement.

Of immigrants residing in North County, 43 percent feel negatively about the way officers treat them. Recounting numerous experiences of being pulled over for broken tail lights, cracked windshields, and unspecified charges of suspicious driving, immigrants explained that they felt targeted by police because of their ethnicity and potential unauthorized status. They also questioned where the line was between police work and immigration enforcement. Tellingly, when immigrants were asked what occurred as a result of the last time (within the last five years) they were stopped by the police in North County, responses were often quite serious, as reflected in Table 3.1 below.

Table 3.1 Consequence of Last Police Stop in North County

Consequence	Percent
Received ticket	48.9
Detained	38.6
Car impounded	31.1
Received warning only	27.9
Reported to Immigration	23.3
Deported	23.3

N=202

Source: MMFRP 2011

Due to anxiety about the consequences of interacting with local police in North County, immigrants in the sample are mostly reluctant to contact police to report a crime or a concern about suspicious activities in their neighborhoods. In order to measure how often immigrants report crime in their North County destinations, respondents were asked whether they had been a witness or victim of crime and, if answering in the affirmative, whether they had communicated with the police about that experience. Surprisingly, of the entire North County sample, only 18 immigrants, or less than one percent, stated that they had encountered crime either as witnesses or victims. Of these 18 immigrants, 12 were unauthorized and only three (one authorized, two unauthorized) reported the crime to the police. Qualitative interviews confirmed the hesitancy of immigrants to contact police. Diego, an unauthorized 30 year old immigrant with five years experience in Vista, connected his apprehension to report crime to a news story he saw about a woman who faced deportation after calling the police during a domestic dispute. After that, he said, "I don't feel safe going to the police or the courthouse. It's hard. But you can't trust that nothing will happen."

Despite the fear associated with contacting the police, in qualitative interviews immigrants also expressed reporting crime in positive terms, as an action taken by responsible community members. "Of course, we also want to live in a safe neighborhood," Yolanda, an immigrant in Vista explained. Other immigrants emphasized their desire to follow the law as much as possible. "The police are the authority. It's best to do what they say" explained Alejandro, who lives in Escondido. The anxiety many immigrants have about interacting with law enforcement is sometimes counterbalanced by their sense of responsibility in reporting crime and their attempt to be law-abiding members of their receiving communities.

Qualitative interviews also revealed an innovative approach that allows immigrants to report crime while keeping the danger of deportation at bay. Rather than personally speaking with police, migrants explained their inclination to ask a documented friend or family member to make the report on their behalf. "I would ask my aunt to do it," Roberto, recently deported from North County after a traffic stop, said when asked about reporting crime. "She has papers, so it wouldn't be a big deal." Similarly Alicia, a 27 year old who recently arrived to Vista, explained that it would be better for her documented friends to contact the police for her because she fears being asked to show identification. Carmen, a documented immigrant living in Escondido with her unauthorized husband, also stressed the importance of reporting anonymously. "If I could do it without giving my name or address then I would call 911 if something happened," she said. "But I wouldn't want them coming to my house because they could take my husband."

FEAR AND ANXIETY IN EVERYDAY LIFE

The efforts of some immigrants to strategically collaborate with local law enforcement in their North County destinations is particularly notable given their description of the anxieties they experience in their restrictive destinations. At the root of most concerns is deportation. Immigrants also experienced worry over the more mundane details of daily life, such as driving, which are complicated by illegal status. Even immigrants with legal documentation or U.S. citizenship expressed similar fears due to the many unauthorized family members and friends in their social networks.[11] During the three year period when Armando was unauthorized in Vista, he was often concerned about "la migra" and the police. "I remember when I didn't have papers I felt anxious all the time—going out to work and getting on the freeway and going to the store. It was stressful and became a part of everything else. A constant worry." Several unauthorized mothers of children born in the U.S. recounted their anxiety about driving with their children. When Lidia, who lives in Vista, moved within walking distance of her U.S. born daughter's elementary school, she was relieved to avoid the risk of her former twice daily drive between school and home.

The everyday fear and anxiety Tlacotepense migrants experience in North County are concretely represented in their ranked responses of the daily activities that are of most concern in their destination locales. As Table 3.2 below indicates, driving is the top worry for Tlacotepenses. Unauthorized migrants without licenses who are pulled over or are subject to a police checkpoint can wind up in the custody of ICE—either through the Secure Communities program, Escondido's ICE-police collaboration, or with Border

---

11 In 2009, Passel and Cohen estimated that approximately 8.8 million people in the U.S. live in a mixed-status home.

Patrol intervention—and face deportation. Being stopped while driving is one of the most common ways in which Tlacotepenses come into contact with local police. Pablo, who migrated illegally to Linda Vista in 1988 and lived there for nearly twenty years, said, "You know that driving a car without documents is a risk. At any moment you could be pulled over by the police." Indeed, Pablo was pulled over in 2008 and, with his unauthorized status discovered, he was ultimately deported.

Table 3.2 Sources of Concern for North County Migrants

Concern	Percent
Driving a car	67.4
Walking in public	64.3
Going to the hospital	37.1
Taking public transit	36.2
Going to work	33.5
Going to or taking kids to school	20.8

N=202

Source: MMFRP 2011

The second source of concern for Tlacotepenses is walking in public. Migrants felt that being out in plain sight left them vulnerable to being stopped by law enforcement. Felipe, who migrated to California when he was thirteen years old, spoke of the high presence of law enforcement in Vista. "My father was in Vista... from 2000 to 2003, and he said that he couldn't go out to the store, he couldn't walk outside, because you would be stopped if they saw you walking." As a result of his father's experiences, Felipe migrated not to Vista but to the city of Madera in the Central Valley instead, where, he reported, the presence of law enforcement is much lower. Going to the hospital was the third top concern, though at 37 percent it was a source of considerably less anxiety than driving (67 percent) and walking in public (64 percent). Researchers Berk and Schur (2001) argue that the fear associated with the lack of legal documentation can deter immigrants from seeking medical attention. It follows that the heightened climate of anxiety in restrictive destinations may also influence immigrants in the study sample to avoid hospitals.

KEEPING THE CURTAINS CLOSED: STRATEGIES OF AVOIDANCE

In response to their restrictive environments and subsequent anxieties, Tlacotepenses living throughout North County develop strategies to avoid law enforcement and other authorities they fear could report their legal status or that of a family member. As migrants recounted in qualitative interviews, these strategies take two general forms. First, Tlacotepenses avoid public places associated with enforcement as much as possible. Second, when being in public is unavoidable, migrants attempt to blend in, presenting themselves to wider society in a manner that does not target them as unauthorized immigrants.

Many Tlacotepenses curtail their daily activities in order to limit public exposure. Jorge, who migrated to Vista in 2008, explained how he reacted when he first arrived: "In the beginning, on the first day, I closed everything up, the whole apartment, the curtains—everything. I didn't know what was going on. There would be noise from a car or something and I didn't want to look outside." Similarly, Lorena recounted a close encounter with the Border Patrol in her Vista neighborhood that left her shaken: "When I was taking my daughter to school, there was *migra* parked there on the corner. I went back home and then I couldn't take her to school. Afterwards I didn't want to go around her school anymore... I stopped walking my daughter to school, because I was afraid." In another instance, Tlacotepenses began to avoid North County Wal-Marts after rumors of ICE raids at the stores ran through the immigrant community in spring 2010. For Marco, a Tlacotepense with legal documents in Escondido who is married to an unauthorized immigrant, the text message he got about the store raids was enough to keep him and his family away. "It's not worth it—we'll never shop there again," he said. "My wife could be sent away."

As Marco's experience illustrates, the tight social networks enjoyed by many Tlacotepense immigrants allow for the rapid flow of information about potential interior enforcement activity in the North County area. When immigration authorities are present or a checkpoint is set up, word quickly passes through the Tlacotepense community, with cell phones playing a central role. "Now, when there's a checkpoint set up here in Escondido, I get a text from my mom, my uncle, and all my friends," recounted Marta, an authorized Tlacotepense married to an undocumented immigrant. "I always forward those texts to my husband and everyone else I know, too." While increased technology benefits the efforts of police officers, ICE, and the Border Patrol, at the same time it also aids the strategies of avoidance developed by fearful immigrants.

Of course, Tlacotepenses who limit the time they spend in public places still must meet the basic needs of their households. Enlisting the help of a documented friend or family member becomes a critical survival strategy for these migrants. Several adult Tlacotepenses remarked that their U.S. citizen children take care of many essential errands for their families. "I used to send my son—he was 17—to the store, or to pick up his sister at school. I wanted to do these things myself, but it was less risky for him," commented Ana, a mother who lived unauthorized in Vista until 2009. In another circumstance, a Tlacotepense housewife residing in Vista without documentation lived with a debilitating fear of "la migra." Without a license, she refused to drive to the grocery store and her husband worked long hours. This migrant therefore relied on an authorized friend to buy her weekly groceries and deliver them to her home. While North County's limited public transportation infrastructure makes cars a necessity, Tlacotepenses seeking to avoid the risks of police stops and checkpoints rely on friends, family, and co-workers for rides. Adan, a 76 year-old unauthorized Tlacotepense who has lived in Vista for over 30 years, said that he has never driven a car in the U.S. "I always looked for rides to get to work from friends," he explained.

When Tlacotepenses do spend time in public places, they take conscious steps to fit in, both in terms of their dress and their demeanor. Luis, for example, said:

> More than anything, I think, you need to look presentable and well dressed, so they don't see you as someone who is looking for work... If immigration or the police see you looking somewhat dirty they will pick you up. But if they see you looking nice going to the store, with clean shoes and everything, they will say 'Ok, maybe this guy lives here.'

Marta, the authorized Tlacotepense in Escondido who is married to an unauthorized immigrant, shared Luis's sense of how to remain under the radar. Her husband works as a landscaper and typically returns home in the evenings with soiled clothing. Worried that he would be targeted as illegal due to this appearance, Marta began packing a change of clothes with her husband every morning. Now, rather than drive home as a dirty landscaper, he dresses in kakis and a dress shirt. "Who knows," mused Marta. "Maybe it means nothing. But I think that he calls less attention to himself with the clean clothes."

Some Tlacotepenses go beyond changing their outward appearances in order to blend in. Migrants make a special effort to remain calm in public in order to mask their unauthorized status or that of their family members. Pablo, who migrated to San Diego in 1988, worked to alter his very body language to a U.S.-style demeanor to avoid calling attention to his foreign roots. "Being [in the United States] you must get rid of the way you walk [in Tlacotepec] … You have to be fearless, walking around the streets as if you were from here." Armando, an unauthorized immigrant in Vista, concurred: "when you're on the street," he said, "you must carry yourself differently." Body language that projects anxiety can be interpreted by law enforcement as suspicious and draw their attention. "The biggest fear is immigration agents," explained Pablo. "If one of them thinks that you're illegal, what [migrants] do is run. I walk like it's no big deal, but many people run. If you're calm, they think maybe this guy has papers." Indeed Jose, an authorized migrant living in Vista, remembered the day he was detained at the San Clemente Border Patrol checkpoint well: "my friend was driving, and he didn't have papers either. As the migra came up to our car, I told him 'it's okay, take it easy, relax.' But he was so nervous he started to shake. They knew right away we were illegal." From avoiding public places to changing dress and physical carriage, Tlacotepense migrants go to great lengths to minimize encounters with authorities by remaining in the shadows of North San Diego County.

CONCLUSION

This analysis identifies the policy mechanisms through which host societies shape immigrants' lives, and demonstrates how Tlacotepenses negotiate policy constraints of their receiving communities. Despite the restrictive stance towards immigrants taken by cities in North County and the pervasive federal enforcement presence in the area, both documented and unauthorized Tlacotepenses continue to live and work in these communities. Rather than return home to Mexico or blindly proceed with life as normal in North County, these migrants struggle to adapt in their unreceptive receiving locales. Though invested in their own well being and that of their immediate neighborhoods, Tlacotepenses are apprehensive about collaborating with police and to report crimes. Instead, they generate unique strategies to "pass" as non-suspect members of their southern California communities. Given their anxieties about deportation and engaging daily activities that demand a public presence, Tlacotepenses keep a low profile, rely on documented friends, share information about interior enforcement activity in the area, and literally change their overall appearance and demeanor. With the rapid growth in subnational immigration and enforcement across the United States, it is likely that migrants residing in other restrictive destinations mirror the efforts of Tlacotepenses to live under the radar.

While actions to avoid detection may indeed ward off the attention of immigration authorities, they also contribute to the exclusion of Tlacotepenses from the broader societies of their North County destinations. Migrants from Tlacotepec recounted the anxiety they experience while engaging in ordinary, everyday activities such as walking their children to school, shopping in the community and driving to work. This study suggests that restrictive subnational measures and aggressive federal interior enforcement may cut off mechanisms of integration like education and community involvement, leaving immigrants and their families isolated within the receiving environment and exacerbating social inequalities generally. Restrictive ordinances like those developed in several North San Diego County cities send a double message to immigrants and their children, one of both urgent assimilation and hostility. As evidenced in the experience of Tlacotepenses in the area, these policy stances help to produce the social divisions that they simultaneously denounce.

WORKS CITED

Berk, Marc L., and Claudia L. Schur. 2008. "The Effect of Fear on Access to Care Among Unauthorized Latino Immigrants," *Journal of Immigrant Health* vol. 3, no.3: 151-56.

Breier, Michelle. 2010. "Checkpoint Debate Continues in Escondido," *San Diego Union-Tribune*, August 20, 2011. http://www.signonsandiego.com/news/2011/aug/20/checkpoint-debate-continues-escondido/

City of Escondido, CA. 2011. Resolution No. 2011-44. http://www.escondido.org/Data/Sites/1/agendas/Council/032311.pdf

City of Hazleton, PA. 2006. Ordinance No. 2006-10. http://www.clearinghouse.net/chDocs/public/IM-PA-0001-0003.pdf

City of Oceanside, CA. 2011. City Council Minutes, April 6 2011. http://www.ci.oceanside.ca.us/pdf/4-6-2011_S.pdf

City of Vista, CA. 2006. Ordinance No. 2006-8.

Cornelius, Wayne. 2010. "Preface," pp. 7-8. In *Taking Local Control: Immigration Policy Activism in U.S. Cities and States*, ed. Monica Varsanyi. Stanford: Stanford University Press.

Department of Homeland Security. 2011. "John Morton Letter Regarding Secure Communities," *The Los Angeles Times*, August 5. http://www.latimes.com/media/acrobat/2011-08/158828360-05134319.pdf

Department of Homeland Security. 2010a. "Press Release: Secretary Napolitano Announces Record-Breaking Immigration Enforcement Statistics Achieved Under Obama Administration," October 6. http://www.dhs.gov/ynews/releases/pr_1286389936778.shtm

Department of Homeland Security. 2010b. "Immigration Enforcement Actions 2010." http://www.dhs.gov/xlibrary/assets/statistics/publications/enforcement-ar-2010.pdf

Department of Justice. 2011. "Press Release. Department of Justice Challenges Alabama Immigration Law," Office of Public Affairs, August 1. http://www.justice.gov/opa/pr/2011/August/11-ag-993.html

Doty, Roxanne. 2003. *Anti-Immigrantism in Western Democracies—Statecraft, Desire, and the Politics of Exclusion*. New York: Routledge.

Englund, Jason. 2007. "Small Town Defenders or Constitutional Foes: Does the Hazleton, PA Anti-Illegal Immigration Ordinance Encroach on Federal Power?" *Boston University Law Review*, vol. 87, no. 883: 884-910.

Espenshade, Jill, Barbara Obrzut, Benjamin Wright, Soo Mee Kim, Jessica Thompson, and Edward O'Conner. 2007. "Division and Dislocation:

Regulating Immigration through Local Housing Ordinances." Washington D.C.: Immigration Policy Center. http://www.immigrationpolicy.org/special-reports/division-and-dislocation-regulating-immigration-through-local-housing-ordinances

Furuseth, Owen, and Heather Smith. 2010. "Localized Immigration Policy: The View from Charlotte, North Carolina, A New Immigrant Gateway," pp. 173-192. In *Taking Local Control: Immigration Policy Activism in U.S. Cities and States*, ed. Monica Varsanyi. Stanford: Stanford University Press.

García, Angela, et al. 2010. "Pressure from the Inside: The Subnational Politics of Immigration." *Recession Without Borders*. Lynne Reiner Publishers.

Guidi, Ruxandra. 2011. "DUI Checkpoints in California May Soon Be Regulated," KPBS Public Broadcasting, September 1. http://www.kpbs.org/news/2011/sep/01/dui-checkpoint-regulated-driver-license-immigrant/

Hadall, Chad. 2010. "Border Security: The Role of the U.S. Border Patrol." Congressional Research Service. http://www.fas.org/sgp/crs/homesec/RL32562.pdf

HoSang, Daniel Martinez. 2010. *Racial Propositions: Ballot Initiatives and the Making of Postwar California*. Los Angeles: University of California Press.

Immigration and Customs Enforcement. 2011. Secure Communities Activated Jurisdictions. http://www.ice.gov/doclib/secure-communities/pdf/sc-activated.pdf

Isackson, Amy. 2006a. "Judge Halts Escondido Landlord Ordinance," KPBS Public Broadcasting, November 17. http://www.kpbs.org/news/2006/nov/17/judge-halts-escondido-landlord-ordinance/

Isackson, Amy. 2006b. "Escondido Landlord Ordinance Is Dead," KPBS Public Broadcasting, December 13. http://www.kpbs.org/news/2006/dec/13/escondido-landlord-ordinance-is-dead/

Isackson, Amy. 2007. "Vista Settles ACLU Suit Alleging Day Laborer Hiring Discrimination," KPBS Public Broadcasting, June 26. http://www.kpbs.org/news/2007/jun/26/vista-settles-aclu-suit-alleging-day-laborer/

Marosi, Richard. 2011. "Escondido's city-federal effort to oust illegal immigrants draws praise, criticism," *The Los Angeles Times*, February 4. http://articles.latimes.com/2011/feb/04/local/la-me-adv-immigrant-crackdown-20110206

Martin, David, and Peter Schuck, eds. 2005. *Immigration Stories*. New York: Foundation Press.

Motamura, Hiroshi. 1990. "Immigration Law After a Century of Plenary Power," *Yale Law Journal*, vol.100, no.3: 545-613.

National Conference of State Legislatures. 2005-2011. "State Laws Related to Immigration and Immigrants," http://www.ncsl.org

Passell, Jeffrey, and D'Vera Cohen. 2009. "A Portrait of Unauthorized Immigrants in the United States." Washington D.C.: The Pew Hispanic Center. http://www.pewhispanic.org/files/reports/107.pdf

Preston, Julia. 2006. "Pennsylvania Town Delays Enforcing Tough Immigration Law," *The New York Times*, September 2.

Ramakrishnan, Karthick, and Tom Wong. 2008. "Immigration Policies Go Local: The Varying Responses of Local Governments to Low-Skilled and Undocumented Migration." Washington D.C.: Woodrow Wilson Center. http://www.karthick.com/working_assets/KR-wilsoncenter-Feb21.pdf

Ramakrishnan, Karthick, and Tom Wong. 2010. "Partisanship, Not Spanish: Explaining Municipal Ordinances Affecting Undocumented Immigrants," pp. 73-96. In *Taking Local Control: Immigration Policy Activism in U.S. Cities and States*, ed. by Monica Varsanyi. Stanford: Stanford University Press.

Rodriguez, Matthew, and Elena Gaona. 2006. "Labor Is Law Likely to Pass in Vista," *The San Diego Union-Tribune*, June 25. http://legacy.signonsandiego.com/news/northcounty/20060625-9999-1mi25curb.html

Secretaría de Relaciones Exteriores. 2011. "Consulado organiza reunión de orientación legal en Escondido," Cónsul General de México en San Diego, February 17. http://portal.sre.gob.mx/sandiego/index.php?option=news&task=viewarticle&sid=452

Semple, Kirk, and Julia Preston. 2011. "Deal to Share Fingerprints is Dropped, But Not Program," *The New York Times*, August 6. http://www.nytimes.com/2011/08/06/us/06immig.html

Singer, Audrey, Jill Wilson, and Brooke DeRenzis. 2009. "Prince William County Case Study: Immigrants, Politics, and Local Response in Suburban Washington." Washington D.C.: Brookings Institution. http://www.brookings.edu/reports/2009/0225_immigration_singer.aspx

State of California. 1994. Proposition 187. California Voter Guide 1994. http://www.calvoter.org/archive/94general/props/187.html

United States Code of Federal Regulations. 8 CFR 287.1 http://ecfr.gpoaccess.gov/cgi/t/text/text-idx?c=ecfr&tpl=/ecfrbrowse/Title08/8tab_02.tpl

Varsanyi, Monica. 2010. *Taking Local Control: Immigration Policy Activism in U.S. Cities and States*. Stanford, CA: Stanford University Press.

Varsanyi, Monica. 2008. "Immigration Policing Through the Backdoor: City Ordinances, the "Right to the City," and the Exclusion of Undocumented Day Laborers," *Urban Geography*, vol. 29, no.1: 29-52.

Wroe, Andrew. 2008. *The Republican Party and Immigration Politics: From Proposition 187 to George W. Bush.* New York: Palgrave Macmillan.

4 The "Parties" Between Us: Migrant Participation In The Politics Of San Miguel Tlacotepec[1]

JORGE HERNÁNDEZ-DÍAZ, JORGE HERNÁNDEZ HERNÁNDEZ

> *I think the social fabric of Tlacotepec hass been ripped ... even within families. My own cousin...is against me.*—A 2010 candidate for municipal president.

INTRODUCTION

Juana's emphatic assertion that she is not in any political party reflects the negative attitudes that Tlacotepenses, and Oaxacans in general, have towards institutionalized politics. A common perception in San Miguel Tlacotepec is that institutionalized politics have only served to split the town's population into interest groups. Both migrants and non-migrants point to organizations and political parties as the cause of the political conflict of Tlacotepec. As one of the main actors in this struggle laments: "This is what political parties bring with them—strong differences."

In this chapter we review the role of migrants in local politics. We pay special attention to actors who play (or played) central roles in the main migrant organization present in Tlacotepec, the Indigenous Front of Binational Organizations, known by its Spanish acronym, FIOB[2]. We contend that Tlacotepec is exemplary of a process occurring in local governments where, paradoxically, the legal recognition in 1995 of the *usos y costumbres* system has dismantled the uniformity and stability with which the appointment of

---

1 We place parties in quotation marks in this title for, as we shall argue in this chapter, the migrant organization that is a main political actor in San Miguel Tlacotepec is not legally registered as a party, even though it carries out many of the roles of the common Mexican political party.

2 Frente Indígena de Organizaciones Binacionales.

authorities was previously carried out in indigenous communities of Oaxaca. Usos y costumbres literally means "usages and customs," but is better understood as common law practices, where the legislative body is the community assembly composed of the citizens of a town.[3] We conclude that the ambiguous state legislation that covers the political system of usos y costumbres has led to multiple interpretations of what the system actually entails (Anaya Muñoz, 2006; Recondo, 2007; Durand Ponte, 2007; Hernández-Díaz, 2007), leading to what we see in San Miguel Tlacotepec as a very flexible mechanism of election and governance which could easily pass as a political party system, even though the rhetoric of those who promote the system presents it as an "authentic" alternative to political parties (authentic in the sense that it is reliable and purportedly linked to an pre-Columbian indigenous past).

In what follows we outline the political system of Tlacotepec and its relation to the changing legal structure of the state of Oaxaca which has enabled the usos y costumbres of the town to become a very flexible mechanism due to the constant amendments in rules. We argue that the rhetoric employed to legitimize usos y costumbres in Tlacotepec has moved away from an ethnic discourse and has increasingly adopted many of the procedures and concepts of the political party system (i.e. voting rights, campaigning, ballot boxes, etc.). We then present a history of the FIOB in the community, as this migrant-founded group is a main element in the local politics of Tlacotepec. Our contention is that, although not officially a political party, this migrant-founded group has acted within the institutionalized political structure by a strategy of alliance with one of Mexico's formally registered parties. We finally review the recent post-electoral conflicts that have afflicted the town of San Miguel Tlacotepec. The line of reasoning we follow is that the usos y costumbres system has become very flexible since its legal recognition in the political constitution of the state of Oaxaca in 1995, which has left towns like Tlacotepec with a mechanism of election open to interpretation and thus prone to be manipulated by incumbent authorities. The resulting disputes have led the political actors of this usos y costumbres town to lean toward the most stable form of legitimacy of power accessible to them: the discourse and practices of the political party system of non-indigenous Mexico.

---

3 Usos y costumbres is a contested term, both in the academic literature and in political debate (Bartra, 1997, 1999; Viqueira 2001, Hernández-Díaz, 2007; Hernández-Díaz y Juan Martínez, 2007). It broadly refers to the different forms of social-political organization present in indigenous communities in Mexico (specifically Guerrero, Oaxaca, and Chiapas). Citizenship in indigenous usos y costumbres communities in Oaxaca is also a much debated topic since it is commonly held only by male heads-of-household or those 18 or older born in the town (Hernández-Díaz, 2007, 2010; Hernández-Díaz y Juan Martínez, 2007).

GOVERNANCE IN SAN MIGUEL TLACOTEPEC

The county of San Miguel Tlacotepec is comprised of a *cabecera*, or county seat, located in the town of the same name; a municipal *agencia* in the town of San Martín Sabinillo; and four village *agencias de policía* in Santiago Nuxaño, Guadalupe Nucate, Xinitioco, and Yosondalla[4] A *municipio* is roughly equivalent to a county, with a hierarchical administrative structure placing the *cabecera*, which is commonly the most populated settlement, above the *agencias* and *agencias de policías*; and entitles the *cabecera* to receive and distribute the moneys received through different tax and tariff collection mechanisms and from the state and federal levels of government..

Since the 1990s, communities in Oaxaca have undergone a political reorganization in which the relationship with the state and federal governments emphasize local power, autonomy, and juridical recognition. The change for indigenous towns in Oaxaca was brought about by the decentralization of the Mexican state (Rodríguez, 1997) and the expansion of groups that promoted indigenous identity and rights (Hernández-Díaz, 2007). This context resulted in clashes between the demands of various interest groups: between political parties and NGOs, between human rights groups and indigenous rights groups, and of special interest to us in this chapter, between migrant organizations and local community interest groups (Fox and Rivera-Salgado, 2004). In San Miguel Tlacotepec this clash of interests is represented, for example, in the conflict between return migrants who wish to participate in local governance and the local political structure which gives precedence to those who have fulfilled community services or *cargos*[5] in Tlacotepec. The local system of Tlacotepec, however, has been adapted to the out-migration of the town, which has left fewer individuals in a position to successfully accomplish the cargo assigned to them (see Perry et al, 2009). This flexibility of the system is a result of the legislation and political structure of the state of Oaxaca, which employs a dual system of local governance.

Usos y costumbres, although in use since at least the colonial period, became a legally recognized form of government in Oaxaca when it was incorporated into the state constitution in 1995 (Velásquez, 2000; Anaya Muñoz, 2006;

---

4 A municipio is roughly equivalent to a county, with a hierarchical administrative structure placing the cabecera, which is commonly the most populated settlement, above the agencias and agencias de policías; and entitles the cabecera to receive and distribute the moneys received through different tax and tariff collection mechanisms and from the state and federal levels of government.

5 The word cargo in Spanish means both "position" and "obligation" or "burden", which handily describes this concept within the usos y costumbres system in which an individual is obligated to serve his community (originally without any form of remuneration) and simultaneously is acknowledged for the fulfillment of his duties and given respect or a "position" within the community. An individual is expected to comply with all the cargos the town assembly bestows upon him throughout his life; each cargo carries more responsibilities and prestige than the previous one.

Recondo 2007; Hernández-Díaz, 2007). Since then, it has formally coexisted and competed with the political party system. However, unlike the uniformity of the political party system across Mexico, usos y costumbres varies greatly from one Oaxacan town to the next. These differences range from the procedural mechanisms employed in a town, to the philosophical principles on which a system is instituted.[6] In communities like Tlacotepec, the two systems – usos y costumbres at the local level and political parties for state and federal elections – coexist, and individuals can simultaneously participate in both.

Previous research in Tlacotepec signaled ethnicity as a "unifying element for community members, shaping the substance of membership practice and underlying their claim to the right to self-govern" (Perry et al, 2009, p.209; Cornelius et al, 2009). But we argue that ethnicity has now lost its central place in the political discourses present in the town.[7] The constitution of the state of Oaxaca has legitimated the employment of usos y costumbres and extended this right to all communities which operated under this system since "time immemorial"… or at least three years prior to the reform in electoral procedures in 1995. This phrasing reinforces the notion that usos y costumbres has ties to an indigenous pre-Colombian past, and simultaneously allows communities which have recently adopted the practice to put forward an interpretation of the system to employ as local government. Among the elements that brought about the electoral reform was the significant percentage of the Oaxacan population speaking an indigenous language (36 percent according to the 2010 census[8]), which linked the defense of usos y costumbres as a form of identity preservation, the 1994 Zapatista armed uprising in Chiapas, which employed a discourse of sovereignty for indigenous communities within the Mexican state and presented the threat of spreading to other densely-populated indigenous regions of southern Mexico, and the pressure from NGO's and other groups which sought to promote the respect for, and reinforcement of, indigenous identities in the face of formal political structures.

Thus, with the official backing of the state usos y costumbres legislation, it became no longer necessary to rely on a discourse of ethnic identity to counter the larger mestizo political apparatus. Our perception it that today, when trying to legitimize procedures and practices, concepts like "traditional" or "democratic" hold more weight in the rhetoric employed in Tlacotepec than "Mixtec" or "indigenous", which have lost their previous presence. Algimiro Morales, a key figure in Tlacotepec politics explains: "the *gente de razón* (people of reason)[9]

---

6 As, for example, the systems that are developed upon the principle of the rights of the group over its members as opposed to those that promote individual rights and liberties.

7 The decrease in the use of the Mixtec language among Tlacotepenses also may be correlated with the disuse of ethnicity in the political discourse.

8 Instituto Nacional de Estadística y Geografía, Censo de Población y Vivienda 2010.

9 The colonial category of gente de razón was employed to distinguish the Spanish-descended elite among the population of San Miguel Tlacotepec, and other indigenous communities of Oaxaca.

disappeared and the Indians no longer feel Indian. (...) To be Indian is a mental state, rather than being it by blood or heritage. Whoever wants to be Indian is Indian, and whoever doesn't [want to be Indian] isn't [Indian]."

In the study of the modifications undergone by the usos y costumbres system, the town of Tlacotepec is of special interest due to the strong presence of the FIOB, a migrant organization that participates in local, state and federal politics. Originally a migrant group founded by Tlacotepenses, FIOB has had members elected to local government positions in Tlacotepec and a FIOB leader even reached a seat in the state congress. Understanding the workings of the FIOB is central to explaining the political processes at work in Tlacotepec. In the next section we outline the history of the organization. We discern that initially the FIOB was crucial in allowing migrants to channel specific demands. But today migrants who wish to participate in local politics do not present themselves as "emigrants" or migrant-organization members, instead preferring to employ a discourse of citizenship, customs, and tradition.

THE ORIGINS OF THE FIOB

Beginning in the mid-1980s, a considerable number of indigenous Mexicans entered the migration stream toward the north (Zabin, 1993; Kearny, 1996). This migration has continued, and today many Oaxacans migrate every year to the northern agricultural fields of Culiacán, Sinaloa; San Quintín, Baja California, and to the state of California in the United States. Some migrants from Oaxaca have reached the state of Oregon and others have crossed two borders to work in Canada (Kearney, 2000, Stephen, 2007).

With increasing numbers of indigenous migrants heading to northern Mexico and the United States, several organizations have been formed to defend labor, land, and cultural rights, and to promote respect for indigenous ethnic identity (Rivera-Salgado, 1999, Fox y Rivera-Salgado 2004). These organizations have based their demands on claims of membership in a distinct cultural group, using a collective identity as a strategy of mobilization and to call for institutional structures that protect and foster their sociocultural particularism. Unlike other indigenous organizations in Oaxaca, several of the groups formed by people from the Mixteca region were founded outside of the state (Velasco Ortiz, 2002a, 2002b, 2005; Rivera-Salgado, 1999)[10]. But regard-

---

10 Some of these organizations are: Indigenous Front of Binational Organizations, Frente Indígena Oaxaqueño Binacional (FIOB); Benito Juárez Civic Association, Asociación Cívica Benito Juárez (ACBJ), Coalition of Indigenous Oaxacan Organizations and Communities, Coalición de Comunidades Indígenas Oaxaqueñas (COCIO); State Coordinator of Indigenous Migrants in Baja California, Coordinadora Estatal de Indígenas Migrantes en Baja California (CEOMBJ), "Carlos Salinas de Gortari" Informal Merchants and Aggregates Union, Unión de vendedores ambulantes y anexos "Carlos Salinas de Gortari" (UVAMACS); "Benito Juárez" Merchants Union, Unión de comerciantes "Benito Juárez" (UCBJ); Community Planning Committee, Comité Comunitario de Planeación (COCOPLA), Unified Day-laborers Movement, Movimiento de Unificación de Jornaleros Independientes (MUJI) (Velasco Ortiz, 2002a; 2002b).

less of their founding place, the organizations from the Mixteca have sought to stay in touch with the problems the indigenous population of this region faces (Hernández Díaz, 1998, 2001). Today, many of these organizations are grouped within large *frentes* or bloc organizations like the Indigenous Front of Binational Organizations (FIOB), the International Network of Indigenous Oaxacans (RIIO)[11], and the New Oaxacan Alliance (NAO)[12], all of which form part of the larger Oaxacan Federation of Indigenous Communities and Organizations in California (FOCOICA)[13].

The FIOB consists of members who live primarily in the states of Oaxaca, Sinaloa, Jalisco, and Baja California in Mexico, and California in the United States. With both migrant and non-migrant members, the FIOB presents itself as a binational organization because it acts politically both in the United States and Mexico. As a binational organization, the FIOB stipulates that its priorities are to strive to improve the human and labor rights of indigenous migrants, strengthen cultural identity, and support the development of infrastructure both in their destinations as well as communities of origin (FIOB, 1995).[14]

FIOB'S ACCESS TO ELECTORAL POLITICS

In 1995, FIOB members began to discuss the possibility of participating in the electoral process. In several meetings, FIOB members analyzed their previous experience in municipal government, to which several members, both in Tlacotepec and in neighboring Tecomaxtlahuaca, had previously been elected through the system of usos y costumbres. The FIOB decided to take part as a group in federal and state elections through a policy of alliances with existing political parties. According to FIOB leader Arturo Pimentel, from the beginning it was proposed that ties with other groups would be accepted as long as the independence of the organization was not jeopardized. In 1997, the FIOB publication *El Tequio* stated the group's position: "indigenous organizations like the FIOB have to adopt a determined position, for this is of vital importance to advance the democratic transformation of the country" (*El Tequio*, 1997)[15].

---

11 Red Internacional de Indígenas Oaxacans (RIIO)

12 Nueva Alianza Oaxaqueña (NAO)

13 Federación Oaxaqueña de Comunidades y Organizaciones Indígenas en California (FOCOICA)

14 Further details on the FIOB's history and work can be found in Rivera Salgado (1997), Hernández-Díaz (2000, 2000b), Ramírez Romero (2000), and Velasco Ortiz, (2002, 2005).

15 The FIOB analyzed its involvement in electoral politics taking into consideration that "political participation serves to consolidate the political and organizational project of the FIOB"; "to consolidate the defense and acknowledgement of indigenous rights...possible electoral alliances must be with political forces committed to the democratic struggle of the country"; and "political alliances must be made with very clear compromises" (El Tequio, 1997).

This type of alliance proved promising early on. In a 1995 election, FIOB support gave the Democratic Revolution Party (PRD),[16] which ran two candidates of Mixtec origin, the highest number of votes the party had ever received in the San Quintín Valley of Baja California. Although the party did not win any seats in that election, the experience was encouraging enough for both the PRD and the FIOB to continue their alliance.

In the 1998 state congressional election the FIOB attained its first electoral triumph in Oaxaca. An alliance between the FIOB and PRD led FIOB member Juan Romualdo Gutiérrez, originally from San Miguel Tlacotepec, to be elected as a state representative from district XXI, representing the region around the city of Juxtlahuaca[17]. The FIOB had achieved its goal of maintaining autonomy while also "seek[ing] political-electoral alliances with the group with the most political strength,"[18] according to then-newly elected Representative Gutiérrez. The FIOB-PRD coalition propelled Gutiérrez to victory, winning with 8,069 votes versus the PRI's 8,029 votes. This was the first time the PRD had won an election in this district, a feat FIOB members argued was due to the votes of its affiliates.

In the 2001 elections the FIOB again sought to put forth its own candidate, but the group's efforts were marred by internal fighting. A rupture emerged in the FIOB leadership between then-congressman Juan Romualdo Gutiérrez and FIOB head Arturo Pimentel, who refused to resign his position within the FIOB as members of the leadership asked him to do in order to back his candidacy for congress[19]. This impasse led a portion of the FIOB leadership to abandon Pimentel's campaign, which weakened his candidacy and left it unable to defeat the PRI. The 2001 election also saw the rise of another important political group in the region, the Unified Movement of Triqui Struggle (MULT)[20]. The MULT called on its members to abstain from voting, leading to an abstention rate of 69% in the 2001 elections, considerably higher than the

---

16 The Partido de la Revolución Democrática PRD was formed in 1989 by a group that splintered off the Institutional Revolutionary Party, Partido Revolucionario Institucional (PRI), which had governed Mexico since 1929 and had effectively consolidated a corporate centralized structure with which it ruled the country. The PRD leans toward the left of the political spectrum and commonly creates alliances with social organization for electoral purposes.

17 The electoral districts are administrative divisions that serve the purpose of ordering state and federal electoral processes in Mexico.

18 "... buscar una alianza político electoral con la fuerza política en dónde la gente estuviera mayoritariamente". (Juan Romualdo Gutiérrez, Interviewed December 14, 2007)

19 In the first internal process of 1998 Arturo Pimentel, the FIOB head, was also a candidate. Pimentel states that Juan Romualdo Gutiérrez initially "didn't even want to participate, at that time I [Pimentel] had the possibility and opportunity to be a candidate both for federal and local congress". (Interviewed December 15, 2007)

20 The Movimiento Unificado de Lucha Triqui (MULT) was born in 1981 as a political group that resisted the PRI bosses. At the beginning it quickly won support among the Triqui people. Since then, the MULT and PRI have been fighting for political control of Triqui communities, resulting in a bloody conflict and several hundred deaths. Currently the MULT is associated with the Popular Unity Party, a local political party that claims to be the only and first indigenous political party in Mexico.

60% rate in the elections held three years before, and particularly crucial. The 1998 election was won by a difference of only 40 votes.

The 2001 election left FIOB split between those who supported Arturo Pimentel and those who supported Juan Romualdo Gutiérrez, whose faction came to be headed by California-based Rufino Domínguez. Arturo Pimental left the FIOB and founded a new organization, the National Front of Indigenous and Peasants[21] (FNIC). Thus fractured, the FIOB has lost its electoral might. The only time the FIOB has been able to defeat the PRI was in 1998, when the group stood together and worked alongside the PRD, which was willing to put a FIOB-backed candidate on the ballot. This leads us to believe that a specific sociopolitical environment led to the PRD's success in the election of 1998, one that was probably leading up to the national context of 2000, when an opposition party (the National Action Party or PAN[22]) defeated the PRI for the first time in a presidential election.

THE FIOB AND LOCAL POLITICS IN TLACOTEPEC

The participation of migrants in local elections in Tlacotepec dates back to the early 1990s, when a group of residents in the *cabecera* who were also members of the FIOB protested against the administration of the municipal president and ousted him from office through a general assembly[23]. Encouraged by this triumph, the group mobilized to promote its own candidates and break the control that the PRI had long held in Tlacotepec. Although the PRI fought back, it was unable to contain the strength of this new group of FIOB members. A general community assembly held on November 12, 1995 saw Tlacotepenses vote FIOB members into municipal government, defeating the PRI candidates. On January 1, 1996 the first non-PRI municipal government in San Miguel Tlacotepec came into office, headed by Abel Carrasco Martínez. Fresh off its victory, the FIOB also formed an official municipal committee in San Miguel Tlacotepec in 1996.[24] The organization grew its ranks by incorporating Tlacotepenses who had not previously been politically engaged, including many women.

---

21 Frente Nacional Indígena y Campesino (FNIC).

22 Partido Acción Nacional (PAN)

23 Through the initiative of a group of youths, a general assembly protested against municipal president Aurio Reyes Salvador. The protest that brought about this recall was carried out on the basis that it was considered anomalous that the elected authorities included the president's father and his son-in-law.

24 In the Mixtec region, the FIOB organized through municipal committees that were formed in several localities of the municipalities of the districts of Tlaxiaco, Juxtlahuaca, and Huajuapam. Their main activity was the search for productive projects and economic support for its membership, in which the women played a crucial role. Later, they spread their activities to seek the legalization of vehicles that were brought from the United States without an import permit, and to obtain public transportation concessions.

During its time in office, the Carrasco administration maintained close ties with the FIOB leadership. Because both he and FIOB leaders Arcángel Pimentel, Juan Romualdo Gutiérrez, and Arturo Pimentel had been teachers and also had ties of *compadrazgo* (fictive kinship), they were closely connected. During this three-year period, the lines between the FIOB and the local government blurred. FIOB leaders were able to modify the dynamic of local politics of Tlacotepec. The organization's discourse initially coincided with that of the local section of the teachers' union,[25] which emphasized social struggle and concern about socially-vulnerable groups. With this focus, the FIOB presented itself as an opposition force to the PRI, which represented the power of the state. But as the FIOB became more ingrained in the local political scene, its leaders were involved as central political actors in fights over elections, resources, and power.

The following election brought about a quarrel over voting procedures. This conflict focused on three aspects of the electoral process: the voting mechanism and eligibility requirements for both candidates and voters. While the FIOB sought to make changes in these areas, PRI supporters argued that this violated local norms. The PRI group argued that the usos y costumbres system in Tlacotepec required ballots to be hand-delivered to the homes of all citizens on the day of voting and declared eligible for office all residents of the municipal agencies as well as the cabecera who had held previous posts. In contrast, the FIOB group sought to carry out elections in a community assembly (and not by the ballot system previously used), to limit voting to inhabitants of the cabecera – not other agencies – and to make any individual living in the cabecera eligible to hold office, no matter whether they had held previous positions or *cargos*. In the traditional model of the usos y costumbres system, or *cargo* system as it is identified in the anthropological literature, eligibility of an individual to a position within the hierarchical structure of the municipal government relies on the performance of that individual in previous positions. Thus, only those who have served (and perceived by the population to have served well) can climb the rungs of the ladder that is local government.[26]

Despite resistance, the FIOB group managed to carry out an election in a community assembly in 1998 in which Ramiro Léon, a young migrant who had recently returned to Tlacotepec, was voted municipal president. For FIOB supporters, this was a great success, given that León won 158 votes of the approximately 200 people in attendance. PRI supporters quickly challenged the result. The PRI membership, hoping to annul the election, abandoned the

---

25 National Union of Workers at the Service of Education (Sindicato Nacional de Trabajadores al Servicio de la Educación, SNTE). In Tlacotepec the first FIOB promoters were teachers of the SNTE.

26 The entry-level position is commonly referred to as the topil (which was cut in Tlacotepec due to the strain produced by out-migration, see Perry et al, 2009). Reaching the age of 18 or becoming the head of a family (normally signaled by becoming a parent) is sufficient to qualify for government service.

assembly when they realized they were the minority. The PRI filed a petition with the state electoral authorities claiming that the election had not been carried out according to the usos y costumbres of the community. The case reached the State Electoral Institute (IEE)[27], which attempted, but ultimately failed, to find a negotiated settlement. In a special session on December 26, 1998, the General Council of the IEE declared that the elections could not be validated due to several irregularities:

> Regarding the municipality of San Miguel Tlacotepec, although it is true that there is a report of the community assembly which notes the participation of 331 citizens and which is signed by the municipal authority and the attending citizens, ... citizens of the same *cabecera*, of the *agencias* of Guadalupe Nucate, San Martín Sabinillo, Santiago Nuxaño and Xinitioco ... argue that the election was not carried out according to usos y costumbres given that not all citizens of the municipality attended, and that the ballots were not handed out in a timely fashion for the citizens of the community to write the names of the proposed candidates to function as municipal authorities, and the urns were not installed to deposit the ballots previously mentioned. The election was carried out through a single candidate list and in the assembly, Mr. Arturo Pimentel, leader of the FIOB, presented himself as an envoy of the State Electoral Institute of Oaxaca. Given this, there is a violation of article 109 paragraphs 3 and 4, as the common law electoral procedure was not respected, a procedure employed to publicly nominate and elect authorities, based on the internal norms in force within the municipality (TEPJF, 2002: 5)[28].

The conflict was finally resolved through political means. The case was turned over to the state congress where local congressman Juan Romualdo Gutiérrez influenced the final decision in favor of the FIOB group. Ramiro León Herrera formally and legally took office as municipal president in February of 1999, putting the municipal government entirely in the hands of the FIOB. The elected municipal president at the time was also president of the municipal committee of the FIOB, and with seven other FIOB members, he took office for a term intended to last until 2002.

However León Herrera was only active one year. The opposition quickly tagged León as inexperienced and unaware of the political reality of the community. As Yolanda Maldonado, current head of the PRI in Tlacotepec, explained, "What I said at the IEE was that Ramiro didn't have any experience, and was going to fail because the young man had been living in the United

---

27 Instituto Estatal Electoral (IEE)
28 Tribunal Electoral del Poder Judicial de la Federación, Electoral Court of Federation's Judicial System, 2002.

States for ten years, and he was going to fail because he didn't even know the usos y costumbres of the town."

As the PRI supporters predicted, León Herrera got off to a difficult start, and the PRI used this to cause a schism within the FIOB. León Herrera was reprimanded for mishandling government funds and behavior unbecoming of a municipal president, as is explained by FIOB leader Arturo Pimentel:

> The problem unleashed a struggle here with the PRI. Ramiro made a mess with the money, and Aquiles Morales was involved; he is from Teotitlán and was a delegate of the PRI government, they ... began to manipulate [Ramiro]. We reprimanded him, but he did not understand. This was when the organization [FIOB] had to face the people; we had to decide whether to face facts or cover up; we decided not to cover up and we began questioning him.

Facing this reprimand, Pimental explains that León was coopted by the PRI, going so far as to openly declare himself a PRI adherent. According to PRI group members, it was Arturo Pimentel himself, leader of the FIOB, who forced León Herrera out, a version of events confirmed by FIOB leader Juan Romualdo Gutiérrez:

> I don't know whether it's true or not, but it is said that [Arturo Pimentel] was asking Ramiro León for a monthly stipend, which Ramiro refused to give him. Arturo then organized the older people and pitted them against Ramiro, who was then replaced by the municipal council led by Alberto Martínez Hernández, a man who can neither read nor write, but who went along with Arturo's interests. We had a very good beginning with Ramiro León Herrera. I obtained resources for him to be able to build infrastructure. I was in congress then. But with this friction, the council decided to support Arturo.

The PRI group, headed by Yolanda Maldonado, backed Ramiro León, who was accused by the FIOB of betrayal and corruption. The PRI bloc argued that it did not defend Ramiro León's actions, but that the manner in which he was removed from office was illegal. Despite the PRI's backing, León was ousted in an assembly organized by the FIOB. Paradoxically, it was now the PRI group which sought to defend León's position as legitimate before state electoral authorities, accusing the FIOB of violating local political rules. In this upheaval, Ramiro León quit the FIOB and requested his acceptance into the PRI. Again, the state congress resolved in favor of the FIOB and León was replaced by another returned migrant.

These different conflicts and upheavals provoked changes, since it became apparent that the local political system of Tlacotepec was not functioning adequately, that is, compromises were not being reached and external actors (like the IEE) had to intervene. Because of the imprecise wording in the constitution that legalized usos y costumbres, the town of Tlacotepec has been able to adapt the system to different circumstances. This led to modifications of the system, most notably the acceptance of the right of women to attend community assemblies and vote for local authorities. As FIOB leader Hilda Hernández puts it, before this time:

> The ballots were handed out to elect authorities and each one wrote down [the name of] their candidates, and we didn't even set foot [in the town hall], but now women participate and everybody [at community assemblies] gets to see the person we elect to town government.

Our perception is that it has recently been women's groups who have been more organized and therefore are able make collective decisions in an assembly. This was the context in which elections took place in 2001. The people of Tlacotepec reacted to the problems that the PRI-FIOB conflict brought about by voting in individuals with no political affiliation. However, in part due to their lack of political ties and experience, the 2001-2003 administration did little to capture resources and build infrastructure, ultimately leaving office with few accomplishments.

In the 2003 election, the FIOB put forth as its candidate Juan Romualdo Gutiérrez, who had previously served in the state congress. With the political experience and the ties created throughout his time in congress, Juan Romualdo Gutiérrez won the popular vote and served during the 2004-2007 period. Juan Romualdo argues that resources for infrastructure were obtained and financial reports were given every three months during his administration. Additionally, he is said to have attended the *mayordomías*, headed the religious processions, summoned the senior *principales* and, in general, covered the forms regarded as usos y costumbres. Juan Romualdo's stance of rigorously observing the procedures of usos y costumbres while delivering quarterly reports and such indicates an attempt at balancing "traditional" politics and institutionalized party politics.

However, the PRI, and especially the women within the group, had reorganized. Had it not been for the campaigning and political maneuvers of Gutiérrez, the PRI would probably have won full control of the municipal government. The 2007 election once again saw a debate about the rules for elections, something unheard of prior to the events described in this chapter. In an assembly leading up to the elections of 2007, a check-list was posted laying out the eligibility requirements for candidates for local government.[29] The day of

---

29 See Perry et al, 2009. 1. Do not vote for who has already served as municipal president. 2. Do not vote for anyone who is in the current municipal council, the committee of communal resources, or the police force. 3. Do not vote for anyone who does not live in the town. 4. Vote for someone who has served the community. 5. Vote for someone who has satisfactorily fulfilled his cargos. 6. You may vote for women who meet the previously listed requirements.

the election one of the favorites to win was Orlando Molina Maldonado, son of Tlacotepec PRI leader Yolanda Maldonado. Although Molina Maldonado won a majority of the votes, a review by the assembly led some to question his eligibility to hold office. Molina Maldonado had a birth certificate from another town and was questioned about not having held any previous cargo. He claimed to have lived in Tlacotepec for several years and had financed a dance group and dressed as a *chilolo* for the dances involved in the town's annual festivities. These arguments for his eligibility were not considered valid by many within the assembly and Molina Maldonado decided to accept the *regiduría de salud* (health office) to avoid problems. A second appeal also marked this election, as those in the municipal *agencias* sought the right to participate in the election of authorities. Among those in the 2007 electoral assembly was a group of *agencia* residents led by Ángel Morales, who in the following election of 2010 would play an important role (see the following section).

During the last 20 years, San Miguel Tlacotepec has seen the development of two groups with well-defined political positions, often ideological opposed to each other. Before this rivalry, the municipality operated under the same model as other usos y costumbres municipalities of Oaxaca. The PRI, which monopolized political power, selected candidates, either through an imposition of the party will or through negotiations with locals, and elected them through the usos y costumbres system. The changes in Tlacotepec are typical of changes throughout the state of Oaxaca (brought on, among other things, by the emergence of indigenous rights groups, decentralization of power, and legal codification of the usos y costumbres system). The specific trends present in Tlacotepec have been a result of the establishment of interest groups within the town that, although they may have external connections (whether it be women with the PRI national structure or migrants with the bi-national FIOB), ultimately respond to the practices and discourses of local interaction.

ELECTION DAY(S)

On November 21, 2010, the municipal election took place in San Miguel Tlacotepec. Arcángel Carlos Pimentel Ocampo came out on top with 203 votes and, thus, was understood to have been elected municipal president. However, five days later, a complaint was brought before the State Electoral Institute, which consisted of five allegations:

- The electoral committee was comprised almost exclusively of family members and supporters of those elected.
- The eligibility requirements were interpreted in an absurd and self-serving manner.
- The votes were not counted correctly, with more votes counted than ballots distributed.
- The election booths remained open two hours beyond the scheduled closing time.

- Many citizens were prevented from voting because the electoral committee claimed not to know them or decided that they had not fulfilled services to the community (TEPJF, 2011)[30]

A second election was ordered by the federal court to be held on December 19, 2011, and this time José Legaria Niño won the office of municipal president. A second complaint was filed on grounds similar to those against the first election. The people of Tlacotepec did not reach an agreement until June 2011.[31] The case ultimately reached the federal government's Regional Court of the Electoral Tribunal, which ordered a third election, to be overseen by the State Electoral Institute of Oaxaca.

On the morning of June 12, 2011, the special election was held in San Miguel Tlacotepec. Heavily guarded by state police with assault rifles, the central plaza of Tlacotepec began to fill with people by 8:00 am. The four ballot boxes for the *cabecera* with the label *Gobernador* began to be set up, next to booths that would allow citizens to submit their vote in secret. Ballots with two options were handed out; on the "green" ticket was José Legaria Niño and on the "red" ticket Arcángel Pimentel. Legaria Niño won with 669 votes to 441 for Pimentel. The contest was close in the municipal *cabecera*, where Legaria Niño prevailed by only 42 votes. The votes from inhabitants of the *agencias* were decisive in providing Niño with the victory, with Sabinillo and Nuxaño combined giving 236 votes to Legaria and only 50 to Pimentel. The votes of the *agencias*, which had been neglected in previous elections, have now become crucial in deciding the local administration of San Miguel Tlacotepec.

A week later, on June 24, 2011, the General Council of the IEE validated the election results, determining that the election "was done by a democratic method, satisfying the principle of universal suffrage in its diverse variants. Likewise, the incorporation of municipal *agencias* into the election was promoted in a real and material manner" (IEEPCO, 2011)[32]. Thus, this "usos y costumbres" election (which was carried out in an indistinguishable fashion from the party system) was deemed valid and accepted by state institutions.

A couple of days after the election, the group led by Arcángel Pimentel filed yet another complaint based on irregularities observed before and during the electoral process, such as the presence of "pressure" groups[33] on election

---

30 Tribunal Electoral del Poder Judicial de la Federación, Electoral Court of Federation's Judicial System, Files SX-JDC-42/2011 and SX-JDC-43/2011.

31 The survey research done in January 2011 for this edition of the MMFRP was carried out in a town without an official government and where two different groups claimed legitimacy to their government positions.

32 Acuerdo CG-RDC-005-2011, Consejo General del IEEPCO, June 24, 2011.

33 For example, groups of people from the agencias sat around the public plaza in front of the municipal building where the voting took place to indicate to others (especially elderly people and those who cannot read) how to vote for Legaria Niño. At some point during the election one of the observers (who were allowed by the State Electoral Institute to observe the election) attempted to take a photograph of one of the groups which immediately became aware and dispersed while commanding the photographer to stop taking pictures.

day, the claim that some of those who voted were not on the official electoral list, and a smear campaign against Pimentel. As of the time of writing there was no response to this complaint and the election was still considered valid by the state electoral authorities. Although the post-electoral struggle is as yet unresolved, even if both groups come to an agreement, the arrangement will likely only be temporary, and the conflict will remain latent within the community.

The significance of the use of political party electoral paraphernalia used in this election reflects our argument that the usos y costumbres system has become so flexible that it can even allow for the same procedures that the political party system implements. The boxes with the label *Gobernador* were obviously the ones employed in the 2010 election for governor of the state of Oaxaca where Gabino Cué, a candidate promoted by a coalition of parties, won against the PRI's candidate, marking the first time in the history of Oaxaca that the PRI did not win the governor's seat. Thus, usos y costumbres has become a chameleonic procedure which can even disguise itself as a political parties system in which *"Tu voto es libre y secreto"* (Your vote is free and secret) is the motto promoted by the federal and state electoral institutes.

The discourse among the various groups in Tlacotepec has now centered on adherence to legal standards and tradition, largely displacing discourses of Mixtec and/or migrant identity. No one, for example, mentioned the fact that at least one member of the new municipal administration is a returned migrant, either to challenge their right to hold office (under previous set of rules, returned migrants were ineligible to do so) or to garner support among the population in Tlacotepec (where everyone knows or is related to a migrant). Rather, the "legality" (based on the political party standards decreed by the State Electoral Institute) by which the different interest groups operated is appealed to as a way to legitimize their positions. This new way to legitimize claims is undoubtedly a response to an ever-changing political context. The convergence of national and state discourses with local interests and struggles illuminate the processes currently present in this community.

CONCLUSION

The case of San Miguel Tlacotepec is exemplary of the ways migrant organizations can interact with local and regional political dynamics. Even though it remains early to make conclusions, we can make some observations that may shed light on general tendencies and point towards future research.

First, the FIOB has carried out, both regionally and locally, the characteristic role of a political party without being rhetorically or legally recognized as such. Thus, even though there is an explicit alliance with the PRD, FIOB members claim their group is politically plural and that, in the words of Juan Romualdo Gutiérrez, within the organization "communities and individuals with different political preferences converge." FIOB's current alliance with the

PRD is strategic, functioning as a means to obtain representation in the state's legislative structure, without fully integrating into a political party structure or adopting its platform. More than an alliance, the FIOB-PRD tie serves as an arrangement in which the political party lends its name and legal registry to an organization that would otherwise be ineligible to compete in elections. The FIOB-PRD arrangement is one of electoral franchise. This arrangement has benefited both groups, with the PRD defeating a PRI candidate in a district where the PRI had never lost, and the FIOB having a voice in congress to promote the rights of indigenous migrants and other interests of the group.

Considering the high percentage of Mixtec migrants and the history of political participation in this region of Oaxaca, it is evident that PRD "candidates" have won precisely because they are members of and backed by the FIOB. That is to say, the Mixtec vote in the Juxtlahuaca region is more in support of the FIOB and less in support of the PRD. This phenomenon is explained by Juan Romualdo Gutiérrez in a 2000 interview:

> ...as indigenous peoples and communities we made an analysis of which party could harbor the aspirations of the organizations and of a candidate that came from [these organizations gathered within the FIOB]... It was the communities that made the decision, but because of the handicap we have [of not being constituted as a political party, and thus not being legally eligible for election], we had to ask the PRD to support us with the registration [of our candidate]. There was no problem, they had their own candidate and I had to run in a primary election, and once I won I was able to run in the election [for state congress].

This FIOB-PRD arrangement is not permanent because the parties' interests at some junctures may differ or even become opposite of those of the organization. As an organization which presents itself as a plural and tolerant and defends a wide variety of principles, the FIOB warns of other attitudes the party may adopt. Again, Juan Romualdo Gutiérrez explains:

> ...as a plural and autonomous organization we are not married to any political party, so that if the PRD implements *cacique* practices, hierarchical decision-making, elitist decisions, imposing candidates, that are not in agreement with our organization and which do not have the support of the communities, we will not share these mechanisms. Not only with the PRD, we would not share these practices with any party. So, what are we interested in? In a political process that is open to society, which considers the opinion of the citizens through participation. If at any point the PRD closes itself off to these mechanisms, at that time the PRD would not be an alternative anymore and we would analyze [the possibility of an alliance with]

the party that would give these opportunities to the indigenous communities.

For FIOB members, no political party can authentically represent the interest of the indigenous population. As a result, according to Gutiérrez, "our greatest aspiration is to promote the autonomous capacities in communities to [be able to] to end the paternalism created by the powerful." To achieve this goal, this organization seeks to strengthen of the usos y costumbres system in Oaxaca in order to weaken the power of political parties within indigenous communities.

The rhetoric employed in these arguments coincides with that of other indigenous organizations which have at some point also sought to defend their group rights presenting themselves as unique cultural groups within the predominantly mestizo Mexican state. But with the FIOB, the elements invoked in this political discourse targeted at claiming rights through group identification (language, ethnicity, and, in the case of the FIOB, labor and migrant conditions) have lost much of their appeal among the population in Tlacotepec. We attribute this loss to the years of poor treatment by political actors and the negativity this engendered in Tlacotepenses (recall Juana's remark at the beginning of this text: "I don't belong to any of those political parties!"). While the rhetoric of indigenous identity may still be an important tool in molding the perceptions of outsiders, within Tlacotepec we find a decrease in adherence to Mixtec identity as an organizing tool.

The discourse of usos y costumbres serves as a linkage to a perceived "traditional" way of organizing a community. However, the practices of actual political organization are not necessarily in tune with the common law forms of social organization commonly identified as usos y costumbres, as seen in the mechanisms employed by political parties in June 2011 elections in San Miguel Tlacotepec. Although, for now, migrant and/or indigenous organizations that wish to participate in elections can only do so through alliances with legally constituted parties, these groups have increasingly inserted themselves in the political party system of mestizo Mexico. In Tlacotepec, they have essentially replicated the party system at the local level in a usos y costumbres town. We will undoubtedly continue to observe new forms of discourse, strategies of organization, and hybridization of political practices by migrants and non-migrants, *indios* and *mestizos*, as they articulate their claims in a struggle for labor, political, and cultural rights and resources.

WORKS CITED

Anaya Muñoz, Alejandro. 2006. *Autonomía indígena, Gobernabilidad y Legitimidad en México. La Legaliz ación de usos y costumbres electorales en Oaxaca. México:* Universidad Iberoamericana y Plaza y Valdés.

Bartra, Roger. 1997. "Violencias Indígenas," *La Jornada Semanal.* 31 de Agosto de 1997.

Bartra, Roger. 1999. *La sangre y la tinta. Ensayos sobre la condición postmexicana.* Océano. México.

Cornelius, Wayne, David Fitzgerald, Jorge Hernández-Díaz, and Scott Borger, eds. 2009. *Migration from Mexican Mixteca. A Transnational Community in Oaxaca and California.* La Jolla, CA: Center for Comparative Immigration Studies, University of California, San Diego.

Durand Ponte, Victor Manuel. 2007. "Prólogo." In *Ciudadanías diferenciadas en un estado multicultural: los usos y costumbres en Oaxaca,* ed. Jorge Hernández-Díaz. México: Siglo Veintiuno – Universidad Autónoma Benito Juárez de Oaxaca.

Fox, Jonathan y Gaspar Rivera Salgado, eds. 2004. *Indigenous Mexican Migrants in the United States.* La Jolla, California: Center for U.S.-Mexican Studies and Center for Comparative Immigration Studies, University of California, San Diego.

Hernández-Díaz, Jorge, ed. 2007. *Ciudadanías diferenciadas en un estado multicultural: los usos y costumbres en Oaxaca.* México: Siglo XXI Editores/ UABJO.

Hernández-Díaz, Jorge y Víctor Leonel Juan Martínez. 2007. *Dilemas de la institución municipal. Una incursión en la experiencia oaxaqueña.* México: Miguel Ángel Porrúa/UABJO.

Hernández-Díaz, Jorge. 2010. *Ciudadanías en conflicto. Política del reconocimiento, expresiones y discursos en una zona urbana.* México: UABJO/Plaza y Valdés.

Instituto Estatal Electoral y de Participación Ciudadana de Oaxaca. 2011. *Acuerdo Cg-Rdc-005-2011. Por el que se Califica la Elección Extraordinaria a Concejales del Municipio de San Miguel Tlacotepec, Oaxaca, Celebrada Bajo el Régimen de Derecho Consuetudinario el Día Doce de Junio de Dos Mil Once.* June 27, 2011. http://www.ieeoax.org.mx/acuerdos/2011/AcdoSanMiguelTlacotepec%2021jun2011.pdf.

Instituto Nacional de Estadística y Geografía, Censo de Población y Vivienda 2010.

Juan Martínez, Victor Leonel. 2011. "Viejos y nuevos conflictos municipales". In *En Marcha, Realidad Municipal de Oaxaca* no. 133.

Kearney, Michael. 2000. "La comunidad rural oaxaqueña y la migración: más allá de las políticas agraria e indígena," *Cuadernos Agrarios* no. 19-20: 11-23, enero-junio 2000. México.

Kearny, Michael. 1996. "La migración y la formación de regiones autónomas pluriétnicas en Oaxaca." En: *Coloquio sobre Derechos Indígenas.* Oaxaca, México: Instituto Oaxaqueño de las Culturas.

Perry, Elizabeth et al. 2009. "Between here and there: Ethnicity, Civic Participation, and Migration in San Miguel Tlacotepec." In *Migration from the Mexican Mixteca: A Transnational Community in Oaxaca and California,* Wayne A Cornelius et al. La Jolla, CA: Center for Comparative Immigration Studies, University of California, San Diego.

Recondo, David. 2007. *La política del Gatopardo. Multiculturalismo y democracia en Oaxaca.* México: CIESAS-CEMCA.

Rivera-Salgado, Gaspar. 1999. "Mixtecactivism in Oaxacaliformia." En *American Behavioral Scientist,* N° 42. Thousand Oaks, CA: SAGE.

Rodríguez, Victoria E. 1997. *Decentralization in Mexico: From Reforma Municipal to Solidaridad to Nuevo Federalismo.* Boulder, CO: Westview Press.

Stephen, Lynn. 2007. *Transborder Lives: Indigenous Oaxacans in Mexico, California and Oregon.* Durham: Duke University Press.

Tribunal Electoral del Poder Judicial de la Federación. 2011. *Juicios para la Protección de los Derechos Político-Electorales del Ciudadano: SX-JDC-42/2011 y SX-JDC-43/2011. Actores: Ricardo Morelia León y otros. Autoridad Responsable: Tribunal Estatal Electoral de Oaxaca. Tercero interesado: Arcángel Carlos Pimentel Ocampo.* June 27, 2011. http://200.23.107.66/siscon/gateway.dll?f=templates&fn=default.htm

Tribunal Electoral del Poder Judicial de la Federación. 2002. *Elección de Concejales al Ayuntamiento del Municipio de Asunción Tlacolulita, Estado de Oaxaca, por Usos y Costumbres,* in Colección de Sentencias Relevantes, núm. 4.

Velasco Ortiz, Laura. 2005. *Desde que tengo memoria. Narrativas de identidad en indígenas migrantes.* El Colegio de la Frontera Norte – Consejo Nacional para la Cultura y las Artes, CONACULTA, México.

Velasco Ortiz, Laura. 2002a. *El regreso de la comunidad: migración indígena y agentes étnicos. Los mixtecos en la frontera México-Estados Unidos,* México, El Colegio de México/El Colegio de la Frontera Norte.

Velasco Ortiz, Laura. 2002b. "Agentes étnicos, transnacionales: las organizaciones de indígenas migrantes en la frontera México-Estados Unidos." In *Estudios Sociológicos,* mayo-agosto, año/vol. XX, número 002: pp. 335-369

Velásquez, María Cristina. 2000. *El Nombramiento. Elecciones por usos y costumbres en Oaxaca.* Oaxaca, México: Instituto Estatal Electoral.

Viqueira, Juan Pedro. 2001. "Los usos y las costumbres en contra de la autonomía." In *Letras Libres.* Marzo de 2001.

Zabin, Carol (coordinadora). 1992. *Migración Oaxaqueña a los Campos Agrícolas de California. Un Diálogo.* La Jolla, California: Center for U.S.-Mexican Studies, University of California, San Diego.

5 Discount Transnationalism: Recession and the Transformation of Cross-Border Ties

ABIGAIL ANDREWS, BRENDA NICOLÁS, LUCIA GOIN, AND MELISSA TALIA
KARAKASH

Indigenous Oaxacan migrants like the people of San Miguel Tlacotepec, a rural
Mixtec community with a more than 30-year history of migration to the United
States, are well-known in politics and academic research for their high levels of
"binationalism," or economic, social, and political engagement with their home
villages (Fox & Rivera Salgado 2004; Stephen 2007). Yet, the "Great Recession"
of 2007-2010 ate away at the economic foundations of this cross-border activity.
From 2007 to 2009, the unemployment rate in the United States rose from 4.7%
to 9.4%, and that in Mexico from 3.5% to 5.4%. Per capita GDP fell 5.6% in
the United States and 6.1% in Mexico.[1] Mexican immigrant communities like
Tlacotepec, many of whose members work in heavily impacted sectors like
construction and manufacturing, were some of the hardest hit (Alarcón et al
2008; Kochhar 2009). As Araceli Chavez, a mother of four who came to the
United States in 1993, described, "How I suffered with the recession! I lost my
job, I lost my house – no, now we're all crammed into this tiny place. It was
hard." Likewise, long-time migrant Roberto Ortiz, who works as a painter, told
us that where before the recession he had logged 60 or 70-hour weeks, he now
struggled to find a few hours of work a day. This hardly yielded enough to
make rent in the United States, let alone send money home.

In this paper, we examine how the economic downturn changed the ways
migrants from San Miguel Tlacotepec and their relatives back home form and
maintain cross-border economic ties, communication, and political and civic
engagement. We argue that while Tlacotepenses sought to continue participating in transnational activities to the greatest extent possible, the recession
placed new constraints on their ability to fund and spend time on such pur-
suits. Our research is based on two community-wide surveys that the Mexican
Migration Field Research Project conducted of Tlacotepenses in the United
States and the hometown, representing more than 850 people each, in 2007
and 2011. Along with more than 40 in-depth interviews, these surveys provide
an ideal foundation for a quasi-longitudinal comparison, illuminating how

---

1 OECD, http://stats.oecd.org/Index.aspx?DataSetCode=SNA_TABLE1 and http://www.
oecd-ilibrary.org/employment/unemployment-rate_20752342-table1

recession affected the nature and volume of cross-border remittances, communication, and politics.

The recession had differential effects in different sectors of transnational activity. While economic flows dropped off, cross-border communication grew. As expected, we found that Tlacotepenses sent fewer remittances, and some stopped sending money altogether. However, migrants maintained enduring attachments to family members across the border, and they refused to drop transnational activity altogether. Rather, in what we call "discount transnationalism," migrants and their families found cheaper ways to remain engaged. While many were unable to afford to return home for visits, increasingly cheaper phone calls and emails enabled them to maintain communication. Likewise, even though Tlacotepenses decreased their economic contributions to political groups and the annual town fiesta, they continued to attend meetings and parties in the United States oriented around hometown themes, thus staying involved with their community in ways that did not require financial costs. Although townspeople contributed less money to political and cultural activities, they continued to attend, showing the strength of members' personal transnational ties and sense of identification with the home community.

TRANSNATIONALISM

In the last two decades, scholarly discussion of immigrant transnationalism has exploded (*e.g.,* Kearney 1991; Levitt 2001; Vertovec 2009). Basch, Glick Schiller and Szanton Blanc (1994, 7) define transnationalism as "the processes by which immigrants forge and sustain multi-stranded social relations that link together their societies of origin and settlement." Scholars have shown that migrants send money, communicate, and exchange ideas across international borders, which helps them maintain long distance social and political ties (Portes 2003). However, debate has often focused on whether or not such a phenomenon exists (Waldinger and Fitzgerald 2004; Schiller and Levitt 2006), how sustained or widespread it is (Portes, Guarnizo, and Landolt 1999; Waldinger and Fitzgerald 2004), or which activities "count" as transnationalism (Levitt and Schiller 2003; Fox 2005; Waldinger 2008). In this paper, we focus on three categories of cross-border participation: economic remittances, interpersonal communication, and cultural and political participation. We argue that theoretical progress can best be made in this field by moving beyond the preoccupation with defining what is or is not "transnational." It is more useful to explore how different forms of cross border activities vary in divergent ways based on the economic context.

Remittances, communication, and political activism across borders are contingent and subject to constraints. As past research has highlighted (Waldinger and Fitzgerald 2004, 1179) the political context, particularly migration policies in sending and receiving countries, strongly influences the nature of transnational activity in different places and time periods. The influence of the political context sparks a question as to how *economic* conditions and constraints may also affect migrant communities' binational activities. Here, drawing on Waldinger and Fitzgerald's approach, we assess how the global economic crisis altered "the use, form, and mobilization of the connections linking 'here' and 'there'" (1177). Our study adds to the existing scholarship by analyzing how the context of economic recession affects remittances, communication, and political activism across the U.S.-Mexico border. In addition, we highlight the ways the economic context has differentiated effects in different arenas of transnational activity.

ECONOMIC TIES

In Tlacotepec, as well as throughout Mexican migrant communities, the economic crisis decreased cross-border remittances, but it did not spark the flood of migrant returns that some experts predicted. According to the National Bureau of Economic Research, the overall volume of remittances from the United States to Mexico dropped from US$25.5 billion in 2006 to $21.2 billion in 2009. As shown in Figure 5.1, while remittances had grown steadily from 1995 until 2007, between 2007 and 2009, the average monthly remittances each family sent to Mexico dropped from $2,172 to $1,765.

Figure 5.1 Average Monthly Remittances to Mexico, 1995-2010

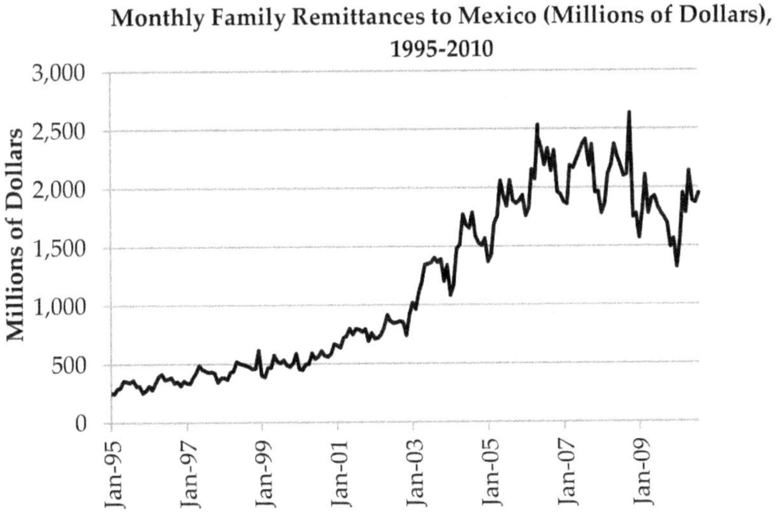

Monthly Family Remittances to Mexico (Millions of Dollars), 1995-2010

Source: Banco de México, 1995-2010

81

In Tlacotepec, echoing national trends, the monthly volume of remittances per family decreased during the economic crisis. Fewer families sent money across the border at all. While 49 percent of people living in the hometown said they had received remittances in 2007, only 36 percent reported remittance income in 2010. Further, the average family reported receiving less money. As Matías Hernández, a municipal official, described, "Before the economic recession two or three years ago, people in Tlacotepec received more money compared to what they receive now, because the remittances [migrants] send them decreased." As shown in Table 5.1, although a plurality of respondents maintained the same level of remittances, 34 percent said they sent less money during the recession, and only 22 percent said they sent more.

Table 5.1 Reported Changes in Remittance Volume among sTlacotepenses, 2007 – 2010

Remittances from the United States to Tlacotepec	Percent of Respondents
Sent less in 2007	34
Sent the same amount	44
Sent more in 2010	22

As some migrants lost their jobs or income, they joined the pool of non-remitting family members. Not surprisingly, unemployment was negatively correlated with remittances: no migrant who was unemployed sent remittances in either 2007 or 2010. Julián García, a member of the town government in Tlacotepec, explained, "Now they send less. They used to send more, but not now, because they don't have work. Or they work one day a week or two, they say. Or for a few hours, and that's it. It's not like before when they used to work the whole week." One sign of the poor economic conditions that migrants face is "reverse remittances," which invert the typical direction of economic support. In 2011, 2.7 percent of respondents reported sending remittances *from* Mexico *to* the United States.[2]

In spite of job losses, Tlacotepec migrants did not flood back home as the media had predicted. Rather, they weighed the rising cost of living in the United States against their poor job prospects back home. From 2005 through 2010, returns to Tlacotepec remained constant at about 15 to 20 respondents per year, consistent with nationwide surveys showing a fairly steady rate of return to Mexico (Passel and Cohn 2009; Rendall, Brownell, and Krups 2010). In 2011, 21 percent of respondents said that someone in their family had returned

---

2 We do not have comparable data from the 2007 survey.

to Tlacotepec in the last three years due to lack of work in the United States. Among U.S.-based respondents, only 6.8 percent said they planned to return to Mexico in the coming year. As many respondents told us, "If the economy is bad in the United States, it's even worse in Mexico." Javier González, a 32-year old migrant explained, "Lots of people say, 'I'm going back.' A lot of people I know said, 'I'm leaving the United States, I'm going to go back home.' But I think no more than five percent actually do it, because it's really hard. It's hard to be in the U.S. and come back. To start with, I'm sure, the first question is, 'What am I going to live off of?'"

On the other hand, people who return to Tlacotepec have much lower expenses than they did in the United States. Mario Sanchez, a migrant who returned in 2009, commented that the low cost of living at home made him reluctant to go back to the United States again. He explained, "Here [in Tlacotepec] I'm calm; here things are mine; here no one evicts me. Here I don't pay rent; I don't pay gas. I don't pay electricity or phone bills or anything. There [in the United States], no. There you have to be on top of everything." While many migrants continued to imagine returning to Tlacotepec, actually doing so seemed most viable for those who no longer expected to earn money in the United States, such as those close to retirement.

Although the number of people returning to Tlacotepec was small, the local, political impact of individual returnees was larger than their numbers would suggest, because several were community leaders. For instance, Josefino Santiago, an older returned migrant and municipal official, argued that the crisis generated returns like his:

> Various people are returning. There are several cases, ... and it's because in the United States they no longer have work nor places to live. Some of my cousins lost their houses, and others are about to lose them because of the economic recession there. There was a drop in employment and they couldn't pay any more, so they lost their property and now, as a result, they're here [in Tlacotepec].

Alfonso and Tonia Mendez, a couple in their late 50s who had lived in the United States for more than twelve years, provide a good example. Long-time leaders among U.S.-based Tlacotepenses, they lost their jobs and house in Vista, California in 2009 and as a result returned to live in Tlacotepec in 2010. Tonia explained, "I was out of work. They laid us both off, so we thought the best thing to do would be come back. We couldn't pay off our house any more; we couldn't keep paying it. We lost it, and we thought, let's go to our *pueblo*." While it was an early retirement for both, staying in the United States a few extra years until they turned 65 no longer seemed worth it.

Although few migrants actually returned, the economic downturn made those in the U.S. more likely to *think* of their hometown as a long-term fallback plan. In 2011, more U.S.-based respondents hoped to return to their hometown one day; the percent of migrants expecting to stay in the United States upon retirement dropped from 19.8 percent in 2007 to 11.4 percent in 2011. Also, fewer people in Tlacotepec said they intended to migrate *to* the United States, down from 18.3 percent in 2007 to 10.8 percent in 2011.

In sum, the economic crisis slowed cross border economic flows: fewer migrants sent remittances, and the average migrant sent less money per month. There was not the predicted flood of migrants returning home. Nevertheless, the idea of being able to return home, where the cost of living was lower than in the United States, became more important as migrants thought about their futures.

COMMUNICATION AND SOCIAL TIES

While Tlacotepenses remitted less during the recession, they began calling and emailing their relatives across the border more regularly. These opposing trends form the core of what we call "discount transnationalism," wherein Tlacotepenses try to maintain transnational ties at a lower cost, cutting down transnational economic activity but, in its place, putting additional time into transnational and hometown-related social activity. Though the recession hurt Tlacotepenses' incomes, it also coincided with the diffusion and diminishing costs of phone and Internet technology. Ever more Tlacotepenses gained access to cellular phones, international calling cards, and Internet communication. In turn, perhaps to mitigate the effects of their spatial separation, make up for their diminished economic support, or invest in a sort of interpersonal "insurance" in case they needed to return home one day, Tlacotepenses – especially those based in the United States - increased the frequency of their cross-border communication.

As anthropologist Steven Vertovec (2004) points out, regular, inexpensive international telephone calls are one of the primary sources of connection in global social networks, acting as "a kind of social glue connecting families and other small-scale social formations across the globe" (2009, 55-56). This is especially true for low-income groups like migrants, who may lack the means to travel or build other forms of ties.

The vast majority of Tlacotepenses make regular transnational phone calls. Of respondents living in the United States, 87 percent place at least one phone call to the hometown per month, and 54 percent receive at least one call a month from their relatives in Mexico. Likewise, among hometown-based respondents, 78 percent receive and 29 percent place at least one call per month with relatives in the United States. To communicate transnationally, most Tlacotepenses use U.S. phone cards, sold for about US$2.00 for 30 minutes of conversation, and call their family members' Mexican cell phones, landlines, or the community telephone run as a private business (*caseta*). Of families in the hometown, 100 have landlines in their homes that were installed in 2006, and another 100 have signed up for service starting in 2011. However, far more

Tlacotepenses have cellular phones, which operate on pre-paid plans and do not charge to receive calls. Elsa Zuñiga, who runs the caseta telephone service in Tlacotepec, said that although the store used to be busy with people waiting for phone calls from the United States, most residents now receive calls on their personal cell phones.

Initially, we expected that tight budgets and lower remittances would mean fewer phone calls; yet Tlacotepenses emphasized that they had been able to find new, cost-effective ways to talk. Elsa, of the telephone service, estimated that perhaps ten out of 100 families had lost their landlines in the recession due to non-payment. Nevertheless, she noted, cellular service had improved in the village, so rather than calling less, most of those whose landlines were cut reverted to communicating on cell phones, which operate on a pay-as-you-go basis. For example, 38-year-old Emilia Bautista, the sole remaining sister of a family mostly based in the United States, spent about US$4.00 a month on a pre-paid cell phone so that she could receive free phone calls from her siblings. Because it was cheaper to place calls from the United States to Mexico, she texted them when she wanted to talk, explaining "My siblings and I are constantly sending each other texts … It's easy and it's cheap."

As in the 2007 MMFRP study, Tlacotepenses in the United States still made the majority of the transnational phone calls. The respondents explained that this reflected the radical difference in the cost of calling from the United States to Mexico. As Israel, a returned migrant with children in the United States, described, "[In Tlacotepec] a phone card costs 200 pesos, and you spent it really fast. The money disappears, and I can't spend that much. So I say, 'You guys call me.' Over there you can buy a phone card for $2.00 and it lasts for 15 or 20 minutes. And from here to there, maybe 200 pesos, which is $20 dollars. I can't pay that cost, so they call me."[3]

When we analyzed the relationship between demographic characteristics and the frequency of transnational phone calls, we found that the recession coincided with a democratization of transnational communication. The regression results reported in Table 5.2 show that among U.S. respondents in 2007, education was the one significant predictor of transnational calling; those with more education made more phone calls. By 2011, this was no longer the case; people of different levels of education were equally likely to make calls across the border. We believe that this change reflects migrants' increasing familiarity with and access to cell phone technology and calling cards, even among less-educated migrants.

---

3 "Una tarjeta cuesta 200 pesos y se la gasta uno facilito. Pues, el dinero se va acabando, y no puedo gastar mucho. Pues yo les digo, 'Llámenme, ustedes.' Por que allá puedes comprar una tarjeta por dos dólares, y alcanza unos 15-20 minutos. Y aquí para allá, unos 200 pesos cuanto es—son 20 dólares. Entonces yo no puedo hacer ese gasto. Pues, me hablan."

Table 5.2 Predictors of Call Frequency among U.S.-based Respondents, 2007 and 2011

	2007	2011
Age	0.14 (0.10)	0.07 (0.13)
Male	-0.14 (0.53)	1.30 (2.68)
Years of education	0.14 (0.07)*	-0.37 (0.27)
Spouse lives elsewhere	1.32 (1.17)	-1.66 (3.60)
At least one child lives elsewhere	3.72 (2.15)	-2.07 (3.75)
Sends remittances	0 .75 (0.63)	-2.05 (2.72)
R-squared		0.04
	N=156	N=100

* p < .05

Among respondents in Mexico, although some inequality in calling rates persisted, we found a similar diffusion of transnational calling. The regression results in Table 5.3 show that in both 2007 and 2011, those who received remittances and those who had more resources exchanged more frequent transnational phone calls. However, whereas age and past migration history had been significant predictors of transnational calling in 2007, by 2011, older people and non-migrants were now just as likely to talk on the phone regularly with people in the United States as were younger people and former migrants. We also found that spousal separation had become a significant predictor of phone call frequency, perhaps as cell phones and calling cards made it ever easier for separated spouses to talk. Perhaps, in the context of recession, they worried that their separation would last longer, and they compensated by talking often.

Table 5.3 Predictors of Call Frequency among Mexico-based Respondents, 2007 and 2011

Mexico-Based Respondents	2007	2011
	(N=580)	(N=545)
Age	-.19 (0.00)*	-0.30 (0.05)
Male	-0.17 (0.66)	1.90 (1.15)
Years of education	0.03 (0.07)	0.07 (0.13)
Spouse lives elsewhere	0 .51 (0.51)	6.07 (1.61)***
At least one child lives elsewhere	0.62 (0.69)	0.93 (1.46)
Receives remittances	2.02 (0.37)**	3.60 (1.08)***
Wealth index	0.03 (0.01)	1.77 (0.84)*
Migrant	2.11 (0.81)*	0.57 (1.25)
R-squared	0.13	0.07

* p < .05 ** p < .01

Finally, even during the recession, Tlacotepenses felt that talking to relatives was worth the cost. Tlacotepenses who did not have phones of their own still went to great length to maintain communication, unwilling to cut phone calls from their budgets. For instance, Maria Ortiz, an elderly woman looking after her young grandchildren, said that communicating with her children (her grandkids' parents) was indispensable. To keep costs low, each week she took the children to a nearby town where telephone service was cheaper. Despite the economic downturn, communication remained a priority.

Figure 5.2 shows that between 2007 and 2011, the average number of calls-per-month of Mexico-based respondents increased, and those among U.S.-based respondents nearly doubled. While U.S.-based migrants reported an average of 2.3 calls home per month in 2007, by 2011 the average reached 4.2. Among those calling from Tlacotepec, the average number of calls made per month increased from 1.2 to 1.5. Exchanging more phone calls during the economic crisis also may have helped Tlacotepenses to stay connected.

Figure 5.2 Average Number of Transnational Phone Calls Per Month by Tlacotepenses, 2007 and 2011

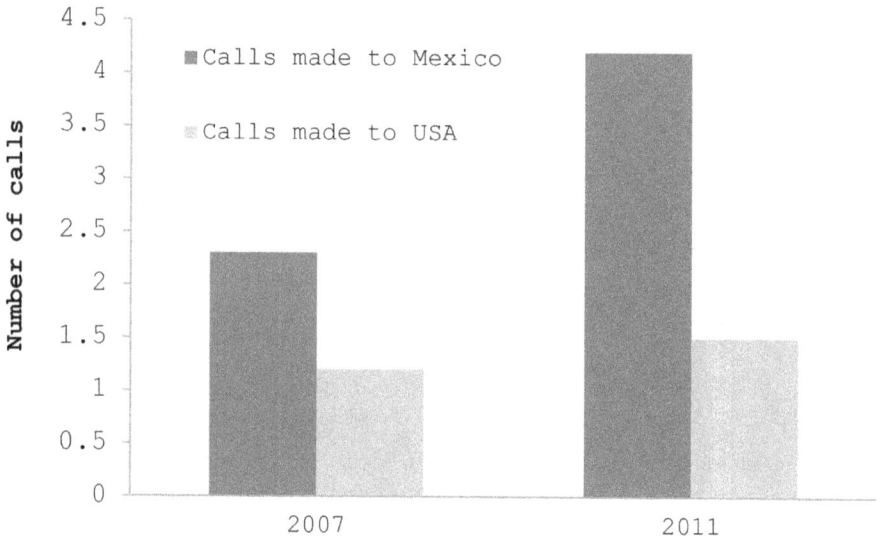

N=13s81

Internet communication—through emails and websites such as Facebook and the San Miguel Tlacotepec online forum—has also become an increasingly important means of communication due to improved technology, infrastructure, and access. Among U.S.-based Tlacotepenses, home Internet access rose from only 42.6 percent of respondents in 2007 to 63.6 percent of respondents in 2011. In the United States, even middle-aged respondents with as little as a third grade education had recently learned to use the Internet. Tlacotepenses in the United States regularly used the Internet to communicate with each other about their hometown, sending a steady stream of emails and Facebook messages with political news, cultural updates, photos, and notices of upcoming events. They used online groups such as Facebook and an online forum to post photos of their events and fiestas and to air successes, news, and grievances. At www.sanmigueltlacotepec.org, migrants could find out about the San Miguel Tlacotepec soccer team's big win, read accusations of corruption in the hometown municipal government, or find out where and when the next community fundraiser would be held. This low-cost, regular exchange of information may keep Tlacotepenses more informed about hometown-oriented activity than they were just a few years earlier.

Although Tlacotepenses in the United States communicated with each other regularly over the Internet, their online interactions with those back in Mexico were somewhat more limited. Though nearly 64 percent of U.S.-based respondents had Internet at home, only a few families in Tlacotepec had Internet in their houses. Among U.S.-based respondents, 24 percent sent emails to relatives in Tlacotepec, while only 16 percent of those in Oaxaca sent email to those in California. Although cross-border Internet interactions are constrained by a lack of familiarity with, or access to, the Internet in Tlacotepec, the Internet was becoming more common there as well. Since the previous study of Tlacotepec in 2007, a new Internet café was established in the community, and an existing Internet café lowered its cost from 12 to 10 pesos (about US$0.90) an hour. Both cafés were very popular with school-aged young people. Those Tlacotepenses who *did* communicate across the border by email did so regularly: emailers based in Tlacotepec sent a message to U.S.-based friends and family on average every two days, while U.S.-based emailers sent one to Tlacotepec about every three days. As with cell phones, the Internet seemed to be growing in Tlacotepec. Although money flows across the U.S.-Mexico border dropped, communication increased, as Tlacotepenses sought methods to maintain transnational ties at a discount.

CULTURAL AND POLITICAL TIES

The trend in transnational political and cultural participation echoes the theme of discount transnationalism: while migrants continued to report participating in such activities, they committed less money to the causes. Many found ways to "participate at a discount," for instance, identifying themselves as members of a civic organization but contributing less money, or choosing to attend the annual community fiesta in the United States instead of making the costly trip home for the event.

Political Ties

Tlacotepenses participate in a variety of civic and political organizations. Politically, Tlacotepenses at home and in the United States are well known for their history of leadership in binational organizations. These organizations, which bring together migrants from numerous villages in Oaxaca and other Mexican states, include the Indigenous Front of Binational Organizations (FIOB), the Coalition of Oaxacan Indigenous Communities (COCIO), and the Indigenous and Peasant National Front (FNIC). FIOB and COCIO operate binationally, promoting migrant rights, cultural awareness, and community development, while FNIC focuses on advocacy and community development for indigenous people within Mexico. In addition to participating in these organizations, Tlacotepec migrants sometimes also organized among themselves for short-term efforts to raise funds or promote hometown development projects, such as installing an irrigation system, paving roads, or building a school. Often, these project-based campaigns arise ad hoc and last only as long as the project takes to complete.

Our survey data suggest that the rates at which migrants participate in binational organizations and contribute to smaller, ad-hoc hometown projects, held steady from 2007 to 2011. As previous research finds (Velasco Ortiz 2005; Rivera-Salgado 2002; Fitzgerald 2006), participation in formal binational organizations is limited to a small percentage of migrants and a few non-migrant activists. In 2011, out of nearly 900 respondents in the U.S. and Tlacotepec, 4% reported participating in FIOB, 2% in COCIO, and 3% in FNIC. Nevertheless, the percentage of people who said they participated in such organizations held steady; the 2007 and 2011 numbers were nearly identical. Likewise, in 2011, 30 percent of U.S.-based respondents contributed to public projects back home, such as a potable water project, approximately the same rate reported in 2007 (33%).

However, while similar numbers of people continued to identify with transnational organizations and attend their events during the recession, their economic contributions to public projects decreased. Before 2007, U.S.-based respondent contributed an average of $51 annually to hometown development efforts; during the recession, the average annual contribution dropped to $18. Likewise, while similar numbers of people considered themselves members of binational organizations in 2011 and 2007, the recession decreased the amount of time members could contribute as volunteers. Benito Nuñez, president of FIOB's operations in his hometown of Tlacotepec from 1996-1999 and again from 2007-2011, reported that the number of participants in the local FIOB chapter remained at around 70 people from 2007 to 2011. However, he said that during the recession these members had been less willing to give time to the FIOB. Benito suggested that many people in Tlacotepec had to work additional hours or take on additional jobs to make ends meet, giving them less time for unpaid FIOB tasks. Though the organization's local projects ostensibly promote economic development, they were not effective enough to replace other forms of work. Benito explained:

> [The income projects generate] is very low, so it's not enough to sustain the economy of a household. I think it's for that reason that we [the FIOB] don't do many projects anymore. Due to the economic situation, people need to work more. They have less time to spend on the organization, because here it's all volunteer work, without pay. Another thing that [the recession] has cut back, I think, is the

training we can give people who support the organization. They say, 'To tell the truth, I have a lot of needs, and I need to make ends meet somewhere else.'

Gloria Lima, a long-time FIOB participant living in San Miguel Tlacotepec, added that nowadays she rarely attends FIOB events, because she needs to spend her time working. She told us, "I'm not really part of the FIOB anymore. I'm a sympathizer, nothing more. They want me to go now, but I don't anymore ... I need to spend more time on my work. My job gives me money to eat; FIOB has never given me either a salary or benefits ... that's why one separates from the FIOB quickly, because you don't get anything from them."

Furthermore, the recession decreased outside support for economic development projects and diminished the funds available to organizations as a whole. The FIOB president, Benito, noted that the FIOB had lost some of its donor support since the early part of the decade, stunting its capacity to promote development activities. From the late 1990s to the early 2000s, the FIOB received support from foundations such as MacArthur and Ford, as well as from the Mexican government, making it possible for the organization to finance a number of projects ranging from chicken coops to roofing to women's microfinance cooperatives (Domínguez Santos 2004).[4] When funding declined, Benito said the FIOB had to limit the scope of its activities:

Lately we have not had big projects here in Tlacotepec. We get very few projects. Like I told you, the last [project] was the one with cement.[5] This was a year ago, already, because we have not had the support. Since Ulises Ruiz [former state governor] was leaving power, the Ministry of Social Development (SEDESOL) no longer had resources to support the organization.

Another organization, COCIO, founded in 1994 in Vista, California, has faced trouble attracting volunteers for similar reasons. According to U.S.-based co-founders of COCIO, José Fernando and Alfonso Mendez, diminishing foundation support did not affect COCIO as much as FIOB, because COCIO earns money exclusively through its own fundraisers. However, Mendez noted, the individuals who were once involved participated less in the recession, because they had less time and money. As of 2011, COCIO was essentially dormant among Tlacotepenses. In contrast, Aida Herrera, the leader of FNIC, a Oaxaca-based organization active in Tlacotepec but not in the United States, hoped that her organization might be re-activated in the context of recession, as migrants returned home with spare time. In short, while

---

4 The INI (Instituto Nacional Indigenista) is now known as the Comisión Nacional para el Desarrollo de los Pueblos Indígenas and its current purpose is promote indigenous peoples' development, using different venues.

5 In this project, the Oaxacan state government donated bags of cement to active members of the FIOB. Each member could use the cement as he or she saw fit.

people still identified with binational organizations at the same rate, decreasing money and volunteer time hampered these organizations' capacity to provide services and mobilize effective political activism.

As a result, the one political area in which migrants grew *more* active during the recession was in the hometown government. Because return migration was concentrated among older migrants, who were often long-time community leaders, these returnees had more influence than their numbers alone might suggest. Many became important political players back home, including involvement in the community government. Of 22 people elected to public office in 2011, ten had returned from the United States within the last three years and another ten had worked there at some point. While few of these people came home for the express purpose of participating in politics, their presence and experience put them in a position to be politically active. For instance, Adrian Martinez, who was elected secretary of education in Tlacotepec in 2011, had gone back and forth to Vista to work in the agricultural fields since 1981. He remained civically involved when living abroad and then served in the municipal government while home. Likewise, long-time migrant Alfonso Mendez, mentioned above, had been an important political leader in binational organizations for almost three decades. Although Alfonso's 2010 return was provoked by the high cost of living in the United States, upon arrival, Alfonso took advantage of his time and influence in the village to campaign for his political allies in the 2010 municipal election. Alfonso hoped that being in Tlacotepec would enable him to influence community politics more directly than he had from the United States.

One challenge of analyzing Tlacotepenses' transnational political engagement is that the impacts of recession intermingle with other, internal political factors. Although Tlacotepenses were key founders of binational organizations such as FIOB and COCIO, they often describe their community as fragmented by political strife and corruption. In addition to recession, this history dissuades people from participating politically or donating money. As José Fernandez, a leader of the water project, commented, such distrust makes it difficult to raise funds for public projects. He explained, "For fiestas and other things people do contribute more, but for [public] projects, like the water project, a great work for our community, they don't want to contribute anymore … they have told us [project leaders] that we are crazy, that we will steal that money again." However, because these political conflicts had been ongoing since well before the economic recession, we believe comparing surveys from 2007 and 2011 shows changes specifically associated with the recession. In addition, in-depth interviews highlighted the economic reasoning behind peoples' shifting political involvement.

Cultural Ties

Participation in cultural activities followed a similar trend to politics, with people continuing to try to participate but seeking "discounted" forms of remaining involved. Although academics have focused attention on transnational political activities (Rivera-Salgado 2004; Fox & Bada 2008), our surveys underscore that a much larger number of Tlacotepenses are involved in cultural activities. Tlacotepenses in Vista, California, in San Diego County – as well as in the northern California community of Brentwood – have hometown associations that bring the community together to celebrate the birthday of their patron saint, San Miguel.[6] These organizations raise funds for the hometown and support each other in times of need, such as when a fellow migrant dies and his or her remains must be repatriated. Since 1991, the Tlacotepec hometown association has organized an annual festival in San Diego County in honor of San Miguel, where Tlacotepenses eat traditional foods and perform traditional dances and music. According to one of the town's websites, the fiesta has drawn as many as 1,200 people per year. The occasion provides a means for Tlacotepenses in the United States to stay connected to each other socially (Fox & Rivera-Salgado 2004; Rivera-Salgado et al. 2005).[7] Some community members also participate in groups that get together to practice the community's traditional dances, which they present at the fiesta and other local cultural events. In addition, Tlacotepenses have formed teams to play in an immigrant soccer league in Vista.

In spite of the recession, attendance at the annual fiesta in honor of San Miguel remained high. Of 133 U.S.-based Tlacotepenses surveyed in 2011, at least 90 (68%) attended this fiesta each year, either in California or in San Miguel Tlacotepec. However, people increasingly participated in this fiesta at a discount by choosing to attend the one in the United States rather than traveling to San Miguel Tlacotepec. In 2007, 17% of U.S.-based respondents made the trip to the fiesta in Tlacotepec, and 49% participated in the fiesta in California. However, by 2011, only 12% returned to Tlacotopec, and 56% attended the California fiesta.

The recession has made fundraising for the California fiesta challenging. Yet, there were still plenty of Tlacotepenses willing to volunteer their labor. As Erminda López, a member of committee responsible for organizing the 2011 fiesta in Vista, explained, "Maybe it's harder to raise funds, but thank God we already have people committed to serve on the festival committee for the next three years. People come; they always come." Of U.S.-based Tlacotepenses, 22 percent reported donating money to the fiestas in Tlacotepec over the last five years, and the average US-based Tlacotepense contributed $25 per year for such fiestas. Seventy-three percent of U.S.-based respondents reported

---

6 The literature shows such hometown associations are a widespread and important part of political transnationalism (Kearney & Nagengast 1989, 1990; Lynn 2007; Fox & Rivera-Salgado 2004, Melero-Malpica 2005).

7 http://www.sanmigueltlacotepec.org/civico_smt.html

serving on the committees that organize dance performances and festivals. Unable to afford participating in more costly transnational cultural activities that require travel and legal documents, Tlacotepenses appear to be focusing their time and money at the local level in the destination, another example of discount transnationalism.

CONCLUSION

Comparing the levels and forms of cross-border action before and after the recession of 2007-2010 shows that economic circumstances like the recent recession shape cross-border economic, social, and political activities in divergent ways. This finding helps make theoretical progress on transnationalism by moving beyond ongoing debates about whether or not "transnationalism" exists and identifying its variations and the circumstances under which it changes.

As we show in this chapter, the economic downturn had differentiated effects on different transnational practices. In particular, the levels of remittances and political contributions were contingent on economic prosperity in ways cross-border communication may not have been, especially as the cost of communicating across borders continued to fall. On one hand, the recession decreased the scope and level of remittances, as well as the amount of money migrants were willing to commit to political projects and cultural events. Nevertheless, migrants compensated by finding cheaper ways to remain involved with their community, through practices we call "discount transnationalism." In particular, they communicated by phone and email at increasingly high rates, keeping in touch even when they could not send as much money or return as often for visits. Also, they continued to formally identify with political organizations at the same rate in spite of having less time to volunteer. And, though fewer migrants went home during the crisis to participate in cultural events, growing numbers of them participated in local versions of the hometown fiesta. While the level and form of transnational activities are contingent on economic well-being, migrants' commitment to home drove them to innovate socially to keep their cross-border connections alive.

WORKS CITED

Alarcón, Rafael et al. 2009. "La crisis financiera en Estados Unidos y su impacto en la migración mexicana," *Migraciónes Internacionales* 16, 5.1 (Enero-Junio).

Basch, L., N. Glick Schiller and C. Szanton Blanc, eds. 1994. *Nations Unbound: Transnational Projects, Postcolonial Predicaments, and Deterritorialized Nation-States*. Gordon and Reach. Switzerland.

September 2010. *Business Cycle Dating Committee, National Bureau of Economic Research*. The National Bureau Of Economic Research. April 2011. http://www.nber.org

Cornelius, Wayne A., David Fitzgerald, Pedro Lewin Fischer and Leah Muse Orlinoff, eds. 2009. *Mexican Migration and the U.S. Economic Crisis: A Transnational Perspective*. La Jolla, CA: Center for Comparative Immigration Studies, University of California, San Diego.

Cornelius, Wayne A., David Fitzgerald, Jorge Hernández-Díaz, and Scott Borger, eds. 2009. *Migration from the Mexican Mixteca: A Transnational Community in Oaxaca and California*. La Jolla, CA: Center for Comparative Immigration Studies, University of California, San Diego.

Conway, Dennis and Jeffrey H. Cohen. 1998. "Consequences of Migration and Remittances for Mexican Transnational Communities." *Consequence of Migration*.

Domínguez Santos, Rufino. 2004. "The FIOB Experience: Internal Crisis and Future Challenges." In *Indigenous Mexican Migrants in the United States*, ed. Jonathan Fox and Gaspar Rivera-Salgado. La Jolla: Center for U.S.-Mexican Studies, University of California, San Diego.

Fox, Jonathan. 2005. "Unpacking Transnational Citizenship," *Annual Review of Political Science* 8: 171–201.

Fox, Jonathan and Gaspar Rivera-Salgado. 2004. "Building Civil Society among Indigenous Migrants." In *Indigenous Mexican Migrants in the United States*. La Jolla: Center for U.S.-Mexican Studies: 1-65.

Fitzgerald, David. 2006. "Rethinking Emigrant Citizenship." *New York University Law Review* 81.117 (April): 90-116.

Kearney, Michael. 1991. "Borders and Boundaries of State and Self at the End of Empire," *Journal of Historical Sociology* 4.1: 52-74.

Kearney, Michael and Federico Besserer. 2004. "Oaxacan Municipal Governance in Transnational Context." In *Indigenous Mexican Migrants in the United States*, ed Jonathan Fox and Gaspar Rivera-Salgado. La Jolla: Center for U.S.-Mexican Studies, University of California, San Diego.

Kochhar, Rakesh. 2009. "Unemployment Rises Sharply Among Latino Immigrants in 2008." *Pew Research Center Report.* Washington, DC.

Levitt, Peggy. 2001. *The Transnational Villagers.* Berkeley: University of California Press.

Levitt, P., and N. G Schiller. 2004. "Conceptualizing Simultaneity: A Transnational Social Field Perspective on Society," *International Migration Review* 38.3: 1002–39.

Levitt, Peggy and Ninna Nyberg-Sørensen. 2004. "The Transnational Turn in Migration Studies." *Global Migration Perspectives* 6. Geneva: Global Commission on International Migration.

Mahler, Sarah J. 2001. "Transnational Relationships: The Struggle to Communicate Across Borders," *Identities: Global studies on culture and power* 7.4: 583-619.

Melero, Daniel Malpica. 2005. "Indigenous Mexican Migrants in a Modern Metropolis: The Reconstruction of Zapotec Communities in Los Angeles." In *Latinos L.A.: Transformation, Communities, and Activism,* ed. Enrique C. Ochoa and Gilda L. Ochoa. Tucson: The University of Arizona Press.

Nagengast, Carole and Michael Kearney. 1990. "Mixtec Ethnicity: Social Identity, Political Consciousness, and Political Activism." In *Latin American Research Review.* California: The Latin American Studies Association 25.2: 61-91.

Passel, Jeffrey S and D'Vera Cohn. 2009. "Recession Slows - but Does Not Reverse - Mexican Immigration." *Pew Research Center Report.* Washington, DC.

Portes, A. 2003. "Conclusion: Theoretical convergencies and empirical evidence in the study of immigrant transnationalism," *International Migration Review* 37(3):874–892.

Rivera Salgado, Gaspar. 2002 "Migration and Political Activism: Mexican transnational indigenous communities in a comparative perspective" [cite thesis]

Rendall, Michael S, Peter Brownell and Sarah Kups. 2010. "Declining Return Migration from the United States to Mexico in the Late-2000s Recession." *Rand Labor and Population Working Paper.* Washington, DC.

Schiller, N. G, and P. Levitt. 2006. "Haven't We Heard this Somewhere Before? A Substantive View of Transnational Migration Studies by way of Reply to Waldinger and Fitzgerald." The Center for Migration and Development.

Stephen, Lynn. 2007. *Transborder Lives: Indigenous Oaxacans in Mexico, California and Oregon.* Durham: Duke University Press.

Velasco Ortiz, Laura. 2005. *Mixtec Transnational Identity.* Tucson: University of Arizona Press.

Vertovec, Stephen. 2004. "Cheap Calls: The Social Glue of Migrant Transnationalism," *Global Networks* 4.2: 219-224.

Vertovec, S. 2009. *Transnationalism.* Abingdon: Routledge, 2009.

Waldinger, Roger. 2008. "Between 'Here' and 'There': Immigrant Cross-Border Activities and Loyalties," *International Migration Review* 42(1):3-29.

Waldinger, R. D, and D. Fitzgerald. 2004. "Transnationalism in question," American Journal of Sociology 109(5):1177–95.

6 A House Divided: Family Separation and Education

COREEN DAVIS, DENISSE FERNANDEZ, TANIA FONSECA, ORIANA MARQUEZ-DAHESA, ALEXIS SMITH

> *If my father were working in the fields [in Tlacotepec] like many other people, I am almost sure that I would not be able to continue studying simply because there is no money to be made working in the fields.* — Mercedes, a first year university student whose father works in the United States

As a student at the Universidad Tecnológica de la Mixteca, Mercedes has gone further in her education than most of her Tlacotepense peers. Yet throughout the years that Mercedes has achieved this success in school, her father has lived in the United States, returning only for brief visits. Over nearly two decades, Mercedes' father has kept in contact through regular phone calls, often inquiring about her progress in school, and consistently sent money to help pay for Mercedes' education. Even while the economic crisis has precluded her father from making return visits to Tlacotepec for the past three years, he has continued to support Mercedes with both phone calls and remittances.

Both of Francisco's parents live and work in California and send money for his education. With both of his parents gone, Francisco has been forced to rely heavily on his grandmother for emotional support in his education. The money from Francisco's parents in the United States and the grandmother's best efforts to support Francisco have not been enough to ensure his success in school. Last semester, failing two classes, Francisco decided to drop out of high school.

For Mercedes, her father's migration has been part of the foundation for her academic success. Yet for Francisco, with both of his parents in the United States and only his grandmother at home to offer emotional support, family separation contributed to him dropping out before completing high school. What explains the success of Mercedes and students like her while others, such as Francisco, struggle in comparison? Why has family separation played such a different role in the educations of these two students? We found that the effects of family separation on education among Tlacotepenses varied by the number of parents absent. Youth with one migrant parent and one parent in Mexico received the parental support and financial resources to achieve higher attainment and grades than those with both parents abroad as well as those with both parents in Tlacotepec.

Family separation[1] is extremely common among Tlacotepenses: 43 percent of those between the ages of 15 and 35 have experienced family separation in some form. Sixteen percent experienced separation from both parents while 27 percent experienced separation from only one parent.[2] The remaining 57 percent of Tlacotepenses in our sample experienced no family separation. Among families in which one parent was absent, in 95 percent of cases it was the father who migrated while the mother remained at home.

Our chapter analyzes the impact of these various types of family separation on the education of young people in Tlacotepec. In order to measure the educational success of such Tlacotepenses, we analyzed students' aspirations (the number of years of schooling current students hope to complete), attainment (actual number of completed years of schooling) and, for those currently in school, their grades.

This chapter begins with an overview of the existing literature on migration, education, and family separation. We then sketch the educational context of Tlacotepec, providing an overview of the school system and how it compares to other parts of Mexico before presenting our empirical findings on the impact of family separation on aspirations, attainment, and grades. We discuss these findings using qualitative interview evidence and explain the factors that allow some students who experience family separation to succeed while hindering the success of others. Finally, we conclude with an overview of the findings and their significance in understanding the effects of family separation on the education of young people in Tlacotepec.

Migration, Family Separation, and Education

A central debate in the literature on migration and education in the United States and Mexico is whether the migration of Mexican parents helps or hurts the education of their children who remain at home. Among studies that argue that migration is a positive factor in education, remittances are often cited as important in allowing students to continue education to levels they might not otherwise be able to afford. A 2007 study conducted in San Miguel Tlacotepec found that remittances help to cover the costs of attending school and have a particularly positive effect on allowing students to complete high school

---

1 We define family separation as the absence of either the mother or father for at least one year when the child is between the ages of six and eighteen.

2 Separation from both parents does not necessarily imply the absence of both parents at the same time.

(Sawyer et al. 2009). Dreby (2010) finds a similar effect of remittances on high school completion. In her work in Oaxaca, children of migrants who remain in their hometowns reap the benefits of the economic stability that remittances provide, including being able to pay for the higher costs of attending high school. The cost of paying for high school, which unlike primary and secondary school is not free in Mexico, can prove particularly challenging for residents of poor communities such as Tlacotepec.

The positive effect of remittances on education mirrors earlier research, including Hanson and Woodruff's (2003) study finding that children in migrant households finish more years of schooling than those without a migrant family member. Hanson and Woodruff attribute this difference to an increase in family income as a result of remittances sent from abroad, which help to ease economic deprivation at home and allow for the children to attend school. Similarly, Kandel and Kao's (2001) work with children in Zacatecas finds that children from a migrant household earned higher grades than those without migrants in their home.

In addition to remittances, several authors have argued that migrant parents establish an "immigrant bargain" with their children who remain at home. Robert Smith defines this phenomenon as the "expectation that the sacrifice made by the parents will be redeemed and validated through the children's achievement" (2006:125). Under this premise, parents migrate to the United States and endure the hardships in order to provide economic support for their children in Mexico in exchange for their academic success and good behavior.

While remittances and the immigrant bargain often have positive effects on the education of children in Mexico, migration can also lead to negative educational outcomes. Sawyer and colleagues argue that migration is a double-edged sword: while remittances help some, seeing the amount that family members who have left Tlacotepec are able to earn leads others to leave school and join them in the United States. This study and others have documented the development of a "culture of migration" in which young people who might otherwise continue their studies follow the community norm and migrate north instead. Kandel and Massey's (2001) study of Zacatecas argues that the culture of migration leads adolescents to see migration as the norm and thus aspire to migrate rather than remain in their towns. This follows the work of Kandel and Kao (2001), which demonstrates that those from families with migrants have lower aspirations of attending college than those from non-migrant households, a fact they attribute to children seeing that migrating north is often more economically beneficial than continuing their studies. Similarly, McKenzie and Rapoport's (2006) work in rural Mexico finds migration has a significantly negative effect on attainment levels for sixteen to eighteen year olds, particularly males, who aspire to migrate rather than attain more schooling. For girls, however, migration significantly increases their attainment, which is consistent with remittances allowing them to pursue more years of schooling.

In addition to the economic draw that leads some children to give up school in order to migrate, the psychological impact of separation from a family member often interferes with students' academic success. Dreby (2010) argues that for some students who experience parental separation, the ensuing depression and sadness can manifest itself in lower academic performance, deviant behavior, and dropping out of school. Additionally, the immigrant bargain, which in good times can lead to academic success, can also have a negative effect on education when migrant parents are not able to fulfill their end of the deal. In her work, Dreby argues that unfulfilled expectations in the "immigrant bargain" may lead to the detachment of children from their absent parents, which results in behavioral problems as well as lower interest in school. Dreby finds that a parent failing to provide an appropriate amount of remittances can trigger a negative response from their children, manifested by disregard for parental authority and poor performance in school.

Our study builds on this work to examine the effects of family separation on students' aspirations, attainment, and grades. Our central questions include: Are the effects of family separation on education positive or negative? What differences exist between students separated from their parents and their united counterparts? What accounts for the struggles of some students separated from their parents while others in similar situations succeed? What specific family arrangements are most conducive to students' academic success?

EDUCATIONAL CONTEXT OF SAN MIGUEL TLACOTEPEC

Although Mexico currently spends about 4.4 percent of its GDP on education, similar to the 4.6 percent average of other countries in the Organization for Economic Cooperation and Development (OECD Family Database 2010), the educational system has many problems, including low enrollment rates and high dropout rates beyond the primary level[3], particularly in rural areas of Mexico (Santibañez, Vernez, and Razquin 2005). As shown in Table 6.1, the average level of attainment in Mexico is 8.6 years (INEGI 2011), or just above completed middle school. The 2010 census reveals that among those fifteen years and older, seven percent nationally, did not receive any formal education. In Oaxaca, the indicators are worse than the country as a whole. The percentage of those not receiving any formal education in Oaxaca – fourteen percent – is double that of the national average. Other variables measuring academic attainment for the population fifteen and older reveal an overall trend of lower educational achievement for Oaxaca in a national comparison.

---

3 The educational system of Mexico is divided into three basic levels: primaria (1st through 6th grade), secundaria (7th through 9th grade), and preparatoria (10th through 12th grade).

Table 6.1 Selected Educational Indicators for Population 15 years and Older, 2005

Indicator	Mexico	Oaxaca	San Miguel Tlacotepec
Average Years of Attainment	8.6	6.9	5
Percent Literate	90.5	80.6	68.2
Percent Attended School	91.6	93.6	87
Percent Incomplete Primary	14.3	20.6	57

Source: Sawyer et al. 2009, INEGI 2010

The indicators on the 2010 census place the state of Oaxaca second to last nationally in educational attainment. At 6.9 years of education, the average attainment in Oaxaca is just above the level of primary school. Despite the low numbers, Oaxaca has in fact made dramatic gains in attainment statewide, with the figure jumping from 4.6 years in 1990 to 5.6 years in 2000, before hitting 6.9 years in the 2010 survey (INEGI 1990, 2000, 2010). This jump coincides with a national educational policy change in 1993 that made secondary education compulsory (Zorilla 2004).

Educational outcomes for the indigenous population in Mexico remain below those of the population as a whole, a relevant factor in Oaxaca, a state where 34 percent of the people speak an indigenous language (nationally, the figure is six percent) (Cuentame Oaxaca 2010). According to the non-governmental monitoring organization *Mexicanos Primero*, 55 percent of indigenous adults nationwide do not attend school or complete a primary education, compared to 29 percent of the total adult population (Mexicanos Primero 2010). The average educational attainment for the indigenous population is four years of school, half of the national average of eight years.

If education outcomes in Oaxaca and among the indigenous populations are low, outcomes in San Miguel Tlacotepec are even lower. As Table 6.1 indicates, Tlacotepec trails behind state and national averages in rates of school attendance, primary completion, and literacy[4]. The 2010 census shows that

---

4 All analyses of our own data presented in this chapter are restricted to people without any education in the United States unless otherwise noted.

Tlacotepec has an average educational attainment of only five years (INEGI 2011). Tlacotepec has seen some improvement in recent years, however, with younger generations of Tlacotepenses attaining far higher levels of education than their older counterparts (see Figure 6.1). Those between the ages of 15 and 29 have an average attainment of nine years, a number that caps a trend of steadily increasing attainment for Tlacotepenses in recent years.

Figure 6.1 Average Years of Education in Mexico by Age Cohort, 2010

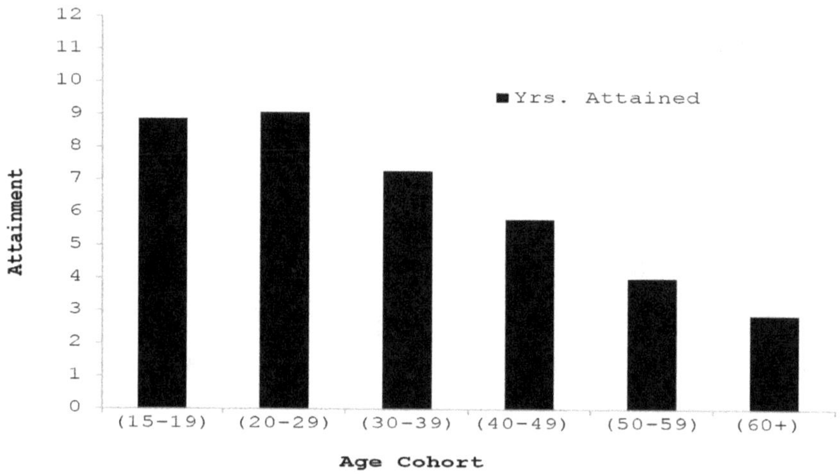

N=803

Source: INEGI 2010

Tlacotepec's preschool, two elementary schools, and middle school feed into the local high school. Known as the CECYTE (*Colegio de Estudios Científicos y Tecnológicos del Estado de Oaxaca*), the high school has played an instrumental role in raising the average attainment level for younger cohorts. Before the CECYTE opened in 2003, the nearest high school was a 30-minute drive away, a distance that required a daily taxi fare for most students, making it impossible for many to attend high school. Today, the accessibility and convenience of the CECYTE allows incoming students from the *secundaria* to enroll in high school, thus contributing to an overall increase in educational attainment for the younger generations.

IMPACT OF FAMILY SEPARATION ON EDUCATION

Aspirations

Asked about their educational aspirations, the vast majority of students (80 percent) in Tlacotepec said they hoped to attend college (see Table 6.2). Separated by whether or not students had experienced family separation, 94 percent of students who experienced separation from both parents aspired to attend college, 88 percent of those who experienced separation from one parent, and 83 percent of students who did not experience family separation aspired to attend college. Among all Tlacotepense students, the average level of aspirations was sixteen years of education, two years higher than the average aspirations in the 2007 study (Sawyer et al. 2009).

Table 6.2 Aspirations of Tlacotepense students separated from none, one or both parents, 2011

	No Separation	One Parent Absent	Both Parents Absent
Aspire to some Middle School	6%	0%	0%
Aspire to some High School	12%	12%	6%
Aspire to some College	82%	88%	94%

N=101

Attainment

There is a wide gap between Tlacotepenses educational aspirations and their actual attainment. The average aspiration of 16 years is seven years above the average attainment for Tlacotepenses between the ages of 15 and 35. Although most people in this age group aspire to pursue higher education, those who experience separation from one parent obtain higher levels of attainment than those who experience separation from both parents and those who do not experience separation at all.

Figure 6.2 Educational attainment by parental residence status for Tlacotepenses aged 15-35, 2011

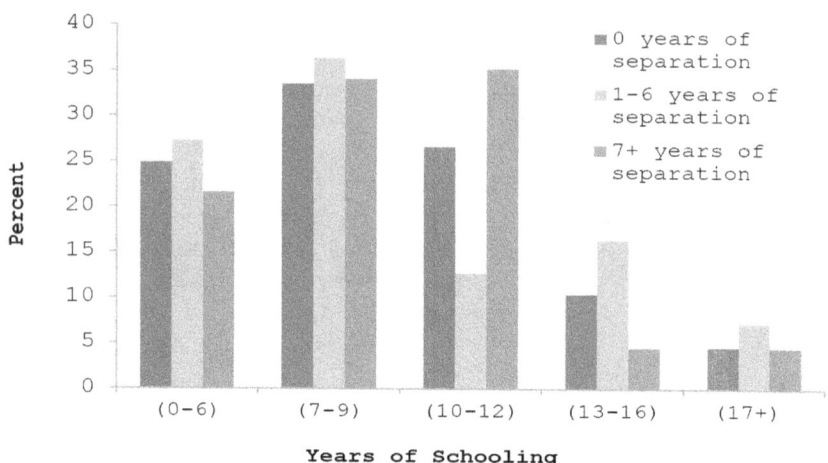

N = 316

In order to analyze the impact of family separation on educational attainment, we divide Tlacotepenses between the ages of 15 and 35 into three groups: those who experience no family separation, those who experience the absence of one parent, and those who experience the absence of both parents. As seen in Figure 6.2, students in the second group – those who experience the absence of one parent – have higher levels of attainment than the other two groups. Eighty-one percent of students who experience the absence of one parent complete at least middle school (the end stage of compulsory schooling in Mexico), compared to only 69 percent of students who experience the absence of both parents and 75 percent of those who experience no separation. Those who experience the absence of one parent attend college at a higher rate (18 percent) than the other two groups (9 percent for those who experience the absence of both parents and 15 percent for those with no separation). The mean level of attainment is also highest for the group who experience the absence of one parent. Young people with one parent in the United States have an average attainment of 9.6 years versus 8.7 years for those with both parents absent and 9.4 years for those with no separation. We hypothesize that this family arrangement, with one parent working in the United States and the other parent at home in Tlacotepec, combines the benefits of increased economic support coming from the migrant parent and the proximate nurturing from the parent at home.

Does the length of parental separation affect years of schooling? Figure 6.3 shows levels of attainment for three groups of students: those who experienced no family separation, those who experienced between one to six years of separation, and those who experienced seven or more years of separation.

Young people who experience no family separation are less likely to complete education (both high school and college) beyond the compulsory middle school level than the other two groups. This may be due to families' lack of resources to continue paying for further education. The fact that neither parent has migrated is an indicator of socioeconomic status because migrating to the United States requires a level of resources the family may not have. The poverty of such families leads many of their children to drop out of school to work and support their family.

Young Tlacotepenses who experience one to six years of family separation demonstrate a different pattern in their levels of attainment. Members of this group complete high school at lower rates than the other two groups but graduate from college at the highest rates of any of the groups. The lower high school completion rates may be explained by the fact that some in this group complete their compulsory education and then migrate instead of continuing their education. The allure of migration is stronger for those with parents and networks already established in the United States than for those who experience no separation. Unlike those who experience seven or more years of separation, those in this group are more likely to still maintain strong connections to those in the United States. For those in this group who choose to continue with their education, the remittances sent from abroad provide much needed funds to pay for high school and college studies.

For young people who experience seven or more years of family separation there is a slightly different pattern. Approximately 35 percent end their studies after middle school and high school. Young people separated from their parents for seven or more years are less likely to pursue higher education than people that experience no separation as well as those who experience one to six years of separation. We hypothesize that this may be due to the fact that those in this group are less likely to have contact with and receive remittances from family in the United States to fund further education.

Overall, it is youth who experience one to six years of family separation who pursue higher education at the highest rates. This follows the "immigrant bargain" phenomenon outlined by Smith (2006) in which children experiencing relatively short periods of separation fulfill their end of the bargain to their migrant parents with educational success. On the other hand, young people that experience prolonged periods of separation may exhibit disillusionment at the long absence of their parent and decide not to pursue higher education.

In order to disentangle the factors that affect attainment, we constructed a linear regression with a series of nested models, using attainment as the dependent variable (see Table 6.3).

Table 6.3 Predictors of Years of Education of Tlacotepenses 15-35, 2011

	m1	m2	m3	m4
(Intercept)	9.358*** (0.293)	8.440*** (1.137)	8.819*** (1.125)	7.170*** (1.114)
one parent gone	0.260 (0.503)	0.972 (0.575)	1.024 (0.564)	1.211* (0.536)
two parents gone	-0.618 (0.601)	-0.825 (0.693)	-0.841 (0.679)	-0.291 (0.652)
age		-0.040 (0.040)	-0.036 (0.039)	0.057 (0.042)
male		-0.325 (0.489)	-0.633 (0.493)	-0.070 (0.480)
father's attainment		0.165* (0.065)	0.150* (0.064)	0.102 (0.062)
wealth			1.051** (0337)	1.425*** (0.328)
migrant				3.280*** (0.644)
adj. R-squared	-0.001	0.223	0.254	0.330
N	316	227	226	226

In Model 1 we analyzed the absence of one and both parents in relation to no parental absence. In this model, parental separation is not statistically significant in predicting attainment. Model 2 controls for basic demographic standards including: age, gender, and parental attainment. Attainment of both the mother and the father are statistically significant and positive predictors of the child's attainment. Model 3 additionally controls for wealth, revealing a statistically significant and positive correlation between wealth and attainment. We attribute this correlation to wealthy families having the resources to pay for schooling as well as to migrate and increase their income through remittances.[5] In this model, parental attainment retains its statistical significance.

Finally, Model 4 controls for whether the person has migrated. We find a statistically significant and negative correlation between attainment and a history of migration which we attribute to the culture of migration that draws youth from school and towards migration. Parental education and wealth maintain their strong and positive correlation. In this model, separation from one parent is a statistically significant predictor of attainment, illustrating that

---

5 As migration is expensive, families in the lower socio-economic levels are unable to afford to make the trip, leaving them without the option of obtaining remittances for higher education.

young Tlacotepenses who have experienced separation from one parent on average attain over a year more education than their peers.

GRADES

In addition to analyzing attainment by different types of family separation, we also sought to measure educational success by analyzing the grades of current students. We created an average of individual student grades and compiled them into two categories: passing and failing[6]. Our data indicate that family separation due to migration negatively affects the grades of students in San Miguel Tlacotepec when both parents are absent from the home. However, when only one parent has migrated, average grades are higher than those of students who experience no absent parents and those who experience two absent parents.

Table 6.4 shows that among those who have experienced the absence of one parent, 87 percent of current students earn passing grades, while only 80 percent of students with both parents absent and 73 percent of students with no migrant parents are passing.

Table 6.4: Grades of Tlacotepense students by parental residence status, 2011

	No Separation	One Parent Absent	Both Parents Absent
Failing	27%	13%	20%
Passing	73%	87%	80%

N=47

Remittances at least partly explain this gap. Money earned by a migrant parent abroad not only helps pay for a young person's schooling, but also provides the student with the necessary materials and supplies to successfully perform in school. Further, the increased income resulting from a migrant parent takes the labor burden off of the students, allowing them to focus on schoolwork and not be pressured to contribute to the household's economy, as Kandel and Kao (2001) have noted. Additionally, the presence of at least one parent, who can provide academic and emotional support in the household, correlates with a higher percentage of passing grades.

---

6 The limited size of our sample made it necessary to include only these two categories of grades.

DISCUSSION

While all young people in Tlacotepec have similar levels of aspirations for their education, those who have experienced the absence of one parent during their educational careers demonstrate better outcomes in terms of attainment and grades than do those who experience the absence of both parents as well as those who experience no family separation. We argue that economic and emotional support are the most important factors in determining students' levels of attainment and grades. Each of the three family arrangements we discuss offer different benefits and drawbacks in providing economic and emotional support.

For students who experience the absence of one parent, a group that has higher attainment and grades than the other two groups, our qualitative interviews reveal that they tend to receive both economic and financial support. They are better equipped to excel in school because they receive money from abroad to fund their schooling, allowing them to focus solely on their education, while also benefiting from the support system maintained at home. The parent in the United States sends remittances that go toward education while the parent at home provides motivation and discipline to keep the student on track.

Mercedes, whose mother remains with her and her siblings in Tlacotepec while her father works in the United States, illustrates the potential benefits of this family arrangement. Mercedes was able to continue to study through high school with funds sent by her father. These remittances also pay for the costs she is currently incurring as part of her university studies. Mercedes is determined to finish her degree in engineering, work after graduation, save money, and ultimately pursue a master's degree in engineering. These lofty goals, which Mercedes, unlike many others, appears likely to achieve, are possible in part because of the emotional and practical support both parents have provided over the years. Her mother has been particularly central in providing this type of support, helping her with daily activities, encouraging her to finish her assignments, and assisting her in finding an apartment near her university. Even though her mother possesses only an elementary school education, her encouragement and backing have been crucial factor in Mercedes' academic success. "She says that the most important treasure a family can have is not a house or land, but education."

Mercedes also receives support from her father, with whom she maintains frequent contact by phone, email, letters, and occasional visits. Her father encourages her to succeed in school, saying "my father has always supported us children. He tells us to keep studying because he had to migrate at a young age and he wants us to have a better life than he has had." The "immigrant bargain" encourages Mercedes to repay her father for the sacrifices by achieving successes in school. Maintaining contact between the child and the parent provides additional support and can encourage a young person to remain in school. Her father is very invested of Mercedes and her siblings and he inquires often about their educational progress, providing encouragement and discipline when necessary. Having one parent in the United States and one in Tlacotepec has made it possible for Mercedes to pursue higher education, as this family arrangement has given her both economic and emotional support.

While for Mercedes, having her father in the United States has been beneficial, for other young Tlacotepenses family separation can create a desire to leave. For some, the allure of migration and the money that can be earned in the United States often causes them to leave school earlier than they might have otherwise. As demonstrated in Table 6.2, migrants between the ages of 15 and 35 attain two years less of schooling on average than do youth who do not migrate.

For two of Francisco's older brothers, the allure of migration was strong enough that they disregarded the advice of their grandmother in Mexico and the long-distance pleadings of their parents in the United States. Although their family members constantly encouraged them to continue with school, with only the grandmother present, there was not enough of an adult presence to provide discipline to ensure Francisco's brothers' academic success. The draw of life in the United States was stronger than any encouragement she could offer, and both brothers dropped out of school and headed north. Even though young Tlacotepenses who have experienced separation from both parents often have the financial resources to continue their educations, they lack enough emotional support to keep them in school.

If having both parents absent can provide economic but not emotional support, having both family members present can provide the opposite: strong emotional but little economic support for education. In a poor, rural Mexican town like Tlacotepec, lack of funds is often one of the main reasons why students end their educational careers. For the Lopez family, all of whom have lived their entire lives in Tlacotepec, the small income they earn from farming and a small store they own has contributed to none of their children studying beyond sixth grade. The mother says that uniforms and other school supplies are expensive and the family simply does not earn enough to pay for these expenses. Aware that their parents cannot afford to put them through more than six years of schooling, the children accept that after completing primary school they stop studying and start working to support the family. Some of the children work in the family store while the older children take care of their younger siblings. Fifteen year-old Sonia, the eldest of the Lopez children, described being frustrated when her parents leave her to care for the younger children, which meant she could not continue with her education. Because there is no possibility for the children to continue their education beyond elementary school, there is also little encouragement to achieve high grades. Children in the Lopez household lack both the economic and emotional support necessary for educational success.

111

Recognizing that money is an obstacle to education for many families, the Mexican government has implemented social programs in recent years to seek to boost educational attainment of youth. *Oportunidades*, one of the main such programs, provides cash transfers to mothers as long as their children remain in school. A comparative study on the outcomes of differential exposure to Oportunidades for Mexican rural youth shows positive impacts of longer exposure on grades of schooling attained. Of students with more exposure to the program, youth (both boys and girls) on average accumulate about 0.5 more years of schooling than students with less exposure (Behrman et al. 2009). In Tlacotepec, 64 percent of the population lives in a household that participates in Oportunidades, and many people mentioned the importance of the cash transfers they receive from the program in allowing their children to continue with their educations.

Although the general pattern we find is that Tlacotepenses who experience the absence of one parent fare better in their educations than do those who experience the absence of both parents and those who experience no separation, there are, of course, exceptions to the rule. Although the family arrangement of having one parent in the United States and one parent in Mexico can often provide both economic and emotional support, this is not always the case. In some cases, a parent working in the United States may be unable to make enough money to provide adequate remittances and/or may also lose contact with his or her family in Tlacotepec and stop providing emotional support to his or her children. One such example is David, whose father is in the United States and in recent years has stopped contacting his family in Tlacotepec. Lacking the emotional and financial support to succeed academically, David has been struggling in school. Despite having his father in the United States and his mother in Tlacotepec, David does not demonstrate the trend of success for such students that we document in this chapter.

Another exception is the opposite of the case of David. Zamany, a student whose mother and father are in the United States, should, according to the general trend, be struggling in school. But despite the fact that both of her parents are absent, she has overcome the difficulties of family separation and is excelling in school. Her grades are above average and she aspires to pursue higher education. Despite their absence, Zamany's parents maintain consistent communication with her and send remittances. While she lacks direct parental support, Zamany gets much guidance from her mother in the United States, with whom she speaks regularly. The immigrant bargain also encourages Zamany to dedicate herself to her studies, as she understands that the hardships her parents have endured have made it possible for her to pursue an education that many cannot afford. What's more, Zamany's parents have left her in the care of her grandparents in Tlacotepec, who provide strong emotional support for her.

For students who lack emotional support at home, teachers can fill this void and provide specific guidance on educational options. Especially because many parents and caregivers in Tlacotepec have little education themselves, teachers are often the only ones around who can provide specific guidance on future educational possibilities. Even though Sandra, a high school student, does not experience family separation, she explains how hard it is to decide what to study in college, especially because her family members know little about higher education. She says that her physics teacher, who has a college degree, gives her and her peers support and is willing to meet after class to discuss different options.

There are many paths that Tlacotepenses can take to be academically successful. A common pattern we have identified involves a combination of economic support coming from a parent abroad and emotional support from a parent in Tlacotepec. Although this family arrangement is most strongly correlated with higher attainment and grades, there are exceptions to this pattern. Some students without remittances get economic support from government programs like *Oportunidades* while others with both parents absent get emotional support from other family members or teachers. Although it is possible to find both types of support in many different ways, in a high emigration town like Tlacotepec, for many families, having one parent absent and parent at home is an avenue to the educational success of their children.

CONCLUSION

Educational aspirations in Tlacotepec are high for all young people, regardless of family separation. Yet some Tlacotepenses come closer to achieving these aspirations than others. Overall, we find that students with one parent in the United States and one parent in Tlacotepec have higher attainment and grades than do any other group. We argue that this family arrangement provides the two necessary elements for educational success: economic and emotional support. Although this type of family separation can provide challenges, the combination of having one migrant parent who provides remittances and one parent at home who provides emotional support to the child is likely to make both types of support possible.

There are situations in which young Tlacotepenses succeed in school without the support of parents in Mexico or without the financial resources from a parent abroad. For those with both parents absent, some academically-successful youth receive their support from an older relative (a grandparent, uncle, aunt) or someone else in the community, often a teacher. They may also be inspired by the immigrant bargain, and knowing the hardships their parents have endured for their benefit may lead them to succeed in school in Tlacotepec. For those with both parents in Tlacotepec, economic resources to continue with their education may be at a premium. But government programs such as *Oportunidades* may provide the economic support for some who otherwise might give up on school to continue with their education.

As a snapshot of a single town, our study is limited and the results may not necessarily apply to other parts of Mexico. A second limitation was the size of our sample, which made it impossible to analyze possible differences between maternal versus paternal separation. Both of these limitations could be resolved by future research with larger samples. Possibilities include a testing of our argument that having one absent parent produces better educational outcomes in different areas of Mexico with different migration histories. We also suggest further study of the potential differential effects between maternal and paternal separation on education.

WORKS CITED

Behrman, Jere, Susan Parker, and Petra Todd. 2009. "Schooling Impacts of Conditional Cash Transfers on Young Children: Evidence from Mexico," *Economic Development and Cultural Change* 57(3): 439-477.

Censo de Poblacion y Viviendo. 2011. *Síntesis metodológica y conceptual del Censo de Población y Vivienda 2010.* Mexico

Cuentame Oaxaca. 2010. "Población. Hablantes de lengua indígena," *Información por Entidad.* INEGI.

Dreby, Joanna. 2010. *Divided by borders: Mexican migrants and their children.* University of California Press.

Hanson, G. H, and C. Woodruff. 2003. *Emigration and educational attainment in Mexico.* University of California, San Diego and NBER National Bureau of Economic Research.

INEE (Instituto Nacional para la Evaluación de la Educación). 2005. "Tablas Estadísticas INEE."

INEGI (Instituto Nacional de Estadística, Geografía e Informática). 2011. "Mexico en Cifras," *Instituto Nacional De Estadistica Y Geografia.* Mexico: INEGI.

Kandel, William, and Grace Kao. 2001. "The Impact of Temporary Labor Migration on Mexican Children's Educational Aspirations and Performance," *International Migration Review* 35:1205-1231.

Kandel, William, and David Massey. 2001. "Culture of Mexican Migration: A Theoretical and Empirical Analysis, The." *Soc. F.* 80:981.

McKenzie, David, and Hillel Rapoport. 2006. "Migration and Education Inequality in Rural Mexico," *Inter-American Development Bank.* Argentina.

Mexicanos Primero. 2010. "Brechas El Estado de la Educación en México 2010." Mexico.

OECD (Organization for Economic Cooperation and Development). 2007. Expenditure by funding source and transaction type. *OECD.StatExtracts.*

Santibañez, Lucrecia, Georges Vernez, and Paula Razquin. 2005. "Education in Mexico." *Rand Corporation.*

Sawyer, Adam, David Keyes, Christina Velásquez, Grecia Lima, and M. Miguel Bautista. 2009. "Going to School, Going to El Norte: Migration's Impact on Tlacotepense Education." In *Migration of the Mexican Mixteca: A Transnational Community in Oaxaca and California,* ed. Wayne A. Cornelius, David S. FitzGerald, Jorge Hernandez-Diaz, and Scott Borger. Boulder, CO: Lynne Rienner Publishers.

Smith, Robert C. 2006. *Mexican New York: transnational lives of new immigrants.* University of California Press.

Zorilla, Margarita. 2004. "La educación secundaria en México: Al filo de su reforma," *Revista Electrónica Iberoamericana sobre Calidad, Eficacia y Cambio en Educación.*

7 Migration and Mental Health in a Binational Mixteco Community

REGINA CALVARIO, WHITNEY L. DUNCAN, DIANA ENRÍQUEZ, GILBERTO LÓPEZ, HUGO SALGADO

> *There's nothing here, not even psychologists. There's nothing. There are a lot of people who need treatment, lots of people who have problems here, so we need services. If there were [psychologists], I think it would help us a lot. I suffered so much, and I wanted someone I could share my troubles with.* — Maria Luisa, San Miguel Tlacotepec, Oaxaca, Mexico

INTRODUCTION

Maria Luisa, a 55-year-old mother of six who lives in San Miguel Tlacotepec, has suffered severe depression and *nervios*[1] on and off for years, beginning when her daughters left for the United States in 2004. At the time, she had never heard of "depression" but the sadness, desperation, and fear she was feeling led her to seek help in the nearby town of Juxtlahuaca, where a private doctor treated her with antidepressants and vitamins. Six years later, Maria Luisa continues to suffer from depression. Four of her children have settled in Vista, leaving her at home with her two other children, one grandchild, and her husband, who recently returned from the United States. While in Vista, Maria Luisa's husband had trouble finding and keeping work, both because of the difficult economic situation and his drinking problems. Maria Luisa's children in Vista have their own families, and, as she put it, "there is little work there, so they can't send much." As a result, she must work to support herself, her husband, and the three kids.

---

1 Nervios, or 'nerves' is a condition reported across a number of cultures that encompasses a wide range of physical, emotional, and existential experiences, from general nervousness and worry to psychosis (Jenkins 1988). In Latin America nervios often refers to an agitated, anxious, or worried state, and can sometimes lead to an attack of nerves, or an ataque de nervios. It is also associated with anger, thinking too much, and high and low blood pressure (Finkler 2001).

117

Maria Luisa attributes her current depression to several interrelated factors, all of which illustrate themes this chapter will examine: being separated from her children in Vista, lack of financial resources, and a dearth of employment options for herself and her family in both Vista and San Miguel Tlacotepec. In addition to the care she continues to receive from the private medical doctor, Maria Luisa has also gone to a nearby village to seek help from a *curandero*, but she reported it did not help her. Maria Luisa, like many Tlacotepenses, wishes there were a psychologist in Tlacotepec.

SIGNIFICANCE AND OVERVIEW

Many studies have examined the mental health status of migrants in the United States, but few examine these topics by including non-migrants and returned migrants in communities of origin (notable exceptions include Salgado de Snyder 1993, Wilkerson et al. 2009, Breslau et al. 2007, 2011, and Silver 2011). In helping fill this gap, our study asks: How do mental health outcomes vary among migrants, returned migrants, and non-migrants? Based on a combination of quantitative and qualitative data, including a mental health scale administered to all study participants, we show that overall, mental health among Tlacotepense migrants is better than that of Tlacotepec residents, including returned migrants. We explain these findings as a combination of various factors: the 'healthy migrant' effect, in which the healthy are more likely to migrate than the unhealthy; and the 'salmon bias' effect, which argues that sick migrants are more likely to return to their places of origin; the buffering effects of strong social networks among migrants; and the stresses of migration-related family separation in Tlacotepec.

Our data on treatment-seeking indicate that when migrants do suffer mental health problems in the United States, they are less likely than Tlacotepec residents to receive treatment and less likely to prefer formal mental health services. These findings lead us to conclude that when mental health symptoms impede migrants' ability to function and work in the United States, they may be more likely to return home and seek treatment there. Migrants who do not return home make use of their social networks in times of distress. Among all three groups, attitudes toward psychological services are positive, but lack of access to such services contributes to the utilization of informal care for mental health problems. Financial struggles contribute to emotional distress and access problems for both Tlacotepec residents and migrants.

MIGRATION AND HEALTH

Epidemiological studies in the United States indicate that newly-arrived Latino immigrants have substantially better overall health—as measured by death rates and infant mortality rates—than groups with whom they share a similar sociodemographic profile, such as African Americans and U.S.-born

Latinos (Hummer et al. 2007; Palloni and Arias 2004; Lara et al. 2005). This frequently cited finding is referred to as the 'Hispanic health paradox,' known as such because low socioeconomic status is expected to correlate positively with elevated mortality and health risk factors. This paradox has been well-documented yet also debated. Several theories have been advanced to explain the paradox, most notably the buffering effects of social support and family networks, the 'healthy migrant' effect, and the 'salmon bias' effect (Palloni & Arias 2004).

Social support and family networks have been shown to be an important mitigating factor in buffering the negative physical and mental effects of stress associated with the migration experience (Arcury et al. 2007; Nandi et al. 2011). *Social support* is defined as "[t]he information leading the subject to believe that he is cared for and loved, esteemed and a member of a network of a mutual obligation" (Cobb 1977). There is also evidence that *perceived* social support from families is related to lower levels of psychological distress among Latino groups (Rivera 2007; Vega et al. 1991).

The 'healthy migrant effect' posits a 'migration of the fittest' in which people with comparatively good health are more likely than others to emigrate (Escobar 1998; Abraido-Lanza et al. 1999; Palloni and Arias 2004). The 'salmon bias effect' theorizes that ill Hispanic migrants are more likely to return to their countries of origin than healthy migrants, and are therefore not accounted for in statistical analyses and epidemiological studies that take place in the United States alone. Alternatively, they may be counted upon returning to the United States after recovering, thus appearing healthier than they actually are (Abraido-Lanza et al. 1999; Hummer et al. 2007; Cornelius, Chávez and Jones 1984). 'Medical returns,' in which migrants return to their country of origin expressly for medical care, are also increasingly reported among Mexican migrants (Bergmark et al. 2008; Horton and Cole 2011; Wallace et al. 2009). Medical returns have been attributed to lack of insurance and other access issues in the United States, unsuccessful treatment in the United States, and preference for Mexican medical practices.

With regard to mental health, the prevailing view is consistent with the Hispanic health paradox: recently arrived Mexican migrants (and foreign-born populations in general) tend to have better mental health than U.S.-natives. This theory is reflected in a nationally-representative sample of Latinos, where U.S.-born Latinos reported higher lifetime rates for most depressive disorders than Latino immigrants (Alegria 2008). When disaggregated by ethnic subgroups, however, the paradox was only reliably observed for Mexican subjects, and only evident for depressive and anxiety disorders (Alegria 2008). Mental health appears to deteriorate with time spent in the United States (Grant et al. 2004, Alderete et al. 2000; Escobar 2000; Vega et al. 1998; Escobar 1998). Acculturation stress (Cuéllar 2000; Cuéllar, Siles, & Bracamontes 2002; Finch, 2003) and economic and social marginality (Vega 2009) are likely contributing factors to that trend.

Very few studies directly compare the mental health of Mexican migrants to that of non-migrating Mexicans. Vega et al. (1998) found that prevalence of mental disorders was lowest among recent Mexican migrants, intermediate among Mexico City residents, and highest among migrants who had spent more time in the United States. Using national epidemiological data from various household surveys conducted in the United States and Mexico, Breslau and colleagues have more recently found higher prevalence for mood and anxiety disorders among Mexican migrants than among both a general Mexico sample (Breslau et al. 2007) and a sample of Mexican migrant sending communities (Breslau et al. 2011). Recently arrived migrants, particularly among younger cohorts, have particularly elevated risk for anxiety and mood disorders, lending credibility to the theory that migration itself presents considerable mental health risks (Breslau et al. 2011).

AVAILABLE SERVICES

Although mental health services in Oaxaca have expanded dramatically in the past decade, they continue to be concentrated in the urban state capital, Oaxaca City—a six-hour drive from San Miguel Tlacotepec. Tlacotepec itself has no formal mental health services, but the government-run community health center is currently being expanded to bring in a psychologist. For now, the closest option is the Juxtlahuaca IMSS[2] hospital (20 minutes away), which recently added psychological counseling to its list of free services. However, it is only staffed by one intern psychologist at a time, and patients must be formally employed to be enrolled in the IMSS system.

Several psychologists have private practices in Juxtlahuaca, but the cost—between 70 and 300 pesos per consultation—is prohibitive for many Tlacotepenses, many of whom earn between 80 and 100 pesos per day. The nearest large city, Huajuapan, a two-hour drive from Tlacotepec, has a range of psychological services, both public and private. However, there are no psychiatric services in the Mixteca region; patients must travel to Oaxaca City and seek care at either the state psychiatric hospital, a general public hospital, or with private practitioners.[3]

The Vista area also has a number of both private and government-subsidized care options, which have increased since the 2004 passage of California's Mental Health Services Act (Proposition 63) that provides more state funding for mental health programs. Mental Health Systems, a publicly funded agency

---

2 Created in 1943, IMSS, or Instituto Mexicano de Seguro Social (The National Institute of Social Services), is Mexico's social security system for workers employed in the formal sector.

3 'Psychological services' refer to services rendered by psychologists and counselors, and may include psychotherapy, counseling, psychological education and awareness building, and group sessions. Psychologists and counselors are not legally authorized to prescribe medications. 'Psychiatric services' refer to services rendered by psychiatrists and also may include therapy and education, usually in addition to psychiatric medications.

providing cost-effective mental health and addiction services, has a number of clinics in North County whose goal is to offer "culturally appropriate" programs for children, adolescents, adults, and families. The non-profit organization North Country Lifeline offers free group and general counseling. The cost of individual sessions is reimbursed through Medi-Cal, California's Medicaid program providing services for low-income families. Staff at Lifeline report that migrants regularly utilize these services and that patients do not need to provide information regarding their immigration status.

The National Alliance on Mental Illness (NAMI) North Coastal San Diego County is a non-profit organization run by local volunteers aimed at educating the populace about mental health and eradicating stigmas surrounding mental illness. NAMI's San Diego County affiliates throughout North County offer family, group, and peer-to-peer support groups run by trained (non-professional) community members who provide education about mental health. Tri-City Medical Center in Vista offers inpatient services for the severely mentally ill as well as a group outpatient program that meets three times a week at a cost of $350 per day without health insurance. The Vista Community Clinic, which provides affordable care for other health problems, does not have psychologists on staff, but primary care physicians there do diagnose mental health problems and prescribe psychopharmaceuticals for depression. Free depression screening is available for all adults in San Diego during National Depression Screening Week in early October. Private services are also plentiful in North County, but tend to be expensive for those without insurance.

MIGRATION AND MENTAL HEALTH STATUS

Depression Scale: The CES-D

We utilized several approaches to measure mental health among Tlacotepenses, one of which was a field-tested and validated depression screening tool widely used in community health studies: the Center for Epidemiological Studies Depression Scale (CES-D) (Radloff 1977). The CES-D focuses on clinical depression, a mood disorder in which feelings of sadness, loss, anger, or frustration interfere with everyday life for a period of two weeks or longer (Fava 2008).[4] The CES-D has been administered in rural communities across the Mexican state of Jalisco, as well as in various community settings in the United States. In both countries, the CES-D has been found to have high internal consistency (Irwin et al. 1999; Maldonado & Salgado-de Snyder 1994), making the use of this instrument particularly appropriate for the cross-sectional and international nature of our study. Originally a 20-item scale, it has been used

---

4 An accurate diagnosis for clinical depression, however, can only be made by a physician or qualified mental health professional.

in many studies as a screening tool for the presence of depressive illness. We chose the shorter 10-item version of the CES-D scale, also designed to measure depressive symptomatology in the general population (Kohout 1993). This short-form version includes items assessing depressive symptoms in the three primary domains of symptomology identified in the longer instrument: (a) depressed affect, (b) interpersonal relations, and (c) positive affect (Radloff 1977). Analyses of data obtained in previous samples of Latino immigrants indicated the 10-item short form of the CES-D has acceptable reliability and validity (Kuptniratsaikul 2002), with those scoring above 11 considered to have depressive symptoms. Greater scores reflect greater levels of depressive symptoms, with a suggested cut-off score of 10 between significant and non-significant symptomology (Irwin et al. 1999).[5]

A binational comparison of self-rated depression symptoms

The mean age of our total sample was 36 (SD=9.07) with an inclusion age range of 15-65 years. The sample consisted of 55 percent female and 45 percent male participants. Twenty percent of our total sample reported significant levels of depressive symptomatology, the same expected percentage in the general population at the time the scale was created (Radloff 1977). Female respondents reported higher levels of depressive symptoms, consistent with literature on depression and other mood disorders (Roberts 1980). United States-based respondents reported the highest depressive symptoms in their late teens, yet they experience a steady drop in depressive symptoms after age 45. On the other hand, Mexico-based respondents reported a steady climb of symptoms after their mid-thirties.

With regard to migration, Tlacotepec residents (i.e., non-migrants and returned migrants) were much more likely to report significant depressive symptomatology than were current migrants. The prevalence of depression was 23 percent for non-migrants, 21 percent for returned migrants, and 9 percent for current migrants (see Figure 7.1). These findings are in line with the 2007 study of Tlacotepec, which found that non-migrants and returned migrants were more than 2.5 times as likely to have been diagnosed with at least one physical illness (Duncan et al. 2009).

---

5 Each item is rated on a 4-point scale ranging from 0 (0 days per week) to 3 (5-7 days per week). A total score was calculated by summing the responses after items 5 and 8 were reversed to account for their positive affect.

Figure 7.1 Percent of Tlacotepense Adults Reporting Depressive Symptoms by Migrant Status, 2011

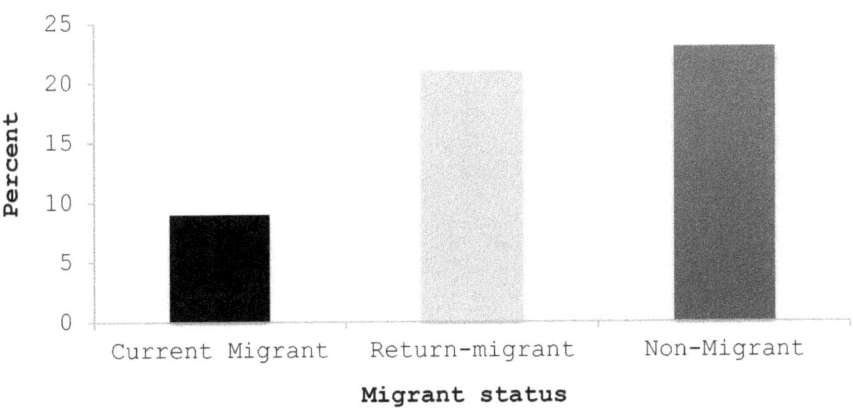

N=774

To further test the impact of migrant status on mental health, we conducted a series of multiple regression analyses using the CES-D scores as our dependent variable and six independent variables: gender, education, wealth, migration status, marital status, and age (see table 7.1). Men and respondents with higher levels of education were less likely to report depressive symptoms, which is what we predicted based on accepted epidemiological literature (Dohrenwend 1975). Consistent with our descriptive data, we find that current migrants are less likely to report depressive symptoms after applying the controls.

Table 7.1 Determinants of Significant Depressive Symptoms among Tlacotepenses, 2011

	Model 1
Determinant	β
Male	-1.490*** (0.414)
Education	-0.143*** (0.045)
Wealth	-0.283 (0.302)

Migrant (Yes)	-1.535*
	(0.643)
Return Migrant	0.382
	(0.498)
Married (Yes)	-0.309
	(0.462)
Age	-0.086
	(0.071)
Age^2	0.001
	(0.001)
Intercept	9.769***
	(1.371)
Adjusted R-squared	0.086

N=720

These results run counter to recent studies comparing the mental health of Mexican migrants with non-migrating Mexicans. Breslau et al. (2011) found that Mexican migrants—particularly from younger birth cohorts—had higher lifetime prevalence rates of depressive and anxiety disorders than did family members of migrants remaining in Mexico (17.4 percent versus 11.7 percent, respectively) (Breslau et al. 2011: 430). Their study provides the "first direct evidence that experiences as a migrant might lead to the onset of clinically significant mental health problems in this population" (ibid). Although they utilize nationally representative samples in the United States and Mexico to identify a transnational sample of migrants and family members of migrants, their study does not directly compare migrants, returned migrants, and non-migrants from the same sending community.

By comparing these three groups, our study allows us to gauge the impacts of sampling bias, familial separation, and social networks. We theorize that migrant mental health is significantly better than that of non-migrants and returned migrants in their hometown due to a combination of the following factors: (a) the healthy migrant and salmon bias effects; (b) social networks that are protective of Tlacotepense migrants; and (c) familial separation which is particularly distressing for Tlacotepec residents. Finally, we discuss the impacts of financial struggles on the emotional health of all Tlacotepenses, regardless of migration status.

Healthy Migrant Effect

The healthy migrant effect—the notion that healthy people are more likely to emigrate than unhealthy people—is a sampling bias that has been put forth as one explanation for the Hispanic health paradox. If sick Latinos do not emigrate, then Latino migrants in the United States should be healthier than others with similar sociodemographic profiles. In line with this hypothesis, our logistic regression analysis (Table 7.2) shows that males with more depressive symptomatology according to the CES-D were less likely to have plans to emigrate in the coming year (p<.01).

Table 7.2 Effect of Depressive Symptoms on Tlacotepenses' Plans to Migrate, 2011

Determinant	β
CES-D	-0.047*
	(0.023)
Age	-0.050
	(0.060)
Age squared	0.000
	(0.001)
Male	-1.155***
	(0.288)
Married	-0.265
	(0.350)
Education	-0.007
	(0.023)
(Intercept)	4.466***
	(1.010)
McFadden's R-squared	0.063

N=600

These results indicate stronger support for the healthy migrant hypothesis than several recent nationally representative studies. Utilizing data from the longitudinal Mexican Family Life Survey, Rubalcava et al. (2008) compared Mexican residents and recently arrived Mexican migrants and found that "[o]verall, associations between the likelihood of migrating to the United States and physical health measurements suggested that migrants were positively selected for health" (81), particularly among females and rural males, but these findings were generally weak. Their data, however, is based on respondents' assessments of overall health and on physical health markers such as body weight index, height, and blood pressure, not on indicators of mental health.

Breslau et al. (2007) use data from the WHO's World Mental Health Surveys in Mexico and the United States and find that pre-existing anxiety disorders are actually predictive of subsequent emigration, thus contradicting the healthy migrant hypothesis. The differences between our findings and those of Breslau et al could be due to the fact that their study is based on retrospective reports of the onset of anxiety disorder, while our study is based on self-reports of current depressive symptomatology. These divergent findings suggest that further studies comparing migrants to non-migrants in their towns of original are needed.

Salmon Bias Effect & Treatment-Seeking

The salmon bias effect explains that Latino migrants appear to have better overall health outcomes than those of a similar demographic profile because those who are unwell are more likely to return to their countries of origin to seek treatment, and are thus undercounted in epidemiological studies in the United States. Studies that propose the salmon bias effect as a factor in the Hispanic Health Paradox compare Latino migrants to other groups in the United States, but one might expect that a similar sampling bias would take place on the other end: if unhealthy migrants are more likely to return home, there would be a disproportionately high number of sick residents in their hometowns. Our data on the relative health of migrants versus Tlacotepec residents suggest that this is a possibility.

Of course, there are many reasons a small, poor, migrant-sending community such as Tlacotepec might be conducive to poorer mental health outcomes than relatively wealthy communities in California. Further, ill migrants returning home might not remain ill, such that the sampling bias would be insignificant. However, if being in Tlacotepec is less conducive to mental health, sick returned migrants might be unlikely to recover upon returning home and thus be more likely to seek treatment. Our treatment-seeking data—which show that current migrants are the least likely to get treatment for self-reported depression[6] while returned migrants are the most likely (see figure 7.2).[7] —indicate that the salmon bias may be a contributing factor to the disparities among Tlacotepec residents and migrants.

---

6 In addition to the CES-D, our survey asked informants whether they had in the last year suffered depression, nervios, anxiety, panic attack, susto, or bilis/coraje. If informants answered in the affirmative, they were asked the primary and secondary cause of the illness, who (if anyone) treated them, and what type of treatment they received.

7 The 2007 study found a similar trend: Tlacotepec residents were considerably more likely to have gotten treatment for reported illnesses than Tlacotepenses in Vista (Duncan et al. 176, 179).

Figure 7.2 Services sought for depression, by type of migration experience, 2011

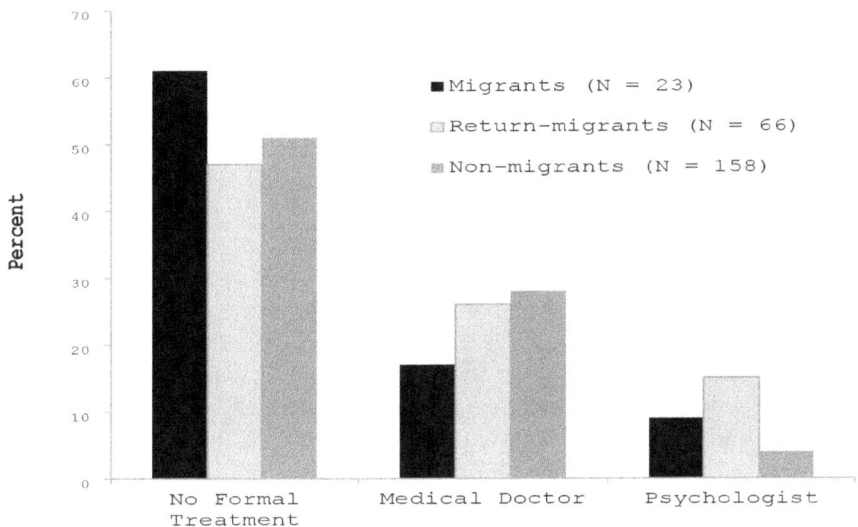

We did not ask people whether sickness was part of their decision to return home, and many other factors are undoubtedly at play in such a decision. However, it is also a possibility that some sick migrants return home in part to seek treatment.[8] Returning from Vista to the Mixteca for treatment would be highly inconvenient, of course, especially given that mental health services are available in North County. However, such services are often affordable only with health insurance, which is relatively uncommon among Tlacotepense migrants (our 2007 study indicated that only 25 percent of current migrants had health insurance). Further, lack of familiarity with the California health system, language barriers, worry about immigration status, and discomfort with unfamiliar medical and psychological practices may prevent sick migrants from utilizing the mental health services available in the Vista area — and lead them to return home for care (Bergmark et al. 2008, Wallace et al. 2009; Horton and Cole 2011).

Several returned migrants in Tlacotepec reported having returned from the United States to Oaxaca and seeking medical and psychological care there.

---

8 The 2007 study found that nearly 21 percent of Tlacotepec residents and 22 percent of Vista residents had returned or had a family member return to Mexico for medical treatment (Duncan et al. 2009: 179).

They cited cost as the main factor, though they found that once they returned to Tlacotepec, access to services was still a problem.

Enriqueta, a 30 year-old Tlacotepec resident with clinically-diagnosed schizophrenia, described the onset of her illness:

> It was in the United States where my relatives started to notice that I wasn't normal; I didn't act right. I didn't pay attention and my family members noticed. I came here [to Mexico] sick from the U.S. and it is here where I got treatment. An uncle put me on a plane and sent me to Oaxaca, alone. My father had to get a loan to travel into the city and get me.

One reason Enriqueta did not get treatment when she lived in Vista was because she and her family members, who were working for minimum wage in agriculture, could not afford it. In addition to the cost, Enriqueta feared losing her job if she took time off to seek treatment. It was not until her relatives started noticing extreme changes in her personality that they decided her illness had become an emergency and sent her back to Oaxaca to receive treatment.

On her arrival in Oaxaca City, she said, "[my parents] took me directly to [the psychiatric hospital] Cruz del Sur." Indeed, psychiatrists at Cruz del Sur estimate that over a third of their patients are former migrants like Enriqueta, and psychologists throughout Oaxaca describe migration-related distress as one of the main reasons for which people—often returned migrants—seek psychological and psychiatric care in the state (Duncan forthcoming). According to these psychologists, returning to Oaxaca from the United States for treatment is not an uncommon practice.

Cruz del Sur is the only public psychiatric hospital in the state, but medications there can be prohibitively expensive. "The government pays for the visit," says Enriqueta, but "the patient pays for the medication … it is very expensive, about 3000 pesos each time I go to the hospital." 3000 pesos is more than many Tlacotepenses make in a month. Unable to afford the costs on her own, Enriqueta has been living with her schizophrenia without the required medical treatment—sometimes going weeks without medicine.

Anselmo, lived in north San Diego County until anxiety and depression made it impossible for him to function and hold down a job, at which point he returned Oaxaca to seek treatment. "I went to a medical doctor [in Tlacotepec]. He told me that I needed medicine to control my *nervios*… it worked. He gave me sleeping pills and some shots to help me control my emotions." Anselmo began to see a psychologist but it became too expensive to continue with that treatment option:

> To see a psychologist one has to go all the way to Huajuapan. It is far. You need some money to go there. The cost depended on whether I

needed lots of treatment or not. When I would go really sick, it would cost $500 or $800 pesos per visit.

Both Enriqueta and Anselmo experienced mental health issues in the United States, but were unable to afford treatment there. Forced to return home to receive treatment, they found that once again the cost was prohibitive. For both, the hope of finding cheaper treatment in Mexico proved as elusive as it had in the United States.

Overall, these findings suggest that the salmon bias effect may be a binational phenomenon best understood by comparing migrants not only to other sociodemographic groups in the United States, but also to Mexican migrant-sending communities. The bias could partially explain disparities among Tlacotepenses in Vista and in Tlacotepec. Treatment-seeking practices and barriers to accessing care for migrants in the United States may shed light on some migrants' reasons for returning home, even if the perception that care might be more accessible in Mexico is inconsistent with the reality upon getting there.

Family Disruption and Social Support

Another explanation for the finding that Tlacotepec residents have poorer mental health than U.S.-based migrants is the stress of family separation for those who stay behind. Existing studies indicate that family separation, lack of circular migration, and disruption in social support and networks are all significantly and negatively associated with mental health status (Bryceson and Vuorela 2002; Dreby 2010; Hondagneu-Sotelo 1997; Menjívar and Agadjanian 2007; Schmalzbauer 2004; Silver 2011).

Although family separation is an important issue for both migrants and non-migrants, the strong networks migrants create in the United States may mitigate some of the emotional impacts of such disruption (Arcury et al. 2007; Nandi et al. 2011). As individuals migrate to new places, they draw support from the closest people in their social networks, who are usually members of their own ethnic group (Erikson 2002). In the case of Tlacotepenses, who have established a strong community in the city of Vista, the constant communication and interaction with other Tlacotepenses allow for the formation of support networks which incorporate family members and fellow community members (we will return to this point in our discussion of informal mental health care below).

Only a handful of studies have examined the mental health of non-migrating spouses and close family members of migrants. These indicate that non-migrating wives in particular tend to suffer emotional and psychological consequences as a result of their husbands' migration (Salgado de Snyder 1993; Maldonado 1993; Duncan et al. 2009; Wilkerson et al. 2011; Silver 2011). Salgado de Snyder shows that 31 percent of wives of migrants residing in rural Jalisco and Michoacán had a negative view of their husband's decision to migrate, since they were forced to deal with problems precipitated by his migration such as family dissolution, fights, new household responsibilities, loneliness, worry about husbands in the United States, and fear of losing children to migration. Forty-three percent of the women in Salgado's study reported internalizing emotions related to their husband's migration, and her sample's median group score for psychological distress (24.3, as measured by the CES-D) indicates high levels of emotional distress (Salgado de Snyder 1993).

Using data from the Mexican Family Life Survey, Silver (2011) also found that "migration has marked adverse psychological repercussions for migrants' close family members remaining at home, and particularly for the wives and mothers of migrants" (Silver 2011, 25). Her results indicate that women are more negatively impacted by the migration of a close family member than are men (ibid, 27), and that emotional distress may be higher in sending communities with high rates of outmigration than those with lower rates, due to the sense of isolation and emptiness (ibid, 9).

In our sample, 32 percent of women living in Mexico whose husbands are in the United States reported significant depressive symptomatology on the CES-D—compared to 25 percent of women whose spouses lived with them in Mexico. In our 2007 study, we found that 27 percent of women whose husbands lived in the United States had sought treatment for depression, compared to 13 percent of women living with their husbands. We also found that Tlacotepenses with a close family member in the United States were over twice as likely to have sought treatment for depression (17.5 percent versus 8.8 percent) (Duncan et al. 2009).

Family separation is a frequent topic of conversation in Tlacotepec. Dr. Francisco, a local medical doctor who heads a private clinic, explains how migration contributes to tensions in marriages and thus to the emotional health of non-migrating wives:

> Couples in Tlacotepec get married. They're together for a couple of years, then the man migrates to the United States and comes back in three or four years. In that time span, problems begin and the onset of sadness occurs, anxiety problems, along with lack of communication and reduction in remittances.

Many Tlacotepenses also mention the disruptive impacts of parental migration on children's development, emotional stability, and academic performance (see chapter 6, this volume). Jorge, a non-migrant in Tlacotepec, observed:

> Parents go to the United States and leave their children with grandparents, aunts and uncles, then the kids feel bad because

although they have material things and a bit of money to solve their problems, they say "I'd like to at least feel the embrace of a father, I'd at least like him to tell me he loves me." They get depressed and feel the need, the anxiety to belong to a family.

José, a returned migrant residing in Tlacotepec, also described some of the pressures of family separation:

I think it's like a chain. You send money, your family eats, and [your kids] go to school. When you don't send money they don't have food and your children have fewer opportunities. Logically, as the head of the family this affects you mentally and it affects your family. Problems start, solitude, and the chain is broken.

Although family separation is a source of distress for migrants as well as their non-migrating counterparts, we suggest that it may particularly impact non-migrants in towns with heavy outmigration such as San Miguel Tlacotepec. The sense of loneliness is quite noticeable, with residents often discussing the rifts caused by family separation as contributors to marital problems and stress among youth. While non-migrants may enjoy some material benefits provided by remittances, such investments cannot offset the sense of loneliness created by the absence of close family members (Silver 2011). Further, as our next section illustrates, even these material benefits seem to be waning in the context of the economic crisis beginning in 2007.

FINANCIAL STRUGGLES

The theme of economic strife was prominent in interviews with Tlacotepenses on either side of the border, and the data indicate a connection between economic and emotional well-being for migrants, return migrants, and non-migrants. Such findings are not surprising given that income is a significant indicator of mental health and ability to access health services (Belle 1990; Gresenz et al. 2001), but are worth emphasizing in light of the economic crisis beginning in 2007 which led to both higher rates of unemployment among Mexican migrants in the United States and reduced remittances (Wilson 2009).

Although we found little quantitative evidence indicating an association between wealth or remittances and mental health outcomes (as measured through the CES-D), 28 percent of the 256 Tlacotepenses who reported having suffered depression in the past year reported money problems as the main cause. Financial problems were the second-most reported cause overall, second only to family problems. This suggests that economic difficulties are regarded as an important factor contributing to depression in this population.

Figure 7.3 Self-reported causes of depression among Tlacotepenses, 2011

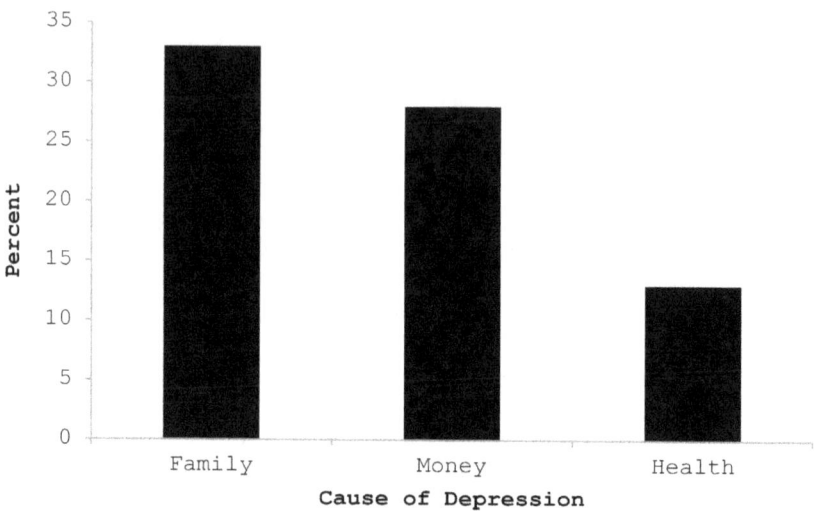

N=263

Our qualitative data suggest that the three main reported causes of depression (family, money, and health problems) are not isolated, but interrelated. Family problems are exacerbated by economic problems, which can subsequently have a negative impact on health and limit access to services.

Financial struggles were a frequent topic of conversation among family members of migrants in Tlacotepec. Dolores, a 64 year-old woman whose husband left her when he migrated to the United States 25 years ago, attributes both her economic and emotional difficulties to her husband's abandonment and lack of financial support. Alone, Dolores has had to struggle to support the family:

> I would work wherever they needed me. I would go wash other people's clothes. I suffered to have enough for everyday expenses for my children [...] My children met [their father], but he has no love for my children. They see him as any man and he sees them as any other person, not as his children. He wasn't here to raise them, to give them advice or lead them on to a good path... My children grew up very poor, with patches on their clothes. When we had beans they would fight over the beans.

Dolores had to rely on support from her in-laws because her husband did not send money to cover her family's expenses. "I would get support from my children's [paternal] grandmother. Their grandfather would make sure that they would eat, but he [her husband] never supported them in any way."

While Dolores' story is the most extreme example of the impact of a migrant parent not contributing to the family income, the theme was far from uncommon. Many women reported that they were no longer receiving the amounts they once had, and were forced to search for new ways of supporting their families. This created stress for both the women and their children. Maria Luisa, whose story began our chapter, reported that since her husband lost his job in the United States, she has been working several informal jobs to try and support the entire family:

> My husband sent very little money and my daughters are married, so my husband sent a little and my son sent a little...but now there's no work there [in the United States] so my son doesn't send anything. He can't because there's very little employment...My husband doesn't worry about a thing and this depresses me, because I want to fight to provide for my kids but I can't do it all alone.

Maria Luisa attributes her depression partially to her economic struggles and need to work constantly, and partially to her family separation, which no longer has the upside of remittances from her children in Vista.

Wages earned by migrants can enable families to afford services that are important to provide a good quality of life (Rose et al. 2008: 105). Without remittances, many Mexican families are at risk of living in poverty and must develop strategies for survival—such as working menial jobs for little pay. However, even with such strategies, health pathologies can result from limited access to basic health care or services. People in Tlacotepec frequently mentioned that lack of remittances has a detrimental impact on Tlacotepenses' mental health and their accessibility to mental health services. As Dr. Gómez from Tlacotepec's local clinic put it, a "bad economic situation affects people's mental and physical health." In addition to the emotional impacts of financial stress, many Tlacotepenses are unable to pay for consultations and medications.

Although the local clinic does offer some medical services, it does not include care for psychological issues, making it difficult if not impossible for many Tlacotepenses to afford mental health services. Elvira, a 50 year-old Tlacotepec resident, says that many Tlacotepenses view psychological treatment as a luxury. "There are mental health services in Huajuapan... [but] imagine, the session alone costs you 800 or 1000 pesos. Where do you get that kind of money?"

Dr. Gómez asserts that economic limitations also impact the quality of treatments that Tlacotepenses receive. When they are unable to afford medicines, doctors must prescribe cheaper, less effective versions. Patient care is also limited by the fact that Tlacotepenses, lacking economic resources, tend to use the closest, rather than the most effective, treatment centers.

> We have patients who need other type of medicines… that we are not able to provide. We tell them that they have to buy a certain medicine and they say that they don't have money. There is anguish because they need the medicine, but we don't have it, we try to change the medicine or make adjustments to try to solve the problem, but the people need a certain medicine and they don't have the resources to buy it. … We have to send them to a hospital in Huajuapan… but they say "I will go to the one in Juxtlahuaca because I don't have enough money to go all the way there [to Huajuapan]."

Financial stress is also an issue among migrants, who often feel extreme pressure to fulfill the role of breadwinner or provider. Ignacio, a teacher in Tlacotepec with a degree in psychology, mentioned the social pressure that migrants endure not only to send remittances while in the United States, but also to come back to Mexico with money. "Everybody expects you to bring something or for you to send them something. If you don't, people even tease you with jokes like: 'look at him, he just went on a trip for fun.'" Migrants often resist returning to Tlacotepec empty-handed: "[T]heir whole world comes to an end, thinking about people in Tlacotepec, who expect them to return with something."

Economic challenges were a prominent theme in our interviews with Tlacotepenses on either side of the border, and the data indicate a connection between economic and emotional well-being among all three migrant categories. Many Tlacotepec residents cannot afford to pay for medical services, medicines, and the expenses that going to an out-of-town psychologist entail. Vista residents also face considerable barriers to access, as our treatment-seeking section showed. Such challenges often lead Tlacotepenses to use informal treatment options to address emotional distress.

INFORMAL CARE

Of the 94 percent of our sample who reported that they would seek help if they suffered an emotional problem, nearly 47 percent said a medical doctor would be their first treatment preference while 32 reported that a psychologist would be their first choice. These preferences differ significantly when analyzed by migration experience, as shown in Figure 7.4. Migrants were less likely to prefer treatment from either a medical doctor or a psychologist than their nonmigrant and returned migrant counterparts, but more likely to prefer friends or family when confronted with mental health issues. Returned migrants were the most likely to prefer medical doctors and psychologists.

Figure 7.4 Preferred services, by type of migration experience, 2011

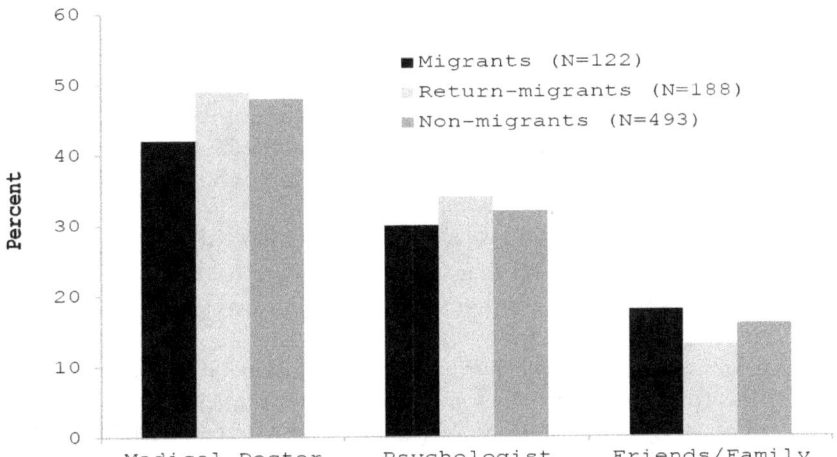

All migrant categories expressed an overall preference for biomedical and psychological treatment, a finding which was reflected in qualitative interviews. In discussing the benefits of seeing a psychologist, Lauro, a non-migrant, said: "well yeah, we'd have to use [a psychologist] because we see that talking with a psychologist changes your life, you can handle depression more, your pain is gone... all that requires a psychologist."

Although we found this strong preference for biomedical and psychological treatments among Tlacotepenses in both Tlacotepec and Vista, factors such as accessibility and affordability of such treatments lead many to seek informal care. We propose that the high reports of "no formal care," the top choice of treatment among migrants, non-migrants, and returned migrants alike (see figure 7.2) may be due to individuals seeking informal channels for treatment. Such treatment options include friends and family (particularly among those with migration experience), faith-based healing, and *curanderos.*

FRIENDS & FAMILYS

Turning to friends or family members was considered an important option in times of emotional distress. Current migrants were more likely (18 percent) than non-migrants (16 percent) and returned migrants (13 percent) to report that they would use family or friends as a first resort for emotional problems. As argued above, migrant networks are strengthened as they establish themselves in new places—which may be one reason that Tlacotepec migrants are more likely to use family or friends for mental health problems.

The theme of family support as a form of coping with emotional distress and mental illness arose in qualitative interviews, especially among individuals who once lived in the United States. Having family support was seen as essential to recovery in a number of cases. Anselmo, the former migrant who returned to Oaxaca to seek treatment, says his wife helped him in many ways: "When my wife was around I would tell her that I felt bad, I felt something, that I didn't feel well." She would provide comfort by talking with him, massaging him, or by preparing herbal teas to soothe his stress and anxiety. Mariana, a return migrant who worked in agriculture when she lived in Vista, discussed how she and her sister felt depressed while living in California: "We didn't seek any help, just us two. We would console one another, give each other strength... 'Let's work hard, as soon as the job dies down we go back to our families'," they told one another. Family support was an important way of coping with depression and anxiety among migrants.

Legal status and low socioeconomic status also create a structure in which access to formal treatments is limited for migrants in the United States (Chávez et al. 1985, 1986). Those who are undocumented and who lack health insurance are less likely to seek formal treatment (Duncan et al. 2009), which also contributes to the use of family or friends as first treatment options. As one returned migrant says about migrants living in the United States, "if one does not go to a psychologist, therapy can be with a friend, a family member, a brother. I think that [also] helps a lot." Overall, friends and family were seen as important sources of support in cases of emotional distress.

FAITH-BASED HEALING

Another theme that emerged from the in-depth interviews is the use of the supernatural as a treatment option in Tlacotepec.[9] Prayer, visits to a *curandero*, and visits to see the priest were all mentioned as treatment options for emotional distress, and sometimes these spiritual practices were utilized in addition to medical treatments. When talking about his faith in God's power to heal, Javier, a non-migrant said: "No, I have not gone [to a medical doctor] because I know that God is the one who helps me. God is first." He went on:

> Well, those who do not believe in God can turn to science, or a psychologist. Those who believe in God can turn to prayer. First turn to God, then to the doctor because we should always put God first. God is the one who gave them the wisdom to be doctors.

In addition to individual prayer, going to religious leaders is a means of addressing illness in Tlacotepec. Julio, who had suffered from depression and

---

9 Interviews focusing on religious practices were not conducted in Vista and little can be said about faith-based healing there. Further research on the topic would complement our findings.

anxiety, states that he turned to the local evangelical church for support. "I went to a Christian church... the pastor told me to pray, and that they too were going to pray for me. To ask the Holy Father to help me, he was going to fix me."

Interviewees often discussed religious and medical practices as going hand-in-hand for treatment of illness, indicating the presence of medical pluralism, or the practice of utilizing more than one approach to healing for the same condition. Chuy, a sixty-something born-again Christian, argued:

> I believe in Jesus Christ who is doctor of all doctors. But God did give us science and doctors. I'm not saying that I will not go [to the local health clinic] because maybe one day I will go. But up until now, I have not gone and I have not thought about going.

The use of faith-based care in addressing mental health problems was not limited to evangelicals. Catholics, too, participated in such approaches. Tlacotepec's priest stated that the Church was actively trying to promote youth groups that would help in the "emotional, mental, and spiritual development" of young adults. Juanito, a 20 year-old college student who has suffered from anxiety and depression, sees his distance from the Church as the cause of his illness. He decided to take an active role in the local youth church group and states that it has helped him develop both mentally and spiritually.

Turning to the supernatural was a prominent theme in our interviews. Some individuals spoke of the supernatural as another way of treating illness, and expressed the belief that God's omnipotence was stronger than any man-made science or medicine. Many others, however, choose to use the supernatural, in conjunction with biomedical and psychological practices, to treat their illnesses.

CURANDEROS

Unlike other towns in the region, Tlacotepec currently has very few options for traditional healing. The town's remaining *curandero*, Martín, grows two plants on his property to treat those who present symptoms of depression, but—unlike medical doctors in the town—he does not believe mental health is a pressing problem. He claims that the majority of his clientele in Tlacotepec consist of people suffering from other types of ailments such as arthritis or high blood pressure. "To be honest, very few people come to me who are suffering from depression," Martín says.

Indeed, while over 90 percent of our Tlacotepec-based sample said they would seek help for an emotional problem, not even two percent claimed they would select a *curandero* as their first, second, or third choice. No migrants reported that they would utilize a *curandero*. Elsewhere in Oaxaca, *curanderos* report frequently treating emotional distress—in cases of both indigenously defined illnesses like *susto*[10] and in cases of depression (Duncan, forthcoming). We theorize that this low number in Tlacotepec is due to diminished utilization and confidence in traditional medicine, especially among younger Tlacotepenses. Idiosyncrasies in Martín's healing approach and doubts about the efficacy of his treatments may also play a part in Tlacotepenses' preference for other types of care.

In summary, we argue that Tlacotepenses who reported receiving no formal treatment for mental health problems likely utilized informal treatment options which include: friends and family, faith-based healing, and *curanderos*. Although there was a strong preference for biomedical and psychological treatments, lack of accessibility and economic means to pay for such treatments lead many to seek informal care.

CONCLUSION

Various studies have examined the mental health status of migrants in the United States, but few have compared them with non-migrants and returned migrants in sending communities to get a more complete picture of the relationship between migration and mental health. In filling this void, our study investigates how mental health outcomes vary among migrants, returned migrants, and non-migrants. Based on a combination of quantitative and qualitative data, we have shown that mental health among Tlacotepense migrants is better than that of non-migrants and returned migrants in Tlacotepec. We explain these findings as a combination of various factors, all of which shed light upon the Hispanic health paradox. These factors include: (a) the 'healthy migrant' effect; (b) the 'salmon bias' effect; (c) the buffering effects of social networks among migrants; and (d) the stresses of migration-related family separation in Tlacotepec.

We complement our data on mental health status with an examination of treatment-seeking practices, which indicate that when migrants are confronted with mental health problems in the United States, they are less likely than Tlacotepec residents to receive treatment and less likely to prefer formal mental health services, despite the availability of such care in the Vista area. These results suggest that migrants may have a propensity to return home and seek treatment when depressive symptoms interfere with their ability to live and work in the United States. Those who remain in the United States make use of social networks in times of distress. Among all three migrant groups, attitudes toward mental healthcare are positive, but lack of access to such

---

10 Susto is a commonly reported condition throughout Latin America in which a severe fright leads to illness, emotional distress, 'soul loss,' and, in some cases, death. Some of the main symptoms associated with susto are "restlessness in sleep, listlessness, loss of appetite, weight loss, disinterest in dress and personal hygiene, loss of energy and strength, depression, introversion, paleness, and lethargy" (Crandon 1983: 156).

services contributes to the utilization of informal care for mental health problems. Financial struggles and a lack of employment options contribute to both mental health problems and access to services for both Tlacotepec residents and migrants.

WORKS CITED

Abraido-Lanza, A.F., B.P. Dohrenwend, D.S. Ng-Mak, and J.B. Turner. 1999. "The Latino Mortality Paradox: A Test of the 'Salmon Bias' and Healthy Migrant Hypotheses," *American Journal of Public Health* 89:1543–48.

Alegria, Margarita, Glorisa Canino, Shrout, Patrick Shrout, Meghan Woo, Naihua Duan, Doryliz Vila, Torres, Maria Torres, Chih-nan Chen, Xiao-Li Meng. 2008. "Prevalence of Mental Illness in Immigrant and Non-Immigrant U.S. Latino Groups," *American Journal of Psychiatry* 165, no. 3: 359-69.

Arcury TA, Quandt SA. 2007. "Delivery of health services to migrant and seasonal farmworkers," *Annual Review of Public Health* 28, no. 1: 345-63.

Alderete, E., et al. 2000. "Effects of Time in the United States and Indian Ethnicity on DSM-III-R Psychiatric Disorders among Mexican Americans in California," *The Journal of Nervous and Mental Disease* 188, no. 2: 90-100.

Belle, Deborah. 1990. "Poverty and Women's Mental Health," *American Psychologist*. 45, no. 3: 385-89.

Bhugra D. Migration and mental health. Acta Psychiatr Scand 2004: 109: 243–58.

Biederman, and S.L. Rauch. Philadelphia: Mosby Elsevie. Grzywacz, ,J., et al. 2010. "Mental Health Research with Latino Farmworkers: A Systematic Evaluation of the Short CES-D," *Journal of Immigrant and Minority Health* 5:652-58.

Bocallao, Martical L., and Paul Smokowski. 2007. "The Cost of Getting Ahead: Mexican Family System Changes After Immigration," *Family Relations* 56, no. 1: 52-66.

Bourdieu, Pierre, ed. 1993. *The Weight of the World: Social Suffering in Contemporary Society*. Stanford University Press.

Bourgois, Philippe. 1995. *In search of Respect: Selling Crack in El Barrio*. Cambridge: Cambridge University Press.

Breslau, Joshua, Guilherme Borges, Daniel Tancredi, Naomi Saito, Richard Kravitz, Ladson Hinton; William Vega; Maria Medina-Mora, and Sergio Aguilar-Gaxiola. 2011. "Migration from Mexico to the United States and Subsequent Risk for Depressive and Anxiety Disorders: A Cross-National Study," *Arch Gen Psychiatry* 68, no. 4: 428-33.

Bryceson, D. and U. Vuorela. 2002. *The transnational family: New European frontiers and global networks*. Oxford and New York: Berg.

Cabassa, Leopoldo J., Marissa C. Hansen, Lawrence A. Palinkas, and Kathleen Ell. 2008. "Azucar y nervios: Explanatory models and treatment experiences of Hispanics with diabetes and depression," *Social Science and Medicine* 66: 2413-24.

Chávez, LR, WA Cornelius; OW Jones. 1985. "Mexican immigrants and the utilization of U.S. health services: the case of San Diego," *Social Science & Medicine* 21, no. 1: 93-102.

_____ 1986. "Utilization of health services by Mexican immigrant women in San Diego," *Women Health* 11, no. 2: 3-20.

Clark, Margaret. 1959. Health in the Mexican-American Culture. Berkeley: University of California Press.

Cobb, S. 1976. "Presidential address-1976. Social support as a moderator of life stress," *Psychosomatic Medicine* 38, no. 5: 300-14.

Coltrane, Scott, Ross D. Parke, and Michele Adams. 2004. "Complexity of Father Involvement in Low-Income Mexican American Families," *Family Relations* 53, no. 2: 179-98.

Cornelius, W. A., L. R. Chávez, and O. W. Jones. 1984. "Mexican Immigration and Access to Health Care." La Jolla, CA: Center for U.S.-Mexican Studies, University of California, San Diego.

Crandon, Libbet. 1983. "Why Susto," *Ethnology* 22, no. 2: 153-67.

Daniulaityte, Raminta. 2004. "Making sense of diabetes: cultural models, gender and individual adjustment to Type 2 diabetes in a Mexican community," *Social Science and Medicine* 59: 1899-1912

Desjarlais, Robert, Leon Eisenberg, Byron Good, Arthur Kleinman. 1995. *World Mental Health: Problems and Priorities in Low-Income Countries*. New York & Oxford: Oxford University Press.

Dohrenwend, Bruce P. 1975. "Sociocultural and social-psychological factors in the genesis of mental disorders," *J Health Soc Behav* 16, no. 4: 365-92.

Dreby, J. 2010. *Divided by borders : Mexican migrants and their children*. Berkeley: University of California Press.

Duncan, Whitney L. Forthcoming 2012. *The Culture of Mental Health in a Changing Oaxaca*. Doctoral Dissertation, University of California at San Diego.

Duncan, Whitney L., Laurel Korwin, Miguel Pinedo, Eduardo González-Fagoaga, and Durga García. 2009. "Lucharle por la vida: The Impact of Migration on Health." In *Migration from the Mexican Mixteca: A Transnational Community in Oaxaca and California*, ed. Wayne A. Cornelius, David

Fitzgerald, Jorge Hernández Díaz, and Scott Borger. La Jolla, CA: Center for Comparative Immigration Studies, University of California, San Diego.

Ecks, Stefan. 2003. "Is India on Prozac? Sociotropic Effects of Pharmaceuticals in a Global Perspective," *Curare* 26, no. 1-2: 95-107

Ericksen, Thomas Hyland. 2002. *Ethnicity and Nationalism: Anthropological Perspectives (2ⁿᵈ Ed)*. London, UK: Pluto Press.

Escobar JI, Hoyos Nervi C, and Gara MA. 2000 "Immigration and mental health: Mexican Americans in the United States," *Harv Rev Psychiatry* 8, no. 2: 64-72.

Fadiman, Anne. 1997. *The Spirit Catches You and You Fall Down: A Hmong Child, Her American Doctors, and the Collision of Two Cultures*. New York, NY: Farrar, Straus and Giroux Publishers.

Farmer, Paul. 1992. *Aids and Accusation: Haiti and the Geography of Blame*. Berkeley: University of California Press.

_____. 2003. *Pathologies of Power: Health, Human Rights, and the New War on the Poor*. Berkeley: University of California Press.

Fava, M., and P. Cassano. 2008. "Mood Disorders: Major Depressive Disorder and Dysthymic Disorder." In *Massachusette General Hospital Comprehensive Clinical Psychiatry*, ed. T.A. Stern, J.F. Rosenbaum, M. Fava, J.

Finkler, Kaja. 2001. *Physicians at Work, Patients in Pain: Biomedical Practice and Patient Response in Mexico*, second edition. Durham: Carolina Academic Press.

_____. 2004. "Biomedicine globalized and Localized: Western medical Practicesin an Outpatient Clinic of a Mexican Hospital," *Social Science and Medicine* vol. 59: 2037-51.

Garcia de Alba Garcia, Javier, Ana L. Salcedo Rocha, Ivette Lopez, Roberta D. Baer, William Dressler, and Susan C. Weller. 2007. "'Diabetes is my companion': Lifestyle and self-management among good and poor control Mexican diabetes patients," *Social Science and Medicine* 64: 2223-35.

Grant BF, Stinson FS, Hasin DS, Dawson DA, Chou SP, and Anderson K. 2004. "Immigration and lifetime prevalence of DSM-IV psychiatric disorders among Mexican Americans and non-Hispanic whites in the United States: results from the National Epidemiologic Survey on Alcohol and Related Conditions," *Arch Gen Psychiatry* 61, no. 12: 1226-33.

Gesenz, Carole Roand; Roland Sturm, and Lingqi Tang. 2001. "Income and Mental Health: Unraveling Community and Individual Level Relationships," *The Journal of mental Health Policy and Economics* vol. 4: 197-203.

Grzywacz, Joseph, et al. 2006. "Leaving Family for Work: Ambivalence and Mental Health among Mexican Migrant Farmworker Men," *Journal of Immigrant and Minority Health* 1: 85-97.

Guarnaccia, Peter J, Roberto Lewis-Fernandez, and Melissa Rivera Marano. 2003. "Toward a Puerto Rican Popular Nosology: *Nervios* and *Ataque de Nervios.*" *Culture, Medicine and Psychiatry* 27: 339–66.

Hahn, Robert. 1995. Sickness and Healing: An Anthropological Perspective. Yale University Press.

Hondagneu-Sotelo, P. and Avila, E. 1997. "'I'm here, but I'm there' The meanings of Latina transnational motherhood," *Gender & Society* 11, no. 5: 548-71.

Hunt, Linda M., Katherine B. de Voogd. 2005. "Clinical Myths of the Cultural 'other': Implications for Latino patient care," *Academic Medicine* 80, no. 10: 918-24.

Irwin, Michael, Kamal Haydari Artin, and Michael N. Oxman. 1999. "Screening for Depression in the Older Adult: Criterion Validity of the 10-Item Center for Epidemiological Studies Depression Scale (CES-D)," *Archives of Internal Medicine* 159, no. 15: 1701-04.

Jenkins, Janis J. 1988. "Ethnopsychiatric Interpretations of Schizophrenic Illness: The Problem of *Nervios* Within Mexican-American Families," *Culture, Medicine, and Psychiatry* 12: 301-29.

Kleinman, Arthur. 1980. *Patients and Healers in the Context of Culture: An Exploration of the Borderland between Anthropology, Medicine, and Psychiatry.* Berkeley, CA: University of California Press.

_____. 1988. *Rethinking Psychiatry.* New York, NY: The Free Press.

Kohout, F. J., et al. 1993. "Two Shorter Forms of the CES-D (Center for Epidemiological Studies Depression) Depression Symptoms Index," *Journal of Aging and Health* 5, no. 2: 179-93.

Kuptniratsaikul, V., S. Chulakadabba, and S. Ratanavijitrasil. 2002. "An Instrument for Assessment of Depression among Spinal Cord Injury Patients: Comparison between the CES-D and TDI." *Journal of the Medical Association of Thailand = Chotmaihet Thangphaet* 85, no. 9: 978-83.

Lock, Margaret and Vinh-Kim Nguyen. 2010. *The Anthropology of Biomedicine.* Oxford: Wiley-Blackwell.

Maldonado, M. 1993. "Apoyo social y su relación con la sintomatología depresiva en esposas de migrantes y no migrantes," *Revista de Psicologia Social y Personalidad* 9, no. 2: 77–84.

Maldonado, M and V. N. Salgado-de Snyder. 1994. "The Psychometric Characteristics of the Depression Scale of the Centro De Estudios Epidemiólogicos in Adult Mexican Women from Rural Areas," *Salud pública De México* 36, no. 2: 200-9.

McArthur, Laura H., Ruben Anguiano, and Kevin H. Gross. 2004. "Are Household Factors Putting Immigrant Hispanic Children at Risk of Becoming Overweight: A community-Based Study in Eastern North Carolina," *Journal of Community Health* 29, no. 5.

Menjivar, C., and V. Agadjanian. 2007. "Men's migration and women's lives: Views from rural Armenia and Guatemala," *Social Science Quarterly* 88, no. 5: 1243-62.

Nandi, Arijit, Sandro Galea, Gerald Lopez, Vijay Nandi, Stacey Strongarone, and Danielle C. Ompad. 2008. "Access to and use of health services among undocumented Mexican immigrants in a US urban area," *American Journal of Public Health* 98, no. 11: 2011-20.

Nichter, Mark. 1981. "Idioms of Distress: Alternatives in the Expression of Psychosocial Distress: A case study from India," *Culture, Medicine, and Psychiatry* 5: 379-408.

Ohnuki-Tierney, Emiko. 1984. Illness and Culture in Contemporary Japan: An Anthropological View. Cambridge University Press.

Palloni, Alberto, and Elizabeth Arias. 2004. "Paradox Lost: Explaining the Hispanic Adult Mortality Advantage," *Demography* 41, no. 3: 385-415.

Petryna, Adriana, and Arthur Kleinman. 2006. "The Pharmaceutical Nexus." In *Global Pharmaceuticals: Ethics, Markets, Practices,* ed. Adriana Petryna, Andrew Lakoff, and Arthur Kleinman. Durham and London: Duke University Press.

Poss, Jane, and Mary Ann Jezewski. 2002. "The role and meaning of susto in Mexican Americans' explanatory model for Type 2 Diabetes," *Medical Anthropology Quarterly* 16, no. 3: 360-77.

Radloff, Lenore Sawyer. 1977. "The CES-D Scale," *Applied Psychological Measurement* 1, no. 3: 385-401.

Rivera, FI. 2007. "Contextualizing the experience of young Latino adults: The Relationship between acculturation and depression," *Journal of Immigrant and Minority Health* 3: 237–44.

Roberts, RE. 1980. "Reliability of the CES-D scale in different ethnic contexts," *Psychiatry Res* 2, no. 2: 125-34.

Rose, Susan, and Robert Shaw. 2008. "The Gamble: Circular Mexican Migration and the Return on Remittances," *Mexican Studies / Estudios Mexicanos* 1: 79-111. University of California on Behalf of the University of California Institute for Mexico

Rubalcava, Luis N., Graciela M. Teruel, Duncan Thomas, and Noreen Goldman. 2008. "The Healthy Migrant Effect: New Findings from the Mexican Family Life Survey," *American Journal of Public Health* 98, no. 1: 78-84.

Salgado de Snyder, V. Nelly. 1993. "Family Life Across the Border: Mexican Wives Left Behind," *Hispanic Journal of Behavioral Sciences* 15, no. 3: 391-401.

Scheper-Hughes, Nancy. 1993. *Death Without Weeping: The Violence of Everyday Life in Brazil.* Berkeley & Los Angeles: University of California Press.

Schmalbauer, L. 2004. "Searching for wages and mothering from afar: the case of Honduran transnational families," *Journal of Marriage and the Family* 66: 1317-31.

Silver, Alexis. 2011. "Families Across Borders: The Emotional Impacts of Migration on Origin Families," *International Migration* 49: no. doi: 10.1111/j.1468-2435.2010.00672.x

Vega, William, Kolodoy Bohdan, Juan Ramon Valle, and Judy Weir. 1991. "Social networks, social support, and their relationship to depression among immigrant Mexican women," *Human Organization* 50: 154–162.

Vega, William A., Kolody Bohdan, and Juan Ramon Valle. 1987. "Migration and Mental Health: An Empirical Test of Depression Risk Factors among Immigrant Mexican Women," *International Migration Review* 21, no.3: 512-530.

Vega, William A., Kolody Bohdan, Sergio Aguilar-Gaxiola, Ethel Alderete, Ralph Catalano, and Jorge Caraveo-Anduaga. 1998. "Lifetime prevalence of DSM-III-R psychiatric disorders among urban and rural Mexican Americans in California," *Arch Gen Psychiatry* 55: 771-78.

Vega, William A., Michael A. Rodriguez, and Elisabeth Gruskin. 2009. "Health Disparities in the Latino Population," *Epidemiologic Reviews* 31, no. 1: 99-112.

Wilkerson, Jared A.; Niwako Yamawaki, and Samuel D. Downs. 2011. "'Effects of Husbands' Migration on Mental Health and Gender Role Ideology of Rural Mexican Women," *Healthcare for Women International* 30: 612-26.

Wilson, Tamara Diana. 2009. "Economic Crisis and the Decline of Remittances to Mexico," *Anthropological Quarterly* 82, no. 2: 587-97.

8 A Town Without Water is Dead: Migration and Responses to Ecological Change

ANDREW HALL, HANNAH P. GIBSON, BETHANY REED, BOANERGES A. RODRIGUEZ ORELLANA, TANIA MONROY

"It is difficult...We migrants always think about returning to our town, but the problem is that there is no water...Look at the land ... Nothing is alive there. To be able to return, we have to do something.— Rosalinda, migrant and member of the *Comité* de Agua

Standing outside his house, Señor Roberto pours beans he has just harvested into a palm leaf basket near his feet. The dry afternoon wind blows, separating the beans from the stalks as they fall. His basket full, Señor Roberto bends his 80-year-old knees and rests on a log. Using a handkerchief to wipe away the sweat and dust that have collected on his forehead, the farmer explains why today beans and corn are nearly the only crops grown in Tlacotepec. "If there were money," he says, "the water could irrigate everything. Then, there would be a lot of agricultural production. We used to plant vegetables like lettuce, cilantro, and tomatoes. The land is good here; everything has been planted here." But now, says Señor Roberto, the lack of water in Tlacotepec has made it impossible to grow these things.

Across town, Señor and Señora Ramirez drag heavy buckets filled with water up a steep hill and down several blocks to their home. This is the second day of the week that water has not arrived at the Ramirez house, as rationing by municipal authorities means that families often go days without running water. Arduous trips to the communal basin are the only way the young parents can get the water they need to bathe, cook, and clean. Although nearly all Tlacotepense homes are connected to the water grid, a large majority reported it was difficult to obtain sufficient water for domestic use. The lack of access to water also affects famers in Tlacotepec, a community that has long relied on small-scale agriculture. Without an established irrigation system, most farmers depend solely on rain to water their crops, leaving them particularly vulnerable to drought and any increase in temperature. In addition, the lack of proper infrastructure for water treatment has led to contamination that threatens local water supplies.

Tlacotepenses are aware of environmental degradation occurring both locally and globally. In response to both real and perceived environmental changes, community members have initiated infrastructure and restoration projects intended to create jobs, curb the flow of out-migration, and improve the quality of life in Tlacotepec. However, a number of social, political, and economic barriers have impeded these efforts.

In this chapter, we first conceptualize the complicated relationship between environmental degradation and migration. Next, we describe changes in local climatic and agricultural conditions over time. We then focus on Tlacotepenses' perceptions of the environment, agriculture, and climate change, examining how education and migration experience can shape attitudes. Finally, we examine five specific projects Tlacotepenses have implemented to improve the ecological and economic sustainability of Tlacotepec. While these projects have had important successes, a number of obstacles have impeded their long-term impact on the town of Tlacotepec.

CONCEPTUALIZING ENVIRONMENTAL MIGRATION

The topic of climate-induced migration received high-profile attention during a 2009 global summit sponsored by the United Nations and the International Organization for Migration. A report by the NGO Cooperative for Assistance and Relief Everywhere (CARE) released at the summit suggests that climate change is likely to push more people to migrate:

> The impacts of climate change are already causing migration and displacement. Although the exact number of people that will be on the move by mid-century is uncertain, the scope and scale could vastly exceed anything that has occurred before. People in the least developed countries and island states will be affected first and worst (Warner et al, 2009, 6).

While the potential impact of climate change on migration is huge, establishing a direct connection between the two can be extremely difficult. Except in situations such as natural disasters or displacement due to large, human-induced projects, migration is usually the result of a combination of factors, of which climate change may be only one. Susan Charnley explains the difficulty in deriving a causal relation between climate change and migration through her work with migrant communities in Tanzania, arguing that environmental conditions are often contributing factors to migration, but "the ultimate cause of displacement often lies in social, political and/or economic conditions" (Charnley 1997, 593).

Further complicating our understanding of environmental migration is the general crisis in the global agriculture sector. Small-scale farmers in the developing world have increasing difficulty carving out livelihoods because of volatile food prices and the growth of the large-scale, agro-business sector (Martin 2010), making the effects of climate change on migration difficult to disentangle from a world-wide crisis in agriculture. Agricultural economist Philip Martin (2010) argues that "climate change, specifically global warming, is likely to compound the challenges faced by agricultural workers in finding sustainable livelihoods." Although changes in global agriculture contribute to migration, so too does environmental degradation. The two are interrelated push factors for many potential migrants in rural agricultural communities such as Tlacotepec.

Graeme Hugo (2008) uses the concept of "carrying capacity" — a term originally used to discuss population equilibrium or the population biology of animal populations — to conceptualize the relationship between migration and changing environmental conditions. In the context of human migration, Hugo describes the carrying capacity of an area as a function of the resources a geographical area contains and the rate at which the resources can replenish themselves after being used. Environmental deterioration makes it difficult to replenish resources, reducing the carrying capacity. When carrying capacity falls, populations have to either create more resources, learn to live with fewer resources, or leave the area. Hugo's application of this theoretical framework to humans has three important caveats: (1) humans have the ability to innovate and increase the carrying capacity of a particular location through increased technology and efficient use of resources, (2) humans can use established infrastructure and transportation to bring resources from areas of surplus to areas of scarcity, and (3) humans require more resources than the food and water that sustain animal life.

This model is useful for understanding out-migration from rural or underdeveloped regions of the world. As over-exploitation of land and natural resources leads to declining environmental conditions, carrying capacity falls. Such areas often lack the capital to import technologies that could reverse or stall these processes, driving migrants toward more sustainable locales. Recognizing this relationship, the UN Water Decade Program on Capacity Development has identified areas suffering from water scarcity and land degradation as being able to sustain decreasing numbers of people and thus particularly susceptible to environmental out-migration. In order to mitigate out-migration, the UN program recommends "empowerment and capacity development of communities and their local institutions" (UN Water Decade Program on Capacity Development 2006, 46).

Ironically, it is sometimes the migrants themselves who are most willing and able to work toward more sustainable environmental practices in the hometowns they have left. While studying attitudes toward environmental degradation and conservation in a migrant-sending community in Wedinoon,

Morocco, Ali Najib (1999, 404) found migrants showed a "high level of concern about environmental issues" compared to non-migrants from the same community. Clark Gray and Richard Bilsborrow's 2011 study of the impact of migrants on agriculture production in a sending community of rural Ecuador argues that migration can improve the local economy through remittances, which inject capital and inspire infrastructure investment. However, increases in carrying capacity driven by migrant investment can sometimes be hindered by migration-induced labor shortages (Gray and Bilsborrow 2011) or by political confrontations between migrant organizations and the sending community's local governing body (Smith 2006).

While the relationship between migration and climate change is complex, many studies agree that climate change plays a role in the decision of millions of people around the world to leave home. With the relationships and carrying capacity model outlined above, we explore how Tlacotepenses are experiencing, perceiving, and responding to changing environmental conditions.

AGRICULTURE AND CLIMATE CHANGE IN TLACOTEPEC

Tlacotepec's economy has traditionally been based on small-scale farming (Erickson, Menéndez, and Nichols 2009). The 885 acres under cultivation, a combination of privately and communally-held land, represent about half of the county's land. The median plot is five acres—often milpa[1] in which beans and corn grow together. In 2011, agriculture continued to play a large role in the daily sustenance of many Tlacotepenses. The majority reported they had participated in agriculture at some point in their lives (65 percent), while most reported that at least someone in their family cultivated milpa in 2010 (65 percent). However, for many Tlacotepenses, agriculture was no longer their main source of income. Only 10.6 percent of respondents reported agriculture was their primary occupation, down from 12.5 percent in 2007 (Cornelius et al. 2009), and following a downward trend of agricultural participation rates in Tlacotepec since 1970 (see figure 8.1). This transformation in Tlacotepec's agricultural sector has been attributed to lack of infrastructure investment, rising food prices, human capital deficiency related to migration, and international agreements such as the North American Free Trade Agreement (NAFTA) which removed tariffs on imported goods and forced small-scale Mexican farmers to compete with industrial farms in the United States and Canada (Cornelius et al. 2009).

---

1 Milpa is a crop-growing system used throughout Mesoamerica in which corn, beans, and pumpkin can be planted together in the same field. The milpa cycle calls for alternating cultivation with letting the area lie fallow. The system is designed to create relatively large yields of food crops without requiring the use of artificial pesticides or fertilizers. Crop yields from this system can become unsustainable if fields are overplanted.

Figure 8.1 Occupational Sectors in Tlacotepec, 1970-2010

Source: INEGI 1970, 1980, 1990, and 2000

*Industry in Tlacotepec is primarily small-scale, independent artisan work.

Changing climate conditions may also contribute to diminishing returns from agriculture, exacerbating difficulties for local farmers and intensifying the trend toward further economic diversification in Tlacotepec. Data from Mexico's National Water Commission (CONAGUA) demonstrate average yearly temperatures have increased across Oaxaca since the early 1980s (see figure 8.2) and predict a continuing increase in the future (Saenz-Romero et al. 2009). This increase of approximately three degrees Fahrenheit between 1983 and 2010 is substantial, as even small changes in temperature can have enormous consequences in the environment (IPCC 2007), especially for agricultural production in regions without irrigation (Saenz-Romero et al 2009). With climate change, Tlacotepenses are relying less heavily on agriculture and working more in the service sector or as small-scale artisans.

Figure 8.2 Average Temperatures in Mexico's South-Pacific Drainage Basin[2]

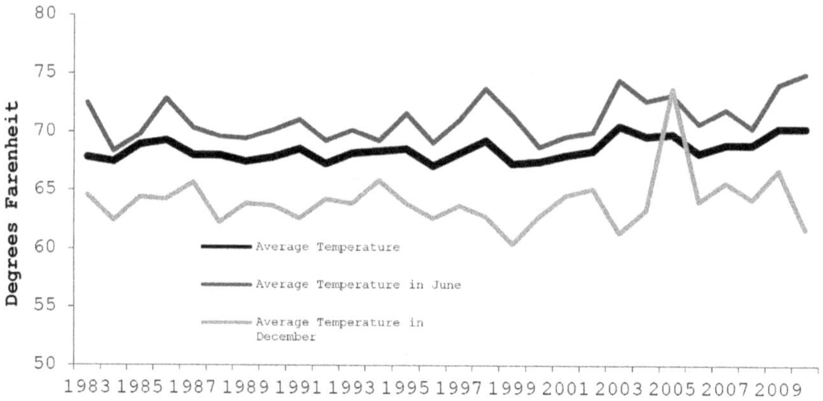

Source: CONAGUA 1983-2009

PERCEPTIONS OF CLIMATE AND AGRICULTURE IN TLACOTEPEC

How do Tlacotepenses perceive the environment and environmental degradation? How do such perceptions shape their daily lives and long-term life choices?

Global Warming

Tlacotepenses are aware of global environmental issues. Asked about the seriousness of global warming, 92 percent felt it was either a "very serious" (75 percent) or "somewhat serious" (17 percent) issue. Only 8 percent said it was "not very serious" or "not serious" (see figure 8.3).

---

2 The South-Pacific Drainage Basin includes the costal areas of Guerrero and Oaxaca as well as inland areas of eastern Guerrero and central Oaxaca.

Figure 8.3 Tlacotepense Perceptions of the Severity of Global Warming, 2011

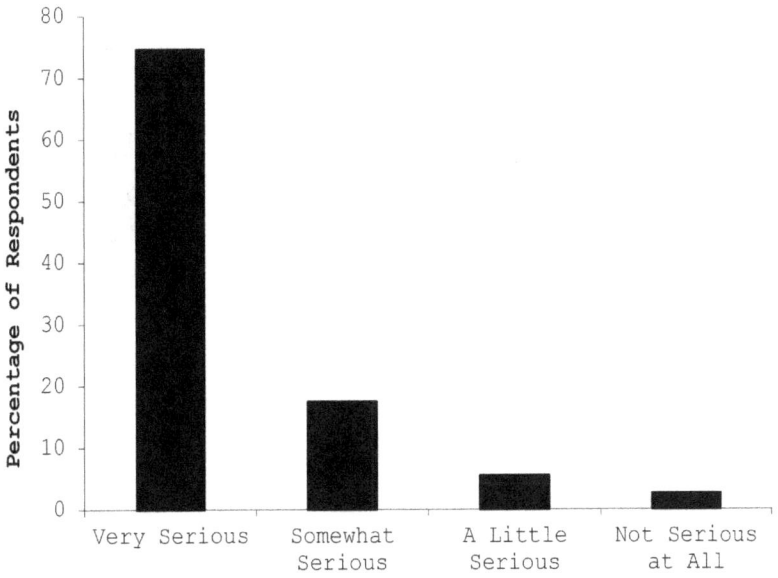

N=827

Source: MMFRP 2011

One reason for high levels of concern over climate change in Tlacotepec may be a perceived increase in local temperatures. Angelica, a 60 year-old grandmother living in Tlacotepec said, "It's drier now. The sun is stronger earlier in the day. When I was growing up, it was not as hot as it is now in the mid-morning. It was not this hot. Everyone wore sweaters, but not anymore." Like Angelica, many Tlacotepenses were concerned that the impacts of global warming and changing climate conditions would have detrimental effects on their hometown.

LAND AND WATER QUALITY

While Tlacotepenses have noticed a rise in temperature, they have also seen a decline in soil quality over the last 25 years. Sixty-seven percent of Tlacotepenses surveyed reported the land was worse in 2011 than it was in 1986, suggesting a profound sense of soil degradation within the community (see figure 8.4)

Figure 8.4 Perceptions of Land Quality and Availability of Irrigation
Water in 2011 vs. 1986

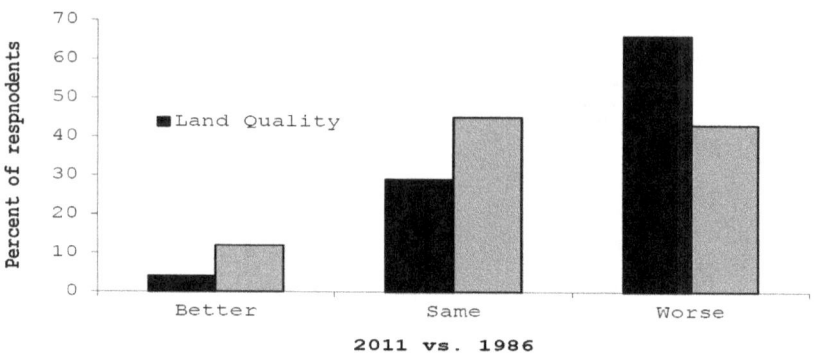

Land Quality N=771
Irrigation Water Availability N=775

Source: MMFRP 2011

Tlacotepenses offered different reasons for declining soil quality and reduced
agricultural output. Maria, a 17-year-old high-school student who has worked
in agriculture told us, "My parents tell me that before some of their plots
produced a lot, and now they barely produce anything. Now, for example, if
you plant three maquilas[3] it will not produce even half of what it did 25 years
ago...sometimes it doesn't rain because of global pollution."

In addition to reporting decreased land quality, many Tlacotepenses noted
that it had become difficult to sufficiently water their crops. With only six percent of the cultivated land in Tlacotepec receiving irrigation in 2009 according to
INEGI, the vast majority of farmers are dependent on often unpredictable rains.
Tlacotepenses recognized this vulnerable position. In our survey, 88.7 percent
of respondents reported it is either "very difficult" or "somewhat difficult" to
access sufficient water for agricultural use. Forty-three percent reported it was
more difficult to obtain water for agricultural use in 2011 than in 1986 (see figure 8.4). Many attribute the decreasing viability of agriculture to reduced levels
of rainfall in Tlacotepec. With an anemic irrigation infrastructure, local farmers
are particularly vulnerable to changing precipitation patterns brought on by climate change.

---

3 A maquila is a unit of land based on the amount of corn seed needed to cultivate that land.
  Ten maquilas is equivalent to one acre. A maquila is also a dry measure of the corn seed
  itself.

MODELING TLACOTEPENSE PERCEPTIONS OF GLOBAL WARMING

In order to determine what factors influence Tlacotepenses' perceptions of climate change, we created an ordinal logistic regression model in which the dependent variable is perceptions of global warming. Controlling for gender, age, wealth, migration status, and time spent working in agriculture, we found education to be the only statistically significant predictor of the perceived severity of global warming. Tlacotepenses with higher levels of education were significantly more likely to report global climate change as more serious than less-educated Tlacotepenses (see table 8.1). Unlike Najib (1999), who found that migrants in Morocco were more aware of environmental degradation than non-migrants, migration history is not a significant predictor of perceptions of global warming among Tlacotepenses when the appropriate controls are applied.

Table 8.1 Ordinal Logistic Regression Modeling Perceptions of Global Warming

Male	0.002
	(0.189)
Education	0.124***
	(0.023)
Wealth4	0.003
	(0.122)
Age	0.000
	(0.007)
Ever worked in agriculture	-0.031
	(0.194)
Ever migrated	0.040
	(0.199)
Intercepts	
poco grave	3.008***
	(0.511)
algo grave	1.700***
	(0.471)
muy grave	-0.277
	(0.460)
McFadden's R-squared	.104
N = 774	

In addition to being more likely to perceive global warming as a grave problem, respondents with higher education were also more likely to report deteriorating land quality and increased difficulty in obtaining sufficient water for agriculture from 1986 to 2011. Seventy-one percent of respondents with at least a high-school education reported worse land quality in 2011 than 25 years prior, compared with 64 percent of those who completed six years of school or less. Forty-four percent of those with a high-school education report it is more difficult to obtain water in 2011 compared with 41 percent of those with 0 to 6 years of education. Although more highly-educated Tlacotepenses are less likely to work in the agricultural sector, potentially making them less knowledgeable of local soil and water conditions, they were more likely to perceive declining land quality and water access.

INFRASTRUCTURE INVESTMENT

A previous study of Tlacotepec (Erickson, Menéndez, and Nichols 2009) identified privatization of land, better access to credit, and better access to irrigation water as changes that could improve Tlacotepec's agricultural economy. In 2011, we asked respondents to rank these three options in order of importance for improving agricultural production. In their ranking, 80.5 percent of Tlacotepenses chose irrigated land as the most important factor, 16.6 percent chose better access to credit, and only 2.9 percent chose privatizing land. Rigo, a 43-year old migrant explains, "There is no irrigation here. If there were a way to get water, there would be a source of jobs in agriculture."

Like Rigo, the majority of Tlacotepenses see the inaccessibility of water as a major limitation to generating sufficient agricultural production in Tlacotepec. Sixty-eight percent of respondents in Tlacotepec who had not worked in agriculture in 2011 said they would be more likely to participate in agriculture if there were a better system of irrigation.

The worsening agricultural conditions often inspire Tlacotepenses to look for work and higher wages elsewhere. According to community members, the lack of water has fueled the decline of agriculture, and the traditional farming lifestyle has slowly become less feasible for supporting their families. Approximately ten percent of Tlacotepenses in 2011 indicated they had plans to migrate to the United States, while many were considering internal migration to more prosperous northern Mexico states like Sinaloa and Baja California. However, according to the 2011 survey, Tlacotepenses reported that improving local infrastructure would create more jobs and leave Tlacotepenses less vulnerable to climatic conditions, potentially mitigating out-migration. When asked what infrastructure improvement would most reduce out-migration, 28.3 percent of respondents reported "more irrigated land for agriculture" as their first choice, second only to "more industry" in Tlacotepec (53.7 percent) as figure 8.5 shows.

Figure 8.5 What would keep most people from leaving San Miguel Tlacotepec?

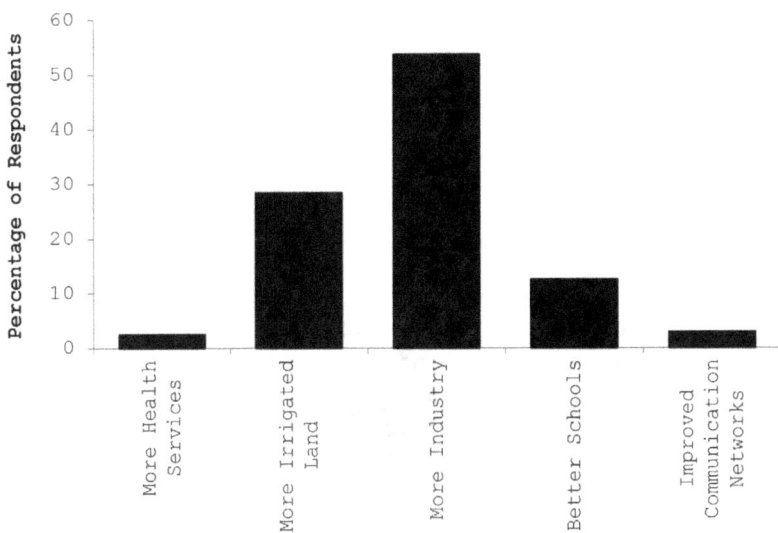

Source: MMFRP 2011v

Ernesto, a 46-year old returned migrant and farmer in Tlacotepec, is optimistic that targeted investments in the agricultural sector, specifically irrigation, could increase sustainability and reduce the flow of emigration. "The most important factor that would keep the people of Tlacotepec from leaving to work in other countries or other states is the creation of jobs in Tlacotepec.... For example, an irrigation system would create jobs. With an irrigation system you can depend on your crops." Like Ernesto, many Tlacotepenses believe community development projects can create jobs and provide better incomes, especially those projects that relate specifically to agriculture and the environment.

Ninety-six percent of Tlacotepenses interviewed in 2011 indicated they would be willing to collaborate in community investment projects that would potentially decrease the community's vulnerability to environmental changes. Further, 90 percent reported they would contribute part of their income to prevent pollution. This suggests a greater willingness to financially support environmental protection efforts compared to a representative sample of the Mexican population (2005) and a representative sample of 58 countries (2005 to 2009) (see figure 8.6). Although differences in when the surveys were carried out may help explain some of the variation among responses, the data suggest that Tlacotepenses may be more willing to make individual financial sacrifices to prevent pollution than respondents in other parts of Mexico and throughout the world, perhaps a result of observing the impact of changing ecological conditions on an agricultural community

Figure 8.6 Willingness to Give Income to Prevent Pollution

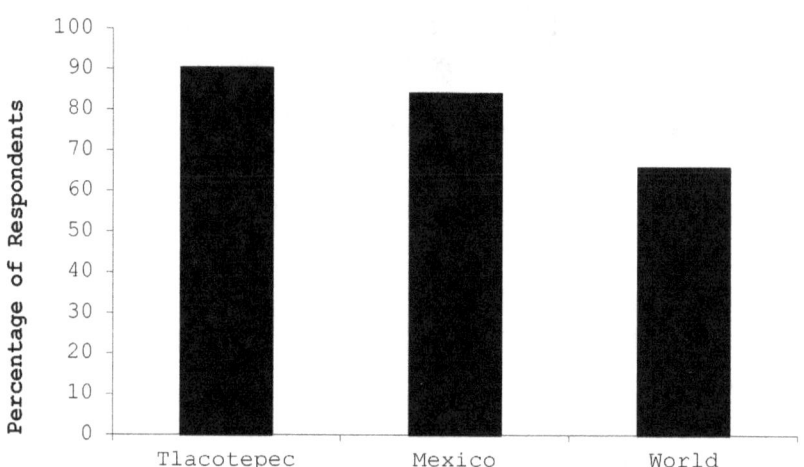

Sources: World Values Survey 2005 (Mexico) and 2004-2008 (World)

The environmental deterioration occurring in Tlacotepec is reducing the town's carrying capacity. Tlacotepenses are responding by leaving the agricultural sector, diversifying their sources of income, and migrating within Mexico or to the United States. Many Tlacotepenses believe community investment projects intended to improve agricultural conditions and water access could reduce out-migration.

WATER AND ENVIRONMENTAL PROJECTS IN TLACOTEPEC

Tlacotepec's current water source is a spring located in a valley approximately two miles from the center of town. The water from the spring is collected in a large tank, from which a small pump sends it up the hill and into the town via a single pipe three inches in diameter. The excess water the system cannot contain flows into the polluted river below the spring.

Closer to the town, water in the pipes reaches another large storage tank, and from there is distributed to smaller neighborhood tanks throughout Tlacotepec. Houses are connected to these local tanks via a network of pipes, and water flow to homes is controlled by opening and closing valves under the street surface. Selected members of the community are given the task of opening and closing the valves every few days during the dry season to allow water to reach a group of several houses at a time.

While this system reaches the majority of homes in Tlacotepec, water flow often does not meet demand. In 2011, 94 percent of respondents reported having running water in their homes, but 74 percent reported it is "difficult" or "very difficult" to obtain sufficient water for domestic use. Many reported inconsistencies in the flow of water and the inadequacy of the flow when it was available.

Scattered throughout the town are water basins built around natural springs that collect spring water as well as rainwater. Town residents do laundry, bathe, and sometimes collect water for domestic use at these basins, although the water is not suitable for drinking. During the dry season residents must rely on water collected in the basins when running water is unavailable in their homes.

In response to these issues surrounding the current water system, residents, government officials, and migrants have formed various groups to organize water infrastructure improvement projects. The projects we discuss below address these issues in different ways, but all face significant financial, logistical, and/or political obstacles.

Well Project

Tlacotepec's municipal government initiated the well project in 2008 to improve access to domestic running water. The municipal government hired a team of engineers from the Technological University of the Mixteca (La Universidad Tecnológica de la Mixteca, or UTM), to locate groundwater in the area around Tlacotepec. The municipal government began drilling a well, expecting to reach water after 20 meters, as the UTM engineers had suggested. But when no water was found at that depth, they kept going. Even after digging to 150 meters at a cost of nearly $129,000, no water was found, leaving the project leaders unsure how to proceed. Another attempted dig would be too costly, and if it failed again, would be politically and financially detrimental to the local government.

In the aftermath of this failure, debate split largely upon partisan lines. Hostile relations between the various political parties active in Tlacotepec and their uneasy coexistence with Tlacotepec's usos y costumbres system of government[4] were a challenge for the well project. Some believe the well project failed because government officials acted to promote their own political interests and did not consider the results of alternative studies (discussed in more detail in "A Migrant Response" below) or the needs of community members— many of whom felt the project was too expensive.

The future of the well project is uncertain. In order to proceed, a new study would have to be conducted to determine where, or if, water actually exists. This would be costly and would again run the risk of incorrectly estimating the location of groundwater. In addition, were the workers to find water, community members would need to be trained and qualified for the maintenance of the completed well, requiring more funds, time, and government and community cooperation. At the time of writing, the large drilling machine sat idle on a hillside above the town, a constant reminder of the failure to find a solution to the town's water problem.

A Migrant Response: The Comité de Agua

The origins of what is today known as the comité de agua stretch back to 1987. In that year, a group of Tlacotepense migrants living in San Diego County formed a committee to improve access to irrigation water in their hometown. An article about their efforts was published in the San Diego Union in 1989, and a couple who read it were inspired to support the group's effort, donating $5,200 to the cause. This donation, combined with $14,000 raised by the committee and another $13,000 supplied by the Oaxacan state government, funded the construction of Tlacotepec's current domestic water system (see above) (San Diego Union Tribune, December 10, 1989).

Over the years, the system has proved difficult to maintain. The electricity powering the pump is unreliable, occasionally overloading the motor and leaving townspeople without running water. In addition, the water's high mineral content corrodes the pipes, and as the demand for water in Tlacotepec increases, the pump and piping have proven insufficient in supporting the town's needs. The municipal government lacks both the financial resources and human capital to maintain or improve the project.

Political conflicts between various factions of Tlacotepenses have affected the work of migrants hoping to improve the water situation in Tlacotepec. Throughout the 1990s, the committee had trouble raising money and support from Tlacotepenses due to political differences and the geographical distance between migrants and non-migrants. Committee members claimed funds were inexplicably disappearing and with dwindling fiscal resources

---

4 The usos y costumbres system of government is based on collective modes of governance, community organization, and conflict resoslution used by the Mixtecos and other indigenous groups in Mexico. See chapter 4, this volume.

and a lack of support from Mexico-based Tlacotepenses, the vitality of the committee slowly diminished.

Nonetheless, the need for water in Tlacotepec has remained and migrants continue their efforts despite the lack of support. In 2008, several migrants decided to reinvigorate the project, and lobbied to become an official comité recognized by Tlacotepec's municipal government. In March 2010, the General Assembly of Tlacotepec officially recognized the Comité Pro-Agua Tlacotepense. Since its return to activity, the Comité has chosen a two-step process, as Manuel, a founder of the original migrant committee and now a leader of the official Comité Pro-Agua, explained. "The first step is to bring running water to every house...the second step, a long-term project, would be to bring irrigation water."

In order to address the issue of water for domestic use, the Comité considered constructing a second, more efficient system to pump water from the spring. They contacted a non-profit organization, Engineers Without Borders (EWB), who sent two engineers, free of charge, to Tlacotepec to evaluate the state of the water system in 2009. In contrast to the work of the UTM engineers who did survey work for the unsuccessful well project, the EWB engineers claimed there was little water to be found near Tlacotepec. Instead of drilling a new well, they suggested an additional pump and storage system similar to the current one would be the most cost-efficient solution. But their work never moved beyond the planning stage. Without funds to move forward with their plans and facing animosity from the municipal president, who opposed the Comité, the engineers returned to the United States. According to some members of the committee, the municipal government has not always been willing to cooperate with the Comité. Manuel felt that "because of municipal presidents' political interests, they are not concerned with the water project. They don't want to spend money." He was especially frustrated that the local administration did not acknowledge the EWB engineers or consider their findings when they designed their project.

Florencio, a founding member of the committee who later retired to Tlacotepec, said that political conflict exacerbated these problems and hindered the Comité's progress:

> Here in Tlacotepec, it is politically unstable. The Comité that we founded didn't have the support of the past president. Even though we held a General Assembly... he didn't recognize us because he considered what we were doing voluntary and not official. When we brought engineers from the United States he didn't consider them important, and when he decided to make a well, he didn't even advise us... Because of political differences his administration preferred to put us aside and dig their well. What a shame, because they didn't find water.

Rosalinda, a member of the Comité, claimed the former municipal president "always refused to talk with us" and that "personal interests" of those in power often determined municipal policy.

Fernando, the former municipal president, sees the matter differently. He told us that the Comité approached him with the engineers' findings too late in his term for him to initiate any projects. "I was going to work with them," he explained, "but they came to me very late...It would have been better if they had come the year our administration started, in 2008. At least we could have started coordinating and working on something."

The Comité has struggled to establish legitimacy in Tlacotepec in part because the local version of the usos y costumbres system of governance requires direct political participation in ways that are impossible for migrants. Community members are expected to participate in general assemblies and to perform civic duties, with recognition given to those who provide continuous community service. Unable to perform these duties, migrants are often denied participation or recognition by other community members when they return to Tlacotepec for brief visits. Margarito, a Tlacotepec-based member of the Comité, also said the majority of those who attend the assemblies are older people who are more interested in receiving immediate benefits, such as the "70 y Más" program which gives economic support to those over 70, than in long-term projects that require financial investment, such as Comité projects.

Florencio said that older people in particular challenged the efforts of the Comité and he sees the town as stuck in its ways. "This town is functioning under a social infrastructure that is not of this age. The customs suffocate Tlacotepense society. They are something that functioned at one time, but now they aren't always helpful...The result is that [Tlacotepenses] devote more time to the fiestas than to financial support for existing programs." Florencio said traditional beliefs and long-standing cultural values are major challenges to the progress of the Comité.

To get around this, the group's goal is to create a privately-owned company that would control and supply water to Tlacotepec. This company would hire its own engineers and administrators to maintain the system and ensure reliability, and residents would pay the company for water service. In Rosalinda's view, the Comité will have succeeded when she and her family can return to Tlacotepec to live permanently: "We are migrants, we live in the United States, but we want to return home. The problem is that there isn't water." To make changes to this situation, the Comité will depend on the relationship it cultivates with government officials at the local, state, and federal level as well as with the Tlacotepense public.

The Reforestation Project

According to Mexico's National Forestry Commission (Comisión Nacional Forestal, or CONAFOR), deforestation and consequent degradation of soil have had serious consequences for the agricultural economies of many small rural towns throughout Oaxaca, including Tlacotepec. In response, CONAFOR has enacted a program to reduce deforestation, promote economic development through sustainable forestry, and provide training and maintenance for such projects to generate employment and income (CONAFOR 2007-2011). Tlacotepec applied for the program in 2007 and received over 20,000 pine seedlings and funds to pay for the labor to plant them.

Tlacotepec's Communal Property Assembly was formed to organize resources and delegate labor through a system of volunteers, which included hundreds of school children. From June to September of 2008, the seedlings were planted and fences erected around them. According to Jorge Rios, treasurer of the Assembly, the reforestation project has been a success. "The seedlings were less than 20 centimeters tall; now they are over two meters." The acres of newly planted trees are expected to increase the fertility of the soil. Their roots and shade will help the soil retain water and replenish lost nutrients. When the trees mature, sustainable models of lumber harvesting could also become a viable source of industry. Jorge believes this project can have lasting benefits for the entire community, "I think that a project like the reforestation project...is for the common good, for all of the community...No one person is going to benefit from this, but everyone."

Although the project has not yet experienced major challenges, some concerns do exist, especially in finding a balance between growing new trees and harvesting existing ones for lumber. If regulations are not clearly established and enforced, cutting down trees for personal consumption or sale could result in additional deforestation.

Environmental Awareness Campaign

In 2009, the local high school initiated an awareness campaign in which 30 high school students and teachers painted four murals throughout the town. The colorful murals painted on the walls of homes and businesses remind residents of the gravity of environmental pollution. One mural portrays a weeping Earth, overtaken by factories and pollution. "Don't contaminate the environment," it implores (see figure 8.7).

Figure 8.7 "Don't contaminate the environment"

Gabriela, a 17 year-old student who participated in the project, says her hope is that the murals will reduce pollution by making people more conscientious about how their actions affect the environment. But Gabriela concedes that the positive effect is limited. "The people know [about pollution], but they do not have the resources to collect the trash and dispose of it correctly," she said. While the mural campaign exposes many Tlacotepenses to the dangers of pollution and subsequent environmental degradation, the financial and social viability of practicing conservation remains an open question.

OBSTACLES

The long-term successes of these projects are uncertain. A lack of economic and human capital, political conflicts, and changing ecological conditions are all threats to their intended outcomes.

The most common obstacle is a lack of financial resources. Although the Water Treatment Plant and the Reforestation project are federally funded, these funds are often difficult to obtain and generally do not cover long-term maintenance costs. The Migrant Comité is dependent on community support, which can be inconsistent during times of economic hardship and hard to secure due to other political and social factors. Without the federal government, projects such as the water treatment plant and reforestation project would not have been possible. But finding consistent funds from the federal or state governments is extremely difficult.

In addition to a lack of economic capital, Tlacotepec lacks the human capital and technical training necessary to ensure the ongoing success of current and potential projects. Maintenance may prove to be problematic for the future of both the water treatment plant and reforestation project. The water treatment plant engineer, who has worked in similar projects in other parts of Mexico, said it was likely the pipes and pumps will eventually need to be replaced. With no one to oversee the plant, problems are likely to go undiagnosed and unresolved. In the case of the reforestation project, knowledge of appropriate harvesting and planting methods is essential to ensure that the trees planted are not cut down at an unsustainable rate, as has happened in the past.

Tlacotepec's tumultuous political environment also makes infrastructure projects difficult. At the time of writing, Tlacotepec was divided by partisan groups at the presidential level who both claimed their candidate had won the election (see Politics chapter, this volume). This conflict took precedence over proposed and ongoing projects. The ban on re-election also makes infrastructure development difficult. With a staff completely remade every three years, there is a lack of continuity, and projects supported by one municipal government are often abandoned by the next administration. In addition, a general community mistrust of the municipal government deters community members from contributing time or funds to proposed projects. One community member voiced her frustration with the municipal government's promise of an irrigation system: "Where is the water? There is none. No more, they turned it off to benefit their own pockets...They fool the people, that's it."

Living so far from Tlacotepec, migrant groups are seen by some residents as out of touch with important community issues. The Comité Pro-Agua has found it difficult to gain legitimacy because many say the migrants no longer understand the town's needs because they no longer live there. Migrant groups advocating public improvements, such as the water project, often have difficulty gaining the attention and legitimacy from their Tlacotepense community. Because migrants no longer participate in community-appointed positions and committees in the town, they are often denied a voice in the community and their projects are dismissed by political opponents.

Although the migrant Comité, the municipality, and Tlacotepec residents all seek improved access to running water and to mitigate environmental degradation, lack of collaboration between all parties inhibits them from achieving results they all desire. The fragmented efforts, with many groups each working independently, impede the long-term success of any of the projects.

In addition to these financial, political, and social challenges, the topography of Tlacotepec and the surrounding area also makes improving water access difficult. The natural spring the town relies on is buried in a valley several miles from Tlacotepec. Its distance from the town and the terrain the pipes must traverse make the repair of the system or construction of new infrastructure costly and logistically challenging.

CONCLUSION

Tlacotepenses broadly share beliefs about the environment, climate change, and the downward trajectory of local agriculture. In 2011, the majority of Tlacotepenses reported Tlacotepec had been experiencing climate change for several decades and global warming was a serious issue. Although residents perceived a slight degradation of soil quality since the 1980s, they still believed the surrounding land was well-suited for agriculture. The greatest obstacle to improved agricultural production was not the quality of the soil, but rather access to irrigation water. Juan, a migrant and permanent U.S. resident, represents the views of many Tlacotepenses when he relates water to the town's prosperity, "Water is a great necessity. Why is the US rich? Because it is so big…there are hills filled with avocados, lemons, oranges, and all of the people are working in the hills. [In Tlacotepec] we can also harvest avocados, lemons, and oranges, but we have no water." If irrigation water were more accessible, residents like Juan, felt the town's agricultural sector and economic viability would dramatically improve.

Projects like the water treatment plant, the well project, the migrant water committee, and the reforestation project are different responses to perceived environmental changes. They have the potential to improve Tlacotepec's economic stability and reduce out-migration, but several factors have slowed or limited their positive impacts. The water treatment plant implemented by the federal government and Tlacotepec's municipality will filter water from the nearby polluted river. The discharged, non-potable water could be suitable for irrigation, which would have positive economic and social implications for the town, but logistical questions remain unresolved. The well project, although ultimately unsuccessful, attempted to locate a closer and more reliable source of water for the town. The migrant Comité hopes one day to develop an improved and privately-controlled water system, both for domestic use and for irrigation, but they lack financial resources and community support. The federal government's reforestation project planted trees meant to improve Tlacotepec's air and soil quality and garnered much community support, but their long-term impact remains unknown.

These and future projects have the potential to increase carrying capacity, reduce out-migration, and sustain or improve Tlacotepec's agricultural economy. Their success, though, depends on the ability of Tlacotepenses to overcome political, financial, logistical, social, and even cultural obstacles. By doing so, Tlacotepenses might begin to establish long-term solutions to the problems that climate change is bringing to their community.

WORKS CITED

Charnley, Susan. 1997. "Environmentally-Displaced Peoples and the Cascade Effect: Lessons from Tanzania," Human Ecology 25: 593-618.

Cornelius, Wayne A., David Fitzgerald, Jorge Hernández-Díaz, and Scott Borger, eds. 2009. Migration From the Mexican Mixteca: A Transnational Community in Oaxaca and California. La Jolla, CA: Center for Comparative Immigration Studies, University of California, San Diego.

Comisíon Nacíonal Del Agua. 1983-2009. Mexico: CONAGUA. http://www. conagua.gob.mx//default.aspx

Comisión Nacional Forestal. 2011. Mexico: CONAFOR. http://www.conafor. gob.mx/portal/index.php/english

Erickson, Emily, Tanya Menéndez, and Peter Nichols. 2009. "The Economics of Migration: Agriculture, Remittances, and Investment." In Migration From the Mexican Mixteca: A Transnational Community in Oaxaca and California, ed. Wayne A. Cornelius, David Fitzgerald, Jorge Hernández-Díaz, and Scott Borger. La Jolla, CA: Center for Comparative Immigration Studies, University of California, San Diego.

Graeme, Hugo. 2008. "Migration, Development, and Environment. Environmentally Induced Population Displacements". PERN Cyberseminar. Nov 2010. http://www.populationenvironmentresearch.org//papers/hugo_ statement.pdf

Gray, Clark, and Richard Bilsborrow. 2011. "Consequences of Out-Migration for Land Use in Rural Ecuador." Presentation at the Population Association of America 2011 Annual Meeting. http://paa2011.princeton.edu/ download.aspx?submissionId=112537

INEGI (Instituto Nacional de Estadística y Geografía). 1970. IX Censo General de Población, Estado de Oaxaca vol. 2. México, D.F.: INEGI.

IPCC (Intergovernmental Panel on Climate Change). 2007. "Summary for Policymakers." In Climate Change 2007: Impacts, Adaptation and Vulnerability. Contribution of Working Group II to the Fourth Assessment Report of the Intergovernmental Panel on Climate Change, edited by M.L. Parry, O.F. Canziani, J.P. Palutikof, P.J. van der Linden and C.E. Hanson, 7-22. Cambridge: Cambridge University Press.

Martin, Phillip. 2010. "Climate Change, Agricultural Development, and Migration." In Climate Change and Migration. Washington D.C.: German-Marshal Fund of the United States.

Najib, Ali B. 1999. "Environmental Knowledge and Environmental Attitudes: Wedinoon, Morocco," Ambio 28: 404-08.

San Diego Union Tribune. 1989. "Piping in Water and a Dream." December 10, 1989.

Saenz-Romero et al. 2009. "Spline models of contemporary, 2030, 2060 and 2090 climates for Mexico and their use in understanding climate-change impacts on the vegetation." Springer Science + Business Media B.V., November 12, 2009.

Smith, Robert C. 2006. Mexican New York: Transnational Lives of New Immigrants. Berkeley: University of California Press.

United Nations Framework Convention on Climate Change. 2009. "Climate Change, Migration, and Displacement: Impacts, Vulnerability, and Adaptation Options." Part of the 5th session of the Ad Hoc Working Group on Long-Term Cooperative Action under the Convention, February 6, Bonn, Switzerland. http://unfccc.int/resource/docs/2008/smsn/igo/031.pdf

Warner, Koko, Charles Ehrnhart, Alex de Sherbinin, Susana Adamo, and Tricia Chai-Onn. 2009. "In Search of Shelter: Mapping the Effects of Climate Change on Human Migration." CARE International.

"Work Plan – II 2010-2013." 2010. UN-Water Decade Programme on Capacity Development. http://www.unwater.unu.edu/file/get/184

www.ingramcontent.com/pod-product-compliance
Lightning Source LLC
Chambersburg PA
CBHW070651290526
45790CB00001B/273